HEARTSMART™ COOKING

for family and friends

Bonnie Stern

RANDOM HOUSE
CANADA

HEART
AND STROKE
FOUNDATION
OF CANADA

Published in Canada by Random House Canada, a division of Random House of Canada Limited, with the co-operation of the Heart and Stroke Foundation of Canada.

Random House Canada and colophon are trademarks.

®HEARTSMART is a registered trademark owned by the Heart and Stroke Foundation of Canada

® **becel** is a registered trademark of Lipton, Toronto, M4W 3R2.

Canadian Cataloguing in Publication Data

Stern, Bonnie
    HeartSmart cooking for family and friends : great recipes, menus and ideas for casual entertaining

On cover: The Heart and Stroke Foundation of Canada
Includes index.
ISBN 0-679-31003-7 (Random House Canada)
ISBN 0-679-31060-6 (Heart & Stroke Foundation of Canada)

1. Heart – Diseases – Diet therapy – Recipes.
2. Low-fat diet – Recipes. 3. Entertaining.
I. Heart and Stroke Foundation of Canada. II. Title.
III. Title: HeartSmart cooking for family and friends.

RC684.D5S72 2000   641.5'6311   C99-932494-2

Project Editor: Shelley Tanaka
Photography: Robert Wigington
Food styling: Olga Truchan
Prop styling: Maggi Jones
Author photograph: Robert Wigington
Illustrations: Jenny Burke
Book design: Andrew Smith
Page layout and composition: Andrew Smith Graphics Inc.

Printed and bound in Canada

10 9 8 7 6 5 4 3 2 1

Front cover photograph: Roast Cornish Hens with Herbs (page 187).
Back cover photographs: Roasted Salmon Salad Niçoise (page 270), Buckwheat Blini with Smoked Trout (page 184), Frozen Lemon Meringue Cake (page 190).

To my parents, Ruth and Max.
They knew the real meaning of entertaining — their home
and hearts were always open to family and friends.

CONTENTS

ACKNOWLEDGEMENTS
FROM THE HEART AND STROKE FOUNDATION OF CANADA

The Heart and Stroke Foundation would like to thank the following people for their assistance in the development and review of the nutrition information for *HeartSmart Cooking for Family and Friends* by Bonnie Stern. Their expertise and advice has been invaluable in transforming the latest scientific information on healthy eating into practical information for all.

Members of the National Nutrition Advisory Committee and Nutrition Taskforce, Ontario: Elaine DeGrandpre, RD; Val Irvine, P.Dt.; Gail Leadlay, RD; Jane Loppe, RD; Bretta Maloff, RD, M.Ed.; Laura Sevenhuysen, RD, M.Ed.

Members of the Heart and Stroke Foundation of Canada's Health Promotion Initiative Review Committee: Sylvia Poirier, RN, MN, Registrar (Chair-HPIR); Dr. Ken Buchholz, MD, CCFP; Karen Fedun; Gail Leadlay, RD; Barbara Riley, M.Sc., Ph.D. Candidate.

A special thanks to: Bonnie Stern for once again creating unbelievably delicious recipes, ideas and more.

Fran Berkoff, RD for doing a stellar job of presenting the nutrition information in a friendly, understandable way.

Rick Gallop, Neila Poscente, Doug MacQuarrie, Mary Elizabeth Harriman, Dominique Mongeon, Carol Dombrow and Wes Clark for supporting this very valuable initiative.

Sharyn Joliat, M.Sc., RD for the nutritional analysis. Katherine Younker, P.Dt., C.D.E., for the Canadian Diabetes Association Food Choice Values.

All those people who worked so hard putting this beautiful book together, especially Shelley Tanaka, Sarah Davies, Anne Collins, Bob Wigington, Olga Truchan, Andrew Smith and their teams of very talented people.

® **becel** is dedicated to educating Canadians about leading a heart healthy life. Supporting the educational initiatives of the Heart and Stroke Foundation forms an integral part of this commitment.

The Heart and Stroke Foundation gratefully acknowledges the generous support of becel ® in helping to make this cookbook possible. The financial support received from our sponsor does not constitute an endorsement by the Heart and Stroke Foundation or the author for the sponsor's products.

AUTHOR'S ACKNOWLEDGEMENTS

HeartSmart Cooking for Family and Friends grew out of the need we all have to socialize and interact with other people. I have found that a good way to interact with other people is to write a book. Creating a book involves so many different components that it seems as if there is a whole army of people at work. And I want to thank all of them.

There is no way to truly measure the influence that other people have on your work. The accumulation of knowledge comes from so many different sources — people you know personally or professionally, authors you read, or food you taste that has been cooked by people you may or may not know.

This is my third collaboration with the Heart and Stroke Foundation of Canada. When I started my cooking school twenty-six years ago, my aim was to help people eat better food and cook more easily; today, whether I am teaching, writing books or articles, or working on a television show, this goal has not changed. Through the Heart and Stroke Foundation I have been able to reach more people than I ever could have done otherwise. So thanks to the volunteers who spread the word and to those who worked on the book, especially Carol Dombrow, Rick Gallop, Doug MacQuarrie and Neila Poscente. Thanks to becel® for their support of the Heart and Stroke Foundation of Canada and this project. Thanks also to Sharyn Joliat from Info Access for the meticulous analysis of the recipes, and to Fran Berkoff for her down-to-earth, common-sense explanations of complex nutritional information.

Random House deserves so much applause for producing another beautiful book. Their support and wisdom have been critical, especially with regard to the change in design and content. I'm grateful to Pat Cairns, Stacey Cameron, Anne Collins, Laurie Coulter, Sarah Davies, David Kent, Maria Madeiros, Doug Pepper, Lorraine Symmes, Susan Roxborough and Alan Terakawa. Thanks also to Joseph Gisini and Andrew Smith, who mastered the design; Jenny Burke for her brilliant illustrations; and Maggi Jones, Olga Truchan and Robert Wigington, who created the beautiful photographs.

My editor, Shelley Tanaka, cooks my recipes as well as my words, and I am always complimented that even when she's in the midst of all that fussy, detailed work, the recipes still engage her enough to get her cooking them. My lawyer, Marian Hebb, is the only person who can keep me relatively calm and focused when life piles up over the top, and I am even more impressed that despite her high-powered, busy schedule, she has started cooking these recipes, too.

Colleagues provide great inspiration, and I am so fortunate to have lots of them: Farina Achuck, Darina Allen, Hubert Aumeier, Susan Bang, Giuliano Bugialli, Biba Caggiano, Sarah Cairns, Hugh Carpenter, Carrie, Leslie and Mitchell Davis,

Susan Devins, Jim Dodge, Arlene Feltman-Sailhac, David Forestell, Madhur Jaffrey, Cherry Kam, Nick Malgieri, Carole Martin, Mark McEwan, Alice Medrich, Hart Melvin, Caprial Pence, Mark Picone, Debi Pratt, Guy Rigby, Mary Risley, Jeffrey Sansone, Nina Simonds, Joanne Weir, Cynthia Wine, Eileen Yin-Fei Lo and Evelyn Zabloski.

I'm especially grateful to family and friends who have taught me so much about hospitality and the spirit of entertaining, including Sydney Bacon, Gwen and Saul Berkowitz, Ruth and Shelley Cohen, Barbara and Morty Glickman, Arnell and Simone Goldberg, Andrea and Jorge Iceruk, Ellen and Sydney Lerer, Earl and Patti Linzon, Jonathon Gus and Lesley Milrod, Joel and Linda Rose, Lynn and Norm Saunders, Ann Sharp and Vernon Shaw, Irene Tam, Ed Hamer and Marsha Werb, Carol and Jim White.

Writing the book is only the beginning. I have been fortunate that the media has always been very supportive of my goal to help people in the kitchen. I would especially like to thank Shelley Ambrose, Julia Aitken at *Elm Street*, Elizabeth Baird at *Canadian Living*, Carla Collins, Carol Ferguson at *Homemaker's*, Alison Fryer and staff at The Cookbook Store, Randy Gulliver, Marion Kane at the *Toronto Star*, Shelagh Rogers and Pamela Wallin. A big thanks to everyone involved with my television show on WTN: Maria Armstrong, Bill Johnston, Ron Lillie and Karen Wookey for giving me the push that I needed; everyone who helps on the show, and everyone at WTN, especially Sue Gravelle, Melanie McCaig, Susan Millican, Julie Smith and Michelle vanBeusekom.

The cooking school has been my home base for twenty-six years, and my staff has always been my backbone. No one could have so many great people working for them as I have been lucky enough to have, and no one could value them more than I do. Thanks to Anne Apps, Dely Balagtas, Jenny Burke, Lorraine Butler, Sadie Darby, Alex Lamb, Letty Lastima, Maureen Lollar, Francine Menard, Emily Richards, Natalina Rinaldi, Linda Stephen, Helen Walker and Allison Weinstein. Special thanks to Rhonda Caplan and Marie Formosa for recipe-testing with a seasoned palate.

Family is there to keep you grounded, but I would never get off the ground at all if it were not for the tremendous support from my husband, Raymond; my kids, Mark, Anna and Fara; Andrew Kiguel, and Jane, Wayne, Meredith and Charles Krangle.

And thanks especially to my students, readers, viewers and visitors to my website (www.bonniestern.com). Thank you for your letters, phone calls and E-mails that let me know how I have helped you and how I can help you more. When you gather your family and friends around the table and cook my recipes for them it makes all my work complete.

BONNIE STERN
TORONTO, 1999

PREFACE

Once again, The Heart and Stroke Foundation of Canada is pleased to offer Canadians another remarkable cookbook. In this informative edition well-known author Bonnie Stern integrates "healthy eating" and "entertaining," concepts commonly considered incompatible. In fact, the more than 200 recipes in this book dispel any notion that compromise in flavour, texture or visual appeal is necessary to create healthy cuisine. The ingenuity of the author's food inventions together with exciting presentation ideas delight both palate and eye while satisfying the goal of healthy eating.

The Heart and Stroke Foundation is committed to helping Canadians improve their nutritional habits. Because Canadians love to cook, we believe one of the simplest ways to cultivate good nutrition practices is for you to be involved in your own kitchen, preparing healthful meals for yourself, family and friends. This book provides you with the incentive to move toward that goal. The cuisine you'll prepare is sure to receive rave reviews along with appreciation for your dedication to good health.

Scientific evidence continues to validate healthy eating as a major contributor to overall good health and to the reduction of the risk for chronic disease. To assist your understanding of the issues, Fran Berkoff, RD provides you with the most up-to-date information on topics such as antioxidants, tea, fat and soy — all in a format that is both easy to understand and actionable. You will find this book to be a valuable resource for key issues that can affect your heart health.

The Foundation will continue to strive to provide you with the tools necessary for a healthy lifestyle. Contact your local office of the Heart and Stroke Foundation to find out about the many programs available to help you maintain a healthy diet. Information is also available on the web (http://www.heartandstroke.ca) and through our information line (1-888-HSF-INFO).

Please enjoy our latest book and I truly hope that it soon shows the signs of being well used.

MR. ALLAN LEFEVER,
VOLUNTEER PRESIDENT
HEART AND STROKE FOUNDATION OF CANADA

HEART-HEALTHY EATING

Some of us use two sets of cookbooks — the ones with healthy recipes for every day and the pull-out-all-the-stops-and-indulge recipes for entertaining. Now you have in your hands a cookbook that gives you recipes and menus that are healthy, delicious and special enough for every occasion. Welcome to *HeartSmart Cooking for Family and Friends*.

As the science of nutrition grows, we're learning more and more about the role food plays not just in treating disease but actually keeping us healthy. There are a number of components in our diet that play a role in lowering the risk of heart disease. Eating more fruits and vegetables, sufficient soluble fibre, foods rich in B-vitamins and less fat, especially saturated fat and trans-fatty acids, are all associated with reducing heart-disease risk. As you read through this book, you'll find the latest cooking tips and nutrition information alongside the delicious HeartSmart recipes. You'll learn not just what is good for you but why. And, as you're digesting the information, you'll have wonderful recipes to make the science come alive.

Too often we blame the risk of heart disease on one factor, such as diet or smoking. While high blood cholesterol, smoking, hypertension, obesity and lack of physical activity are all major risk factors, it is the combination of these factors that can place an individual at particularly high risk. A heart-healthy strategy has to address all these factors — not simply diet and cholesterol.

A heart-healthy diet should be based on Canada's Food Guide to Healthy Eating. The principles are:
- enjoy a variety of foods
- eat more cereals, breads, grains, fruits and vegetables
- choose lower-fat dairy products, leaner meats and foods prepared with little or no fat
- achieve and maintain a healthy body weight by enjoying regular physical activity and healthy eating
- limit salt, alcohol and caffeine

Heart-healthy eating translates into a lifelong eating pattern that everyone can enjoy.

Adopting a nutritious heart-healthy diet doesn't have to be a neverending fight. Because a good diet calls for variety, there's plenty of room for catering to your own tastes and lifestyle.

For many years, the Heart and Stroke Foundation of Canada has provided you with a variety of tools to make heart health easier to achieve. This latest book takes you into the world of entertaining — sharing good health with your family and friends.

FRAN BERKOFF, RD

ABOUT THE NUTRIENT ANALYSIS

Nutrient analysis of the recipes was performed by Info Access (1988) Inc., Toronto, Ontario, using the Nutritional Accounting component of the CBORD Menu Management System.

- The nutrient database was the 1997 Canadian Nutrient File, supplemented when necessary with documented data from reliable sources.

- The analysis was based on:
  - imperial measure and weight (except for foods typically packaged and used in metric quantity)
  - the smaller number of servings (i.e., larger portion) when there was a range, and
  - the first ingredient listed when there was a choice of ingredients.

- Unless otherwise specified, canola vegetable oil, 1% milk, homemade unsalted stocks, regular white rice (not parboiled) and enriched pasta were used throughout.

- Calculations of meat recipes assumed that only the lean portion was eaten. Analysis of poultry recipes assumed that the skin was not consumed.

- Optional ingredients and garnishes in unspecified amounts were not calculated.

- Specific measures of salt were included in the analyses but "salt to taste" was not.

- When previously prepared dried legumes, rice or pasta were called for, they were assumed to have been prepared without salt.

- Good and excellent sources of selected vitamins (A, C, thiamine, riboflavin, niacin, B_6, folacin, B_{12}) and minerals (calcium, iron, zinc) have been identified according to the reference standards developed for the nutrition labelling of foods in Canada (Guide to Food Labelling and Advertising, Agriculture and Agri-Food Canada, March 1996). These standards are known as the Recommended Daily Intakes (RDI), and are based on the Recommended Nutrient Intakes for Canadians (Health and Welfare Canada, 1983). They represent the highest recommended intake of each nutrient for all age/sex groups, omitting supplemental needs for pregnancy and lactation.

- A serving that supplies 15% of the Recommended Daily Intake for a vitamin or mineral (30% for vitamin C) is a good source of that nutrient. An excellent source must supply 25% of the RDI (50% for vitamin C).

HeartSmart Cooking for Family and Friends

In this day and age, people are isolated from each other more than ever. We work in home offices, without daily interaction with colleagues. We bank from home, pump our own gasoline, order take-out food, do our shopping on the Internet. Even those who work in large companies often communicate with their office mates by E-mail.

In such a mechanical society, entertaining family and friends has become more important than ever. We need the opportunity to be more social, to visit one another in our homes.

Entertaining is really just about sharing and welcoming friends and family into your life and taking care of them while they are with you. The pretty tablecloths, fancy recipes and vintage wines are really just trimmings. Good hosts concentrate on their guests' well-being rather than worrying about whether the party will be successful. Still, most of us are a little nervous when we have people over for a meal. This book should help make your entertaining more relaxed, easy and successful.

There are many ways to use this book. You can follow the recipes exactly or use them as a guideline, adapting them according to your mood, your own taste and the tastes of your guests, and what you have in your refrigerator or pantry (sometimes the best recipes are discovered this way!). As with *HeartSmart Cooking* and *More HeartSmart Cooking*, there are plenty of delicious and healthful recipes for everyday meals. But each one of these dishes will also stand up to any special occasion. Use the suggested menus, or plan your own. Use the serving suggestions and presentation ideas or let them inspire you to be original. The work plans and make-ahead tips will help you stay organized and spread out the work, making even a large dinner party perfectly manageable.

It's always easy to find an excuse not to entertain. I hope this book will encourage you to stop obsessing and just do it. Have a plan, stay organized and keep your sense of humour, and you will be well on your way to entertaining happiness.

GETTING ORGANIZED

The key to successful entertaining is to have a plan and be organized. Seasoned hosts know that when you are having a party, it is even more important to be a good organizer than it is to be a good cook. If you write things down nothing is left to chance. If something goes wrong, you will have the time and energy to handle it. Being organized will make you calm, and your company will think you are marvellous.

Make lists for everything. Have a running list of anything you will need at the last minute, and pick up everything at once instead of making several trips. Stick a list on the refrigerator door with the meal schedule, mapping out the timing of serving and order of dishes. (That way there is less chance that the salad will still be in the refrigerator the next morning.)

Before the guests arrive, make sure the dishwasher is empty, the counters are as clear as possible, and there is an empty garbage container at hand. Place a big tub of soapy water in a corner and put all dishes in it as you clear. This will keep sinks free and dishes will be out of the way and soaking until after the guests go home. Allocate sections of the kitchen for appetizer, soup, salad, main course and dessert, with the plates and serving utensils you will need for each course. I like to put sticky notes on the platters, indicating which plate goes with which dish — a helpful reminder for both myself and anyone who is helping me serve.

Some people keep an entertaining diary or scrapbook — a record of the date, menu, guest list (and guests' food allergies), wines and a photograph of the table. It is a wonderful souvenir but also a useful reference for future entertaining.

MISE EN PLACE

When I was in chef training I learned the importance of a mise en place — everything in place. Before you start cooking, have a plan and assemble everything that you'll need.

Setting up a mise en place will take a little effort, but will save you time in the end. Trust me.

- Food doesn't get better when it is frozen, but most things can be frozen fairly successfully.

- Wrap food very well to help prevent flavour transfers and freezer burn.

- Freeze individual pastries, cookies, etc., in a single layer on baking sheets and then transfer to a bag or container so they can be removed individually and thawed quickly.

- Unless otherwise specified, thaw food in the refrigerator, or partially defrost in the microwave

- Be sure the temperature in the freezer is at the freezing point; use a freezer thermometer.

- Don't overfill the freezer.

- Don't refreeze previously frozen food.

- Freeze things such as egg whites, chipotles, tomato paste and fresh lemon juice in ice cube trays for small premeasured portions. Transfer to sealed containers or heavy plastic bags when frozen.

KITCHEN EQUIPMENT

The entertaining chef will appreciate a few extra kitchen tools that will make cooking for company easier and help you to present food beautifully.

- ice cream scoops in different sizes for sorbets, shaping muffin batter, hollowing out vegetables to use as containers, and moulding mashed potatoes and other vegetables
- plastic squirt bottles for decorating soups, garnishing plates and food, decorating cakes
- non-aerosol spray bottle for oiling pans and for spraying oil on roasts, vegetables, salads and bread for even browning
- shaker bottle for dusting icing sugar, cocoa, etc.; it can also be used for dusting paprika and spices over food and plates
- scissors for cutting chives, dill and other herbs for garnishing
- zig-zag knife for cutting melons and other fruits
- melon baller
- toothpicks
- bamboo skewers for kebabs, satays and decorations
- crinkled pastry cutter
- mini blowtorch for brûlées

ENTERTAINING CUPBOARD

When I was growing up, on special occasions my mother sometimes hired a server to help her. We were always amazed when this person found things in our cupboards that we hadn't used in years and made them look gorgeous on the table. Your cupboards probably hold hidden treasures, too (pretend you are at someone else's garage sale and you'll be amazed at what you will see with fresh eyes!).

Keep baskets, candles and other serving items in one place so you don't have to look all over the house for things when you need them.

Although it may seem convenient and inexpensive to use paper napkins, cups and plates, cloth napkins and extra place settings will soon pay for themselves if you entertain regularly and will look more welcoming.

- baskets in various shapes and sizes to use for serving, as trays and as fruit/bread baskets
- placemats for everyday and special occasions
- tablecloths for everyday and special occasions
- serving platters and bowls (oval/round/square/long)
- pedestal plates

- serving spoons
- cake server
- candlesticks and candles
- votives
- napkins (cloth dinner napkins and paper cocktail napkins)
- napkin rings (page 26)
- trays
- table pads
- trivets

THE HEARTSMART PANTRY

If you entertain often, it is a good idea to keep your pantry (and your refrigerator and freezer) well stocked. If you have the basics on hand, you can entertain more easily without having to do an enormous amount of sudden shopping; you can also accommodate last-minute company or decide to entertain on the spur of the moment.

IN THE PANTRY
pasta
rice noodles
short-grain Italian rice for risotto (page 141)
basmati rice or Thai scented rice
sushi rice (page 37)
brown rice (preferably wehani)
cornmeal for polenta
couscous
dried beans

canned tomatoes
canned chickpeas
canned sockeye salmon
canned water-packed white tuna

all-purpose flour
whole wheat flour
granulated sugar
brown sugar
icing sugar
baking powder
baking soda
cocoa
vanilla
cream of tartar
rolled oats
wheat bran
cornstarch

olive oil
unflavoured vegetable oil (canola or sunflower)
sesame oil*
balsamic vinegar
sherry vinegar or red wine vinegar
rice wine
rice vinegar
soy sauce
fish sauce*
hoisin sauce*
black bean sauce*
oyster sauce*
Worcestershire sauce
hot red pepper sauce
mustards* (Dijon, Russian-style, powdered)
horseradish*
honey
ketchup*

salt
pepper
hot chili paste
cayenne
hot red pepper flakes
chipotles or jalapeños
spices and herbs
curry powder

* Refrigerate once opened.

tea (herbal and regular)

onions
garlic
fresh ginger root
crackers
artichoke hearts
chicken broth
vegetable broth
sun-dried tomatoes
dried porcini mushrooms
peanut butter
chocolate

IN THE REFRIGERATOR
eggs
milk
fruit juices
vegetable juices
fresh herbs (e.g., chives/green onions, parsley, cilantro, rosemary)
lemons
limes
salad greens
mayonnaise
salsa
pickles
olives
pesto
capers

maple syrup
yogurt and yogurt cheese (page 303)
fresh fruits and vegetables
cheeses
light miso paste

IN THE FREEZER
coffee (decaf and regular)
sorbets
frozen juice concentrates
chicken breasts
salmon fillets
shrimp
nori
dumpling wrappers
flour and corn tortillas
focaccia
bread
homemade cookies
homemade cake
sesame seeds
frozen peas
frozen corn
frozen blueberries
frozen raspberries
nuts
phyllo pastry
fresh breadcrumbs

COOKING FOR KIDS
It can be difficult deciding what to cook when you are entertaining families with children. If you have picky eaters in your own family, you already know how hard it can be to find something everyone loves. On these occasions, I like to cook in layers. I might make a soup that is very basic but provide an interesting pesto or salsa that more adventurous eaters can add. Or I might make a stir-fry for the main course and remove some chicken and one vegetable with a little soy sauce for the plain eaters and then add other vegetables and another sauce for the rest of the party. Pizzas, pastas and grilled meats can all be treated this way — a simple version and more flavourful version — so you are not really cooking two completely different dinners, and everyone feels as if they are eating the same dish.

THE GUEST LIST

If you are nervous about inviting new people, balance out the guest list with close friends. For added excitement, try inviting a surprise guest. Don't worry about mixing couples with people who are single or having an uneven number of guests. Also remember that a slightly crowded house can make a party feel more festive.

INVITATIONS

For a casual party you can phone, fax or E-mail. Mail invitations with an RSVP for formal parties. Specify the date by which guests should RSVP (including phone/fax and/or E-mail address) and follow up with a phone call if you haven't received a reply by then. Try to send an actual piece of paper that can be put on a fridge or bulletin board. Send out invitations sufficiently in advance; if the occasion is formal or people are busy, more advance notice is required — six weeks for a large party.

Make the invitation enticing; personalize it with a quotation, poem, picture or photograph. Include a small jar of salsa or box of cookies with the invitation. Include the date, time and place (with a map, if necessary, and instructions on parking), dress code, the occasion, theme and/or guest of honour.

PLANNING THE MENU

When you are planning the menu, take into account your available time, your ability and budget, your guests' tastes and appetites, seasonal ingredients, food allergies and the occasion or theme.

Variety is the key to an interesting and successful menu. Try to vary the temperatures of the food (e.g., one cold course, one hot course), the colours (everything should not be white), cooking methods, tastes and textures (don't flavour every dish with basil; avoid serving several pureed dishes at the same meal). If one dish is spicy, the others should be milder. Use seasonal ingredients and local specialties, especially if you are entertaining guests from other cities or countries.

Plan a menu that allows you to enjoy the party, too, and doesn't force you to spend the whole evening in the kitchen. Consider dishes that can be made ahead and reheated or served cold or at room temperature. Try to plan a menu where only one dish needs your attention at the last minute. If one recipe requires a more involved preparation, the others should be simpler.

When you are planning the number of courses, consider where people are coming from and where they are going. For example, don't serve a huge multi-course meal if people are moving on to a night at the theatre; don't worry about appetizers if you know your guests have just come from a cocktail party; don't serve a heavy meal too late in the evening. Plan on more food if you are serving family style or buffet style, where people tend to eat more. If the evening is long (e.g., New Year's Eve), plan more courses.

Dessert is the last thing guests will have in your house, so you'll want to make it special. Serve a more substantial dessert after a light meal and a light dessert after a more substantial meal. You might also consider serving two desserts, giving guests a choice.

As a final tip, you may want to serve only tried-and-true dishes to new guests. Save experiments for close friends or family. Above all, don't panic. Remember that your guests are coming over because they like you and you have extended your hospitality; they are not coming to judge the food (you hope!).

HeartSmart Menu-Planning Tips

- Consult the recipe analyses and use as a guideline for menu planning approximately 30 percent of calories from fat when you are putting together dishes. If one recipe is a little higher in fat or calories, don't worry — simply serve small portions and balance it with other dishes that are lower.
- Keep meat portions relatively small; the meat should fill about one-quarter of the plate, with side dishes and vegetables filling the rest.
- Place on the table a small dish of hummos (page 34), flavoured yogurt cheese (page 303) or one of the other dips to use as a spread instead of butter or margarine.
- Serve the meal slowly, allowing everyone time to digest properly and avoid overeating.
- Keep portions small, especially if you are serving many courses.
- A good menu has variety, but when you are choosing appetizers, side dishes and desserts, it can be better to serve one or two items rather than several (if you offer many different kinds of appetizers or desserts, for example, guests will want to try some of everything, which could lead to overloaded plates!).
- Use the best ingredients you can find. Best-quality balsamic vinegar, for example, is less acidic than less expensive versions, so your salad dressing will require less oil.

Beverages

Featuring Tips from Jeff Sansone

Jeff Sansone is as versatile at making mocktails as he is at whipping up his famous cocktails. As bartender of Canoe, he heads one of the hottest bars in Toronto. Here are some of his tips for serving drinks at home.

> You may decide to serve a variety of non-alcoholic mocktails that go beyond the standard mineral waters and soft drinks. You may also decide to serve alcohol, wine or beer. Why not set up a fresh juice bar and let your guests mix their own concoctions from an array of colourful and tasty juices? Serve mocktails in Champagne flutes and martini glasses and offer fresh berries and fruit slices as garnishes. Virgin Caesars are always popular and can be premixed in pitchers (go easy on spices and let guests adjust their drinks to their own tastes). Fruit juice spritzers (juice, soda and ice) always look and taste good.

Afraid of Entertaining or No Time?

Everyone is a little intimidated by the thought of entertaining. Identify what your difficulties might be — there is always a solution. If you are still overwhelmed by the thought of entertaining, don't give up.

- Consider hiring a caterer to prepare all or part of the meal; hire a high school or cooking school student to help serve or help clean up.
- Serve take-out or a favourite restaurant dish for part of the meal.
- Start the meal at a restaurant and finish with dessert at home.
- Start at home with appetizers at home and then go to a restaurant.

Don't Forget the Washroom

Don't forget to have the washroom clean, tidy and well-stocked. You might want to consider a few extra niceties such as fresh flowers, hand lotion and fresh soap.

- Plan on 6 to 8 items per
  hour per person.
- Make 2 to 4 different
  items if you are entertaining 8 people or less.
- Make 3 to 6 different
  items if you are entertaining 8 to 16 people.
- Make 4 to 8 different
  items for 16 to 20 people.
- For more than 20 people
  make 8 to 10 different
  items.
- Have a selection of hot
  and cold foods. Set up
  food at more than one
  spot in the room, or pass
  food on trays.

See Alcohol (page 274).

THE ESSENTIALS
- Corkscrew: Try for a "waiter's version," a professional corkscrew that opens wine,
  bottles and cans.
- Cocktail Shaker: The Boston shaker works best. It consists of a mixing glass and
  stainless-steel core that overlaps the glass.
- Strainer: The Hawthorn strainer works best.
- Ice Bucket and Scoop: Tongs are too unwieldy. Buy a scoop at any kitchen store.
- Cutting Board/Paring Knife: You can cut and twist garnishes much more quickly
  if you use the proper utensils.
- Pitcher: Comes in handy for juices, water, pop, etc. Keep a couple on hand.
- Napkins and Coasters: Protect your furniture!
- Straws: Someone will always ask for one.
- Blender.
- Ice: Estimate how much you'll need and then double the amount (you'll need
  about 1 lb/500 g per person). Make sure the ice that goes in the drinks is fresh.
  Have separate tubs of ice for chilling bottles.

SETTING UP
- At an appetizer party, serve drinks away from the food. This cuts down on conges-
  tion and keeps your guests moving. Sometimes the best spot to serve beverages is
  the kitchen; that way you're close to the fridge and sink, and clean-up is easier.
- Think about offering a special drink for the night. You can pre-mix batches and
  save time later. Name the drink after the guest of honour.
- Have lots of extra clean glasses on hand. For appetizer parties, have twice as many
  glasses as guests. Consider renting glassware. It's not that expensive and you can
  send the glasses back unwashed! If your party is outdoors, party supply stores offer
  a large assortment of good-quality plastic glasses in all sizes and colours.
- Have boxes ready to hold empties. Allocate a protected spot for dirty glasses.
- Place a plastic liner under the tablecloth to protect the bar table. Protect the floor
  under ice buckets and tubs with plastic.
- When in doubt, hire a professional bartender.

MATCHING FOOD WITH WINE*

FEATURING TIPS FROM SADIE DARBY

Sadie Darby, a discriminating wine taster and wonderful teacher, has worked with me
for twenty years. She also loves to cook and is especially good at pairing wine with food.
Should you choose to serve wine, she offers the following tips on serving wine at home.

- Store bottles on their sides, so that the cork remains in contact with the wine (if the
  cork dries out, the seal may break and the wine may oxidize).

- Store wines at 15°C to 16°C in a dark, vibration-free spot with reasonable humidity.
- There is a tendency to drink white wine too cold and red wine too warm. Put red wines in the refrigerator for about 30 minutes before serving. Take white wines out of the refrigerator 15 minutes before serving. To chill wines quickly, place the bottle in a bucket with plenty of ice and water. Do not prechill the wine glasses.
- In general, serve white wine before red, light-bodied before full-bodied, dry before sweet, young before old, sparkling before still.
- Be sure to offer alternatives to wine or to combine it with club soda as a spritzer if appropriate.
- When serving wine with food, match the wine to the strongest flavour in the dish.
- Hot, spicy foods go well with low-tannin wines, or consider serving beer. Sweet and sour dishes require a high-acid wine. Deep-fried foods marry well with high acid and/or sparkling wines; saltier foods also go well with high-acid wines.
- If you are serving wine with dessert, make sure the wine is sweeter than the dessert.
- Count on 5 glasses of wine per bottle.
- Serve wine in clear, untinted glasses.
- Serve Champagne in flutes to preserve the bubbles.
- Serve wine in large enough glasses to enhance the bouquet; the colder the wine, the more elusive the bouquet.
- Fill glasses two-thirds full if the glasses are small; fill large glasses less than half full.
- Hold a glass of wine by the stem.
- Ask for help if you are unsure of what to serve; consult an expert at the liquor store — take your recipes with you.

MUSIC TO EAT BY

FEATURING TIPS FROM SHELAGH ROGERS

Shelagh Rogers and I date back to the *Morningside* days, when we cooked and laughed together on the radio. She is now the host of CBC's *Take Five* and TVO's *Saturday Night at the Movies*. Here are some of her tips on how to choose music for a dinner party.

Shakespeare said, "If music be the food of love, play on." Around the same time, a poet named George Lillo wrote, "There's sure no passion in the human soul, but find its food in music." There is a deep and abiding connection between food and music: two sensual pleasures, too soon over!

I love food, I love music and I love to have people over for both. But at most memorable dinner parties, you can't remember the music. This is absolutely as it should be. Chances are if the music stood out, it was too loud or it distracted the guests from their meals. Music is an accompaniment, like a perfect chutney or salsa. It is not the main event. That doesn't mean it has to be boring.

WINE-SERVING TEMPERATURES
- sparkling and sweet white wines: 10°C to 12°C
- white, rosé and light red wines: 15°C to 16°C
- full-bodied red wines: 19°C to 20°C

BE A RESPONSIBLE HOST
- Designate someone to be in charge of serving drinks. Guests tend to drink more when they serve themselves.
- Always serve food when offering alcohol. Ensure non-alcoholic drinks are available.
- As the host, drink moderately if at all. Be aware of how your guests are going home. Remember that a good party has a safe ending.

- blankets
- drapes
- bedspreads
- throws
- rugs
- grass (page 267)
- scarves
- designer sheets
- enlarged photographs
- laminated blow-ups of
  magazine pages
- newspaper or magazine
  pages
- netting (for a seafood
  dinner)
- burlap (for a harvest
  dinner)
- fabric remnants (try
  organza or velvet runners)
- large towels (for a spa
  luncheon)
- antique or embroidered
  tea towels
- banana leaves or palm
  leaves

Here are a few hints for choosing music to enhance a dinner party.
- Consider the age of the group and play music of their time (i.e., if your guests are in their fifties, don't play Nine Inch Nails!).
- Plan your music according to the style of food. If it's a Cajun night, throw on a little zydeco or Dixieland band music. If it's Caribbean, try reggae. You get the idea.
- Watch out for the overly familiar. I once put the Beatles on and everyone ended up singing "When I'm Sixty-four" while the Bearnaise congealed.
- For the most part, you're better off with instrumentals. When you put on a vocal, a part of the brain will always try to listen.
- Be creative. Change music as you change courses. Upbeat for the appetizer, subtle for the main, jazz for dessert.
- When in doubt, go with the classics. You can't lose with Telemann's Tafelmusik (which means "music for the table"), Mozart's serenades or Haydn's symphonies. Keep it light, bright and in a major key. Wagner's "Twilight of the Gods" really only works on Hallowe'en.
- For divine inspiration, or if all else fails, keep in mind Santa Cecilia. She is the patron saint of music. She is only a prayer away.

LIGHTING
Lighting can help to set the mood. Your dining room (and your guests!) look better in softer light. If you don't have a dimmer, buy one.
- Dim the dining-room lights and eat by candlelight.
- Do not use scented candles in the dining area.
- Use glasses to hold votives; just put a little water in the bottom of each glass. Votive candles also look cosy nestled in antique muffin pans.
- If candles have been frozen for a few hours, they will burn more slowly. Cutting down the wicks will also make them burn more slowly.
- If your candle is slightly too small for the holder, wrap the base with aluminum foil.
- Use candles in flower arrangements.
- Try placing candles of different heights all over the table.
- For a casual dinner, place votives in tiny earthenware flower pots.
- Place candles in a line down the centre of the table.
- Place candles on or in front of mirrors to create more light.

PLACECARDS AND SEATING ARRANGEMENTS
It may seem odd, but everyone wants to know where to sit. If the party is small, you can just tell people, but if there are more than six people, it is a good idea to have placecards.

Use traditional placecards, have children decorate them or use gift tags or labelled take-home gifts. Other ideas include ribbon, names attached to glasses with clothespins, leaves or stones with names inscribed with marker, guests' photos (recent or old), or wooden plant markers in a little potted plant or cup of fresh herbs or cress. Use traditional holders or place the tags on the plate, tuck them into a napkin or cut a slit in apples or other fruits to hold the cards.

Although there are traditional "rules" about who sits where, I usually arrange the seating casually, according to the situation. Sometimes I place the children together at one end of the table, seat quiet people next to outgoing guests to keep conversation moving, or keep apart guests who are likely to get into heated arguments. Alternating male and female guests also usually works well. If there is more than one table, it's a good idea to appoint acting hosts at each additional table.

CENTREPIECES

Keep centrepieces low so that guests can see over them (or elevated so that guests can see through them). Sometimes small jugs of flowers all over the table are nicer than something really big in the centre. And who says a centrepiece has to be flowers? Try some of the following ideas:

- arrangements of photos
- fruit or vegetable basket
- basket of gourds or squash
- use glasses or bottles with one or two stems in each and set them down the middle of the length of the table
- teapots or baking pans full of flowers
- goldfish bowl

- fill little cups with wheat grass and place at each place setting
- candles (try wedging votives in sand in an urn, statue or dish)
- strew fresh flowers over the centre of the table and nestle candles among them
- driftwood or rocks

SETTING THE TABLE

Table settings are becoming more informal and casual. There are some traditions, but many rules are broken. I rarely provide a separate bread and butter plate or separate salad plate (unless the salad is a separate course) these days, and I seldom have a salt and pepper shaker for every two or three place settings, as some books instruct. Don't be afraid to mix and match china and cutlery — you can combine antique china with modern serving pieces on lacy tablecloths.

There are rules for setting cutlery, however, and they are based on common sense, so it is easy to follow them. In general, you arrange the cutlery from the outside, in the order in which the pieces will be used. Forks are placed to the left of the plate; knives and spoons are placed to the right. Knives should always be placed with the sharp edge facing the plate.

Glasses start above the knife and go to the right, beginning with the water glass and followed by wine glasses, in the order in which they will be used.

SOUVENIR TABLECLOTH
For a souvenir of the party, have everyone write their names and greetings (with fabric crayon or indelible marker) on a plain tablecloth. Add the menu, date and comments for a great keepsake.

OUTDOOR TABLECLOTHS
If you are dining outdoors, sew stones into the corners of the tablecloth to keep it from blowing in the wind. Or attach shells or rocks to the ends of ribbons and crisscross over the table to hold the tablecloth in place.

French service is the most formal and elegant, but it usually requires professional help. Waiters serve seated guests from large platters.

Plated service is best for smaller dinner parties. Individual plates of food are assembled in the kitchen and then brought to the table and placed in front of each guest, restaurant style. Plates are traditionally served from the diner's left and removed from the diner's right (lower on the left, raise on the right) unless you are serving soup, water or wine, which should also be served from the right.

If you are serving **family style**, platters are placed on the table and guests pass the platters and serve themselves. Or the host or hostess places food on individual plates, serving from large platters.

At a **buffet**, guests serve themselves from a buffet table.

You can also combine different kinds of service, depending on what is practical and comfortable for you. For example, you can serve the salad and soup at the table and then have guests help themselves to main course and dessert from a buffet. With close friends and family, you can serve and/or eat in the kitchen and let guests help you cook and serve.

GARNISHING

FEATURING TIPS FROM OLGA TRUCHAN

Olga Truchan is Canada's top food stylist. She brings to every photo shoot a brilliant artistic sense, enormous experience and a passion for food. Here are some of her tips on how to make your food look as wonderful as it tastes.

The visual appeal of the food we eat enhances our dining experience by delighting our eyes as well as our palates. Gone are the days when a sprig of curly parsley would constitute culinary art. A combination of good raw ingredients, careful cooking, arrangement and garnishes results in wholesome dishes that are a joy to make and share.

Look beyond traditional table settings to containers around your house and garden. Keep it simple and clean but don't be inhibited. There are no prescriptions, no rules or regulations — experiment and have fun!

Try these suggestions to start:

- Let nature be a guide. Use a piece of slate or flat rock as a platter for hors d'oeuvres, appetizers or kebabs. Try clean pebbles or beach stones as a base for platters; use slightly moist sea salt to anchor oysters and mussels on your platters and keep them stable.
- Instead of pedestal plates, set your bowls or plates on driftwood, in willow or other branches.
- For kebabs, use the woody stems of rosemary, sharpened sticks of bamboo or maple twigs, or sugar cane.

EDIBLE FLOWERS

Here is a partial list of edible flowers. It is best if the flowers have been organically grown. CAUTION: If you choose to use flowers not listed here, DO CHECK and ensure they are edible.

SPRING
- violets
- pansies
- johnny jump-ups
- lilac
- tulips

SUMMER
- roses
- herb flowers (sage blossoms, chive blossoms, lavender, bergamot)
- squash blossoms
- sunflowers
- nasturtiums
- impatiens
- daisies
- day lilies

AUTUMN
- pot marigolds (calendula)
- chrysanthemum

- Don't just skewer meat and vegetables; use skewers for tiny breads and cheeses, tiny sandwiches, sushi.
- Tie food bundles with blanched leeks, green onions or chives.
- Make use of edible flowers from your (or a friend's) garden. Garnish plates and platters with petals or whole flowers, throw them in your salad, pin them on your tablecloth, freeze them in ice cubes.
- Line trays, baskets or platters with fresh herbs, lettuce, cabbage or banana leaves; use parsley or herbs to keep food steady. Use hardier lettuces and herbs next to hot foods and more delicate leaves for cold dishes and desserts.
- For an unusual look, serve food in hollowed-out rocks, on grass, in garden pots or urns, children's buckets, toys, soda fountain glasses… the list is endless.
- If you are using mushrooms in the menu, buy or gather green moss and arrange a huge portobello mushroom on it for the centrepiece.
- Provide contrast by using large and small platters, filled sparsely or generously; keep it monochromatic or multicoloured.

SOUP GARNISHES

TWO-TONE SOUP
Use two different-coloured pureed soups of the same thickness. Place each soup in a separate measuring cup. Pour both soups into the bowl at the same time. The liquids should meet in a straight line.

STARBURST GARNISH
Place a 1-inch/2.5 cm drop of contrasting soup or puree (e.g., yogurt, sour cream, tomato sauce) on the surface of the soup. Pull the tip of a knife through the circle to create a star pattern.

SQUIGGLE GARNISH
Place the contrasting-coloured puree in a squeeze bottle and squeeze a zigzagged line down the centre of the soup.

HEARTS
Make large polka dots of contrasting colour. Starting at the outside of one dot, drag the tip of the knife right through the centre.

SPLASH GARNISH
Drop a splash of contrasting-coloured puree onto the surface of the soup.

SWIRLS
Whatever design you have made with the contrasting colour can be embellished by dragging the tip of your knife through the lines.

BACKS OF CHAIRS

The backs of chairs have become fashionable to decorate. Rental companies provide special covers for chairs for a different look, or if you want the chairs to match the tablecloths and napkins. For other chair decorations try ivy, flowers or herbs, towels, draped material tied with ribbon or raffia, scarves, rugs, sweaters, ribbons, plain fabric that has been stamped or stenciled.

CHOOSING A THEME

- Celebrate a season (summer nights, spring brunch), holiday (Thanksgiving, Passover) or special occasion (birthday, going-away party, graduation).
- Plan a menu around your favourite food (an all-potato meal, seafood celebration).
- Plan a meal around a sports or TV event (the big game, Oscar night).
- Try a fun theme (spa luncheon, fifties dinner).
- Feature a specific ethnic cuisine (Italian, Moroccan, Thai).

TABLESCAPING

FEATURING TIPS FROM MAGGI JONES

Maggi Jones worked as a prop stylist with top food photographer Robert Wigington — the team that has been responsible for the photographs in five of my cookbooks. She was also the table stylist for "Bonnie Stern Entertains," seen on WTN.

Here are just some of her tips on how to get ideas for setting up your table.

- Look through magazines and books for ideas. When you see a presentation you like, make a note of it or keep a copy of the picture. Browse through art books for ideas on how to put together colours and shapes. If you are cooking food from a certain country, or to celebrate a particular event, go to the library and seek out reference books that will give you ideas and information related to your theme.
- Look around at the things you already own, to see if they can be used in new ways. Find a different use for that vase!
- Bring back things from your travels, whether you're going to another country or just to the cottage. Find something new and bring it into your home (e.g., a piece of driftwood, a basket of smooth stones, pine boughs).
- Keep an idea diary. Date the entries so you will know when things were popular. Keep a menu diary, photos of your table and a description of the table. Try to remember flower arrangements, special napkin folds or food presentations you see in friends' homes or in restaurants.
- Consider renting or borrowing dishes, cutlery, tablecloths, etc., to achieve the look you want and a different look each time you entertain.

NAPKIN FOLDING

Use cloth napkins if possible; they should be at least 20 inches/50 cm in diameter. Try one of the folds described below; tuck a flower, twig, pine cone, holly, etc., into napkins to make them look more festive.

KNOT

Open the napkin completely and, starting at one corner, roll up. Tie as flat a knot as possible in the centre. Arrange the napkin vertically on the plate. (For a layered look, use two contrasting-coloured napkins together.)

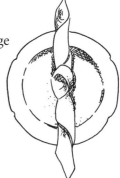

BUFFET FOLDS

There are many ways to enfold cutlery for a buffet so it is easy to carry. Here are two examples:

1) Triangle: Open the napkin completely and fold in half to form a triangle. Fold the napkin in half three times more in the same direction to form a narrow triangle. Place the cutlery in one of the pockets created by the folds. Fold down the top edge and tuck it in so the cutlery is completely enclosed.

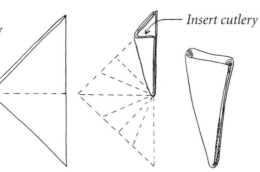

Insert cutlery

2) Rolled: Open the napkin completely. Place the necessary cutlery vertically at one end. Fold the top and bottom edges in and roll up tightly. You can secure the roll with ribbon or twine.

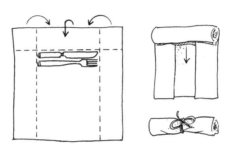

ARTICHOKE LINER

This is a great way to fold a napkin when you are serving soup and the bowl is either very hot or risks slipping on the bottom plate. I also use this liner with hot appetizers served in individual dishes.

Open the napkin and fold all four corners into the middle. Holding the centre securely, carefully flip napkin over and fold each corner into the centre again. Transfer the napkin to serving plate. Holding the centre, gently pull out the flaps from under each corner to form a container for a soup bowl or ramekin.

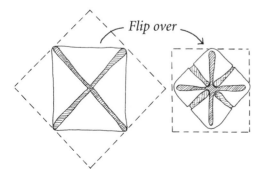

Flip over

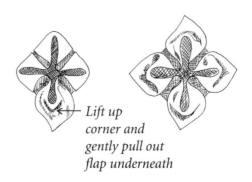

Lift up corner and gently pull out flap underneath

- Do not use strongly scented flowers at the table.
- Use an oasis in the bottom of the vase or container to hold flowers. Or criss-cross tape over the opening of the vase to keep flowers in place; wrap tape around the rim of the vase to secure the cross (florist's tape works well).
- Cut stems on the diagonal.
- Cut stems while holding them under warm water.
- Remove any leaves that will be under water.
- Arrange greenery first, then add the flowers.
- Try an arrangement of flowers of the same colour.
- Keep flowers in a cool place away from sun or light until guests arrive.
- To revive flowers, place the stems in warm water and then cool water.
- To open roses, blow gently and quickly into the centres.

- ivy
- grape vines
- flowers
- herbs
- ribbon
- bagels (for brunch)
- raffia or string
- corrugated cardboard secured with raffia

TRIANGLE FOLD

Open the napkin completely and fold in half to form a triangle. Bring two sides up to centre point to form a diamond. Fold diamond in half to form a triangle, so folds are on the outside. Fold in half again and place the napkin on the plate, resting on the folded edge.

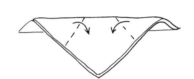

TUXEDO

Open the napkin completely and fold in half to form a triangle. Fold down the folded edge about 1 inch/2.5 cm. Flip the napkin over and fold down the two sides to meet in the middle. Fold back the bottom third of the napkin. Fold back the two sides. Place the napkin on a plate. A rose or other flower can be inserted.

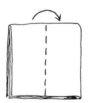

PLAIN FOLD

Open the napkin completely and fold in half to form a rectangle. Fold in half twice more. Place the napkin on the table or plate vertically, with the open edge on the right and the folds at the top.

FOLD WITH NAPKIN RING

Fold the napkin in quarters. Starting at one corner, roll up. Insert in a napkin ring. You can also open the napkin completely, simply pick up the napkin in the centre and tuck the point into the napkin ring.

FOLD IN WINE GLASS

Open the napkin completely and, starting at one corner, roll up. Fold in half and insert the folded end into a wine glass. Allow the "ears" to flop over if you wish.

Carving

FEATURING TIPS FROM HUBERT AUMEIER

It is so hard to find good information on carving that for this book I turned to Hubert Aumeier, my good friend and colleague in Canmore, Alberta. He is a master chef and part owner of Valbella Meats, a meat-processing plant and butcher store featuring game and specialty meats.

Here are just some of his invaluable tips on how to carve traditional cuts of meat.

BASIC TIPS

- You need four basic pieces of equipment for successful carving — a carving knife, a sharpening steel, a wooden carving board and a large fork to hold meat in place.
- Make sure your carving knife is sharp. Hold the steel horizontally in your left hand. Holding the knife in your right hand, run it along the top side of the steel from the base to the tip. Place the steel underneath the knife to sharpen the other side.

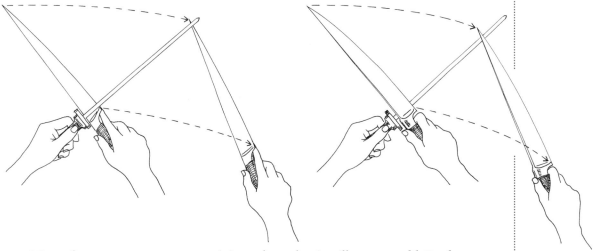

- Most of us carve meat as soon as it is ready so that it will not get cold. But large pieces of meat do not get cold for a while! A roast that is more than 3 lb/1.5 kg will be much easier to carve if you let it rest for at least 15 to 20 minutes. The meat will lose less juice and will be more evenly coloured. Smaller roasts should rest for at least 5 minutes.
- For easier carving, always ask the butcher to remove the chine bone when you are buying rack of lamb or pork, crown roasts and rib roasts.
- Do not stab meat with a fork as this will allow the juices to run out. Simply use a fork to hold the meat in place while you carve.
- To prevent juices from dripping over the carving board onto your table, place board on a larger tray lined with a tea towel.

LEG OF LAMB

For some reason (probably so that it will fit in your roasting pan), butchers cut the end of the shank bone off the leg of lamb. Ask yours to leave the bone on and to clean it so that you will have something to hold on to while you are carving. Also ask that the aitch bone be removed for easier carving.

After the lamb has rested for about 15 minutes, hold the end of the bone (wrap a napkin around it) with the leg resting on the cutting board. Carve the meat from the end of the bone down to the carving board. Rotate the bone a quarter turn and carve again. Repeat until all the meat is off the bone. (Do not worry about carving against the grain!)

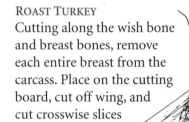

ROAST TURKEY

Cutting along the wish bone and breast bones, remove each entire breast from the carcass. Place on the cutting board, cut off wing, and cut crosswise slices from each breast.

Remove the legs from the carcass by cutting through the hip joints. Cut the thigh from the drumstick. Cut the meat off each side of the thigh bone and then carve crosswise. Do the same with each drumstick.

Thigh bone

FLANK STEAK

Flank steak is a tougher cut of meat but it can be grilled and served rare if it is marinated and carved thinly. To carve it properly, slice the meat very thinly against the grain on the diagonal (a boneless turkey breast can also be carved this way).

PRIME RIB ROAST

Although you can buy a boned rolled rib roast, there is something very regal about cooking and serving it on the bone. Cooking it on the bone also gives it more flavour, keeps it juicier, and there will be very delicious bones to divvy up.

Roast the meat bone side down. Let it rest for 15 to 20 minutes before carving. Holding the ends of the bones up, cut the meat off the bones in one piece. Carve the meat off each bone. Place the roast on the carving board, cut side down. Hold the meat in place with a fork and carve in thick or thin slices as you wish.

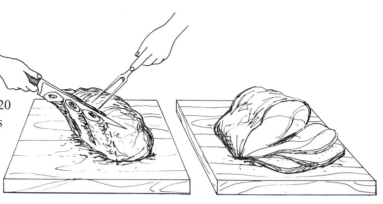

CROWN ROAST OF PORK OR LAMB

When ordering a crown roast, make sure the chine bone has been removed. If the ends of the bones have been Frenched (cut to a point), the roast will look even nicer. Order the rack by the number of ribs you need. I usually order one pork chop per person and two or three lamb chops per person. To shape a crown roast the butcher twists a large rack or two racks into a crown and ties it together. When you carve, remove the twine and carve between the bones.

BONING A WHOLE FISH

Lift the fish to a platter with a large spatula or debone in the pan. Remove the skin on top side. Using a fork and a spoon, separate the two fillets down the length of the fish and gently fold them back to expose the bone. Carefully lift up the head and pull towards the tail to remove the entire skeleton. Gently reassemble the fish and serve.

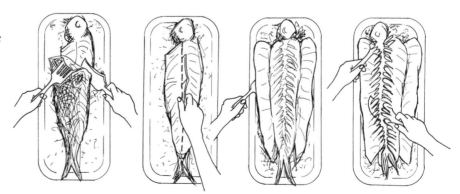

HOW TO BE THE PERFECT HOST, AND THE PERFECT GUEST

FEATURING TIPS FROM GUY RIGBY

Guy Rigby, Executive Assistant Manager of Toronto's Four Seasons Hotel, says he owes his career to good manners — he got his first big promotion when he impressed his boss by automatically standing up when a woman (the boss's mother, as it turned out!) walked into the room. Guy has been in the hospitality business ever since, and he knows better than anyone that good manners is really all about showing respect for others.

THE PERFECT HOST

- A great host is always sensitive to the needs of the guests. When planning a menu, think carefully about who your audience is. Today, many people have health or cultural dietary considerations. If your guests are vegetarian, find out what type of vegetarian. If your guests have food allergies, it is their responsibility to advise you in advance. It is your responsibility to try to prepare a meal that is suitable for everyone to eat.
- If you are really unsure how guests are going to react to your menu, serve the meal family style by putting all the food on the table, or buffet style by placing food on a side table so guests can help themselves. This way it is easier for them to refuse something they don't like without attracting attention.
- People often bring a bottle of wine but it is not compulsory to serve it. If you arrange for guests to bring an item such as a dessert or a salad, then you should definitely serve it.
- Don't assume your guests are fond of animals. Be prepared to remove your pets from the room if your guests are uncomfortable or allergic.
- Unplug the telephone and turn off the television (a good idea for everyday family dinners, too).
- Adjust the temperature of the room so it is cool — it will heat up in a hurry when guests arrive.
- Take coats (clear a space in the coat closet or have a designated bedroom) and introduce your guests to each other right away. Offer a drink as soon as guests arrive; getting people involved in the kitchen or helping can also make them feel more comfortable and relaxed.
- Do not be inconsiderate to your other guests if someone is late. Inform them that you are still waiting for more guests, make an excuse on their behalf and announce how long you intend to wait. You should certainly not wait more than 45 minutes.
- Light candles, serve water and have the first course on the table (if cold) before guests sit down.
- The female guest of honour is traditionally served first, then other women, then men and the host last. However, your home is not a restaurant, so do whatever is most convenient and comfortable for your guests.

HOST/HOSTESS GIFT IDEAS

- disposable or instant camera for taking pictures at the party
- photo album
- picture frame
- basket of fruit
- vase with flowers
- candles
- specialty teas or coffees
- specialty oils or vinegars
- cookbook or wine book
- latest bestseller
- bath oils or soaps
- stationery
- tea towels
- small serving platter or bowl
- travel diary or blank journal

- Traditionally, you should wait until all your guests have finished eating before you begin clearing the table. You should not plan to race through dinner anyway, so this should not be a problem. You may well need to get up from the table to finish the preparation of the next course — this will indicate to the slow eater that their time is up!
- When you are clearing the table, try not to stack dishes in front of guests; remove them two at a time. Remove everything from the table that is not needed for the next course.
- Designate a helper beforehand so guests do not feel the need to get up and help.
- If your party completely loses its energy and you think emergency action is needed, change the seating arrangement between courses, move to the living room or den for dessert and coffee, or even bring in a board game or surprise guest (neighbour or relative).

THE PERFECT GUEST

- Common courtesy dictates that you should RSVP at least one week before a party.
- If you have dietary restrictions, politely inform your host in advance to avoid any uncomfortable situations. Everyone has a different interpretation of what a vegetarian can eat, so be specific. Don't make your host guess.
- A well-mannered guest never arrives early, never very late; up to 15 minutes from the time the invitation states is the perfect time.
- Although it is not compulsory, bringing a gift shows how much you appreciate your host's hospitality. Wine and edible gifts are usually good choices but do not expect them to be served that evening unless you prearrange it with the host. (A plate of cookies or chocolates that can be served as an add-on with coffee would be a better choice than a cake or tart.) You may even say on a card that the gift is for the host and hostess to enjoy another time. If you bring flowers, bring an arrangement or plant rather than cut flowers, which will distract the host while a vase is found, etc. (It is very nice to send flowers on the day of the dinner or the day after, especially if you have forgotten to bring something.)
- Do not rearrange your host's seating plan.
- Unless specifically invited to do so by your host or hostess (and even then you should wait), do not start eating before everyone is served.
- Pass food around the table in one direction to keep things organized.
- If the table has been correctly set, the general rule is to start from the outside of your place setting and work your way towards the plate (page 21). If you are not sure, wait and follow the lead of your host or hostess.
- Soup should be sipped from the side of a spoon without slurping. You should never insert the entire bowl of the spoon in your mouth. To reach the last spoonfuls, soup bowls should be tilted away from the body, not towards.

TAKE-HOME FAVOURS

Take-home gifts are definitely an "extra," but if the occasion is very special, guests will be delighted to receive something that reminds them of the party.
- homemade cookies
- candied ginger or orange peel
- placecards or copies of the menu
- photographs
- photo album
- flowers
- bouquet of herbs
- candles
- soap (especially fruit-scented)
- stationery (with a food theme)

• Do not sit with your elbows on the table.

• If the meal is served family style, pick up a dish and hold it for the guest on either side of you, if they have not already served themselves.

• If you are at a more formal dinner, either in someone's home or at a restaurant, gentlemen should stand as other guests arrive (male or female). It is impolite to greet someone from a sitting position.

• On more formal occasions, when it is time to sit down for dinner, gentlemen should pull out the chairs for the women sitting on either side of them. Gentlemen should never sit before ladies are seated. A man should always stand whenever a lady sitting on either side of him stands to leave the room. When the woman returns, the man should again stand and assist her with her chair.

• Once a knife, fork or spoon has been used, it should never again touch the table. Between bites, place the knife and fork on the plate.

• The correct way to eat bread is to tear off a small piece, spread a small amount of butter on it if desired and then eat it. You should transfer the butter to your side plate from the butter dish first, rather than double-dipping into the butter dish. It is considered improper to spread the entire piece of bread or roll as if you are about to make a sandwich, or to cut the bread with your knife.

• While it may be a compliment, asking for seconds is a faux pas. You can mention how delicious the dish was in the hope that you will be offered more, but do not put your host in an embarrassing situation. There may not be enough for everyone to have seconds!

• When you have finished your meal, place your knife and fork (or spoon and fork) side by side on the plate, with the handles at 4 o'clock or 6 o'clock.

• There is never any expectation that a guest must help clear the table. You may want to offer and a good host will decline. If everyone gets up from the table and piles into the kitchen with dirty dishes, it tends to break up the atmosphere of the party.

• Traditionally you should pick a time to leave when dinner and coffee have been completely served and there is a natural lull in the conversation. Begin by thanking your host graciously, make your apologies and leave. Never be the last one to say goodbye.

• Be sure to send a handwritten thank-you note.

APPETIZERS

HUMMOS WITH ROASTED SQUASH *34*
CARAMELIZED ONION DIP WITH ROASTED POTATOES *35*
SHRIMP AND ASPARAGUS SUSHI ROLLS *36*
SHRIMP MOUSSE ON SUGAR CANE STICKS *38*
QUESADILLAS WITH CARAMELIZED ONIONS AND GRILLED PEPPERS *39*
ROASTED TOMATO AND GARLIC BRUSCHETTA *40*
SUSHI PIZZA *42*
CHICKPEA BRUSCHETTA *44*
BAKED CHÈVRE ON BLACK BEAN SALSA *45*
SPICED LAMB CIGARS *46*
CORN PANCAKES WITH SALSA *48*
CURRIED CHICKEN POT STICKERS *50*
GRILLED SHRIMP WITH CHARMOULA *52*
SOUTHWEST CHOPPED SHRIMP COCKTAIL *53*

MORE APPETIZERS

ASIAN EGGPLANT DIP *57*
ROASTED GARLIC AND POTATO CROSTINI *58*
TERIYAKI-GLAZED CHICKEN MEATBALLS *59*
BAKED SPRING ROLLS *60*
CHICKEN SATAYS WITH PEANUT MARINADE *62*
SMOKED SALMON SUSHI BALLS *108*
SAMOSAS WITH CILANTRO CHILI DIP *110*
SESAME-SEARED TOFU SALAD ROLLS *144*
BLACK BEAN AND CORN HUMMOS *146*
BUCKWHEAT BLINI WITH SMOKED TROUT *184*
SPICY THAI SHRIMP *217*
DOUBLE-WRAPPED SHRIMP SALAD ROLLS *248*
SPARKLING ORANGE JUICE JELLY *268*

HUMMOS WITH ROASTED SQUASH

Here's a delicious variation of hummos. Use any cooked legumes instead of chickpeas. Leftover hummos can be used as sandwich spread, or add stock to turn it into a soup.

If you are in a hurry, use 2 cups/500 mL diced frozen squash. Simmer for 5 minutes instead of roasting. You could also use 1 or 2 minced garlic cloves or 1 head roasted garlic.

Makes about 3 cups/750 mL

SERVING SUGGESTION
• Serve as a dip with pita chips, tortilla chips or on potato crostini (page 58).

MAKE AHEAD
• This can be made a few days ahead and refrigerated.

Tortilla Chips
Cut four 8-inch/20 cm corn or flour tortillas into wedges (scissors work well) and arrange in a single layer on a baking sheet. Bake in a preheated 400°F/200°C oven for about 8 minutes, or until lightly browned and crisp. Makes about 3 cups/750 mL.

1 lb	peeled butternut squash, cut in 2-inch/ 5 cm chunks (about 4 cups/1 L)	500 g
2 tbsp	olive oil, divided	25 mL
1 tsp	chopped fresh rosemary, or ¼ tsp/1 mL dried	5 mL
1	19-oz/540 mL can chickpeas, drained and rinsed	1
2 tbsp	lemon juice	25 mL
1 tsp	ground cumin	5 mL
¼ tsp	hot red pepper sauce	1 mL
	Salt and pepper to taste	

1. Place squash on a baking sheet lined with parchment paper. Sprinkle with 1 tbsp/15 mL olive oil and rosemary. Bake in a preheated 400°F/200°C oven for 40 minutes, or until tender and well browned. Cool.

2. Place chickpeas in a food processor and chop finely. Add lemon juice, cumin, remaining 1 tbsp/15 mL oil and hot pepper sauce. Combine well. Add squash and combine. Add salt and pepper. If mixture is too thick, add a little yogurt or water to thin.

Hummos with Roasted Red Peppers
Roast 2 sweet red peppers (page 49). Peel, seed and dice. Use instead of the squash.

Hummos with Roasted Squash and Pesto
Add ⅓ cup/75 mL pesto to the hummos.

Devilled Eggs with Hummos
Use hummos as a filling for devilled eggs. Shell hard-cooked eggs, cut in half and remove yolks. Fill egg whites with hummos. Garnish with whole chickpeas and sprinkle with paprika.

PER TABLESPOON

Calories	20
Protein	0.7 g
Fat	0.7 g
Saturates	0.1 g
Cholesterol	0 mg
Carbohydrate	3 g
Fibre	0.4 g
Sodium	18 mg
Potassium	41 mg

CARAMELIZED ONION DIP WITH ROASTED POTATOES

This is an up-to-date, fresher version of potato chips with onion soup mix dip. The potatoes can also be very thinly sliced, spread on a parchment-lined baking sheet and roasted at 425°F/220°C for 25 to 30 minutes until browned. Season very lightly with oil, salt and pepper. When the chefs from Canoe — Anthony Walsh and Todd Clarmo — taught at my school, they made incredible paper-thin potato chips baked with an herb leaf sandwiched between two.

You can use sweet potato chunks in this recipe instead of baking potatoes. Leftover potatoes can be made into potato salad, with the leftover dip as a dressing. The dip can also be used as a sandwich spread.

Makes 8 servings

2 lb	baking potatoes or Yukon Gold potatoes, peeled	1 kg
3 tbsp	olive oil, divided	45 mL
1 tbsp	chopped fresh rosemary, or ½ tsp/2 mL dried	15 mL
½ tsp	salt	2 mL
¼ tsp	pepper	1 mL
2	large Spanish onions (about ¾ lb/375 g each), chopped	2
1 cup	yogurt cheese (page 303) or thick low-fat yogurt	250 mL

1. Cut potatoes into 1-inch/2.5 cm chunks (or use whole or halved unpeeled baby potatoes). Toss in a large bowl with 2 tbsp/25 mL oil, rosemary, salt and pepper. Place in a single layer on baking sheets lined with parchment paper. Roast in a preheated 400°F/200°C oven for 45 to 50 minutes, or until browned.

2. Meanwhile, heat remaining 1 tbsp/15 mL oil in a large skillet on high heat. Add onions and do not stir until onions begin to brown. Reduce heat to medium, stir and then leave them alone again until they are brown on the bottom. Then cook, stirring often. If they begin to burn or stick, add a little water and keep cooking until onions are very brown. Cool completely.

3. Combine onions with yogurt cheese. Taste and add salt and pepper if necessary. Serve with roasted potatoes.

SERVING SUGGESTIONS
- Serve dip in a bowl with potatoes on a bed of parsley. Serve potatoes with toothpicks or rosemary sprigs.
- Serve dip in a hollowed-out loaf of black bread, with squares of the bread for dipping instead of potatoes.

MAKE AHEAD
- The dip can be made a day ahead.
- The potatoes can be roasted a few hours ahead. If you roast the potatoes a day ahead, store them in an airtight container overnight in the refrigerator. Serve at room temperature.

PER SERVING

Calories	178
Protein	5.3 g
Fat	6.1 g
Saturates	1.3 g
Cholesterol	3 mg
Carbohydrate	26.7 g
Fibre	2.4 g
Sodium	176 mg
Potassium	486 mg

Good: Vitamin B_6; Vitamin B_{12}

SHRIMP AND ASPARAGUS SUSHI ROLLS

Some people hesitate to eat sushi because they think it always involves eating raw fish. But sushi refers to the vinegar flavouring of the rice (sushi actually means vinegared things), and sushi can be made with many ingredients, including raw or cooked seafood, tofu or vegetables.

This is a wonderful appetizer to serve at a sushi party or any special dinner. If you can't find extra-large shrimp, just use more smaller ones, or substitute smoked salmon, cooked crab or grilled tofu. Leftover sushi can be broken up and served as a salad.

Barry Chaim, owner of EDO, one of Toronto's best Japanese restaurants, likes to add 2 tbsp/25 mL pickled ginger juice to the shrimp-cooking liquid fore extra flavour.

Makes 4 rolls or 24 pieces

8	extra-large shrimp, cleaned (about 1 oz/30 g each)	8
8	spears asparagus, trimmed and peeled	8
4	sheets toasted nori (about 8 x 7 inches/20 x 18 cm)	4
4 cups	cooked sushi rice (page 37)	1 L
¼ cup	Russian-style mustard or 4 tsp/20 mL wasabi	50 mL
¼ cup	yogurt cheese (page 303) or mayonnaise	50 mL
8	pieces of lettuce, about 4 inches/10 cm long	8
8	fresh chives or strips of green onion	8

1. Insert skewers lengthwise through shrimp to keep shrimp straight. Cook shrimp in a deep skillet of simmering water for 3 to 4 minutes until pink, opaque and cooked through. Cool. Remove skewers.

2. Cook asparagus in a separate skillet of boiling water for 2 to 3 minutes until just cooked and bright green. Drain, rinse with very cold water and pat dry.

3. Cut asparagus spears to same length as nori; if shrimp are not long enough, cut them in half lengthwise.

4. To roll sushi, arrange one sheet of nori at a time on a bamboo mat (sudari) or a tea towel. Bumpy side of nori should be face up to help the rice stick. Gently pat about 1 cup/250 mL rice over nori, leaving about ½ inch/1 cm clear space at the top. (Dip your fingers in a bit of cold water if rice is very sticky.)

SERVING SUGGESTIONS

- Arrange sushi on a square glass plate or bamboo mat with some slices facing up and some standing.
- When you are assembling sushi, let a bit of asparagus and shrimp hang out on either side of the rolls so those pieces look wild.
- Serve with dipping sauce or soy sauce.

MAKE AHEAD

- These are best made close to serving, but they can be made a few hours in advance.

Dipping Sauce for Sushi
In a small bowl, combine ½ tsp/2mL wasabi with 2 tbsp/25mL water. Stir in ¼ cup/50mL soy sauce, 1 tbsp/15mL chopped fresh ginger root and 2 tbsp/25mL rice vinegar. Makes ½ cup/125mL.

PER PIECE

Calories	60
Protein	2.9 g
Fat	0.5 g
Saturates	0.1 g
Cholesterol	11 mg
Carbohydrate	10.7 g
Fibre	0.3 g
Sodium	48 mg
Potassium	54 mg

5. In a small bowl, combine mustard or wasabi and yogurt cheese. Adjust the amount of mustard or wasabi according to your taste.

6. Across centre of rice, spread a bit of mustard mixture. Place a piece of lettuce on mustard, top with two shrimp in a line, asparagus and two chives. Wet the strip of nori at the top and, using mat or towel to help you roll, roll up sushi. Repeat until you have four rolls. If you are not serving immediately, wrap each roll in plastic wrap.

7. Just before serving, using a knife dipped in cold water, trim off the ends of each roll (a treat for the chef or see serving suggestions). Cut each roll in half and then cut each half in thirds. Dip knife before each cut or wipe with a wet cloth.

Southwest Sushi Rolls

Combine 1 tsp/5 mL chopped chipotles (page 73) with ⅓ cup/75 mL yogurt cheese (page 303) or mayonnaise and 2 tbsp/25 mL chopped fresh cilantro. Spread on rice in place of mustard/yogurt mixture.

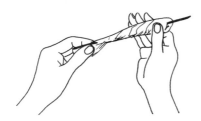

Skewering Shrimp

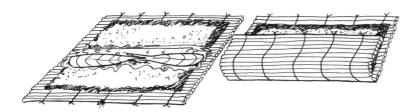

Sushi Rice
For sushi, use medium-grain Japanese rice. It absorbs less water than other rices and when cooked it should be sticky but not mushy. Rinse it in plenty of cold water before cooking. Soaking for 30 minutes before cooking also improves the texture.

Homemade Shrimp Stock
If you buy shrimp in the shell, use the shells to make stock. Place the shells in a pot and cover generously with cold water. Bring to a boil and skim off scum. Add a coarsely chopped carrot, onion, celery stalk and leek, some parsley stems, a pinch of thyme and a bay leaf and cook gently for about 20 minutes. Strain and freeze. Use any time fish stock or clam juice is called for.

Shrimp Mousse on Sugar Cane Sticks

Serving Suggestions

- Mousse mixture can also be moulded into patties. Broil, barbecue or cook in a non-stick pan.
- Use the mixture as a filling for dumplings (page 50) or spring rolls (page 60).

Make Ahead

- Make and shape the mousse ahead and refrigerate until ready to cook. You can also cook ahead and serve warm or at room temperature, or reheat at 350°F/180°C for about 15 minutes.

These look spectacular moulded onto the sugar cane, but you can also use lemongrass, popsicle sticks or skewers. Look for sugar cane in Asian or Caribbean markets; you may also be able to buy some from a Thai or Vietnamese restaurant. Serve with soy sauce or Thai hot sweet sauce for dipping.

You can also use boneless, skinless chicken breasts instead of shrimp. Leftover mousse can be diced and added to clear soups or salads.

Makes 24 pieces

1¼ lb	shrimp, cleaned (page 249) about 1 lb/500 g after cleaning	625 g
1	clove garlic, minced	1
1	green onion, finely chopped	1
1 tbsp	granulated sugar	15 mL
1 tbsp	Thai fish sauce or soy sauce	15 mL
1 tbsp	vegetable oil	15 mL
1 tsp	hot chili paste	5 mL
¾ tsp	salt	4 mL
1 tbsp	chopped fresh cilantro or chives	15 mL
3	pieces sugar cane (each about 4 inches/10 cm long), peeled and cut lengthwise into 8 sticks	3

1. Combine shrimp, garlic, green onion and sugar in a food processor and chop finely. Add fish sauce, oil, hot chili paste, salt and cilantro. (This can also be done by mincing mixture finely into a paste with a knife or cleaver.)

2. Lightly dip hands in cold water. For each appetizer, take about 1½ tbsp/20 mL shrimp mixture and shape it around the top half of each piece of sugar cane.

3. Cook shrimp on the grill or in a grill pan for 3 to 4 minutes per side until browned and cooked through. Or place on a baking sheet lined with parchment paper and bake in a preheated 400°F/200°C oven for 20 to 30 minutes, turning once.

Per Piece

Calories	27
Protein	3.7 g
Fat	0.9 g
Saturates	0.1 g
Cholesterol	27 mg
Carbohydrate	0.9 g
Fibre	0 g
Sodium	158 mg
Potassium	28 mg

QUESADILLAS WITH CARAMELIZED ONIONS AND GRILLED PEPPERS

Poblano peppers are similar to green peppers but have much more flavour and are only slightly hot. They are sold at Mexican or South American markets. If you cannot find them, use canned poblanos or regular sweet red peppers.

Makes 24 to 30 pieces

1 tbsp	olive oil	15 mL
3	onions, thinly sliced (about 1 lb/500 g)	3
1 tbsp	brown sugar	15 mL
1 tbsp	balsamic vinegar	15 mL
	Salt and pepper to taste	
4	large poblano or sweet red peppers	4
1½ cups	grated part-skim mozzarella or smoked mozzarella cheese	375 mL
½ cup	chopped fresh cilantro or basil	125 mL
6	10-inch/25 cm flour tortillas	6

1. Heat oil in a large skillet on medium-high heat. Add onions and cook until they start to brown. Lower heat and cook for 10 minutes.

2. Add sugar and vinegar to skillet and continue to cook until onions are very tender and browned. Season with salt and pepper and cool.

3. Meanwhile, cut peppers in half lengthwise, remove seeds and place on a baking sheet, cut sides down. Broil until blackened. Cool. Remove skins. Slice into ½-inch/1 cm strips.

4. Combine cooled onions with peppers, cheese and cilantro.

5. Arrange 3 tortillas on work surface in a single layer. Divide mixture among tortillas and spread as evenly as possible. Top each with another tortilla to form "sandwiches." Press together firmly but gently.

6. Grill quesadillas on barbecue or in grill pan until cheese melts. Allow to rest for 2 minutes. Cut each quesadilla into 8 to 10 wedges.

SERVING SUGGESTIONS
- Serve quesadillas whole for a brunch or light meal.
- Serve quesadilla in wedges on a salad.

MAKE AHEAD
- These can be assembled ahead and grilled just before serving. Or they can be cooked ahead and reheated in a single layer on a baking sheet — place in a 400°F/200°C oven for about 10 minutes. They are also delicious at room temperature.

PER PIECE

Calories	88
Protein	3.6 g
Fat	2.9 g
Saturates	1 g
Cholesterol	4 mg
Carbohydrate	12.2 g
Fibre	1.1 g
Sodium	106 mg
Potassium	99 mg

Excellent: Vitamin C

ROASTED TOMATO AND GARLIC BRUSCHETTA

Tomatoes become intense and flavourful when they are roasted. Combined with garlic and herbs, they make a great topping.

Leftover grilled bread can be diced and used as croutons, or you can combine it with salsa to make bread salad.

Makes 20 pieces

SERVING SUGGESTIONS

- Serve on top of a salad or soup.
- Use the roasted tomato mixture as a crêpe or omelette filling, sandwich topping, pasta sauce or pizza topping, or stir into rice or other grains.

MAKE AHEAD

- The topping can be made a few days ahead, but grill bread on the same day and add topping just before serving. Serve warm or at room temperature.

Roasted Tomato Topping

8	plum tomatoes, quartered lengthwise (about 1½ lb/750 g)	8
1 tbsp	olive oil	15 mL
½ tsp	salt	2 mL
¼ tsp	pepper	1 mL
2	heads garlic	2
2 tbsp	chopped fresh basil	25 mL
2 tbsp	chopped fresh mint or basil	25 mL
2 tbsp	balsamic vinegar	25 mL

Grilled Bread

20	slices French stick, about ½ inch/1 cm thick and 2 inches/5 cm in diameter	20
1 tbsp	olive oil	15 mL
1 tbsp	chopped fresh rosemary, or ½ tsp/2 mL dried	15 mL
¼ tsp	salt	1 mL
¼ tsp	pepper	1 mL

PER PIECE

Calories	70
Protein	1.9 g
Fat	1.9 g
Saturates	0.3 g
Cholesterol	0 mg
Carbohydrate	11.6 g
Fibre	0.8 g
Sodium	176 mg
Potassium	103 mg

1. Place tomato wedges, cut side up, on a baking sheet lined with parchment paper. Spray or drizzle with olive oil. Sprinkle with salt and pepper.

2. Cut top quarter off heads of garlic. Wrap garlic in foil.

3. Roast tomatoes and garlic in a preheated 400°F/200°C oven for 40 to 50 minutes, or until garlic is squeezable and tomatoes have dried a bit and are slightly browned on the bottom. Cool.

4. Chop tomatoes roughly and place in a medium bowl. Squeeze garlic from cloves and add to tomatoes. Add basil, mint and vinegar. Combine well. Taste and adjust seasonings if necessary.

5. Arrange bread slices on a baking sheet. Brush with olive oil. Sprinkle with rosemary, salt and pepper. Barbecue, broil or grill for 1 minute on each side until outside is crusty but inside is still chewy.

6. Top each slice with a spoonful of topping just before serving.

Roasted Tomato and Garlic Bruschetta with Cheese
Top grilled bread and tomato mixture with ½ cup/125 mL grated Fontina, smoked mozzarella cheese or ½ cup/125 mL crumbled goat cheese. Place bruschetta on baking sheet and broil for 1 minute just to melt cheese. Watch it closely.

Roasting Garlic
To roast garlic, cut the top quarter off the head. Remove any parchment-like skin that comes away easily. Wrap the garlic head in foil and bake at 400°F/200°C for about 40 to 45 minutes, or until tender. When cool, turn the head upside down and gently squeeze the garlic out of the head with your hands or using a potato ricer.

SUSHI PIZZA

SERVING SUGGESTIONS

- This can also be made in an 8- or 9-inch/20 or 23 cm springform pan. Use additional sheets of nori cut to fit if necessary.
- Make individual moulds using small ring moulds or washed tuna or salmon tins with the tops and bottoms removed.
- For a spectacular garnish, use flying fish roe or green wasabi caviar.

MAKE AHEAD

- This can be made up to a few hours ahead. If you have to refrigerate it, wrap it very well so the rice does not dry out.

This makes a great appetizer or brunch dish. Leftovers can be tossed together to make a sushi salad. You can use thinly sliced prosciutto ham instead of smoked salmon.

The secret to making sushi rice is adding the right amount of vinegar. Add some vinegar and taste. When the rice tastes perfect, add a bit more vinegar, as the flavour will dull slightly as the rice sits.

Makes 16 pieces

2 cups	sushi rice (page 37)	500 mL
2¼ cups	cold water	550 mL
¼ cup	seasoned rice vinegar (page 132), or more to taste	50 mL
16	thin slices English cucumber, unpeeled	16
¼ lb	smoked salmon	125 g
2 tbsp	Russian-style mustard	25 mL
¼ cup	yogurt cheese (page 303), thick yogurt or mayonnaise	50 mL
1	sheet toasted nori (about 8 x 7 inches/20 x 18 cm)	1
3	green onions or small bunch chives, thinly sliced on the diagonal	3
1 tbsp	sesame seeds, toasted (page 245)	15 mL
½	lemon, very thinly sliced	½

1. Place rice in a bowl and cover with cold water. Swish rice around and drain. Repeat until water is clear. Drain rice well.

2. Place rice in a medium saucepan and add 2¼ cups/550 mL cold water. Cover. Bring to a boil on medium-high heat. Boil for 1 minute. Reduce heat to low and cook for 10 minutes. Remove from heat and allow to rest for 10 minutes. (Do not lift the lid at any time during cooking and resting!)

3. Toss rice gently with vinegar. Cover rice with a damp towel if you are not using it right away.

4. Line an 8-inch/20 cm square baking dish with plastic wrap. Arrange cucumber slices in a single layer over the bottom. Arrange smoked salmon slices on top of cucumber.

PER PIECE

Calories	115
Protein	3.7 g
Fat	1 g
Saturates	0.2 g
Cholesterol	2 mg
Carbohydrate	22.2 g
Fibre	0.4 g
Sodium	219 mg
Potassium	66 mg

Good: Vitamin B$_{12}$

5. In a small bowl, combine mustard with yogurt cheese. Spread over salmon.

6. Pat half the sushi rice on top of salmon and sauce. Place nori on top of rice (cut to fit if necessary). Pat in remaining rice. Cover with plastic wrap. Weight the rice down with cans of food or bricks covered with foil. Allow to rest at room temperature for 15 to 30 minutes.

7. To serve, unwrap and unmould onto a serving platter. Scatter chives and sesame seeds over top and garnish with lemon slices.

Nori
According to Japanese cooking expert Elizabeth Andoh, nori is made from laver, a type of sea vegetation that has been compressed and dried in thin sheets. Buy the pretoasted variety and store it in the freezer.

B-VITAMINS

There is strong evidence that eating a low-fat, high-fibre diet that includes adequate amounts of folic acid and vitamins B_6 and B_{12} will lower the risk of heart disease.

Folic acid, one of the B-vitamins, plays a role in lowering the risk of heart disease by regulating homocysteine levels in the body. Homocysteine is a protein substance found in the blood. Some scientists say that high levels of homocysteine may be even more risky to heart health than high levels of cholesterol. High levels have been shown to damage the lining of the artery walls, potentially leading to a buildup of plaque and increasing risk of heart attack or stroke.

The best food sources of folic acid are dark green leafy vegetables (e.g., broccoli, spinach, Romaine lettuce, peas and Brussels sprouts), orange juice, liver, peas and beans. White flour, enriched pasta and enriched cornmeal are now fortified with folic acid.

Some research suggests that folic acid is even more effective when it is taken with vitamins B_6 and B_{12}. Vitamin B_6 is abundant in whole grains and cereals, bananas, lentils, beans, meat, fish, poultry, nuts and soybeans. B_{12} is plentiful in all animal products — meat, fish, poultry, dairy and eggs. People who avoid all animal products or have a particular anaemia that prevents them from absorbing B_{12} may not be getting enough. Also, 10 to 30 percent of older adults lose their ability to adequately absorb the naturally occurring form of B_{12} found in food. These people should meet most of their recommended intake with synthetic B_{12} found in fortified foods or vitamin supplements. Some soy products are fortified with B_{12} but most aren't, so read labels carefully. B_{12} is also found in some brands of nutritional yeast.

CHICKPEA BRUSCHETTA

SERVING SUGGESTION
• Serve as a garnish on soups or salads.

MAKE AHEAD
• Make topping and toast bread ahead but put together just before serving; otherwise bread will become very soggy.

Bruschetta is so popular that there are now restaurants in Italy that specialize in it. This is an easy and delicious version. Use leftover topping in sandwiches, or add more stock or yogurt and serve as a dip.

Makes 26 pieces

2 tbsp	olive oil, divided	25 mL
1	small onion, chopped	1
3	cloves garlic, finely chopped	3
pinch	hot red pepper flakes	pinch
1	19-oz/540 mL can chickpeas or white beans, drained and rinsed	1
1 tsp	chopped fresh rosemary, or ¼ tsp/1 mL dried	5 mL
1 tsp	chopped fresh thyme, or ¼ tsp/1 mL dried	5 mL
2 tbsp	chopped fresh parsley	25 mL
1 tbsp	lemon juice	15 mL
½ tsp	pepper	2 mL
½ cup	homemade vegetable stock (page 69), chicken stock (page 79) or water	125 mL
1	16-inch/40 cm baguette, cut in ½-inch/1 cm slices (about 26 slices)	1

1. Heat 1 tbsp/15 mL oil in a large skillet on medium-high heat. Add onion, garlic and hot pepper flakes. Cook for a few minutes until tender.

2. Add chickpeas, rosemary, thyme, parsley, lemon juice and pepper. Cook for a few minutes. Add stock and bring to a boil.

3. Mash chickpea mixture with a potato masher until spreadable but not pureed. Taste and adjust seasonings if necessary.

4. Brush one side of bread slices with remaining 1 tbsp/15 mL oil. Grill bread on each side until lightly browned. Spread oiled side of bread with about 1 tbsp/15 mL chickpea mixture.

PER PIECE

Calories	64
Protein	2.2 g
Fat	1.7 g
Saturates	0.2 g
Cholesterol	0 mg
Carbohydrate	10.2 g
Fibre	0.7 g
Sodium	99 mg
Potassium	38 mg

BAKED CHÈVRE ON BLACK BEAN SALSA

This appetizer is especially appropriate for a Southwest menu or a casual barbecue.
Serve with baked tortilla chips (page 34).

Makes 5 cups

1	19-oz/540 mL can black beans, drained and rinsed	1
1 cup	corn niblets	250 mL
1	sweet red pepper, roasted (page 49), peeled, seeded and diced	1
2	tomatoes, seeded and diced	2
1	chipotle (page 73) or jalapeño, finely chopped	1
1	clove garlic, minced	1
½ cup	chopped fresh cilantro or basil	125 mL
1 tbsp	lime juice	15 mL
½ tsp	salt	2 mL
¼ tsp	pepper	1 mL
6 oz	chèvre (goat cheese)	175 g

1. In a medium bowl, combine black beans, corn, red pepper, tomatoes, chipotle, garlic, cilantro, lime juice, salt and pepper. Spoon into a 12 x 8-inch/2.5 L baking dish.

2. Cut goat cheese into rounds or chunks and place on top of salsa. Just before serving, place under broiler for 3 to 4 minutes (watch closely) until lightly browned and warm.

3. Serve warm with tortilla chips.

SERVING SUGGESTION
• Puree the cheese and salsa and serve as a dip, sandwich filling or spread.

MAKE AHEAD
• This can all be assembled ahead and broiled at the last minute.

PER TABLESPOON

Calories	15
Protein	0.9 g
Fat	0.5 g
Saturates	0.3 g
Cholesterol	1 mg
Carbohydrate	1.8 g
Fibre	0.4 g
Sodium	34 mg
Potassium	29 mg

SPICED LAMB CIGARS

SERVING SUGGESTIONS
• Serve lamb cigars with charmoula (page 52) or thick yogurt as a dip.
• Serve lamb cigars as a garnish on a salad.
• Stack cigars high on a platter with layers criss-crossed, or arrange in a circle on a platter.

If you want these slightly bigger, just cut the phyllo in half instead of thirds — you will end up with 24 pastries. You can use lean ground beef, chicken or turkey instead of the lamb.

Makes 36 pastries

2 tsp	olive oil	10 mL
1	small onion, finely chopped	1
2	cloves garlic, finely chopped	2
1 tsp	ground cumin	5 mL
1 tsp	paprika	5 mL
pinch	cayenne	pinch
1 lb	lean ground lamb	500 g
⅔ cup	tomato sauce	150 mL
1	egg, beaten	1
1 tbsp	honey	15 mL
12	sheets phyllo pastry	12
⅓ cup	olive oil	75 mL
¾ cup	dry breadcrumbs	175 mL
1 tbsp	sesame seeds	15 mL

1. Heat 2 tsp/10 mL oil in a large skillet on medium-high heat. Add onion and garlic and cook for a few minutes until tender. Add cumin, paprika and cayenne and cook for 30 seconds until fragrant.

2. Add lamb to skillet and cook until lamb loses its raw appearance. Add tomato sauce and simmer for 5 minutes. Taste and adjust seasonings if necessary. Transfer to a bowl to cool.

3. Add egg and honey to lamb mixture and combine well.

4. Cut stack of 12 phyllo sheets in thirds crosswise (each strip should be about 12 x 5 inches/30 x 12 cm). Cover with plastic wrap and then a damp tea towel.

PER PASTRY

Calories	90
Protein	3.5 g
Fat	5.3 g
Saturates	1.4 g
Cholesterol	15 mg
Carbohydrate	7.1 g
Fibre	0.3 g
Sodium	93 mg
Potassium	66 mg

5. Working with one or two pieces of phyllo at a time, arrange phyllo pieces in a single layer on work surface. Brush oil over phyllo and sprinkle with breadcrumbs.

6. Form about 1 tbsp/15 mL filling into a small log about 3 inches/7.5 cm long. Place on sheet of phyllo at bottom. Fold edges over filling and roll up. Place on baking sheet lined with parchment paper. Brush top with olive oil and sprinkle with sesame seeds. Repeat until all filling is used.

7. Bake rolls in a preheated 400°F/200°C oven for 15 to 20 minutes, or until brown and crisp.

Spiced Vegetarian Cigars

Use 2 cups/500 mL cooked rice instead of lamb in the filling. Taste and adjust seasonings if necessary (the filling should be very well seasoned).

MAKE AHEAD
• Pastries can be made ahead and frozen unbaked on a baking sheet lined with plastic wrap. When pastries are frozen, transfer to a plastic bag and store in freezer. Bake on parchment-lined cookie sheets from the frozen state; add about 10 minutes to the cooking time.
• You can also freeze the baked pastries and reheat at 350°F/180°C for 15 to 20 minutes.
• Pastries can be made ahead and served cold or at room temperature.

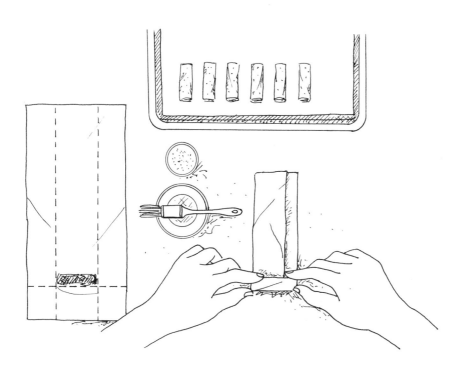

CORN PANCAKES WITH SALSA

MAKE AHEAD
• These pancakes can be made a day ahead, refrigerated and warmed in a 350°F/180°C oven for about 10 minutes.

These pancakes are very tender, with a sweetness that is the perfect foil for a spicy topping. Other spreads and dips such as guacamole, roasted garlic and goat cheese spread (page 58) or hummos (page 34) make good toppings. Cooked and diced fennel or zucchini can be used instead of corn and peppers in the pancakes. Leftovers can be sliced and sprinkled on salads or soups. Plain pancakes make a great side dish.

Makes about 24 pancakes

3	eggs	3
1 cup	buttermilk	250 mL
1 cup	all-purpose flour	250 mL
½ cup	cornmeal	125 mL
2 tbsp	granulated sugar	25 mL
1 tsp	baking soda	5 mL
½ tsp	ground cumin	2 mL
½ tsp	pepper	2 mL
½ tsp	salt	2 mL
1 tbsp	vegetable oil	15 mL
¾ cup	corn niblets, cooked and very well drained	175 mL
¼ cup	diced roasted sweet red pepper (page 49)	50 mL

Hot Tomato Salsa

3	plum tomatoes, seeded and chopped	3
1	jalapeño or chipotle (page 73), seeded and finely chopped	1
1	clove garlic, minced	1
1 tbsp	olive oil	15 mL
1 tbsp	lime juice	15 mL
¼ cup	chopped fresh cilantro	50 mL
2 tbsp	chopped fresh chives	25 mL
	Salt and pepper to taste	

PER PANCAKE AND 1 TBSP SALSA

Calories	64
Protein	2.2 g
Fat	2 g
Saturates	0.4 g
Cholesterol	27 mg
Carbohydrate	9.4 g
Fibre	0.5 g
Sodium	116 mg
Potassium	63 mg

1. In a large bowl, combine eggs and buttermilk.

2. In separate bowl, combine flour, cornmeal, sugar, baking soda, cumin, pepper and salt. Mix together well.

3. Whisk dry ingredients into egg mixture. Stir in oil, corn and red pepper.

4. Brush a large non-stick skillet with vegetable oil and heat on medium-high. Add batter (use 2 tbsp/25 mL batter per pancake — they should be about 2 inches/5 cm in diameter). Cook just until surface loses its sheen. Turn. When second side is cooked, remove from pan. Continue until all pancakes are cooked (arrange pancakes in a single layer on serving platter).

5. In a small bowl, combine tomatoes, jalapeño, garlic, olive oil, lime juice, cilantro, chives, salt and pepper. Taste and adjust seasonings if necessary. Spoon some salsa on each pancake.

Breakfast Corn Pancakes

Omit the red pepper and cumin from the pancake batter. Serve pancakes with maple syrup insead of salsa.

Roasting Peppers
There are many ways to roast peppers, but one of the easiest methods is to cut the peppers in half, remove the ribs and seeds and place on a baking sheet, skin side up. Place under the broiler until black, cool and remove the charred skins. Roast peppers when they are in season and then freeze them for future use. Cut the peeled peppers into strips or chunks and place on a baking sheet in a single layer. When frozen, pack into freezer bags or containers. The pieces will stay separate, allowing you to defrost small amounts at a time. You can also buy roasted and peeled peppers in jars.

CURRIED CHICKEN POT STICKERS

SERVING SUGGESTIONS
- Serve these in individual bowls as a first course, or place in a large serving bowl and serve with toothpicks as an hors d'oeuvre with drinks.
- Serve dumplings on skewers stuck into a whole pineapple or melon.
- Turn the dumplings into wontons by folding the dough into triangles and sealing closed.
- Shape the filling into balls and poach in soups or cook and serve with sweet and sour sauce (page 94).

MAKE AHEAD
- These can be made ahead and frozen uncooked. Cook from the frozen state but for twice the cooking time. They can also be cooked ahead and reheated, but you will have to add a bit of water or stock to the skillet.

PER DUMPLING

Calories	42
Protein	3.6 g
Fat	0.8 g
Saturates	0.1 g
Cholesterol	8 mg
Carbohydrate	4.7 g
Fibre	0.2 g
Sodium	71 mg
Potassium	75 mg

Whenever Hugh Carpenter, a favourite cookbook author, teaches at my school, everyone who attends his classes, including me and my staff, rushes home afterwards to cook. Hugh makes great dumplings, and these are Hugh-inspired. (You can also use shrimp or scallops instead of chicken — chop finely in a food processor.)

Leftovers can be served on top of a salad or added to Asian-flavoured soups.

Makes about 35 dumplings

1 lb	lean ground chicken breast	500 g
1	egg white	1
1 tbsp	cornstarch	15 mL
1 tsp	sesame oil	5 mL
1 tbsp	soy sauce	15 mL
¼ tsp	salt	1 mL
¼ tsp	hot chili paste	1 mL
1	small carrot, finely chopped or grated	1
2	green onions, chopped	2
1 tsp	chopped fresh ginger root	5 mL
½ cup	chopped cooked spinach, wrung out until very dry	125 mL
35	Chinese dumpling wrappers, approx.	35
1 tbsp	vegetable oil, divided	15 mL
1 tsp	sesame seeds, toasted (page 245)	5 mL
¼ cup	chopped fresh cilantro or chives	50 mL

Curried Tomato Sauce

⅓ cup	pureed tomatoes, tomato sauce or low-fat coconut milk	75 mL
⅓ cup	water or stock	75 mL
1 tbsp	dry sherry	15 mL
1 tbsp	oyster sauce or hoisin sauce	15 mL
1 tbsp	curry powder	15 mL
1 tsp	granulated sugar	5 mL

1. In a large bowl, combine ground chicken, egg white, cornstarch, sesame oil, soy sauce and salt. Stir in chili paste, carrot, green onions, ginger and spinach. Mix well.

2. Place a few dumpling wrappers on the work surface in a single layer. Place a teaspoon of filling in centre of each wrapper. Place one dumpling in the palm of your hand, and bring up sides of wrappers to cover filling but leave top open. Squeeze slightly around the middle to give each dumpling a "waist." Flatten filling that is exposed on top. Place dumplings, open side up, on a baking sheet lined with waxed paper and brushed with a little of the vegetable oil. Continue until all filling is used.

3. To prepare sauce, combine pureed tomatoes, water, sherry, oyster sauce, curry powder and sugar. Reserve.

4. To cook, brush a large non-stick skillet with remaining vegetable oil. Arrange dumplings, open side up, in skillet. Cook on medium-high heat until lightly browned on the bottom.

5. Spoon sauce over and between dumplings and cover pan. Cook for 3 to 5 minutes, or until tops feel firm and cooked through. Shake pan gently to prevent sticking.

6. Toss dumplings and sprinkle with sesame seeds and cilantro.

GRILLED SHRIMP WITH CHARMOULA

SERVING SUGGESTIONS
• Serve shrimp on a bed of
fresh herbs.
• Serve as a salad on arugula.

MAKE AHEAD
• Shrimp can be made
ahead and served cold
or at room temperature.

Maureen Lollar, who runs my cooking school and organizes my cookware shop, isn't easy to impress, but she loves charmoula — an exotic blend of spices and herbs that can be used as a marinade, dressing, dipping sauce or sandwich spread. If you use olive oil instead of mayonnaise, the mixture will be less firm but just as delicious.

You can use grilled salmon or chicken instead of the shrimp. If you are using wooden skewers, soak them in cold water for 30 minutes before using.

Makes 6 to 8 servings

16	extra-large shrimp (about 1 lb/500 g), cleaned (page 249)	16

Charmoula

3	cloves garlic, minced	3
1 tsp	ground cumin	5 mL
1 tsp	paprika	5 mL
¼ tsp	cayenne	1 mL
3 tbsp	lemon juice	45 mL
¼ cup	mayonnaise or olive oil	50 mL
¼ cup	yogurt cheese (page 303)	50 mL
¼ cup	finely chopped fresh cilantro	50 mL
	Salt and pepper to taste	

1. Pat shrimp dry and thread on skewers. Place in a large shallow baking dish.

2. In a medium bowl, combine garlic, cumin, paprika, cayenne and lemon juice. Stir in mayonnaise, yogurt cheese, cilantro, salt and pepper. Taste and adjust seasonings.

3. Combine half of charmoula mixture with shrimp. Marinate for 5 minutes or up to a few hours in refrigerator.

4. Grill shrimp on barbecue, under broiler or in a grill pan for 2 to 3 minutes on each side, or until shrimp curl and are cooked through.

5. Serve shrimp with remaining charmoula as a dip.

PER SERVING

Calories	144
Protein	12.9 g
Fat	8.8 g
Saturates	1.1 g
Cholesterol	93 mg
Carbohydrate	2.9 g
Fibre	0.2 g
Sodium	143 mg
Potassium	134 mg

Excellent: Vitamin B_{12}
Good: Niacin

Southwest Chopped Shrimp Cocktail

This is the shrimp cocktail reinvented, and actually a great way to stretch a pound of shrimp. Serve it as an appetizer or as a luncheon or light supper dish.

Makes 8 servings

1 lb	shrimp, cleaned (page 249)	500 g
1 tbsp	olive oil	15 mL
2	cloves garlic, minced, divided	2
1 tbsp	chopped fresh rosemary, or ½ tsp/2 mL dried	15 mL
½ tsp	ground cumin	2 mL
½ tsp	salt, divided	2 mL
pinch	hot red pepper flakes	pinch
¼ cup	lime juice	50 mL
½ tsp	pepper	2 mL
1	jalapeño, seeded and diced	1
3	plum tomatoes, seeded and diced	3
2	sweet red peppers, roasted (page 49), peeled, seeded and diced	2
2 cups	corn niblets	500 mL
½ cup	chopped fresh cilantro	125 mL
8	8-inch/20 cm flour tortillas	8

1. In a large bowl, combine shrimp with oil, 1 minced clove garlic, rosemary, cumin, ¼ tsp/1 mL salt and hot pepper flakes. Marinate for up to 2 hours in refrigerator.

2. Grill shrimp on barbecue, in grill pan or under broiler. Cut each shrimp into 3 or 4 pieces. Place in a large bowl.

3. In a small bowl, combine lime juice with remaining minced garlic, pepper and remaining ¼ tsp/1 mL salt. Add to shrimp. Add jalapeño, tomatoes, sweet peppers, corn and cilantro. Toss well. Taste and adjust seasonings.

4. Wrap tortillas in foil and place in a preheated 350°F/180°C oven for 10 minutes. Fold each tortilla in quarters. Put into martini glass with point at the bottom. Open one pocket to make a cone. Fill with shrimp.

Serving Suggestions

- Leave the shrimp whole. Omit from the salad and hang over the edge of the bowl like a classic shrimp cocktail.
- Hang a twist of lime over the edge of the glass.

Per Serving

Calories	217
Protein	13.2 g
Fat	5.2 g
Saturates	0.8 g
Cholesterol	65 mg
Carbohydrate	30.6 g
Fibre	2.6 g
Sodium	364 mg
Potassium	297 mg

Excellent: Vitamin C; Niacin; Vitamin B$_{12}$
Good: Vitamin A; Thiamine; Iron

HOLIDAY OPEN HOUSE

Sparkling Passionfruit Berry Punch
or Assorted Mocktails

Asian Eggplant Dip

Roasted Garlic and Potato Crostini

Teriyaki-glazed Chicken Meatballs

Baked Spring Rolls

Chicken Satays with Peanut Marinade

Chewy Spice Cookies

Fruit Platter

Hosting an open house is a great way to entertain lots of people. Always put a beginning and end time on the invitation so you know how much food to have on hand (and so that guests don't assume they are staying on for dinner!). Everyone loves this kind of party because the food is cute and easy to eat. Plan on six to eight appetizers per person per hour. Serve a variety of dishes to allow for vegetarians and guests with different tastes or food allergies. Make sure you have lots of ice and non-alcoholic beverages on hand and consider having a bartender if you are entertaining a large crowd.

WORK PLAN

MAKE AHEAD

• Cookies can be made up to one month ahead and frozen. Defrost the day of serving.

• Spring rolls can be made up to two weeks ahead and frozen cooked or uncooked. Bake or reheat just before serving. To bake from the frozen state, add 5 to 10 minutes to the cooking time, or reheat at 350°F/180°C for 20 to 25 minutes. (They can also be served warm or at room temperature.)

• Eggplant dip can be made up to a few days before serving.

• Crostini topping can be made a day ahead.

• The meatballs can be made a day ahead.

• Marinate and assemble the satays a day ahead and cook just before serving, or they can be cooked about an hour ahead of time and served at room temperature. They can also be cooked ahead and reheated (place on a baking sheet in a single layer, cover with foil and reheat at 350°F/180°C for 15 to 20 minutes).

SAME DAY

- Combine all the punch ingredients except for the ginger ale and ice, which should be added just before serving.
- Roast potatoes for crostini a few hours ahead. Smear topping on potatoes just before serving.
- Bake spring rolls and cook or reheat satays just before serving.
- Reheat meatballs in the sauce. Add water if the sauce is too thick.

PRESENTATION IDEAS

- Buy inexpensive fabric and cut it into 6-inch/15 cm squares with pinking shears. Use the swatches as cocktail napkins.
- Have some platters of food on tables and some platters for passing; hand out cocktail napkins as you serve appetizers.
- Put the food and drinks in different areas.
- Prepare two platters of the same dish so that you can replace a dish quickly when it is empty or running low.
- Garnish platters with fresh herbs and edible flowers (page 22).
- Use rosemary stems instead of skewers and toothpicks.
- Freeze lemon or lime slices, edible flowers or fresh herbs in ice cubes for drinks.
- Freeze cranberry or orange juice into ice cubes for the punch so that it doesn't become diluted with water.
- Use hollowed-out vegetables as sauce dishes or as little vases for herbs.
- Serve dips and sauces with roast potatoes as well as other vegetable dippers.
- Have the music on low; decorate the room with lots of dim candles.

MATCHING FOOD WITH WINE*

If you want to serve wine: Wines with a touch of sweetness will complement the Asian spices and heat of the food. Off-dry Riesling (Germany, Ontario, New York State) and Gewürztraminer (Alsace, South Africa, Ontario) are fruity wines that marry well with the sweeter ingredients used in these recipes. The berry-fruit flavours and low tannins of Gamay (Beaujolais, Cool Climate New World) make it a crowd pleaser and a good match for the spicy heat of the food. Always serve Gamay slightly chilled.

See Alcohol (page 274).

SPARKLING PASSIONFRUIT BERRY PUNCH

*For a spirited version of this punch, use sparkling white wine in place of the ginger ale
and Alizé® (a relatively new Cognac-based passionfruit drink from France) instead of
the passionfruit juice (if you cannot find Alizé®, add ½ cup/125 mL Cognac or brandy
to the other ingredients).*

Makes 12 to 16 servings

1½ cups	passionfruit juice	375 mL
3 cups	ginger ale	750 mL
2 cups	cranberry juice	500 mL
2 cups	orange juice, tangerine juice or mango juice	500 mL
2 cups	sliced strawberries	500 mL
2 cups	cranberries	500 mL
2 cups	ice	500 mL

1. Combine passionfruit juice, ginger ale, cranberry juice and orange juice.

2. Add strawberries, cranberries and ice.

PER SERVING

Calories	82
Protein	0.5 g
Fat	0.1 g
Saturates	0 g
Cholesterol	0 mg
Carbohydrate	20.3 g
Fibre	0.2 g
Sodium	9 mg
Potassium	173 mg

Excellent: Vitamin C

ASIAN EGGPLANT DIP

This unusual dip is one of the most popular I have ever served, even with people who think they dislike eggplant. Serve it with rice crackers or sesame crisps. I like to use it as a sauce on grilled chicken or pork tenderloin. It can also be served in rice paper wrappers with cooked vegetables or chicken as fresh spring rolls, or it can be combined with rice to make a wrap filling (page 166). It also makes a good garnish for soups.

Makes 1½ cups/375 mL

1	large eggplant (about 1½ lb/750 g)	1
2 tbsp	soy sauce	25 mL
2 tbsp	brown sugar	25 mL
1 tbsp	rice vinegar	15 mL
1 tbsp	water	15 mL
1 tsp	vegetable oil	5 mL
4	cloves garlic, finely chopped	4
1 tbsp	finely chopped fresh ginger root	15 mL
4	green onions, chopped	4
½ tsp	hot chili paste	2 mL
1 tsp	sesame oil	5 mL
2 tbsp	chopped fresh cilantro	25 mL

1. Place eggplant in a baking dish and pierce in a few places with fork or tip of knife. Roast in preheated 425°F/220°C oven for 45 to 50 minutes or until tender. Eggplant can also be roasted on a grill for 10 to 15 minutes per side for a smoky flavour, or it can be microwaved for about 10 minutes on High. (Be sure to pierce it.) Cool.

2. Peel eggplant and chop finely (do not try to remove seeds).

3. In a small bowl, combine soy sauce, sugar, vinegar and water.

4. In a wok or large skillet, heat oil on high heat. Add garlic, ginger, green onions and chili paste. Cook for about 30 seconds or until fragrant. Add soy sauce mixture. When bubbling, add eggplant. Stir to combine well and heat thoroughly.

5. Remove wok from heat and stir in sesame oil.

6. Place dip in serving bowl and sprinkle with cilantro. Serve cold or at room temperature.

MAKE AHEAD
• This dip can be made up to a few days ahead and refrigerated.

PER TABLESPOON
Calories	18
Protein	0.4 g
Fat	0.5 g
Saturates	0.1 g
Cholesterol	0 mg
Carbohydrate	3.4 g
Fibre	0.8 g
Sodium	89 mg
Potassium	84 mg

ROASTED GARLIC AND POTATO CROSTINI

Sliced roasted potatoes make a great base for salsas and other spreads. My daughter, Fara, came up with the idea of topping potatoes with this luscious spread. You can also cut up the potatoes, toss with the topping and serve as a potato salad.

Makes 32 appetizers

SERVING SUGGESTION
• Garnish each crostini with a sprig of parsley or a dab of salsa.

MAKE AHEAD
• The garlic topping can be made a day ahead. The potatoes can be roasted a few hours before serving.

4	baking potatoes or Yukon Gold potatoes	4
2 tbsp	olive oil	25 mL
½ tsp	salt	2 mL
¼ tsp	pepper	1 mL
1 tbsp	chopped fresh thyme, or pinch dried	15 mL
1 tbsp	chopped fresh rosemary, or pinch dried	15 mL

Roasted Garlic Topping

4	heads garlic	4
2 oz	chèvre (goat cheese), about ½ cup/125 mL	60 g
¼ cup	yogurt cheese (page 303) or thick yogurt	50 mL
½ tsp	pepper	2 mL
1 tbsp	balsamic vinegar	15 mL
2 tbsp	chopped fresh basil or parsley	25 mL

1. Slice potatoes into rounds about ½ inch/1 cm thick. Toss with olive oil, salt, pepper, thyme and rosemary. Arrange in a single layer on baking sheets lined with parchment paper.

2. Cut top quarter off each head of garlic. Wrap garlic in a single layer in foil. Roast garlic and potatoes in a preheated 400°F/200°C oven for 40 to 45 minutes, or until potatoes are brown and crisp and garlic is soft and tender.

3. Squeeze garlic into a food processor or bowl and mash with goat cheese, yogurt cheese, pepper and vinegar. Stir in basil. Smear some of topping on each potato.

Potato Crostini with Smoked Salmon

Omit garlic topping. Whisk together ½ cup/125 mL yogurt cheese (page 303) and 1 tsp/5 mL Russian-style mustard. Smear over cooked potatoes. Top with ½ lb/250 g thinly sliced smoked salmon, fresh chives and freshly ground pepper.

PER APPETIZER

Calories	41
Protein	1.2 g
Fat	1.3 g
Saturates	0.4 g
Cholesterol	1 mg
Carbohydrate	6.3 g
Fibre	0.5 g
Sodium	46 mg
Potassium	100 mg

TERIYAKI-GLAZED CHICKEN MEATBALLS

Meatballs are making a big comeback on the cocktail party circuit. Comfort food while you are trying to work a room can't be beat! These are also great for dinner, served over rice, couscous, or udon or soba noodles.

If you can't find ground chicken breasts, ask your butcher to grind boneless, skinless chicken breasts, or do it yourself in the food processor. You can also use lean ground beef or lamb.

If you have any leftovers, cut the meatballs into halves or quarters, add chicken stock and chopped greens and serve as a soup.

Makes about 40 meatballs

1 lb	ground lean chicken or turkey breast	500 g
1	egg, beaten	1
¾ cup	fresh breadcrumbs, or ½ cup/125 mL dry	175 mL
⅓ cup	soy sauce, divided	75 mL
⅓ cup	rice wine, divided	75 mL
2 tbsp	granulated sugar, divided	25 mL
2 tbsp	finely chopped onion	25 mL
2 tbsp	finely chopped carrot	25 mL
2 tsp	vegetable oil	10 mL
1 cup	homemade chicken stock (page 79) or dashi	250 mL

1. In a large bowl, combine chicken, egg, breadcrumbs, 2 tbsp/25 mL soy sauce, 2 tbsp/25 mL rice wine, 1 tbsp/15 mL sugar, onion and carrot. Knead together with your hands or a spoon.

2. Shape mixture into 1-inch/2.5 cm balls and place on a baking sheet lined with parchment paper.

3. In a large, deep non-stick skillet, heat oil on medium-high heat. Add meatballs and brown on all sides, in two batches if necessary.

4. In a small bowl, combine stock, remaining ¼ cup/50 mL soy sauce, remaining ¼ cup/50 mL rice wine and remaining 1 tbsp/15 mL sugar. Add to skillet and bring to a boil. Reduce heat and simmer gently, shaking pan often, until meatballs are thoroughly cooked and juices are slightly syrupy and reduced by about one-quarter. This should take about 10 minutes. Remove to a serving platter.

• The meatballs can be made a day ahead. Reheat in the sauce just before serving.

Dashi
Dashi is a clear, mild, slightly smoky Japanese soup stock made from kelp and dried fish (most often bonito). Instant dashi is available in powdered or cube form, and can be found in Japanese or Asian markets.

PER MEATBALL

Calories	32
Protein	2.6 g
Fat	1.6 g
Saturates	0.4 g
Cholesterol	14 mg
Carbohydrate	1.5 g
Fibre	0 g
Sodium	152 mg
Potassium	34 mg

MAKE AHEAD
• Spring rolls can be made
  up to two weeks ahead
  and frozen cooked or
  uncooked.

BAKED SPRING ROLLS

You can also make these using 6-inch/15 cm spring roll wrappers or egg roll wrappers instead of the phyllo. Secure the last fold with a little egg white and brush with a bit of oil before baking at 375°F/190°C for 25 to 30 minutes.

Use leftovers as a garnish on salads.

Makes about 32 appetizers

2 tsp	vegetable oil	10 mL
2	cloves garlic, finely chopped	2
1	small onion, sliced	1
2	carrots, cut in very thin sticks	2
1	stalk celery, thinly sliced on the diagonal	1
¼ lb	green beans, thinly sliced on the diagonal (about 1 cup/250 mL)	125 g
10	shiitake or regular mushrooms, stemmed and thinly sliced	10
2 cups	chopped napa cabbage	500 mL
2 cups	bean sprouts	500 mL
3	green onions, sliced on the diagonal	3
2 tbsp	chopped fresh cilantro or parsley	25 mL
2 tbsp	oyster sauce or hoisin sauce	25 mL
1 tsp	sesame oil	5 mL
16	sheets phyllo pastry	16
¼ cup	vegetable oil	50 mL

Dipping Sauce

1 cup	liquid from vegetables above (add stock or water if necessary)	250 mL
1 tbsp	cornstarch	15 mL
2 tbsp	cold water	25 mL
½ tsp	hot chili paste	2 mL

PER APPETIZER

Calories	66
Protein	1.5 g
Fat	3 g
Saturates	0.3 g
Cholesterol	0 mg
Carbohydrate	8.7 g
Fibre	0.8 g
Sodium	113 mg
Potassium	87 mg

1. Heat oil in a large non-stick skillet on medium-high heat. Add garlic and onion and cook for 2 minutes until fragrant. Add carrots, celery and green beans. Cook for 2 minutes.

2. Add mushrooms and cabbage and cook for 2 minutes. Add bean sprouts. Heat. Stir in green onions, cilantro, oyster sauce and sesame oil. Taste and adjust seasonings if necessary. Cool.

3. Place filling in a strainer set over a bowl to catch any juices. You should have about 4 cups/1 L filling.

4. Working with one sheet of phyllo at a time (keep the rest covered with a piece of plastic wrap and a damp tea towel), cut phyllo in half. Fold each piece in half. Place 1½ tbsp/20 mL filling on phyllo and fold up bottom point. Fold in two sides and roll up. Brush with oil. Arrange on baking sheet in a single layer. Repeat with remaining phyllo and filling.

5. Bake spring rolls in a preheated 375°F/190°C oven for 25 to 30 minutes, turning once, until browned and crisp.

6. Meanwhile, to make sauce, measure liquid from vegetables and add enough stock or water to measure 1 cup/250 mL. Heat in a small saucepan. Combine cornstarch with cold water in a small bowl. Add to sauce and heat until thick. Stir in hot chili paste. Taste and adjust seasonings if necessary. Serve dipping sauce with spring rolls.

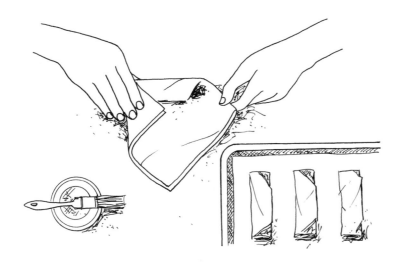

CHICKEN SATAYS WITH PEANUT MARINADE

- Marinate and assemble satays a day ahead and cook just before serving. They are also good served at room temperature.

Nutty Chickpea Sauce
This sauce contains no nuts, though it does contain tahini. Use it any time a peanut sauce is called for.

Puree ½ cup/125 mL cooked chickpeas, 1 tbsp/ 15 mL tahini, 2 tbsp/25 mL honey, 2 tbsp/25 mL water, 2 tbsp/25 mL soy sauce, 2 tbsp/25 mL rice wine and dash of hot pepper sauce. Makes about ¾ cup/175 mL.

I like to serve these on a round platter with a sauce in the middle (double the marinade recipe and serve half as a dipping sauce, or serve with chickpea sauce). Or you can serve these with some sauce and wrapped in a flour tortilla. Leftovers can be chopped and used as a filling for wontons or dumplings, or added to soups. For a main dish, serve the chicken over rice. You can also use salmon or shrimp instead of chicken.

For an even easier technique, grill or broil whole chicken or turkey breasts and then slice and thread the strips on skewers before serving. That way the skewers don't burn.

Makes 16 to 20 appetizers

1 lb	boneless, skinless chicken or turkey breasts	500 g
2	cloves garlic, minced	2
1 tbsp	finely chopped fresh ginger root	15 mL
1 tbsp	peanut butter	15 mL
1 tbsp	honey	15 mL
1 tbsp	soy sauce	15 mL
¼ cup	hoisin sauce	50 mL
½ tsp	sesame oil	2 mL

1. Remove chicken filets and cut remaining breast into 3 or 4 pieces crosswise.

2. Puree or combine garlic, ginger, peanut butter, honey, soy sauce, hoisin sauce and sesame oil.

3. In a large bowl, combine chicken and marinade and refrigerate for at least 30 minutes.

4. Thread strips of chicken lengthwise on 6-inch/15 cm skewers. (If you are using wooden skewers, soak them in cold water for at least 30 minutes before using.) Grill, broil or cook in a non-stick skillet for 3 to 4 minutes per side until chicken is cooked through.

Tofu Satays with Peanut Marinade

Instead of chicken, use extra-firm tofu cut in strips. Cook for 2 to 3 minutes per side.

PER APPETIZER

Calories	42
Protein	6.7 g
Fat	0.8 g
Saturates	0.2 g
Cholesterol	17 mg
Carbohydrate	1.7 g
Fibre	0.1 g
Sodium	82 mg
Potassium	88 mg

Excellent: Vitamin B$_6$
Good: Niacin

CHEWY SPICE COOKIES

This recipe was adapted from one of Marianne Saunders, a professional baker in Calgary. Even adapted to use margarine and part whole wheat flour, these cookies are delicious.

Makes about 64 cookies

½ cup	soft non-hydrogenated margarine	125 mL
1 cup	granulated sugar	250 mL
1	egg	1
¼ cup	molasses	50 mL
1½ tbsp	strong liquid coffee	20 mL
1 tsp	cinnamon	5 mL
1 tsp	ground ginger	5 mL
½ tsp	ground cloves	2 mL
1 tsp	baking soda	5 mL
1 cup	all-purpose flour	250 mL
1 cup	whole wheat flour	250 mL
½ cup	raisins	125 mL
½ cup	chopped dried apricots	125 mL
¼ cup	chopped candied ginger	50 mL
2 tbsp	granulated sugar	25 mL

1. In a large bowl, cream margarine and sugar until light. Beat in egg, molasses and coffee.

2. In a separate bowl, mix or sift together cinnamon, ginger, cloves, baking soda, all-purpose flour and whole wheat flour.

3. Stir dry ingredients into batter. Stir in raisins, apricots and ginger. Knead dough and refrigerate for 1 to 2 hours.

4. Divide dough into 8 equal pieces. Roll each piece into a log about 1 inch/2.5 cm in diameter. Each log should be about 16 inches/40 cm long.

5. Place logs on baking sheets lined with parchment paper. Press flat. Bake in a preheated 350°F/180°C oven for 8 to 10 minutes. Logs should still be soft. (Do not overbake or cookies will not be chewy.)

6. Sprinkle cookies with sugar. Cut on the diagonal into 1-inch/2.5 cm slices. You should have about 7 or 8 cookies per strip. Cool cookies on racks.

MAKE AHEAD
- Cookies can be made up to one month ahead and frozen.

FRUIT PLATTER IDEAS
- Line a basket with banana or palm leaves and place fruit on top.
- Hollow out cantaloupe, pineapple or honeydew halves to use as containers. Fill with balls of fruit.
- Serve a variety of fruits or just one — a bowl or basket of glistening grapes or fresh strawberries with their hulls on.
- Cut top and bottom off melon, peel sides and cut melon in half vertically. Scoop out seeds. Place melon cut side down and slice thinly. Gently fan out slices on a plate.

PER COOKIE

Calories	53
Protein	0.7 g
Fat	1.6 g
Saturates	0.2 g
Cholesterol	3 mg
Carbohydrate	9.6 g
Fibre	0.5 g
Sodium	39 mg
Potassium	69 mg

SALT/HIGH BLOOD PRESSURE

We've known for a long time that reducing salt intake can be an effective way for some people to lower their blood pressure.

The salt in the shaker is sodium chloride. The sodium part of the salt is the culprit. Sodium is also found in MSG (monosodium glutamate), garlic salt and other seasoned salts, sea salt, meat tenderizers, commercially prepared sauces and condiments like ketchup, soy sauce, Worcestershire sauce, fish sauce, chili sauce and steak sauce, bouillon cubes, dried soup mixes, instant soups, cured or smoked foods, olives and pickles. In general, the more processed a food is, the higher the sodium content.

If you want to reduce your sodium intake, here are some tips:

- Use flavourings that don't contain sodium, such as fresh or dried herbs, garlic powder or fresh garlic, onion flakes (instead of onion salt), dry mustard, lemon, spices such as ground coriander, cumin, chili powder and curry powder, ginger, hot peppers and pepper. Make your own salad dressings rather than using the bottled ones, and try using flavoured vinegars instead of adding salt.
- Eat more fresh or frozen fruits and vegetables. If you use canned vegetables, buy sodium-reduced products. Use fresh potatoes rather than instant, fresh cucumbers instead of pickles. Omit salt from the cooking water when you are boiling pasta, rice or vegetables.
- Eat fresh or frozen fish instead of canned or dried varieties; choose sliced roast beef or chicken instead of bologna, salami or other processed meats.
- Re-educate your taste buds. Taste food before adding salt. Cook from scratch instead of packages. Try using half the amount of salt specified in your favourite recipes.

Soups

Carrot and Ginger Soup   *66*
Barbecued Tomato and Corn Soup   *67*
Roasted Tomato Soup   *68*
Split Pea Soup with Cilantro Salsa   *70*
Celeriac and Potato Soup   *71*
Caramelized Onion and Parsnip Soup   *72*
Sweet Potato Chowder with Red Chile Paint   *73*
Pasta e Fagioli   *74*
Mexican Lentil Soup   *76*
Wheat Berry Minestrone   *77*
Chicken Soup with Matzo Balls   *78*
Ruby Red Beet Borscht   *80*
Japanese-style Chicken Noodle Soup   *81*

More Soups

French Onion Soup   *85*
Roasted Squash and Garlic Soup with Beet Splash   *147*
Asparagus Soup with Fresh Tarragon   *250*

CARROT AND GINGER SOUP

SERVING SUGGESTIONS
- Garnish with a yogurt swirl (page 23).
- Combine ¼ cup/50 mL shredded fresh mint, basil or cilantro, 1 grated carrot and 1 tbsp/15 mL toasted sesame seeds. Sprinkle on each serving and drizzle with 1 tsp/5 mL honey.

MAKE AHEAD
- The soup can be made a few days ahead and refrigerated, or it can be frozen for a few weeks. It is also great cold.

This golden orange soup is delicious on its own or as part of a "two soup" presentation (page 23) served with a deep red tomato soup (page 68) or cream-coloured parsnip soup (page 72).

Freeze or refrigerate any leftovers, or use as a garnish to swirl in another soup.

Makes 8 servings

1 tbsp	olive oil	15 mL
1	onion, chopped	1
2	cloves garlic, chopped	2
1 tbsp	chopped fresh ginger root	15 mL
1 tsp	ground cumin	5 mL
1 tsp	paprika	5 mL
pinch	cayenne	pinch
1½ lb	carrots (about 6 large), peeled and chopped (about 3 cups/750 mL)	750 g
1	large potato (about 12 oz/375 g), peeled and diced (about 2 cups/500 mL)	1
6 cups	homemade chicken stock (page 79), or 1 10-oz/284 mL can chicken broth plus water	1.5 L
1 tbsp	honey	15 mL
1 tbsp	lemon juice	15 mL
	Salt and pepper to taste	

1. Heat oil in a large saucepan or Dutch oven on medium heat. Add onion, garlic and ginger. Cook gently until very fragrant, about 5 minutes. Add cumin, paprika and cayenne. Cook for 30 to 60 seconds until fragrant, stirring constantly.

2. Add carrots, potato, 4 cups/1 L stock, honey and lemon juice. Cook until vegetables are very tender, about 30 to 40 minutes.

3. Puree soup in a food processor or blender and return to heat. Season with lemon juice, salt and pepper. If soup is too thick, add additional stock and reseason.

Mixed Vegetable and Ginger Soup
Use a combination of vegetables such as carrots, sweet potatoes and squash instead of just carrots.

PER SERVING

Calories	121
Protein	5.3 g
Fat	3 g
Saturates	0.6 g
Cholesterol	1 mg
Carbohydrate	18.7 g
Fibre	2.7 g
Sodium	75 mg
Potassium	459 mg

Excellent: Vitamin A
Good: Niacin; Vitamin B$_6$

BARBECUED TOMATO AND CORN SOUP

I like to make this recipe in barbecue classes so people will know that they can add wonderful smoky barbecue flavours to soups as well as salads, pasta dishes and sandwiches.

Leftovers can be used as a pasta sauce or made into a stew by adding cooked chicken, shrimp, meat or chickpeas.

Makes 8 servings

3 lb	plum tomatoes, halved and seeded (12 to 15)	1.5 kg
2	onions, cut in ½-inch/1 cm slices	2
3	ears corn, husked	3
1 tbsp	olive oil	15 mL
4	cloves garlic, finely chopped	4
1 tbsp	finely chopped chipotle (page 73) or jalapeño	15 mL
4 cups	homemade chicken stock (page 79), or 1 10-oz/284 mL can chicken broth plus water	1 L
1 tbsp	balsamic vinegar	15 mL
	Salt and pepper to taste	
¼ cup	chopped fresh basil	50 mL

1. Place tomatoes on grill and cook for a few minutes on each side until soft and brown. Reserve.

2. Grill onion slices until brown on both sides. Dice and reserve.

3. Cook corn directly on grill until browned, turning to cook all sides. Cut or break ears in half and stand upright on cutting board. Cut niblets off cob from top to bottom. Reserve with onions.

4. Heat olive oil in a large saucepan or Dutch oven on medium-high heat. Add garlic and cook until tender and fragrant. Add chipotle and tomatoes. Stir and cook until hot.

5. Add stock and bring to a boil. Cook for about 15 minutes. Puree and return soup to pot. Add onions and corn. Cook for 5 minutes.

6. Add vinegar and season to taste with salt and pepper. Serve garnished with chopped basil.

SERVING SUGGESTION
• Slice a couple of tomatoes, grill and reserve. Garnish each serving of soup with a slice of tomato, a sprig of fresh basil or crumbled goat cheese.

MAKE AHEAD
• This can be made up to two days ahead and refrigerated, or it can be made in advance and frozen. It is also delicious cold.

Handling Hot Chiles
If you have sensitive skin, wear plastic gloves (or just cover your hands with plastic bags) when you are handling hot chiles. If you prefer a milder taste, remove the ribs (and the seeds), which are the hottest parts.

PER SERVING

Calories	130
Protein	5.9 g
Fat	3.4 g
Saturates	0.6 g
Cholesterol	1 mg
Carbohydrate	22.5 g
Fibre	4.2 g
Sodium	38 mg
Potassium	611 mg

Excellent: Vitamin C
Good: Vitamin A; Thiamine; Niacin; Folacin

ROASTED TOMATO SOUP

SERVING SUGGESTIONS

- Omit the chives and goat cheese and serve this with another soup in a two-tone presentation (page 23).
- Omit the garnish. Spoon some yogurt on the centre of each serving and swirl as a decoration (page 23).
- Sprinkle each serving with chopped toasted pine nuts.
- Serve a spoonful of fresh tomato salsa on top of each serving.

MAKE AHEAD

- This can be made up to two days ahead and refrigerated, or it can be made weeks ahead and frozen. The soup can also be served cold.

PER SERVING

Calories	151
Protein	5.7 g
Fat	4.6 g
Saturates	1.3 g
Cholesterol	3 mg
Carbohydrate	25.7 g
Fibre	4.6 g
Sodium	253 mg
Potassium	719 mg

Excellent: Vitamin A; Vitamin C; Vitamin B$_6$
Good: Thiamine; Iron

Roasting the tomatoes transforms a traditional tomato soup into something spectacular. If you use a food mill to puree the soup, it will remove the skins and seeds of the peppers and tomatoes. If you use a food processor or blender, they will just be chopped into tiny bits. You can also use two 28-oz/796 mL cans of plum tomatoes instead of the roasted tomatoes. Simply drain and add them to the pot with the roasted onions and peppers. Cook the soup for 15 minutes after adding the stock.

Use leftovers as a sauce on pasta, or combine with vinegar and olive oil and use as a salad dressing.

Makes 6 to 8 servings

3 lb	plum tomatoes (12 to 15), quartered lengthwise	1.5 kg
3	sweet red peppers, halved and seeded	3
1	jalapeño, halved and seeded, or 1 chipotle (page 73), pureed	1
1	onion, cut in chunks	1
1 tbsp	olive oil	15 mL
½ tsp	salt	2 mL
¼ tsp	pepper	1 mL
1 tbsp	chopped fresh thyme, or ½ tsp/2 mL dried	15 mL
1 tbsp	chopped fresh rosemary, or ½ tsp/2 mL dried	15 mL
4	heads garlic	4
2 ½ cups	homemade vegetable stock (page 69) or water	625 mL
2 tbsp	balsamic vinegar	25 mL
¼ cup	crumbled chèvre (goat cheese)	50 mL
1	bunch fresh chives	1

1. Arrange tomatoes cut side up on baking sheets lined with parchment paper. Arrange peppers and jalapeño (if using) skin side up alongside tomatoes (if you are using a chipotle, add to soup in step 3). Break up onion and scatter over all. Drizzle vegetables with oil and sprinkle with salt, pepper, thyme and rosemary.

2. Cut top quarter off each head of garlic and wrap garlic in foil. Place vegetables and garlic in a preheated 400°F/200°C oven and roast for 30 to 45 minutes or until vegetables are brown and garlic is very squeezable. Peel peppers if skin comes off easily, otherwise don't worry.

3. Place roasted tomatoes, peppers and onion in a large saucepan or Dutch oven. Squeeze in garlic. Add stock and bring to a boil. Cook, uncovered, for 5 minutes.

4. Puree vegetables. If soup is too thick, add more stock; if it is too thin, cook, uncovered, until reduced to a thicker consistency.

5. Add vinegar and simmer for a few minutes. Taste and adjust seasonings if necessary.

6. Spoon soup into wide shallow bowls. Spoon a little crumbled goat cheese on top of each serving. Chop chives or hold bunch of chives over each serving and snip 2-inch/ 5 cm lengths over the soup so they fall like old-fashioned pick up sticks.

Homemade Vegetable Stock
In a large pot, combine 2 onions, 2 carrots, 2 stalks celery, 2 leeks and ¼ lb/ 125 g mushrooms (all cut in chunks). Add 3 qt/3 L cold water, 1 bay leaf, ½ tsp/2 mL dried thyme, handful of fresh parsley, 4 peeled cloves garlic and 6 peppercorns. Bring to a boil and remove any scum. Cover and simmer gently for 1½ hours. Strain stock and freeze. Makes about 3 qt/3 L.

Homemade Roasted Vegetable Stock
For a more strongly flavoured version of the recipe above, place the vegetables in an oiled roasting pan and sprinkle with 1 tbsp/15 mL granulated sugar. Roast at 450°F/230°C for 40 to 50 minutes, or until well browned. Use roasted vegetables and browned scrapings from pan to make stock as above.

SPLIT PEA SOUP WITH CILANTRO SALSA

You can puree this or serve it chunky (if you puree, it may need more stock). You can also puree only half to make it thicker but still chunky.

Makes 6 to 8 servings

SERVING SUGGESTION
• Serve in large wide bowls for a main course or in small cups for an appetizer.

MAKE AHEAD
• This soup will get thicker if it is made ahead and refrigerated; simply add more stock or water and reseason when reheating. This soup also freezes well.

1 cup	dried yellow or green split peas or lentils	250 mL
1 tbsp	vegetable oil	15 mL
1	onion, chopped	1
2	cloves garlic, finely chopped	2
1 tbsp	finely chopped fresh ginger root	15 mL
1	carrot, diced	1
1	parsnip, peeled and diced	1
1	potato, peeled and diced	1
1 tbsp	ground cumin	15 mL
6 cups	homemade vegetable stock (page 69) or water	1.5 L
1 tbsp	red wine vinegar or lemon juice	15 mL
	Salt and pepper to taste	

Cilantro Salsa

2	plum tomatoes, seeded and chopped	2
1	jalapeño, seeded and diced	1
¼ cup	chopped fresh cilantro	50 mL
1 tbsp	red wine vinegar or lemon juice	15 mL
	Salt and pepper to taste	

PER SERVING

Calories	215
Protein	10.3 g
Fat	3.8 g
Saturates	0.3 g
Cholesterol	0 mg
Carbohydrate	37 g
Fibre	5 g
Sodium	56 mg
Potassium	704 mg

Excellent: Vitamin A; Folacin
Good: Thiamine; Niacin; Iron

1. Rinse peas and pick over. If you have time, soak in cold water for 1 or 2 hours. Drain.

2. Heat oil in a large saucepan or Dutch oven on medium-high heat. Add onion, garlic, ginger, carrot, parsnip and potato. Cook for 5 minutes, or until vegetables are tender. Sprinkle vegetables with cumin and cook for 2 to 3 minutes.

3. Add peas and stock and bring to a boil. Reduce heat and cook gently for 50 to 60 minutes, or until soup is thick and peas are very tender. Taste and add vinegar, salt and pepper. Add more stock if soup is too thick.

4. Meanwhile, for salsa, combine tomatoes, jalapeño and cilantro in a small bowl. Season with vinegar, salt and pepper. Serve soup with a spoonful of salsa on top.

CELERIAC AND POTATO SOUP

Celeriac is available in nearly all supermarkets and many specialty markets. It has a wonderfully intense celery flavour. I use it in roasted vegetable mixtures, mashed potatoes, in mixed vegetable soups and in potato soups like this one. See if your guests can guess the secret ingredient.

Makes 6 to 8 servings

MAKE AHEAD
• This can be made ahead and reheated. It can also be frozen.

1 tbsp	olive oil	15 mL
1	onion, chopped	1
1	clove garlic, finely chopped	1
1 lb	celeriac, peeled and diced	500 g
1 lb	baking potatoes or Yukon Gold potatoes, peeled and diced	500 g
6 cups	homemade chicken stock (page 79), or 1 10-oz/284 mL can chicken broth plus water	1.5 L
1 tbsp	chopped fresh thyme, or ½ tsp/2 mL dried	15 mL
	Salt and pepper to taste	

1. Heat oil in a large saucepan or Dutch oven on medium-high heat. Add onion and garlic. Cook for a few minutes until tender.

2. Add celeriac and potatoes. Cook for a few minutes. Add stock and thyme. Bring to a boil, reduce heat and simmer gently, uncovered, for 20 minutes. Remove about ½ cup/125 mL diced vegetables and reserve for garnish.

3. Puree the soup. Add more liquid if soup is too thick. Taste and season with salt and pepper. Garnish soup with reserved vegetables.

Celery and Potato Soup

Use celery instead of the celeriac. The flavour and texture will be different, but it will still be good. You can also use turnip or rutabaga instead of the celeriac.

PER SERVING

Calories	140
Protein	7.1 g
Fat	3.9 g
Saturates	0.7 g
Cholesterol	1 mg
Carbohydrate	19.8 g
Fibre	2.3 g
Sodium	97 mg
Potassium	585 mg

Excellent: Niacin
Good: Vitamin B$_6$

CARAMELIZED ONION AND PARSNIP SOUP

MAKE AHEAD

- This can be made several days ahead and refrigerated, or it can be made several weeks ahead and frozen. When reheating, you may have to add stock or water.

One winter night when there was so much snow that the city was virtually closed down, I made this soup to warm up my guests and family as they literally came in from the cold. My son was just starting to experiment with eating different foods. He loves potato soup, so I said this was a caramelized onion and potato soup. My husband said, "Isn't it parsnip?" I said it was caramelized onion and potato. This went on until Ray finally got the message — careful eaters don't always need to know everything. Sometimes I think mothers speak a different language!

You can also use sweet potatoes and turnips instead of potatoes and parsnips. Leftover soup freezes and reheats well. It can also be used as a dip or spread.

Makes 8 servings

1 tbsp	olive oil	15 mL
1	large onion, or 3 shallots (about 12 oz/375 g), sliced	1
1 lb	parsnips, peeled and diced (about 4)	500 g
1 lb	baking potatoes or Yukon Gold potatoes, peeled and diced (about 3)	500 g
6 cups	homemade chicken stock (page 79) or 1 10-oz/284 mL can chicken broth plus water	1.5 L
	Salt and pepper to taste	
3	green onions, sliced very thinly on the diagonal	3

1. Heat oil in a large saucepan or Dutch oven on medium-high heat. Add onion and cook, without stirring, until brown. Lower heat to medium and cook slowly, stirring occasionally, for 10 to 15 minutes until very brown. If onions seem to be burning a bit, add about ½ cup/125 mL water. Cook until water evaporates. Remove half the onions and reserve for a garnish.

2. Add parsnips and potatoes to saucepan and combine with onions. Add stock and bring to a boil. Reduce heat and simmer gently, covered, for about 25 minutes or until vegetables are very tender.

3. Puree soup until smooth. Taste and add salt and pepper. Serve with reserved onions and green onions on top.

PER SERVING

Calories	128
Protein	5.3 g
Fat	3 g
Saturates	0.6 g
Cholesterol	1 mg
Carbohydrate	20.5 g
Fibre	2.5 g
Sodium	32 mg
Potassium	502 mg

Good: Niacin; Folacin

BEET RISOTTO *(page 140)*

HOLIDAY OPEN HOUSE MENU

Sparkling Passionfruit Berry Punch

or Assorted Mocktails

Asian Eggplant Dip

Roasted Garlic
and Potato Crostini

Teriyaki-glazed Chicken Meatballs

Baked Spring Rolls

Chicken Satays
with Peanut Marinade

Chewy Spice Cookies

Fruit Platter

(see recipes starting page 56)

SHOWN HERE:
ASSORTED MOCKTAILS
POTATO CROSTINI WITH ASSORTED TOPPINGS
CHICKEN SATAYS WITH PEANUT MARINADE
SPICY THAI SHRIMP *(page 217)*

SPARKLING ORANGE JUICE JELLY

PHYLLO BASKETS WITH MANGO ICE

ROASTED SALMON SALAD NIÇOISE
(*page 270*)

FLAVOURS OF ASIA
BUFFET MENU

Smoked Salmon Sushi Balls

Samosas with Cilantro Chile Dip

Lamb Biryani

Ginger Curry Grilled Chicken

Grilled Vegetable Salad
with Tomato Soy Dressing

Raita with Tomatoes and Cucumber

Caramelized Pears
with Tiramisu Cream

(see recipes starting page 108)

SHOWN HERE:
SMOKED SALMON SUSHI BALLS
SAMOSAS WITH CILANTRO CHILE DIP
LAMB BIRYANI
GINGER CURRY GRILLED CHICKEN
GRILLED VEGETABLE SALAD
WITH TOMATO SOY DRESSING

PHYLLO NESTS WITH CARAMELIZED FRUITS
(page 288)

SWEET POTATO CHOWDER WITH RED CHILE PAINT

This is delicious on its own or as part of a Southwestern menu. Omit the corn if you prefer a silky smooth texture.

Makes 8 servings

1 tbsp	olive oil	15 mL
2	onions, chopped	2
4	cloves garlic, finely chopped	4
2 lb	sweet potatoes, peeled and cut in 2-inch/5 cm chunks (about 3 large)	1 kg
1 lb	baking potatoes or Yukon Gold potatoes, peeled and cut in chunks (about 2 large)	500 g
8 cups	homemade vegetable stock (page 69) or water	2 L
1½ cups	corn niblets	375 mL
	Salt and pepper to taste	

Red Chile Paint

2	sweet red peppers, roasted (page 49), peeled and chopped	2
1	chipotle or jalapeño, seeded and chopped	1
½ cup	unflavoured low-fat yogurt	125 mL

1. Heat oil in a large saucepan or Dutch oven on medium heat. Add onions and garlic. Cook gently until very fragrant and tender.

2. Add sweet potatoes and potatoes. Stir well. Add 6 cups/1.5 L stock and bring to a boil. Cook for 20 to 30 minutes until very tender.

3. Puree soup. Add more stock if it is too thick. Add corn, salt and pepper and heat thoroughly. Taste and adjust seasonings if necessary.

4. Meanwhile, to make the chile paint, puree red peppers and chipotle until very smooth. Serve soup in wide shallow bowls and drizzle each serving with a little chile mixture (thinned with water if necessary) and some yogurt.

MAKE AHEAD
• The soup can be made up to 2 days ahead and refrigerated, or it can be frozen.

Jalapeños and Chipotles
Jalapeño chiles are medium-hot (although individual chiles can vary greatly). Chipotles are jalapeños that have been dried and smoked. They have a sensational smoky taste and are very hot.

Dried chipotles need to be reconstituted in hot water. Canned chipotles, once opened, can be transferred to a jar and refrigerated for up to a few months; they can also be frozen.

PER SERVING

Calories	203
Protein	4.9 g
Fat	2.9 g
Saturates	0.4 g
Cholesterol	1 mg
Carbohydrate	41.4 g
Fibre	4.4 g
Sodium	62 mg
Potassium	625 mg

Excellent: Vitamin A; Vitamin C
Good: Vitamin B$_6$; Folacin

PASTA E FAGIOLI

Frico

Frico are Parmesan wafers that you can serve as a garnish or appetizer. You can make them plain or add little bits of hot peppers or olives. Use the best Parmesan cheese, such as Parmigiano Reggiano.

Spoon grated Parmesan in mounds on a baking sheet lined with parchment paper. Bake at 350°F/180°C for 4 to 5 minutes. Watch carefully, as the wafers burn easily (1 tbsp/15 mL grated cheese will make a 2-inch/ 5 cm wafer; 2 tbsp/25 mL cheese will make a 3-inch/ 7.5 cm wafer).

PER SERVING

Calories	186
Protein	10.2 g
Fat	3.7 g
Saturates	0.8 g
Cholesterol	2 mg
Carbohydrate	29 g
Fibre	6.4 g
Sodium	371 mg
Potassium	516 mg

Excellent: Vitamin A
Good: Niacin; Folacin

This soup is delicious and heart-warming. Serve it in smaller portions as an appetizer or in large bowls as a whole meal with crusty bread and a salad. Traditionally the soup contains triangular pieces of pasta cut from larger sheets, but any shapes can be used as long as you break them into smaller pieces. You could also use any leftover cooked pasta (use about 2 cups/500 mL). For a vegetarian version, omit the ham and use vegetable stock or water instead of chicken stock.

Any leftover soup will be very thick. You can reheat the soup and thin it with extra liquid. Or add cubes of bread and more cheese and bake it in a casserole at 350°F/180°C for about 30 minutes. (It will be like a ribollita — a casserole made with leftover minestrone.)

Makes 8 servings

1 tbsp	olive oil	15 mL
2	onions, chopped	2
3	cloves garlic, finely chopped	3
1	carrot, chopped	1
¼ tsp	hot red pepper flakes, optional	1 mL
1	28-oz/796 mL can plum tomatoes with juices	1
4 cups	homemade chicken stock (page 79), or 1 10-oz/284 mL can chicken broth plus water	1 L
2 oz	smoked ham, in one piece, trimmed of any fat, optional	60 g
1	19-oz/540 g can cannellini (white kidney beans), rinsed and drained	1
1 cup	small pasta (about 4 oz/125 g), such as little bows, shells or macaroni	250 mL
	Salt and pepper to taste	
2 tbsp	grated Parmesan cheese	25 mL

1. Heat oil in a large saucepan or Dutch oven on medium-high heat. Add onions, garlic and carrot and cook until tender — 5 to 7 minutes. Add hot pepper flakes.

2. Add tomatoes with their juices and break them up with a wooden spoon. Add stock and bring to a boil. Add piece of ham (if using). Reduce heat and simmer gently for about 30 minutes.

3. Add beans and cook for 10 minutes. Remove ham (dice and use as a garnish if you wish). Puree half the soup. Return all soup to pot. Bring to a boil.

4. Add pasta and cook for about 10 minutes until pasta is very tender. Stir often, as the pasta easily sticks to bottom of pan. If soup is too thick, add some water.

5. Taste and add salt and pepper. Serve sprinkled with Parmesan cheese.

Soup Stocks

Salt-free, fat-free homemade stocks are the best, but if you do not have homemade stocks, there are substitutes.

- Frozen stock is usually salt free, with the fat removed. It can be quite expensive, so dilute it with water.

- There are newly available stocks sold in Tetrapaks. They can be resealed and stored in the refrigerator.

- Canned broth, bouillon cubes and powdered soup bases usually contain a lot of salt; they can also contain MSG, fat and food colouring. Of the three, I prefer to use canned broth (buy lower-salt, lower-fat products if possible) and refrigerate it before opening — the fat will solidify on the surface. Remove it before using. I then dilute the canned broth more than the directions recommend, and freeze any extra.

- If you use bouillon cubes or powdered soup bases, dilute them with lots of water, and look for lower-salt, lower-fat brands.

- Water can be a good substitute for stock when there are many other flavourful ingredients in the recipe.

MEXICAN LENTIL SOUP

SERVING SUGGESTION
• Serve the soup in hollowed-out vegetables, such as small pumpkins or squash.

MAKE AHEAD
• This soup can be made ahead and reheated.

Lentils

There are many types of lentils. The small red (pink or orange) lentils are commonly used in soups because they soften quickly and act as a thickener. The large greeny-brown lentils or tiny green French lentils are usually used when you want the lentils to keep their shape — e.g., in salads and casseroles.

There are many types of lentil soups. This is a new favourite modelled after one I tasted at a restaurant in Banff called the Coyotes Deli and Grill. Green lentils are used in this soup so they retain their shape and texture. I like the tiny French ones the best.

Makes 8 to 10 servings

1 tbsp	olive oil	15 mL
2	onions, chopped	2
2	cloves garlic, finely chopped	2
1 tbsp	ground cumin	15 mL
1	chipotle (page 73) or jalapeño, finely chopped	1
2	carrots, diced	2
2	stalks celery, diced	2
2	parsnips, peeled and diced	2
1	potato, peeled and diced	1
2 cups	green lentils, rinsed well and picked over	500 mL
8 cups	homemade vegetable stock (page 69) or water	2 L
1	head roasted garlic (page 41)	1
1½ cups	corn niblets	375 mL
2 tbsp	lemon juice	25 mL
	Salt and pepper to taste	
3 oz	chèvre (goat cheese)	90 g
3 tbsp	milk	45 mL
¼ cup	chopped fresh cilantro or basil	50 mL

PER SERVING

Calories	322
Protein	18 g
Fat	5.7 g
Saturates	1.9 g
Cholesterol	5 mg
Carbohydrate	53.6 g
Fibre	9.2 g
Sodium	113 mg
Potassium	948 mg

Excellent: Vitamin A; Thiamine; Vitamin B$_6$; Folacin; Iron; Zinc
Good: Niacin

1. Heat oil in a Dutch oven or large saucepan on medium-high heat. Add onions and garlic and cook until tender. Add cumin and chipotle and cook for 30 seconds longer.

2. Add carrots, celery, parsnips and potato. Cook for about 5 minutes. Stir in lentils and stock. Squeeze in roasted garlic. Bring to a boil. Reduce heat and simmer gently, uncovered, for about 30 minutes, or until lentils are very tender.

3. Add corn. Cook for 3 minutes. Add lemon juice. Season with salt and pepper.

4. In a small bowl, combine chèvre and milk until smooth. Drizzle on soup and sprinkle with cilantro.

WHEAT BERRY MINESTRONE

This soup makes a delicious first course, or it can be a whole meal when it is served with a salad and crusty bread. You can easily make it vegetarian by using vegetable stock or water. You can also use faro (spelt), barley or rice instead of the wheat berries.

If you have any leftovers, add some bread or cooked pasta, place in a casserole and sprinkle with grated cheese. Bake at 350°F/180°C for about 30 minutes, or until heated through.

Makes 8 servings

2 tbsp	olive oil, divided	25 mL
1	onion, diced	1
1	carrot, diced	1
1	stalk celery, diced	1
2	cloves garlic, finely chopped	2
1	potato, peeled and diced	1
2 cups	chopped cabbage	500 mL
1 cup	pureed canned tomatoes	250 mL
6 cups	homemade chicken stock (page 79), or 1 10-oz/284 mL can chicken broth plus water	1.5 L
3 cups	cooked wheat berries (page 149)	750 mL
2 cups	whole wheat bread cubes (2 large slices bread)	500 mL
	Salt and pepper to taste	
¼ cup	chopped fresh parsley	50 mL

1. Heat 1 tbsp/15 mL oil in a Dutch oven or large saucepan on medium heat. Cook onion, carrot, celery and garlic until tender and fragrant, about 5 minutes.

2. Add potato and cook for 5 minutes longer. Add cabbage, tomatoes, stock and wheat berries. Bring to a boil. Cook gently for 20 to 30 minutes, or until soup is thick. (If soup becomes too thick, add more stock or water.)

3. Meanwhile, in a large bowl, toss bread cubes with remaining 1 tbsp/15 mL olive oil. Spread bread on a baking sheet. Bake in a preheated 350°F/180°C oven for 15 to 20 minutes until crispy.

4. When soup is ready, season with salt and pepper to taste. Serve sprinkled with croutons and parsley.

MAKE AHEAD
- If you make this ahead and refrigerate, it will thicken. Add more stock or water when you reheat it and reseason to taste.
- This is also delicious served cold. Garnish with a spoonful of yogurt.

Homemade Croutons
Cut crusty French or Italian bread into cubes and spread on a baking sheet. Bake in a preheated 350°F/180°C oven for 12 minutes or until crisp.

PER SERVING

Calories	189
Protein	7.9 g
Fat	5.1 g
Saturates	0.9 g
Cholesterol	1 mg
Carbohydrate	29.9 g
Fibre	5.3 g
Sodium	86 mg
Potassium	538 mg

Excellent: Vitamin A; Niacin
Good: Vitamin C

CHICKEN SOUP WITH MATZO BALLS

SERVING SUGGESTION
• Add 1 bunch fresh dill and/or 1 peeled and sliced bulb celeriac to the soup with the other vegetables.

MAKE AHEAD
• It is better to make this soup a day ahead. When you refrigerate it overnight, the fat will solidify on the surface and can easily be removed.

Matzo
Matzo is an unleavened flatbread traditionally served at Passover. Matzo meal is ground matzo. Both can be purchased at any time at Jewish delicatessens and most supermarkets.

PER SERVING
Calories	104
Protein	10 g
Fat	2.8 g
Saturates	0.8 g
Cholesterol	29 mg
Carbohydrate	8.4 g
Fibre	0.3 g
Sodium	715 mg
Potassium	338 mg

Excellent: Niacin
Good: Vitamin B$_{12}$

Chicken soup with matzo balls has almost become a Jewish cliché. But matzo balls break down all ethnic barriers — everyone seems to love them.

Texturally, there are two kinds of matzo balls — hard ones and soft fluffy ones. I have always preferred the latter, but I never seemed to be able to have any control over whether mine turned out hard or fluffy. Then Rhonda Caplan, who works with me on the TV show, told me about her mother's recipe. So I started making Sally Caplan's double-light matzo balls, and my problem was solved. They are not only fluffy, but also lighter in calories and fat.

When it comes to the soup, it is imperative that you use the best chicken you can. If it is not a kosher chicken, it should be organic or free-range. Leftover soup can be used as chicken stock — I usually dilute it a bit.

I love to use a pasta pot when making stock, as the insert automatically acts as a strainer and lifts out the bones.

Makes 8 to 10 servings

1	4-lb/2 kg chicken	1
12 cups	cold water (approx.)	3 L
2	onions, quartered	2
2	stalks celery with leaves, sliced	2
2	carrots, sliced	2
2	parsnips, peeled and sliced	2
1	bay leaf	1
1	bunch fresh parsley	1
¾ tsp	salt	4 mL
¼ tsp	pepper	1 mL

Matzo Balls

1	egg	1
2	egg whites	2
½ cup	matzo meal	125 mL
1½ tsp	salt	7 mL
2 tbsp	chicken soup	25 mL
2 tbsp	chopped fresh parsley	25 mL

1. Cut chicken into 8 pieces. Remove and discard any visible fat. Place chicken in a large pot and add cold water just to cover. Bring to a boil and skim off scum that rises to surface.

2. Add onions, celery, carrots, parsnips, bay leaf, parsley, salt and pepper. Bring to a boil again, reduce heat and simmer very gently, uncovered, for 2 hours. Keep chicken covered with water.

3. Strain soup into another pot. Remove chicken from bones and use in the soup or in sandwiches if you wish. If you are serving soup right away, skim fat off top with a big spoon.

4. Meanwhile, to prepare matzo balls, in a medium bowl, beat egg with egg whites. Add matzo meal, salt, chicken soup and parsley. Cover and refrigerate for 30 minutes.

5. Wet your hands with cold water and shape mixture into 10 to 12 balls.

6. Bring a large pot of water to a boil. Add matzo balls gently and simmer for 40 minutes. Remove from water and serve in strained chicken soup.

Homemade Chicken Stock
Cut 4-lb/2 kg chicken into pieces and remove visible fat (leave skin on for extra flavour). Place chicken in a large pot and add enough cold water to cover by 2 inches/5 cm. Bring to a boil and skim off any scum. Add 2 onions, 2 carrots, 2 stalks celery and 2 leeks (all cut in chunks). Return to a boil and skim again if necessary. Add 1 bay leaf, ½ tsp/2 mL dried thyme, 6 whole peppercorns and a small handful of fresh parsley. Reduce heat and simmer, uncovered, for 1½ hours. (If necessary, add water to keep chicken covered.) Strain stock and chill. Skim off surface fat before freezing. Makes about 3 qt/3 L.

RUBY RED BEET BORSCHT

MAKE AHEAD
• This can be made ahead,
but add garnishes just
before serving.

Low-fat Sauteing Tip
If you are sauteing onions
and/or garlic in a small
amount of oil and the
onions begin to brown too
much, add up to ¼ cup/
50 mL water to the skillet.
The water will cool down
the pan but eventually
evaporate. Continue to
cook until the onions are
tender.

Borscht is an Eastern European specialty. Some people think it is a beet or cabbage soup, but it actually refers to a vegetable soup that can include many different types of vegetables. Here's a great version. The potatoes are usually added at the end so that they do not discolour too much.

Makes 6 to 8 servings

1 tbsp	vegetable oil	15 mL
1	large onion, cut in chunks	1
3	beets (about 1 lb/500 g), peeled and cut in chunks	3
4 cups	chopped red cabbage	1 L
1 cup	chopped canned tomatoes	250 mL
6 cups	homemade vegetable stock (page 69) or water	1.5 L
¼ cup	balsamic vinegar, sherry vinegar or red wine vinegar	50 mL
2 tbsp	brown sugar	25 mL
	Salt and pepper to taste	
1	large baking potato or Yukon Gold potato, peeled, cooked and diced (about ½ lb/250 g)	1
½ cup	unflavoured low-fat yogurt or light sour cream	125 mL
3	green onions, thinly sliced	3
2 tbsp	chopped fresh dill	25 mL

1. Heat oil in a large saucepan or Dutch oven on medium heat. Add onion and cook for a few minutes until slightly wilted. Add beets and cabbage and cook for 5 minutes longer. Add tomatoes and mix in well.

2. Add stock and bring to a boil. Reduce heat and simmer, uncovered, for about 30 minutes, or until beets are tender.

3. Add vinegar and sugar and cook for 10 minutes. Season to taste with salt and pepper. Serve chunky, puree or puree half so that soup is partly smooth and partly chunky.

4. Serve in large bowls topped with cooked potato, yogurt, green onions and dill.

PER SERVING

Calories	156
Protein	4.3 g
Fat	3.7 g
Saturates	0.4 g
Cholesterol	1 mg
Carbohydrate	28.4 g
Fibre	3.6 g
Sodium	170 mg
Potassium	589 mg

Excellent: Folacin
Good: Vitamin C

JAPANESE-STYLE CHICKEN NOODLE SOUP

This is a very soothing soup with the twist of Asian flavours. A big bowl of it makes a very satisfying meal, or have it in smaller portions as a starter. Use chopsticks for the noodles, chicken and vegetables and drink the rest right out of the bowl, or provide spoons if you think your guests would not be comfortable slurping!

When I am serving a clear soup with pasta in it, I like to cook the pasta separately so the broth stays clear.

Makes 6 to 8 servings

MAKE AHEAD
• This soup can be made ahead, but strain the stock and refrigerate the vegetables and noodles separately. Reheat together quickly.

8 cups	homemade chicken stock (page 79), or 1 10-oz/284 mL can chicken broth plus water	2 L
2	1-inch/2.5 cm pieces fresh ginger root, smashed	2
¼ cup	rice wine	50 mL
2 tbsp	soy sauce	25 mL
¾ lb	udon noodles, soba noodles or spaghetti	375 g
½ lb	boneless, skinless chicken breasts, cut in ½-inch/1 cm chunks	250 g
8	fresh shiitake mushrooms, stemmed and sliced	8
6 oz	fresh spinach, broken in pieces	175 g
1 cup	peas	250 mL
2	carrots, grated	2
¼ lb	regular tofu, cut in ½-inch/1 cm cubes	125 g
8	green onions, sliced on the diagonal	8
¼ cup	coarsely chopped fresh cilantro	50 mL

1. Place stock, ginger, rice wine and soy sauce in a large saucepan or Dutch oven. Bring to a boil, reduce heat and simmer gently for 10 minutes. Remove and discard ginger.

2. Meanwhile, cook noodles in a separate pot of boiling water for 5 to 6 minutes, or until almost tender. Rinse with cold water to help prevent sticking. Drain well.

3. Add chicken and mushrooms to stock and cook for 2 minutes. Add spinach, peas, carrots, tofu, green onions and noodles. Heat thoroughly for about 5 minutes.

4. Taste and adjust seasonings, adding soy sauce if necessary. Sprinkle with cilantro.

PER SERVING

Calories	350
Protein	24.8 g
Fat	4.8 g
Saturates	0.8 g
Cholesterol	24 mg
Carbohydrate	50.2 g
Fibre	3.4 g
Sodium	752 mg
Potassium	770 mg

Excellent: Vitamin A; Niacin; Folacin; Iron
Good: Riboflavin; Vitamin B$_6$; Vitamin B$_{12}$; Zinc

COSY WINTER DINNER

Hot Apple Cranberry Drink

French Onion Soup

Pot Roast of Beef
with Root Vegetables

Succotash

Apple Crisp Strudel

*Whether it is dinner after skiing or after a cold commute,
a hearty, hot meal in winter is always appealing. The scent of cinnamon makes a
warm welcome. Offer guests a hot apple cranberry drink when they walk in the door.
For a simpler meal, just serve the onion soup with a salad, or the
pot roast with biscuits or crusty bread.*

WORK PLAN

MAKE AHEAD

• Make the soup and croutons up to two days ahead.
Soup can also be frozen.

• Make the pot roast up to two days ahead and refrigerate. Remove the fat when the pot roast is cold and
reheat in the oven. (The pot roast can also be made
further in advance and frozen.)

• Succotash can be made one day ahead.

SAME DAY

• Top the soup with croutons and sprinkle with cheese.
Place on soup and bake 15 minutes before serving.

• Reheat the succotash briefly just before serving.

• Assemble the crisp in the morning and bake during
dinner or just before your guests arrive (your house
will smell incredible!).

PRESENTATION IDEAS

- Use a tapestry tablecloth (old drapes or bedspreads can work well). Use tapestry ribbon as napkin rings.
- Use large winter scarves as runners/placemats.
- Use a plaid or striped Hudson's Bay blanket as a tablecloth.
- If you have a fireplace, use it.
- Use stoneware and earthenware platters and dishes.
- Drape blankets, sweaters or capes over the backs of chairs.
- Decorate the table with nuts in the shell and winter fruits such as apples, crabapples and pears.
- Use lanterns instead of candles.
- Use tea towels for extra-large napkins.
- Light lots of candles.
- Decorate the table with pine cones and pine boughs.
- Decorate a winter table with a dried flower arrangement.
- Use antique Mason jars as vases.
- Fill an antique muffin pan with tea lights or votive candles for a beautiful effect.

MATCHING FOOD WITH WINE*

If you want to serve wine: The hearty pot roast requires a mouth-filling, tummy-warming wine such as a French Côte du Rhône, which can contain flavours such as black pepper, smoke, plums, licorice and blackberries. The apple crisp is a wine-friendly dessert, and would go well with a Late Harvest Riesling (New World). When you are serving wine with dessert, make sure the wine is sweeter than the dessert; otherwise the wine will taste flat.

See Alcohol (page 274).

HOT APPLE CRANBERRY DRINK

This is a perfect way to welcome guests on a wintery night! To turn this into mulled wine, use a dry Spanish or Italian red wine instead of the apple juice. Add ¼ cup/50 mL brandy or orange liqueur if desired. If you are using wine, be sure to heat it gently and only until warm.

Makes 8 servings

3 cups	apple juice	750 mL
2 cups	cranberry juice	500 mL
1	orange, sliced	1
¼ cup	cranberries	50 mL
¼ cup	granulated sugar	50 mL
1	cinnamon stick, broken, or ½ tsp/2 mL ground	1
4	whole cloves, or pinch ground	4
4	whole allspice, or pinch ground	4
pinch	grated nutmeg	pinch
8	cinnamon sticks	8

1. Place apple juice, cranberry juice, orange slices, cranberries and sugar in a saucepan. Add broken cinnamon stick, cloves, allspice and nutmeg.

2. Heat until sugar dissolves. Serve in mugs with cinnamon sticks as stirrers.

PER SERVING

Calories	110
Protein	0.2 g
Fat	0.1 g
Saturates	0 g
Cholesterol	0 mg
Carbohydrate	27.9 g
Fibre	0.4 g
Sodium	5 mg
Potassium	151 mg

Excellent: Vitamin C

FRENCH ONION SOUP

This is delicious with or without the croutons and cheese. The sliced onions will look like a truckload, but don't worry; they cook down to less than half. If you have leftovers, transfer to a baking dish, bake until the bread absorbs the liquid and serve as a casserole.

Makes 8 servings

2 tsp	olive oil	10 mL
3 lb	onions, thinly sliced (about 9)	1.5 kg
1 cup	dry white wine or additional stock	250 mL
1 tbsp	red wine vinegar or sherry vinegar	15 mL
8 cups	homemade chicken stock (page 79), or 1 10-oz/284 mL can chicken broth plus water	2 L
	Salt and pepper to taste	

Croutons

8	3-inch/7.5 cm rounds French or Italian bread, about ½ inch/1 cm thick	8
1 tbsp	olive oil	15 mL
1	clove garlic, minced	1
1 tsp	chopped fresh thyme, or pinch dried	5 mL
	Salt and pepper to taste	
½ cup	grated Parmesan, Fontina, Asiago or Monterey Jack cheese	125 mL

1. Heat oil in a large, deep skillet or Dutch oven on high heat. Add onions but do not stir. When onions begin to brown, stir, reduce heat to medium and cook for 15 to 20 minutes until onions are tender and evenly browned.

2. Add wine and bring to a boil. Reduce heat again and cook gently until wine has evaporated, about 15 minutes. Add vinegar and cook for a few minutes longer. Add stock, bring to a boil and cook for 20 minutes. Season with salt and pepper.

3. Meanwhile, arrange bread in a single layer on a baking sheet. In a small bowl, combine oil, garlic, thyme, salt and pepper. Brush on top side of bread. Bake in a preheated 400°F/200°C oven for 10 minutes, or until lightly browned.

4. To serve, ladle soup into 8 ovenproof onion soup bowls. Place a crouton on each. Sprinkle evenly with cheese. Bake for 10 minutes. Allow to rest for 5 minutes before serving.

MAKE AHEAD
- The soup and croutons can be made ahead, but bake together just before serving. The soup also freezes well.

PER SERVING

Calories	201
Protein	10.7 g
Fat	6.8 g
Saturates	2.1 g
Cholesterol	6 mg
Carbohydrate	23.2 g
Fibre	2.4 g
Sodium	240 mg
Potassium	464 mg

Excellent: Niacin
Good: Vitamin B$_{12}$

POT ROAST OF BEEF WITH ROOT VEGETABLES

Homemade Beef Stock
Place 3 lb/1.5 kg beef bones, 3 lb/1.5 kg veal bones and 3 lb/1.5 kg chicken pieces in a large roasting pan. Roast at 425°F/220°C for 1½ hours until browned. Add 4 large onions, 4 large carrots, 3 stalks celery and 2 leeks (cut in chunks) and brown for 30 minutes longer. Transfer everything to a large pot. Cover with cold water, bring to a boil, skim off scum. Add 2 bay leaves, ½ tsp/2 mL dried thyme and 6 whole peppercorns. Simmer for 8 to 10 hours or overnight. Add more water if necessary.

Strain and place stock in clean pot. Cook until reduced to 4 qt/4 L. Refrigerate, remove fat and freeze.

For many people, pot roast means beef, but this roast will work well with lamb or pork, too. Leftovers can be made into shepherd's pie (page 201).

Makes 10 to 12 servings

1 tbsp	olive oil	15 mL
4 lb	boneless cross-rib roast of beef, tied	2 kg
½ tsp	salt	2 mL
¼ tsp	pepper	1 mL
2	onions, chopped	2
2	cloves garlic, finely chopped	2
2 tbsp	chopped fresh rosemary, or 1 tsp/5 mL dried	25 mL
2 tbsp	chopped fresh thyme, or 1 tsp/5 mL dried	25 mL
2 cups	dry red wine or homemade beef stock	500 mL
2 tbsp	balsamic vinegar or red wine vinegar	25 mL
2 cups	homemade beef stock or water	500 mL
2	onions, cut in chunks	2
2	carrots, cut in chunks	2
2	parsnips, peeled and cut in chunks	2
4	baking potatoes or Yukon Gold potatoes, peeled and cut in chunks	4
1	sweet potato, peeled and cut in chunks	1
1 tbsp	all-purpose flour, optional	15 mL
1 tbsp	soft non-hydrogenated margarine, optional	15 mL
2 tbsp	chopped fresh parsley	25 mL

PER SERVING

Calories	353
Protein	34.2 g
Fat	11.4 g
Saturates	3.9 g
Cholesterol	74 mg
Carbohydrate	27.8 g
Fibre	3.6 g
Sodium	302 mg
Potassium	919 mg

Excellent: Vitamin A; Niacin; Vitamin B_6; Vitamin B_{12}; Iron; Zinc
Good: Vitamin C; Riboflavin; Folacin

1. Heat oil in a heavy Dutch oven on high heat. Pat roast dry, season with salt and pepper and brown well on all sides (this should take 10 to 15 minutes). Remove roast from pan.

2. Discard all but 2 tsp/10 mL oil from pan. Add chopped onions and garlic. Cook until tender, about 4 minutes. Add rosemary, thyme and wine and bring to a boil. Cook, uncovered, until wine reduces to about 1 cup/250 mL. Add vinegar and stock. Bring to a boil and return beef to pot. Cover tightly and cook in a 350°F/180°C oven for 1½ hours.

3. Arrange onions, carrots, parsnips, potatoes and sweet potato around roast. Cover and continue to cook for 1½ hours or until vegetables and beef are both tender.

4. Remove beef to a carving board and vegetables to a serving platter. Skim any fat from juices and simmer juices on top of stove. If juices are not thick enough, cook, uncovered, until thick, or mix flour and margarine in a small bowl. Add to simmering liquid a teaspoon at a time, stirring, until juices are just slightly thickened.

5. Slice meat, arrange over vegetables and spoon juices on top. Sprinkle with parsley.

SUCCOTASH

There are many variations of this old-fashioned vegetable medley. You can use fresh shelled soybeans (page 133) or sliced green beans instead of lima beans. You can also add diced winter squash. For a heartier version, cook two diced strips of bacon until crisp and discard the fat. Add garlic and onions and continue as per the recipe. (This is a great way to add a smoky bacon flavour without adding too much fat.)

Makes 8 servings

1 tbsp	olive oil	15 mL
2	cloves garlic, finely chopped	2
1	onion, finely chopped	1
1	sweet red pepper, peeled, seeded and chopped	1
2 cups	frozen lima beans, unthawed	500 mL
½ cup	homemade vegetable stock (page 69), chicken stock (page 79) or water	125 mL
2 cups	corn niblets	500 mL
3	green onions, chopped	3
	Salt and pepper to taste	

1. Heat oil in a large skillet on medium-high heat. Add garlic and onion and cook until fragrant. Add red pepper and cook for 5 minutes until pepper wilts and becomes tender.

2. Add lima beans and stock and cook for 5 minutes. Add corn and cook for 3 minutes. Add green onions and salt and pepper to taste.

SERVING SUGGESTION
• Serve in hollowed-out tomato or pepper halves. Place on a baking sheet and heat at 400°F/200°C for 10 minutes.

MAKE AHEAD
• This can be made ahead and reheated before serving.

PER SERVING

Calories	112
Protein	5 g
Fat	2 g
Saturates	0.3 g
Cholesterol	0 mg
Carbohydrate	20.7 g
Fibre	3.7 g
Sodium	60 mg
Potassium	324 mg

Excellent: Vitamin C

APPLE CRISP STRUDEL

For a more nutty oat taste, toast the rolled oats on a baking sheet at 350°F/180°C for 10 minutes before using.

The apple mixture can also be used as a pie filling. Pears, mangoes, pineapple, kiwi or papaya can be used instead of apples for an exotic variation.

Makes 8 to 10 servings

SERVING SUGGESTION
• Serve with sweetened yogurt cheese (page 303), vanilla ice cream or frozen yogurt.

MAKE AHEAD
• This can be made ahead and frozen for up to one month either baked or unbaked. To reheat the frozen baked strudel, bake at 375°F/190°C for 40 to 45 minutes. To bake the unbaked frozen strudel, double the baking time (if the top becomes too brown, cover with foil and reduce the heat to 350°F/180°C).

4	apples, peeled, cored and chopped	4
½ cup	brown sugar	125 mL
1 tsp	cinnamon	5 mL
pinch	grated nutmeg	pinch
pinch	allspice	pinch
1 cup	rolled oats (five-minute kind)	250 mL
¼ cup	chopped candied ginger or dried cranberries	50 mL
2 tbsp	unsalted butter, melted	25 mL
3 tbsp	water	45 mL
⅓ cup	dry breadcrumbs	75 mL
2 tbsp	finely chopped toasted walnuts	25 mL
2 tbsp	granulated sugar	25 mL
6	sheets phyllo pastry	6

1. In a large bowl, combine apples with brown sugar, cinnamon, nutmeg, allspice, oats and ginger. Toss together well.

2. In a small bowl, combine melted butter and water. In a separate bowl, combine breadcrumbs, nuts and granulated sugar.

3. Arrange a sheet of parchment paper on a large, heavy baking pan. Place one sheet of phyllo on parchment. Brush with butter/water mixture and sprinkle with crumbs. Repeat until all 6 sheets are stacked. Spoon apple mixture along long side of pastry. Roll up.

4. Cut shallow diagonal slices through top layer so that cutting and serving will be easier after strudel is baked. Brush top with any extra butter.

5. Bake in a preheated 375°F/190°C oven for 40 to 45 minutes, or until apples are very tender and pastry is brown and flaky. Serve warm or at room temperature.

PER SERVING

Calories	273
Protein	3.9 g
Fat	6.3 g
Saturates	2.3 g
Cholesterol	8 mg
Carbohydrate	52 g
Fibre	3.3 g
Sodium	131 mg
Potassium	354 mg

Good: Thiamine; Iron

SALADS

Roasted Potato, Chickpea and Arugula Salad   *90*

Antipasto Pasta Salad   *91*

Serious Syrian Salad   *92*

Russian Beet and Potato Salad   *93*

Green Mango Salad   *94*

Marinated Vegetable Salad   *95*

Roasted Vegetable Pasta Salad   *96*

Warm Breaded Chicken Salad   *98*

Salsa Spaghetti Salad   *99*

Asian Chopped Salad   *100*

Noodle Salad with Barbecued Chicken and Peanut Sauce   *102*

Rice Noodle Salad with Lemongrass Chicken   *104*

More Salads

Grilled Vegetable Salad with Tomato Soy Dressing   *116*

Raita with Tomatoes and Cucumber   *117*

Fennel, Endive and Red Pepper Salad   *189*

Wheat Berry and Grilled Corn Salad   *219*

Grilled Tomato Salad   *220*

Potato and Arugula Salad with Mustard and Roasted Garlic   *252*

Chopped Salad Niçoise   *301*

ROASTED POTATO, CHICKPEA
AND ARUGULA SALAD

SERVING SUGGESTION
- Serve this salad as a base for sliced steak or lamb chops.

MAKE AHEAD
- This can be made a day ahead and refrigerated, but I like it best served the same day it is made. Serve warm or at room temperature, and add the greens just before serving.

Whenever I roast potatoes for dinner, I often roast extra so I can make this salad with the leftovers.

Makes 8 servings

3 lb	new or baby potatoes, halved (or larger potatoes, peeled and cut in 1-inch/2.5 cm chunks)	1.5 kg
2 tbsp	olive oil, divided	25 mL
2 tbsp	chopped fresh rosemary or thyme, or ½ tsp/2 mL dried	25 mL
1 tsp	salt	5 mL
½ tsp	pepper	2 mL
2	heads garlic, cloves broken apart and peeled (about 26 cloves)	2
2 tbsp	balsamic vinegar, red wine vinegar or sherry vinegar	25 mL
1	clove garlic, minced	1
	Salt and pepper to taste	
1	19-oz/540 mL can chickpeas, drained and rinsed	1
1	bunch fresh arugula or watercress, trimmed and coarsely chopped (about 6 cups/1.5 L)	1

1. Toss potatoes with 1 tbsp/15 mL oil, rosemary, salt and pepper.

2. Place potatoes on a baking sheet lined with parchment paper and roast in a preheated 400°F/200°C oven for 30 minutes.

3. Add cloves of garlic to baking sheet and toss with potatoes (If garlic is added too soon it will burn.) Continue to roast potatoes and garlic for 20 to 30 minutes longer, until potatoes are very tender, brown and crisp.

4. Meanwhile, combine vinegar with minced garlic and remaining 1 tbsp/15 mL oil. Add salt and pepper. Toss hot potatoes, garlic and chickpeas with dressing. Add greens just before serving.

PER SERVING

Calories	244
Protein	7.9 g
Fat	4.7 g
Saturates	0.6 g
Cholesterol	0 mg
Carbohydrate	44.8 g
Fibre	4.5 g
Sodium	409 mg
Potassium	792 mg

Excellent: Vitamin B$_6$; Folacin
Good: Vitamin C; Thiamine; Niacin; Iron

ANTIPASTO PASTA SALAD

This salad is so versatile; you can use any leftover cooked vegetables, pasta, cold cuts or cheese in it. Serve it as a light main course or side salad. Leftovers can be added to frittatas (page 269).

Makes 8 servings

1	19-oz/540 mL can chickpeas, drained and rinsed	1
1	14-oz/398 mL can artichoke hearts, drained, rinsed and quartered	1
2	sweet red peppers, roasted (page 49), peeled and cut in strips (about ¾ cup/175 mL), or ½ cup/125 mL chopped pimiento	2
2 tbsp	chopped hot banana pepper or jalapeño, optional	25 mL
2 cups	cooked small pasta (e.g., little bows or shells)	500 mL
4 oz	lean ham, trimmed, cut in thin strips (about 1 cup/250 mL)	125 g
4 oz	smoked turkey roll, cut in thin strips (about 1 cup/250 mL)	125 g
3 tbsp	red wine vinegar, sherry vinegar or balsamic vinegar	45 mL
2	cloves garlic, minced	2
2 tbsp	olive oil	25 mL
2 tbsp	chopped fresh parsley	25 m
	Salt and pepper to taste	

1. In a large bowl, combine chickpeas, artichokes, red peppers, hot pepper (if using), pasta, ham and turkey.

2. To make dressing, in a small bowl, combine vinegar, garlic, olive oil and parsley.

3. Combine dressing with salad. Taste and add salt and pepper.

SERVING SUGGESTIONS
- Serve as a base for grilled chicken breasts or lamb chops.
- Serve in cup-shaped lettuce leaves.

MAKE AHEAD
- This can be made a few days ahead and marinated in the refrigerator, but bring the salad to room temperature before serving.

PER SERVING

Calories	207
Protein	12.2 g
Fat	6.2 g
Saturates	1.1 g
Cholesterol	17 mg
Carbohydrate	27 g
Fibre	4.2 g
Sodium	417 mg
Potassium	326 mg

Excellent: Vitamin C; Folacin
Good: Thiamine; Vitamin B$_6$

SERIOUS SYRIAN SALAD

SERVING SUGGESTIONS
• Serve the salad moulded in different shapes. Use empty tuna cans or pack into custard cups and invert.
• Serve the salad in hollowed-out tomato halves.

MAKE AHEAD
• This salad can be made up to two days ahead.

Sam Linton, a producer from the Discovery network, asked me to develop a recipe for a TV series with archaeologist Julian Siggers on how prehistoric people lived. Surprisingly, some of the foods they gave me to work with, such as wheat berries and barley, were on my Y2K hitlist of trendy foods. The more things change the more they stay the same! I did take a few liberties including the olive oil.

Makes 8 to 10 servings

1 cup	wheat berries, rinsed	250 mL
1 cup	barley, rinsed	250 mL
1 cup	small dried green lentils, rinsed and picked over	250 mL
1	19-oz/540 g can chickpeas, drained and rinsed	1
¼ cup	chopped toasted pistachio nuts	50 mL
¼ cup	toasted sliced almonds	50 mL
¼ cup	diced dried figs	50 mL
¼ cup	diced pitted dates	50 mL
2 tbsp	pitted black olives	25 mL
½ cup	chopped fresh cilantro	125 mL
1 tsp	chopped fresh rosemary	5 mL
1 tsp	chopped fresh thyme	5 mL
½ cup	lemon juice or seasoned rice vinegar	125 mL
2 tbsp	olive oil	25 mL
	Salt and pepper to taste	
8 cups	arugula	2 L

1. Cook wheat berries in at least 12 cups/3 L boiling water for 1 to 1½ hours or until tender. Drain well and rinse.

2. Meanwhile, cook barley in 12 cups/3 L boiling water for about 30 minutes. Drain well and rinse. Cook lentils in about 12 cups/3 L boiling water for 20 to 25 minutes or until tender. Drain well and rinse.

3. In a large bowl combine wheat berries, barley, lentils, chickpeas, pistachios, almonds, figs, dates, olives, cilantro, rosemary, thyme, lemon juice and olive oil. Season with salt and pepper, and serve on a bed of arugula.

PER SERVING
Calories	421
Protein	16.7 g
Fat	9.5 g
Saturates	1.2 g
Cholesterol	0 mg
Carbohydrate	72.9 g
Fibre	11.3 g
Sodium	144 mg
Potassium	832 mg

Excellent: Thiamine; Niacin; Vitamin B$_6$; Folacin; Iron; Zinc

RUSSIAN BEET AND POTATO SALAD

The colour and taste of this salad are awesome. Serve it as an appetizer or side dish. Cooked shrimp or chicken can be added if you want to serve it as a main course. If you prefer, use a vinaigrette instead of the yogurt dressing.

Makes 8 servings

1	English cucumber	1
1 tsp	salt	5 mL
1 lb	beets, cooked, peeled and diced (about 3)	500 g
1 lb	potatoes, cooked, peeled and diced (about 2 large)	500 g
3	hard-cooked egg whites, diced	3
1	dill pickle, diced	1
2 tbsp	chopped fresh dill	25mL
2 tbsp	chopped fresh parsley	25 mL
2 tbsp	chopped fresh chives or green onions	25 mL
1 cup	yogurt cheese (page 303), thick yogurt or light sour cream	250 mL
2 tbsp	mayonnaise	25 mL
1 tbsp	horseradish	15 mL
	Salt and pepper to taste	

1. Cut cucumber in half lengthwise. Scoop out seeds. Dice cucumber. Place in a colander, toss with salt and allow to drain for 30 minutes. Rinse cucumber well to remove salt and pat dry.

2. In a large bowl, combine cucumber, beets, potatoes, egg whites, pickle, dill, parsley and chives.

3. In a small bowl, combine yogurt cheese, mayonnaise and horseradish. Taste and add salt and pepper if necessary.

4. Toss yogurt mixture with salad.

SERVING SUGGESTION
• Garnish with sprigs of fresh dill.

MAKE AHEAD
• This can be made ahead, but stir in the dressing just before serving. If the dressing has become a little watery, drain it before using.

PER SERVING

Calories	125
Protein	6.1 g
Fat	3.8 g
Saturates	0.8 g
Cholesterol	5 mg
Carbohydrate	17.3 g
Fibre	2 g
Sodium	493 mg
Potassium	468 mg

Excellent: Folacin
Good: Vitamin B$_{12}$

Green Mango Salad

SERVING SUGGESTIONS
• Wrap salad in rice paper
wrappers (alone or with
diced cooked fish) and
serve as salad rolls
(page 248).

SERVING SUGGESTIONS
• Wrap salad in rice paper
wrappers (alone or with
diced cooked fish) and
serve as salad rolls
(page 248).
• Place some salad in a
cocktail glass and hang
cooked shrimp off the
edge of the glass. Or
skewer chicken or shrimp,
grill and arrange on top of
the glass like chopsticks.

MAKE AHEAD
• You can make the salad a
few hours ahead, but
assemble on lettuce leaves
just before serving.

Thai Hot Sweet Sauce
Thai hot sweet sauce con-
tains red chiles, sugar, garlic, vinegar and salt. Use it
on its own or in Asian-
flavoured sauces, dips and
marinades. You can find it
at Asian markets.

PER SERVING

Calories	99
Protein	2.1 g
Fat	1.8 g
Saturates	0.3 g
Cholesterol	0 mg
Carbohydrate	20.9 g
Fibre	2.3 g
Sodium	747 mg
Potassium	258 mg

Excellent: Vitamin A
Good: Vitamin C

This delicious salad is surely one of the reasons Thai cooking has become so popular. Serve it as an appetizer or side salad.

Green mangoes are firm and crisp. They can be hard to find, but look for them in Asian markets or, if you have a local Thai restaurant, they may be willing to sell you a couple. If you can't find green mangoes, use green papayas or even tart green apples. You can also add other shredded vegetables or cooked shrimp or chicken.

Makes 6 servings

¼ cup	thinly sliced red onion	50 mL
2	green mangoes, peeled, seeded and grated	2
1	large carrot, peeled and grated	1
¼ cup	chopped fresh cilantro	50 mL
2 tbsp	shredded fresh mint	25 mL

Thai Dressing

3 tbsp	Thai fish sauce or soy sauce	45 mL
3 tbsp	lime juice	45 mL
1 tbsp	rice vinegar	15 mL
1 tbsp	vegetable oil, optional	15 mL
1½ tbsp	granulated sugar	20 mL
1	small clove garlic, minced	1
1 tbsp	Thai sweet hot sauce, or ½ tsp/2 mL hot chili paste	15 mL
6	leaves Boston lettuce	6
2 tbsp	chopped roasted peanuts	25 mL

1. Soak red onion in ice water for 30 minutes (this step is optional, but soaking does soften the raw onion taste).

2. In a large bowl, combine mangoes, carrot, onion, cilantro and mint.

3. In a small bowl, combine fish sauce, lime juice, rice vinegar, oil (if using), sugar, garlic and hot sauce. Toss mango mixture gently with dressing.

4. Line serving bowls with lettuce leaves. Place salad on lettuce and sprinkle with peanuts.

MARINATED VEGETABLE SALAD

The beautiful colours, textures and flavours of this salad are irresistible. You could also add olives or marinated or canned artichokes.

If you use balsamic vinegar, it may darken the colour of the veggies. Don't worry — they will still taste great.

Makes 12 servings

1 lb	broccoli, trimmed and cut in ½-inch/2 cm chunks	500 g
2 lb	cauliflower, broken in florets	1 kg
1 lb	green beans, trimmed and halved	500 g
1 lb	carrots, trimmed and sliced on the diagonal	500 g
2	large sweet red peppers, seeded and cut in chunks	2

Dressing

½ cup	rice vinegar, balsamic vinegar or red wine vinegar	125 mL
2	cloves garlic, minced	2
2 tsp	Dijon mustard	10 mL
1 tbsp	Worcestershire sauce	15 mL
½ cup	homemade chicken stock (page 79) or vegetable stock (page 69)	125 mL
2 tbsp	olive oil	25 mL
	Salt and pepper to taste	
2 tbsp	chopped fresh dill	25 mL
2 tbsp	chopped fresh parsley	25 mL
12 cups	mixed greens	3 L

1. Blanch broccoli, cauliflower, beans and carrots by cooking each vegetable separately in a large pot of boiling water for 2 to 4 minutes, or until barely tender. Rinse vegetables immediately with cold water to stop the cooking and set colour. Drain well. Place in a large bowl. Add red peppers.

2. To make dressing, in a saucepan, combine vinegar, garlic, mustard, Worcestershire, stock and oil. Heat just until dressing comes to a boil. Add salt and pepper.

3. Pour dressing over vegetables. Stir in dill and parsley. Marinate for a few hours or up to overnight in refrigerator.

4. Bring salad to room temperature before serving. Serve on a bed of mixed greens.

SERVING SUGGESTION
- Serve in a glass trifle bowl without the greens.

MAKE AHEAD
- You can make this up to three days ahead and allow to marinate in the refrigerator. The green vegetables will start to lose their colour but the salad will still taste fine.

PER SERVING

Calories	94
Protein	4.6 g
Fat	3 g
Saturates	0.4 g
Cholesterol	0 mg
Carbohydrate	15.2 g
Fibre	4.9 g
Sodium	77 mg
Potassium	706 mg

Excellent: Vitamin A; Vitamin C; Folacin
Good: Vitamin B$_6$; Iron

ROASTED VEGETABLE PASTA SALAD

MAKE AHEAD
- If you are making this salad more than two hours ahead, refrigerate but bring to room temperature before serving.

When we made this salad in our roasting class, students would go home and make it right after the class — the night class! I make it at least once a week. You can serve it as a pasta dish or a salad. Leftovers can be used in a frittata (page 269).

Makes 6 to 8 servings

8	plum tomatoes (about 2 lb/1 kg), cut in wedges	8
2	sweet red peppers, preferably peeled, cut in chunks	2
2	sweet yellow peppers, preferably peeled, cut in chunks	2
4	thin eggplants (about 1 lb/500 g), cut in 1-inch/2.5 cm chunks	4
1	bulb fennel, trimmed and cut in wedges	1
1	large onion, peeled and cut in wedges	1
1 tbsp	olive oil	15 mL
1 tbsp	chopped fresh rosemary, or ½ tsp/2 mL dried	15 mL
1 tbsp	chopped fresh thyme, or ½ tsp/2 mL dried	15 mL
½ tsp	salt	2 mL
¼ tsp	pepper	1 mL
2	heads garlic	2
1 lb	penne	500 g

Balsamic Basil Dressing

3 tbsp	balsamic vinegar	45 mL
½ tsp	salt	2 mL
¼ tsp	pepper	1 mL
2 tbsp	olive oil	25 mL
¼ cup	shredded fresh basil or chopped parsley	50 mL
2 tbsp	chopped fresh mint	25 mL

PER SERVING

Calories	459
Protein	13.8 g
Fat	9 g
Saturates	1.2 g
Cholesterol	0 mg
Carbohydrate	83.9 g
Fibre	10.1 g
Sodium	423 mg
Potassium	954 mg

Excellent: Vitamin A; Vitamin C; Thiamine; Niacin; Vitamin B$_6$; Folacin; Iron
Good: Zinc

1. Arrange tomatoes, cut side up with peppers, eggplants, fennel and onion in a single layer on baking sheets lined with parchment paper. (You will need 2 baking sheets.) Drizzle vegetables lightly with oil and sprinkle with rosemary, thyme, salt and pepper.

2. Cut top quarter off heads of garlic. Wrap garlic in foil.

3. Roast garlic and vegetables in a preheated 400°F/200°C oven for 40 to 45 minutes until vegetables are tender and brown and garlic is very soft. Place vegetables in a large bowl. Squeeze garlic out of cloves, add to vegetables and toss.

4. Meanwhile, cook pasta in a large pot of boiling water. When tender, drain well and add to vegetables.

5. For dressing, combine vinegar, salt, pepper and oil in a small bowl. Add dressing, basil and mint to vegetables and pasta and toss well. Taste and adjust seasonings if necessary. Serve warm or at room temperature.

WARM BREADED CHICKEN SALAD

The idea for this recipe was inspired by Giuliano Bugialli. This version is less elaborate and considerably lower in fat but still sensational. The fennel can be used raw, grilled or roasted.

Although you could use boneless, skinless chicken breasts, I find the chicken is much juicier and less likely to overcook if it is roasted on the bone.

Leftovers can be cut up and served in a pita.

Makes 8 servings

SERVING SUGGESTION
• I like to bring this to the table on a large platter, but it can also be served on individual plates. The ingredients themselves make the garnish.

MAKE AHEAD
• You can make this ahead and serve it at room temperature, but toss the salad with the dressing just before serving.

Panko Breadcrumbs
Panko breadcrumbs are used in the fast-food industry when a crispy coating is desired. They are incredible for chicken fingers. They are made only from bread whites; the crumbs have been puffed under pressure to crisp them. Look for them in Japanese or Asian markets.

3 cups	fresh breadcrumbs or Panko breadcrumbs	750 mL
¼ cup	chopped fresh parsley	50 mL
1 tbsp	chopped fresh rosemary, or pinch dried	15 mL
3	cloves garlic, minced	3
1 tsp	salt	5 mL
½ tsp	pepper	2 mL
8	single chicken breasts, bone in but skin removed	8
3 tbsp	Dijon mustard	45 mL
¼ cup	lemon juice	50 mL
8 cups	curly endive (frisée) or Romaine	2 L
1	bulb fennel, trimmed and thinly sliced	1
2 cups	cherry tomatoes	500 mL
2 tbsp	red wine vinegar or balsamic vinegar	25 mL
2 tbsp	olive oil	25 mL
	Salt and pepper to taste	
¼ cup	chopped fresh basil or parsley	50 mL

1. In a large, shallow baking dish, combine breadcrumbs, parsley, rosemary, garlic, salt and pepper.

2. Pat chicken dry and brush with mustard. Press chicken into breadcrumbs on both sides and place, bone side down, in a single layer on a baking sheet lined with parchment paper. Bake in a preheated 375°F/190°C oven for 15 minutes.

3. Drizzle chicken with lemon juice. Bake for 20 to 25 minutes longer or until chicken is browned and crisp and cooked through. (If chicken is boneless, second baking will only take about 15 minutes.)

PER SERVING

Calories	259
Protein	33.5 g
Fat	6.8 g
Saturates	1.2 g
Cholesterol	77 mg
Carbohydrate	15.4 g
Fibre	2.4 g
Sodium	554 mg
Potassium	783 mg

Excellent: Niacin; Vitamin B_6; Folacin
Good: Vitamin B_{12}; Zinc

4. Meanwhile, combine endive, fennel and cherry tomatoes in a large, shallow serving bowl. In a small bowl, combine vinegar, olive oil, salt, pepper and basil. Toss with salad. Arrange chicken on top of salad and serve.

SALSA SPAGHETTI SALAD

This salad travels well to picnics and potluck dinners. It is easier to serve and eat when made with a shorter pasta, but there is something really fun about spaghetti. You can also break the spaghetti into 2-inch/5 cm lengths. (Wrap the spaghetti in a tea towel and, holding one end of the towel in each hand, run the length of the towel down the edge of the counter.)

Makes 8 servings

¼ cup	olive oil	50 mL
3	cloves garlic, minced	3
¼ tsp	hot red pepper flakes	1 mL
1 tsp	salt	5 mL
½ tsp	pepper	2 mL
¼ cup	chopped fresh parsley	50 mL
¼ cup	chopped fresh basil	50 mL
¼ cup	chopped fresh chives or green onions	50 mL
8	ripe tomatoes, seeded and chopped (about 2 lb/1 kg)	8
2	sweet red peppers, roasted (page 49), peeled and diced	2
1 lb	spaghetti, penne or bows	500 g

1. Place oil in a large bowl. Add garlic, hot pepper flakes, salt, pepper, parsley, basil and chives. Add tomatoes and peppers. Allow to marinate until pasta is ready or up to 2 hours at room temperature.

2. Cook spaghetti in a large pot of boiling water just until tender. Drain well and toss with oil and vegetables. Taste and adjust seasonings if necessary. Serve warm or at room temperature.

MAKE AHEAD
• You can make this salad ahead, but if it has been refrigerated, bring it to room temperature before serving.

PER SERVING

Calories	305
Protein	8.5 g
Fat	8.2 g
Saturates	1.1 g
Cholesterol	0 mg
Carbohydrate	50.2 g
Fibre	4.4 g
Sodium	300 mg
Potassium	372 mg

Excellent: Vitamin C; Thiamine; Folacin
Good: Vitamin A; Iron

ASIAN CHOPPED SALAD

SERVING SUGGESTION
• Serve in big bowls as a meal.

MAKE AHEAD
• Make and marinate everything ahead but add the lettuce just before serving.

Chopped salads are wonderful because every bite is full of different tastes and textures. In this recipe, the tofu is incognito, so for those who think they don't like tofu, this is a perfect introduction (you could also use grilled chicken, shrimp or steak). If you do not have or like all the salad ingredients, just use more of some or introduce new ones. (Grilled or roasted tomatoes and/or fennel would be a great addition.)

If it's too cold to barbecue, just roast the vegetables and tofu on a baking sheet at 400°F/200°C for 30 to 40 minutes until browned. Serve leftovers in pita bread or use in wraps (page 166) or salad rolls (page 248).

Makes 6 to 8 servings

¾ lb	extra-firm tofu	375 g
3 tbsp	teriyaki sauce (page 194)	45 mL
1	red onion, peeled and cut in ½-inch/1 cm slices	1
2	zucchini, cut lengthwise in ½-inch/1 cm slices	2
1 lb	asparagus, trimmed	500 g
2	thin eggplants, cut lengthwise in ½-inch/1 cm slices	2
2	ears corn, husked	2
2 tbsp	olive oil, optional	25 mL
2	sweet red peppers, halved and seeded	2
4 cups	chopped Romaine lettuce	1 L
½ cup	chopped fresh herbs (e.g., parsley, cilantro, basil, mint or chives)	125 mL

Orange Sesame Dressing

1	clove garlic, minced	1
3 tbsp	orange juice	45 mL
3 tbsp	balsamic vinegar	45 mL
1 tbsp	soy sauce	15 mL
1 tbsp	honey	15 mL
1 tbsp	sesame oil	15 mL
½ tsp	hot chili paste	2 mL

PER SERVING

Calories	251
Protein	12 g
Fat	7 g
Saturates	1 g
Cholesterol	0 mg
Carbohydrate	41.2 g
Fibre	7.7 g
Sodium	439 mg
Potassium	895 mg

Excellent: Vitamin A; Vitamin C; Thiamine; Folacin
Good: Riboflavin; Niacin; Vitamin B$_6$; Iron; Zinc

1. Cut tofu into slices about ¾ inch/2 cm thick. Place in a shallow dish and pour teriyaki sauce over top. Allow to marinate for at least 30 minutes.

2. Brush onion, zucchini, asparagus, eggplants and corn with oil (if using). Grill on both sides until browned. Cut onion, zucchini, asparagus and eggplants into ½-inch/ 1 cm cubes and place in a large bowl. Cut corn off cobs and add to other vegetables.

3. Grill peppers skin side down until blackened; cool and remove skins. Dice and add to other vegetables. Pat tofu dry and brush or spray with oil. Grill for a few minutes per side until browned. Dice and add to vegetables. Reserve lettuce and herbs.

4. To prepare dressing, in a small bowl, whisk together garlic, orange juice, vinegar, soy sauce, honey, sesame oil and chili paste. Combine with vegetables.

5. Just before serving, add lettuce and herbs. Taste and adjust seasonings if necessary.

FIBRE

Fibre is the part of the plant we don't digest. It contains no vitamins, minerals or calories but is still an important part of our diets. There are two main categories — soluble and insoluble. Soluble fibre can be dissolved in water; insoluble can't. Most foods contain both. Apple skins, for example, contain insoluble fibre, while the flesh of the apple contains soluble fibre.

When most people think of fibre, they think of preventing and relieving constipation. This is one role of insoluble fibre. It also helps to lower risk of colon, rectal and stomach cancer and is recommended for people with diverticular disease. Insoluble fibre is found in wheat and corn bran, whole wheat breads, grains and cereals, nuts, vegetables such as carrots, broccoli and corn, and the skins of fruit.

Soluble fibre is often called the sticky kind of fibre. It has been shown to help lower cholesterol levels and to help control blood sugar levels in people with diabetes. It is found in oats, oat bran, pectin-containing fruits such as apples, strawberries and pears, flax, barley, beans and lentils.

Both kinds of fibre are important. If you are troubled with constipation, you may want to include more insoluble fibre in your diet. If your cholesterol is elevated, you may want to have more soluble fibre. But it's best to have a mixture. Some scientists have shown that the best protection against some cancers may come from a combination of the two.

Eating a high-fibre diet is filling and helpful if you are trying to lose weight. The added bonus is that most higher-fibre foods are also lower in fat.

Healthy adults should be aiming for 25 to 35 grams of total fibre daily. When you start to increase your fibre intake, start slowly. Too much too quickly can give you lots of abdominal discomfort. And be sure to drink plenty of fluids — at least 8 glasses a day.

NOODLE SALAD WITH BARBECUED CHICKEN AND PEANUT SAUCE

SERVING SUGGESTIONS
• Serve in big bowls as a complete dinner.
• Serve salad in wraps (page 166) or salad rolls (page 248).

MAKE AHEAD
• This can be made a day ahead. Allow to come to room temperature for 30 to 60 minutes before serving.

Noodle salads with peanut sauce are a mainstay in my kitchen. This is a great version. The peanut sauce can also be used as a dip.

Makes 6 servings

1 lb	boneless, skinless chicken breasts	500 g
2 tbsp	lemon juice	25 mL
1 tsp	chopped fresh thyme, or pinch dried	5 mL
½ tsp	salt	2 mL
¼ tsp	pepper	1 mL
2 tsp	sesame oil	10 mL
2	sweet red peppers, halved and seeded	2
2	zucchini, cut lengthwise in ¼-inch/5 mm slices	2
½ lb	asparagus, trimmed	250 g
2	carrots, cut in matchstick pieces	2
2 cups	bean sprouts	500 mL
½ lb	dried udon noodles, or 1 lb/500 g fresh noodles	250 g
½ cup	chopped fresh cilantro	125 mL
2	green onions, thinly sliced	2

Asian Peanut Sauce

2	cloves garlic, minced	2
2 tsp	grated fresh ginger root	10 mL
½ cup	cooked chickpeas	125 mL
2 tbsp	peanut butter	25 mL
1 tbsp	sesame oil	15 mL
2 tbsp	soy sauce	25 mL
2 tbsp	rice wine	25 mL
2 tbsp	honey	25 mL
2 tbsp	red wine vinegar or balsamic vinegar	25 mL
1 tsp	hot chili paste	5 mL
¼ cup	water	50 mL

PER SERVING

Calories	380
Protein	26.6 g
Fat	8.8 g
Saturates	1.5 g
Cholesterol	45 mg
Carbohydrate	49.7 g
Fibre	4.1 g
Sodium	778 mg
Potassium	743 mg

Excellent: Vitamin A; Vitamin C; Niacin; Vitamin B$_6$; Folacin
Good: Thiamine; Iron; Zinc

1. In a shallow dish, combine chicken, lemon juice, thyme, salt, pepper and sesame oil. Marinate for about 10 minutes.

2. Grill chicken until cooked through — about 3 to 4 minutes per side, depending on thickness. Cool and slice thinly.

3. Grill peppers until skins are black. Cool and peel. Slice into thin strips.

4. Grill zucchini slices until browned. Slice into thin strips. Grill asparagus until lightly browned. Cut spears in half lengthwise (unless very thin) and then crosswise.

5. In a large bowl, combine red peppers, zucchini, asparagus, carrots and bean sprouts.

6. Meanwhile, cook noodles according to package directions. Rinse with cold water, drain well, and combine with vegetables. Reserve cilantro and green onions.

7. To make dressing, in a food processor, combine garlic, ginger and chickpeas and chop. Add peanut butter, sesame oil, soy sauce, rice wine, honey, vinegar, chili paste and water. Puree until smooth.

8. Combine dressing with noodles and vegetables and toss well. Serve topped with chicken, cilantro and green onions.

Noodle Salad with Barbecued Tofu and Peanut Sauce
Use ½ lb/250 g tofu instead of chicken. Cut in slices, marinate and grill. Cool and dice.

RICE NOODLE SALAD
WITH LEMONGRASS CHICKEN

SERVING SUGGESTION
• This looks the most
  impressive served on
  a large platter, but you
  could also serve it on
  individual plates.

MAKE AHEAD
• You could make this salad
  ahead and serve it cold or
  at room temperature.

*This recipe has a lot of steps but they are all easy. It is very fresh-tasting and looks
beautiful, too. Instead of serving the chicken over the noodles and salad, you could just
serve it over rice. The chicken and noodles are also great on their own.*

*In Asian cooking, vermicelli refers to any kind of pasta, but in this recipe use the very
thin rice noodles. (You could also use cooked spaghettini or angelhair pasta.)*

*Leftovers can be chopped, rolled in rice paper wrappers and served as salad rolls
(page 248).*

Makes 8 servings

Lemongrass Chicken

½ cup	granulated sugar	125 mL
½ cup	water, divided	125 mL
1	clove garlic, minced	1
1 tbsp	finely chopped lemongrass, or grated lemon peel	15 mL
2	shallots or 4 green onions (white part only) thinly sliced	2
2 tbsp	Thai fish sauce or soy sauce	25 mL
1½ lb	skinless, boneless chicken breasts, cut in 1-inch/2.5 cm cubes	750 g
1 tbsp	vegetable oil	15 mL

Rice Noodle Salad

½ lb	thin vermicelli noodles	250 g
2 cups	shredded lettuce	500 mL
2 cups	very fresh bean sprouts	500 mL
½	English cucumber, thinly sliced	½
1	large carrot, grated	1
2 tbsp	chopped roasted peanuts	25 mL
½ cup	mixed fresh herbs (e.g., cilantro, basil and mint)	125 mL

PER SERVING

Calories	320
Protein	24.1 g
Fat	4.6 g
Saturates	0.7 g
Cholesterol	49 mg
Carbohydrate	45.4 g
Fibre	1.7 g
Sodium	932 mg
Potassium	487 mg

Excellent: Vitamin A; Niacin;
Vitamin B$_6$
Good: Folacin; Vitamin B$_{12}$;
Zinc

Thai Lime Dressing

¼ cup	boiling water	50 mL
3 tbsp	Thai fish sauce	45 mL
3 tbsp	granulated sugar	45 mL
3 tbsp	rice vinegar (page 132)	45 mL
3 tbsp	lime or lemon juice	45 mL
½ tsp	hot chili paste	2 mL
1	clove garlic, minced	1

1. To prepare marinade for chicken, combine sugar and half the water in a saucepan. Bring to a boil and, without stirring, allow mixture to brown but not burn — it will smell like caramel. Carefully, standing back, add remaining water, garlic, lemongrass, shallots and fish sauce. Cool.

2. Combine marinade with chicken and allow to marinate for 10 minutes or overnight in refrigerator.

3. Place vermicelli in a bowl and cover with boiling water. Allow to rest for 10 minutes until softened. Drain well. Rinse and cool.

4. Line a platter with lettuce. Arrange bean sprouts, cucumber and carrot on top. Place noodles on vegetables. Reserve peanuts and herbs.

5. Make dressing by combining boiling water, fish sauce, sugar, rice vinegar, lime juice, chili paste and garlic in a small bowl. Just before serving, pour over noodles and vegetables.

6. To cook chicken, drain it and reserve marinade. Heat oil in a large non-stick skillet or wok. Add chicken and brown. Add reserved marinade and cook until sauce is syrupy and chicken is cooked. Spoon chicken and juices over noodles. Sprinkle with peanuts and herbs.

Thai Fish Sauce
Thai fish sauce is the Thai and Vietnamese equivalent of soy sauce. It is made by layering fish (usually anchovies, but sometimes crab or shrimp) and salt. The Thai version is called nam pla and the Vietnamese version is nuoc nam. The sauce keeps for a long time but, like soy sauce, it is high in sodium, so should be used sparingly.

FLAVOURS OF ASIA BUFFET

Smoked Salmon Sushi Balls

Samosas with Cilantro Chile Dip

Lamb Biryani

Ginger Curry Grilled Chicken

Grilled Vegetable Salad
with Tomato Soy Dressing

Raita with Tomatoes
and Cucumber

Caramelized Pears with
Tiramisu Cream

*No matter how large or small your house is, there is always a time when you
want to entertain more people than you can accommodate around the table.
That's when you have a buffet. Whether you have a central table or several food stations,
buffets can be a practical and exciting way to entertain.*

WORK PLAN

MAKE AHEAD

• Make the biryani and chicken a day ahead and
refrigerate, or freeze.

• Make grilled vegetables and salad dressing a day
ahead.

• Samosas can be made ahead and frozen baked or
unbaked.

• Cook pears a day ahead and refrigerate.

SAME DAY

• The sushi balls are best made about two hours ahead
and served at room temperature.

• Make the raita.

• Reheat the biryani and chicken.

• Bring the grilled vegetable salad to room temperature
and sprinkle with fresh basil just before serving.

• Bake the samosas about one hour before serving and
serve warm.

• Make filling for the dessert and assemble a few hours
before serving.

PRESENTATION IDEAS

- Make many levels on the serving table by using milk crates or boxes covered with complementary-coloured tablecloths.
- Use pedestal platters or rocks or glass bricks to raise a dish.
- Wrap cutlery in napkins (page 25).
- Place dishes at the beginning of the buffet line and cutlery and glasses at the end so guests can serve themselves more easily.
- Have two platters of each dish. When one is almost empty, you can substitute it quickly with a fresh platter.
- Line appetizer platters with banana leaves.
- Decorate the table with pomegranates.
- If you are entertaining lots of people, have someone help serve food at the buffet to keep the line moving more quickly.
- Decorate the table with lots of candles and different flowers in different vases. Vary the heights.
- Use a large tablecloth (or several) that comes right down to the floor.
- Dishes and cutlery can be mixed and matched.
- A wonderful garnishing idea from Linda Stephen: Remove the top and bottom from a red pepper so it stands upright. Fill the hollow with fresh herbs and/or asparagus spears.
- Decorate the table with vines and/or palm leaves.

MATCHING FOOD WITH WINE*

You may want to serve a selection of wines and beers to go with the different cuisines represented in this menu. Try a Gewürztraminer and off-dry Riesling as whites (Alsace or New World). Gamay from Beaujolais would be a good choice for a red, as it is low in tannin and high in crowd appeal.

See Alcohol (page 274).

SMOKED SALMON SUSHI BALLS

SERVING SUGGESTION
• Stack sushi balls on a
pedestal plate.

MAKE AHEAD
• Sushi tastes best made no
more than a few hours
before serving and left at
room temperature.

This is a really easy type of sushi to make, but since many people are unfamiliar with it, you will be a culinary star when you serve it. I first learned this style from Elizabeth Andoh, my mentor in all things Japanese. The balls look fabulous and taste wonderful. Serve them with bowls of soy sauce for dipping.

Always dip the salmon side of sushi rather than the rice side. The rice absorbs the soy sauce instantly, making it very salty, and the liquid can cause the rice to fall apart. If you have any leftovers, break everything up and serve as a sushi salad.

Makes 32 balls

2 cups	sushi rice (page 37)	500 mL
2¼ cups	cold water	550 mL
¼ cup	seasoned rice vinegar, approx.	50 mL
½ lb	smoked salmon, thinly sliced	250 g
3	sheets toasted nori	3
2 tbsp	wasabi or Russian-style mustard	25 mL

1. Place rice in a bowl and cover with cold water. Swish rice in water, drain and repeat until water is clear. Drain rice well. Place in a medium saucepan with 2¼ cups/ 550 mL cold water. Cover and bring to a boil on medium-high heat. Boil for 1 minute. Reduce heat to low and cook for 10 minutes. Remove pot from heat and allow to rest for 10 minutes. At no point should you remove lid!

2. Gently fluff rice and transfer to a large bowl. Stir and toss rice while sprinkling with vinegar. Taste rice. If it tastes perfect, add a bit more vinegar, as flavour will dull slightly as the rice cools. If not using right away, cover with a damp tea towel.

PER BALL

Calories	57
Protein	2.2 g
Fat	0.4 g
Saturates	0.1 g
Cholesterol	2 mg
Carbohydrate	10.6 g
Fibre	0 g
Sodium	123 mg
Potassium	29 mg

3. Cut salmon into 1½-inch/4 cm pieces. Cut nori into 1-inch/2.5 cm pieces. Cut plastic wrap into 32 6-inch/15 cm squares.

4. Arrange plastic wrap in a single layer on work surface. You may have to do about 6 at a time if you do not have a lot of counter space. Arrange a piece of nori in the centre of each piece of plastic wrap. Place a piece of smoked salmon on top of nori. Smear smoked salmon with a tiny bit of wasabi.

5. Using about 2 tbsp/25 mL cooked rice, mould into a rough ball and place on salmon. Gather corners of plastic together and twist so that rice forms a nice ball.

6. Just before serving, unwrap each ball and place on serving platter.

Vegetarian Sushi Balls

Use a thin slice of English cucumber or cooked carrot instead of salmon. Or make thin egg omelettes, cut them into squares and use in place of salmon.

Wasabi

Wasabi is made from green horseradish root. It usually comes in paste or powdered form (reconstitute the powder with warm water and allow to rest for a few minutes before using). Wasabi is very hot, but you recover quickly. Use with caution.

SAMOSAS WITH CILANTRO CHILE DIP

These Indian-inspired appetizers are usually deep-fried, but using egg roll or spring roll wrappers (or even phyllo pastry as Linda Stephen does in her Taste of India class) and then baking makes them much less oily but still delicious. Serve with this cilantro dip (which is also great with salad rolls, lamb chops and satays) or mango chutney. Leftovers freeze well.

Makes about 36 samosas

1 tbsp	olive oil	15 mL
2	baking potatoes or Yukon Gold potatoes, peeled and diced	2
2	carrots, diced	2
1	onion, chopped	1
2 tsp	chopped fresh ginger root	10 mL
2 tsp	curry powder	10 mL
1 tsp	garam masala	5 mL
1 cup	peas	250 mL
1	jalapeño, seeded and diced	1
½ cup	water	125 mL
1 cup	cooked chickpeas, partially mashed	250 mL
	Salt and pepper to taste	
36	egg roll or spring roll wrappers	36
2 tbsp	olive oil	25 mL

Cilantro Chile Dip

1	clove garlic, minced	1
2 cups	fresh cilantro leaves	500 mL
1	jalapeño, seeded and diced	1
3	green onions, coarsely chopped	3
¼ cup	fresh mint leaves	50 mL
1 tbsp	granulated sugar	15 mL
2 tbsp	rice vinegar (page 132)	25 mL
¼ cup	boiling water	50 mL

1. Heat oil in a large skillet on medium-high heat. Add potatoes, carrots, onion and ginger. Allow to brown on bottom and then reduce heat to medium. Stirring often, cook until almost tender — about 10 minutes.

2. Add curry powder and garam masala and cook for about 30 seconds. Add peas, jalapeño and water and cook until liquid evaporates, about 2 to 3 minutes.

3. Add chickpeas, combine well and season with salt and pepper.

4. Arrange wrappers on counter. Place 1 to 2 tbsp/15 to 25 mL filling in the centre of each wrapper. Moisten edges of wrapper with water and fold in half to form a triangle. Press edges together to seal. Arrange on a baking sheet and brush lightly with oil.

5. Bake in a preheated 375°F/190°C oven for 20 to 25 minutes, or until browned.

6. Meanwhile, to prepare dip, combine garlic, cilantro, jalapeño, green onions, mint, sugar, vinegar and boiling water in a blender or food processor. Blend until smooth. Taste and adjust seasonings if necessary.

LAMB BIRYANI

This is a special dish — very exotic and mysterious. Although the recipe has several steps, it really isn't hard at all and the results are well worth the trouble.

Roasting spices before grinding brings out many levels of flavour, but if you do not have the whole spices, you can combine the ground spices and add them to the onions, ginger and garlic before adding the lamb. Alternatively, you could use 2 tbsp/25 mL curry powder instead of the individual spices.

Makes 8 to 10 servings

SERVING SUGGESTIONS
• Serve in a shallow bowl or large platter. Biryanis are festive dishes, sometimes decorated with edible silver or gold leaf (available in East Indian markets or art supply stores).
• Serve with Fresh Cilantro and Mint Chutney (page 260).

MAKE AHEAD
• The biryani can be assembled ahead and baked before serving, or it can be baked ahead of time. Reheat, covered, at 350°F/180°C for about 30 to 45 minutes or until hot.

PER SERVING

Calories	428
Protein	33 g
Fat	10.5 g
Saturates	3.1 g
Cholesterol	87 mg
Carbohydrate	48.9 g
Fibre	1.9 g
Sodium	239 mg
Potassium	550 mg

Excellent: Riboflavin; Niacin; Zinc
Good: Vitamin B$_6$; Folacin; Vitamin B$_{12}$; Calcium; Iron

1 tsp	whole black peppercorns	5 mL
5	whole cloves	5
½ tsp	cardamom seeds (removed from the pods)	2 mL
1½ tsp	cumin seeds	7 mL
1 tsp	coriander seeds	5 mL
1	1-inch/2.5 cm piece cinnamon stick	1
¼ tsp	grated nutmeg	1 mL
½ tsp	cayenne	2 mL
½ tsp	salt	2 mL
½ tsp	saffron threads	2 mL
2 tbsp	boiling water	25 mL
2 tbsp	vegetable oil	25 mL
3	large onions, very thinly sliced	3
1 tbsp	chopped fresh ginger root	15 mL
3	cloves garlic, finely chopped	3
2 lb	lean leg of lamb, cut in 1-inch/2.5 cm cubes	1 kg
1½ cups	yogurt cheese (page 303) or tomato puree	375 mL
2 cups	basmati rice	500 mL
2 tbsp	sliced almonds, toasted (page 295)	25 mL
2 tbsp	currants or raisins, plumped in boiling water for 5 minutes, drained	25 mL
2	jalapeños or banana peppers, chopped	2
2 tbsp	fresh mint leaves	25 mL
2 tbsp	fresh cilantro leaves	25 mL

1. To make the spice mixture, in a small bowl, combine peppercorns, cloves, cardamom, cumin, coriander, cinnamon stick and nutmeg. Heat a small, heavy skillet on medium-high heat. Add spices and cook for 30 to 60 seconds, shaking pan, until very fragrant. Do not burn. Cool. Grind in a spice grinder, old coffee grinder, or with a mortar and pestle. Stir in cayenne and salt.

2. In a small bowl crush saffron with the back of a spoon or pestle. Pour boiling water over top and reserve.

3. Heat oil in a large, deep skillet or Dutch oven on medium-high heat. Add onions and do not stir until they start to brown. Cook until well browned — about 10 minutes. Remove half the onions and reserve for garnish.

4. To the remaining onions in pan, add ginger and garlic. Cook for a few minutes. If pan is too hot, add about ¼ cup/50 mL water. Cook until water evaporates.

5. Add lamb to skillet. Do not stir for about 2 minutes to allow it to brown. Add spice mixture (not saffron) and combine well. Add yogurt cheese. Cover and cook gently for about 1 hour, or until lamb is tender.

6. Meanwhile, rinse rice until water runs clear. Place rice in a bowl of cold water and soak for about 30 minutes. Drain well. Bring a large pot of water to a boil. Add rice and cook for 5 minutes after water returns to a boil. Drain well. Drizzle with saffron mixture.

7. To a lightly oiled 5-qt/5 L casserole dish, add one-third of the rice. Spread half the lamb on rice. Add one-third more rice. Spread with remaining lamb. Top with remaining rice.

8. Cover casserole tightly with foil and then cover with lid. Bake in a preheated 350°F/180°C oven for 40 minutes. Taste and adjust seasonings if necessary.

9. To serve, remove top layer of marbled rice. Combine remaining lamb and rice. Mound on a serving plate. Top with reserved marbled rice. Garnish with reserved fried onions, toasted almonds, plumped currants, jalapeños, mint and cilantro.

Chicken Biryani
Use chicken instead of lamb. Cook in yogurt for only 30 minutes.

Saffron
Saffron is the most expensive spice in the world. It is made from the dried stigmas of a crocus flower. Don't add too much of it to your cooking, as it has a strong medicinal taste if overused.

GINGER CURRY GRILLED CHICKEN

• Serve this in pineapple boats or on a bed of banana leaves.

MAKE AHEAD
• Make this all ahead and reheat, covered, at 350°F/ 180°C for about 30 to 45 minutes, or until very hot.

I rarely entertain more than about thirty people, but years ago I did invite about seventy-five people to a special party for my daughter, Fara. I cooked for days. Everyone loved the food, but because they expected it to be good, they didn't bother telling me. I was very depressed until the pianist came up to me and said, "I don't know who catered this, ma'am, but this is the best food I have ever had at one of these parties!" He made my day. Be sure to always compliment your host .

This was the main course at that party (you could also make it with shrimp or tofu). Leftovers make great wraps mixed with the couscous (page 243).

Makes 12 servings

1 tbsp	vegetable oil	15 mL
4	cloves garlic, finely chopped	4
3 tbsp	chopped fresh ginger root	45 mL
1½ tbsp	curry powder	20 mL
¼ tsp	hot red pepper flakes	1 mL
½ tsp	allspice	2 mL
½ tsp	cinnamon	2 mL
4	leeks or 2 large onions, trimmed and chopped	4
3	potatoes, peeled and cut in 1-inch/2.5 cm cubes	3
1	28-oz/796 mL can plum tomatoes, drained and pureed	1
2 cups	homemade chicken stock (page 79) or water	500 mL
2 lb	butternut squash, peeled and cut in 1-inch/2.5 cm cubes	1 kg
3	sweet red peppers, peeled, seeded and cut in 1-inch/2.5 cm cubes	3
2 cups	mango nectar	500 mL

PER SERVING

Calories	580
Protein	46.8 g
Fat	5.5 g
Saturates	1.1 g
Cholesterol	89 mg
Carbohydrate	84.6 g
Fibre	7.1 g
Sodium	297 mg
Potassium	1134 mg

Excellent: Vitamin A; Vitamin C; Thiamine; Niacin; Vitamin B$_6$; Folacin
Good: Riboflavin; Vitamin B$_{12}$; Iron; Zinc

1 tbsp	sesame oil	15 mL
1 tbsp	Thai hot sweet sauce (page 94), or 1 tbsp/15 mL seasoned rice vinegar and ¼ tsp/1 mL hot chili paste	15 mL
½ tsp	salt	2 mL
10	boneless, skinless chicken breasts (about 4 lb/2 kg)	10
½ cup	chopped fresh cilantro	125 mL
16 cups	cooked couscous or rice	4 L

1. Heat oil in a large, deep skillet or Dutch oven on medium-high heat. Add garlic, ginger, curry powder, hot pepper flakes, allspice, cinnamon and leeks. Cook for a few minutes until tender. Add about ½ cup/125 mL water if ingredients begin to stick or burn. Cook until water has evaporated.

2. Add potatoes, tomatoes and stock. Cook for 10 minutes. Add squash and peppers. (If there is not enough liquid to just cover vegetables, add a bit of water.) Cook for 10 minutes. Add mango nectar and cook for 10 to 15 minutes longer, or until vegetables are tender.

3. Meanwhile, in a small bowl, combine sesame oil and hot sweet sauce. Rub into chicken. Season with salt.

4. Grill, broil or pan-fry chicken until barely cooked — about 5 minutes per side. Cut chicken into 2-inch/5 cm chunks.

5. Add chicken to sauce. Cook for 5 to 10 minutes. Taste and adjust seasonings if necessary. Sprinkle with cilantro and serve over couscous.

GRILLED VEGETABLE SALAD WITH TOMATO SOY DRESSING

SERVING SUGGESTIONS

Ideally I like to combine lots of different vegetables in this salad for an assortment of tastes and textures, but if I don't have a lot of time I only use two or three.

Use an inexpensive balsamic vinegar to make the marinade. Or, if you prefer, brush the vegetables with olive oil.

This salad tastes fabulous in sandwiches or as a topping for a barbecued chicken sandwich or burger. The dressing can also be used on mixed green salads.

Makes 8 servings

SERVING SUGGESTIONS
- Arrange sprigs of herbs around salad.
- Toss vegetables together instead of arranging on a serving platter.

MAKE AHEAD
- Make this up to one day ahead and marinate in the refrigerator, but serve warm or at room temperature.

2 cups	balsamic vinegar	500 mL
1 tbsp	brown sugar	15 mL
2	sweet red peppers, seeded and cut in one long strip	2
1	bulb fennel, trimmed and cut in wedges	1
2	zucchini (about 6 oz/175 g each), cut on the diagonal in ½-inch/1 cm slices	2
2	thin eggplants (about 6 oz/175 g each), cut on the diagonal in ½-inch/1 cm slices	2
1	large red onion (about ½ lb/250 g), peeled and cut in ½-inch/1 cm slices	1
¾ lb	asparagus (about 16 spears), trimmed and peeled about 1 inch/2.5 cm up stems	375 g

Tomato Soy Dressing

2	cloves garlic, minced	2
1 tsp	Dijon mustard	5 mL
1 tsp	honey	5 mL
2 tbsp	soy sauce	25 mL
2 tbsp	balsamic vinegar	25 mL
2 tbsp	olive oil	25 mL
¼ cup	tomato juice	50 mL
¼ cup	torn fresh basil leaves	50 mL

PER SERVING

Calories	130
Protein	2.7 g
Fat	3.8 g
Saturates	0.5 g
Cholesterol	0 mg
Carbohydrate	23.5 g
Fibre	4 g
Sodium	317 mg
Potassium	493 mg

Excellent: Vitamin C; Folacin

1. Combine vinegar and brown sugar in a saucepan. Bring to a boil and cook until reduced by half — about 20 minutes on medium heat.

2. Brush red peppers, fennel, zucchini, eggplants, onion and asparagus with vinegar mixture.

3. Grill peppers, cut sides up, until blackened; cool and peel. Cut into strips and arrange on a large platter.

4. Grill fennel, zucchini, eggplants, onion and asparagus for a few minutes on each side. (Turn onion carefully so it does not completely fall apart.) Arrange on platter with peppers.

5. To make dressing, in a small bowl, combine garlic, mustard, honey and soy sauce. Whisk in vinegar, oil and tomato juice. Taste and adjust seasonings if necessary.

6. Drizzle dressing on vegetables and sprinkle with basil.

RAITA WITH TOMATOES AND CUCUMBER

Raitas are East Indian yogurt salads. They are usually served with Indian meals to cool spicy tastes, but also make a refreshing addition to a picnic or barbecue.

Makes 8 servings

1	English cucumber, seeded, peeled and grated (about 2 cups/500 mL)	1
½ tsp	salt	2 mL
1 cup	yogurt cheese (page 303) or thick yogurt	250 mL
1	green onion, chopped	1
½ tsp	ground cumin	2 mL
pinch	cayenne	pinch
1	large tomato, seeded and diced (about 1½ cups/375 mL)	1
2 tbsp	chopped fresh cilantro	25 mL
2 tbsp	chopped fresh mint	25 mL

1. In a colander or strainer, combine cucumber with salt. Allow to drain for 20 minutes. Rinse cucumber well. Wrap in a tea towel, squeeze out excess liquid and discard.

2. In a medium bowl, stir yogurt cheese until smooth. Stir in green onion, cumin and cayenne. Add cucumber, tomato, cilantro and mint. Taste and adjust seasonings if necessary.

SERVING SUGGESTIONS
• Serve in mini pitas as appetizers.
• Serve in hollowed-out tomato halves.

MAKE AHEAD
• If you use yogurt cheese, this salad can be made a few hours before serving as it doesn't get as watery as when made with regular yogurt.

PER SERVING

Calories	41
Protein	3.5 g
Fat	1 g
Saturates	0.6 g
Cholesterol	3 mg
Carbohydrate	5.1 g
Fibre	0.7 g
Sodium	173 mg
Potassium	208 mg

Good: Vitamin B$_{12}$

CARAMELIZED PEARS WITH TIRAMISU CREAM

Tiramisu is a wonderful Italian dessert that has been the rage for about ten years. It is a kind of trifle that layers sponge cake, coffee, liqueurs, zabaione, mascarpone cheese and chocolate. Not too shabby but almost indecently rich. In this recipe I have made a creamy mixture reminiscent of tiramisu's flavours and combined them with pears that have a marvellous caramel taste. To be completely true to the name you should use mascarpone, but here I actually prefer the taste and lightness of ricotta.

Makes 8 servings

SERVING SUGGESTIONS

- For a buffet, place the pear halves in a single layer on a large platter. Garnish pears with a sprig of mint and a sprinkle of gold dust (page 289).
- Serve the pears and cream over angel cake (page 294).
- Fill the pears with sorbet or rice pudding (page 292) instead of the tiramisu cream.

MAKE AHEAD

- The pears can be made a day in advance, but make the filling on the day you are serving.
- Assemble as you serve or a few hours ahead.

4	pears, firm but ripe (preferably Bartlett or Bosc)	4
⅔ cup	granulated sugar	150 mL
2 tbsp	chopped candied ginger	25 mL
1	lemon, thinly sliced	1

Filling

½ cup	light ricotta cheese (drained if necessary)	125 mL
2 tbsp	granulated sugar	25 mL
½ tsp	vanilla	2 mL
2 tsp	dark rum, coffee liqueur or extra-strong coffee	10 mL
2 tbsp	chopped bittersweet or semisweet chocolate	25 mL
2 tbsp	icing sugar, sifted	25 mL

1. Cut pears in half lengthwise. Scoop out cores (a melon baller works well).

2. Sprinkle sugar over the bottom of a large skillet that will hold all the pears in one layer. Cook, uncovered, on medium-high heat, until sugar begins to brown, but be careful not to burn. Add pears cut side down. Sprinkle with ginger and arrange lemon slices over top. Reduce heat and cook gently for about 10 minutes. Cover. Remove from heat and allow to rest for 30 minutes.

3. Meanwhile, to prepare filling, in a small bowl, combine ricotta, sugar, vanilla and rum.

4. Place chopped chocolate in a strainer to remove any chocolate "dust" (this prevents the ricotta from discolouring). Stir chocolate pieces into filling.

5. To serve, place a pear half, cut side up, on each plate. Scoop or spoon some cheese onto each half. Drizzle pear and plate with any syrup from cooking. Arrange a cooked lemon slice on each and dust with icing sugar.

PER SERVING

Calories	179
Protein	2.3 g
Fat	2.2 g
Saturates	1.1 g
Cholesterol	5 mg
Carbohydrate	39.6 g
Fibre	2.8 g
Sodium	22 mg
Potassium	226 mg

MEATLESS MAIN COURSES

VEGETARIAN PAD THAI NOODLES

Pad Thai is one of Thailand's most popular dishes. It is easy to prepare at home and every-one always loves it. Serve it as a side dish or appetizer as part of an Asian meal.

Be sure to use really fresh bean sprouts. You can add diced grilled tofu to this or, for a non-vegetarian version, grilled chicken or shrimp.

Makes 6 servings

MAKE AHEAD

• The noodles can be soaked ahead, and the dish can be made ahead up to adding the eggs. You can also make everything ahead and serve the pad Thai at room temperature.

½ lb	rice noodles (about ¼ inch/5 mm wide)	250 g
⅓ cup	ketchup or tomato sauce	75 mL
3 tbsp	soy sauce or Thai fish sauce (page 105)	45 mL
3 tbsp	lime juice	45 mL
3 tbsp	rice vinegar (page 132)	45 mL
3 tbsp	brown sugar	45 mL
½ tsp	hot chili paste	2 mL
1 tbsp	vegetable oil	15 mL
3	cloves garlic, finely chopped	3
1	small onion, thinly sliced	1
2	eggs, lightly beaten	2
1 cup	bean sprouts	250 mL
3 tbsp	chopped peanuts	45 mL
2	green onions, chopped	2
⅓ cup	chopped fresh cilantro	75 mL

1. In a large bowl, soak noodles in very hot water for approximately 8 to 10 minutes until softened but still firm. Drain well. If not using immediately, rinse with cold water and drain.

2. In a small bowl, combine ketchup, soy sauce, lime juice, vinegar, brown sugar and chili paste.

3. Heat oil in a large non-stick skillet or wok on medium heat. Add garlic and onion. Stir-fry until lightly browned and tender. Add reserved sauce and bring to a boil. Add eggs. When they start to set, stir mixture together. Add noodles and heat thoroughly. Add bean sprouts. Sprinkle with peanuts, green onions and cilantro.

PER SERVING

Calories	270
Protein	7.8 g
Fat	6.6 g
Saturates	1.1 g
Cholesterol	72 mg
Carbohydrate	46 g
Fibre	1.6 g
Sodium	728 mg
Potassium	280 mg

Good: Vitamin B$_6$

PORTOBELLO EGG CUPS WITH SALSA

I love the idea of using big mushroom caps as large cups for stuffing. Leftovers can be chopped up and used as a sandwich filling or in salads.

Makes 6 servings

6	portobello mushrooms, about 4 inches/10 cm in diameter	6
4 tsp	olive oil, divided	20 mL
½ tsp	salt	2 mL
½ tsp	pepper	2 mL
1 tbsp	chopped fresh rosemary, or ½ tsp/2 mL dried	15 mL
1 tbsp	chopped fresh thyme, or ½ tsp/2 mL dried	15 mL

Plum Tomato Salsa

3	plum tomatoes, seeded and diced	3
1	clove garlic, minced	1
½	small onion, finely chopped	½
1	jalapeño, finely chopped	1
¼ cup	chopped fresh basil or cilantro	50 mL
6	eggs	6
3	English muffins, halved	3

1. Remove stems from portobellos and save to use in stir-fries, soups or grilled salads. Very gently, with a small spoon, clean out gills (page 197).

2. In a small bowl, combine 2 tsp/10 mL olive oil, salt, pepper, rosemary and thyme. Brush over mushroom caps. Arrange mushrooms in a single layer on a baking sheet. Bake in a preheated 400°F/200°C oven for 10 to 15 minutes until cooked through.

3. Meanwhile, prepare salsa. In a medium bowl, combine tomatoes, garlic, onion, jalapeño and basil. Heat remaining 2 tsp/10 mL oil in a large non-stick skillet. Add salsa. Cook for 1 to 2 minutes until hot.

4. Bring a large, deep skillet of water to a boil. Add eggs and poach for 3 to 5 minutes until whites are firm and yolks are just slightly runny. Remove eggs from pan with a slotted spoon and drain well. Place on a tray lined with paper towels and trim edges.

5. Meanwhile, toast English muffins. Place each mushroom cap on half a muffin. Place an egg in each cap and spoon salsa over top.

MAKE AHEAD

- This can all be made ahead. Undercook the eggs slightly and then reheat in a 350°F/180°C oven for 10 to 15 minutes. Toast the English muffins just before serving.

PER SERVING

Calories	199
Protein	10.2 g
Fat	9.5 g
Saturates	2.2 g
Cholesterol	215 mg
Carbohydrate	18.8 g
Fibre	1.8 g
Sodium	345 mg
Potassium	345 mg

Excellent: Riboflavin; Niacin
Good: Folacin; Vitamin B_{12}; Iron

PASTA WITH CARAMELIZED ONION SAUCE

MAKE AHEAD
• Make the sauce ahead and reheat just when you cook the pasta.

This is a wonderful recipe inspired by Caprial Pence, cookbook author, restaurateur and popular cooking show host. For a non-vegetarian version, you could add 1 cup/250 mL slivered smoked chicken or turkey to the sauce. A mild blue cheese would also taste great in this. Use leftovers as a frittata filling (page 269).

Makes 4 to 6 servings

2 tbsp	olive oil	25 mL
4	large onions, sliced (about 2 lb/1 kg)	4
½ cup	dry sherry or vegetable stock	125 mL
½ cup	dry red wine or vegetable stock	125 mL
2	cloves garlic, finely chopped	2
1 cup	homemade vegetable stock (page 69)	250 mL
1 tbsp	chopped fresh thyme, or ½ tsp/2 mL dried	15 mL
1 tbsp	chopped fresh rosemary, or ½ tsp/2 mL dried	15 mL
¾ lb	penne	375 g
½ cup	grated Gouda or Parmesan cheese	125 mL
	Salt and pepper to taste	
3 tbsp	chopped fresh parsley	45 mL

1. Heat oil in a large, deep skillet on high heat. When pan is very hot, add onions. Do not stir until they begin to brown. Stir, reduce heat to medium-high and cook for about 10 minutes until they are golden.

2. Add sherry and wine, bring to a boil and cook until about half the liquid has evaporated.

3. Add garlic and stock and bring to a boil. Cook until liquid has evaporated by half. Add thyme and rosemary. Onions should be a deep brown colour.

4. Meanwhile, cook pasta in a large pot of boiling water until just tender. Drain and add to onions. Toss gently. (If sauce is too thick, add about ½ cup/125 mL pasta cooking liquid.) Add cheese and toss again. Season to taste with salt and pepper. Sprinkle with parsley.

PER SERVING

Calories	547
Protein	17.1 g
Fat	12.8 g
Saturates	3.7 g
Cholesterol	16 mg
Carbohydrate	84.4 g
Fibre	6.7 g
Sodium	141 mg
Potassium	470 mg

Excellent: Thiamine; Folacin
Good: Niacin; Vitamin B$_6$; Calcium; Iron; Zinc

BUCATINI WITH FENNEL AND CHICKPEAS

Bucatini is like spaghetti but thicker and with a thin hollow inside. It takes slightly longer to cook but has a really wonderful texture.

Although this makes a great main course, I also like to serve it in small portions as an appetizer. For a non-vegetarian version you can add 2 oz/60 g chopped pancetta to the onions and garlic. If you have a few smoked sun-dried tomatoes you could chop them and add for a vegetarian smoky taste.

Use leftovers in a frittata (page 269) or add dressing and serve as a salad.

Makes 6 to 8 servings

1 tbsp	olive oil	15 mL
1	red onion, chopped	1
4	cloves garlic, finely chopped	4
1	carrot, diced	1
1	large bulb fennel, trimmed and chopped	1
1	28-oz/796 mL can plum tomatoes with juices	1
1	19-oz/540 mL can chickpeas, drained and rinsed	1
¼ cup	chopped fresh parsley, divided	50 mL
	Salt and pepper to taste	
¾ lb	bucatini or spaghetti	375 g

1. Heat oil in a large, deep skillet on medium heat. Add onion, garlic, carrot and fennel. Cook for 8 to 10 minutes until fennel is tender and mixture is beginning to brown.

2. Add tomatoes. Break them up with a spoon and cook gently, uncovered, for about 10 minutes.

3. Add chickpeas, 2 tbsp/25 mL parsley, salt and pepper.

4. Just before serving, cook pasta in a large pot of boiling water. Drain, reserving about 1 cup/250 mL pasta-cooking liquid. Toss pasta with sauce and about ½ cup/125 mL cooking liquid, adding more if necessary. Cook for 2 to 3 minutes on low heat, tossing pasta lightly while cooking. Add remaining 2 tbsp/25 mL parsley and adjust seasonings if necessary.

MAKE AHEAD
- Make the sauce ahead and reheat it when you are cooking the pasta.

Pasta Tip
To serve piping hot pasta, cook the sauce in a large pot. When the pasta is ready, add to the sauce pot and toss together for a few minutes. If you are transferring the pasta to a serving bowl it should be hot, or serve directly into individual bowls that have been warmed. Rush the pasta to the table and tell guests to start eating right away!

PER SERVING

Calories	390
Protein	14.6 g
Fat	4.9 g
Saturates	0.6 g
Cholesterol	0 mg
Carbohydrate	74 g
Fibre	8.7 g
Sodium	393 mg
Potassium	768 mg

Excellent: Vitamin A; Thiamine; Vitamin B$_6$; Folacin
Good: Vitamin C; Niacin; Iron; Zinc

CRAZY LASAGNA

SERVING SUGGESTION
• Bake in a rectangular dish and serve in squares, or bake in a round dish and serve in wedges.

MAKE AHEAD
• This can be made two days ahead and refrigerated, or it can be made a few weeks ahead and frozen. It is also wonderful served at room temperature.

Casseroles are a treasure for any cook. Leftovers of this lasagna can be used in a frittata (page 269).

Makes 8 servings

2 lb	plum tomatoes, seeded and quartered	1 kg
1 lb	thin eggplants (about 4) or 1 large eggplant, cut in ½-inch/1 cm slices	500 g
1 lb	zucchini (about 2), sliced	500 g
½ lb	portobello mushrooms, trimmed and cut in chunks	250 g
2	sweet red peppers, cut in chunks	2
1	large onion, cut in chunks	1
2 tbsp	olive oil	25 mL
	Salt and pepper to taste	
2	heads garlic	2
¾ lb	lasagna noodles, broken up	375 g
2 cups	pureed tomatoes or tomato sauce	500 mL
½ lb	light ricotta cheese (1 cup/250 mL)	250 g
¼ cup	shredded fresh basil or parsley	50 mL
1 tbsp	chopped fresh oregano, or ½ tsp/2 mL dried	15 mL
½ lb	part-skim mozzarella, cut in small chunks	250 g
2 tbsp	grated Parmesan cheese	25 mL

1. Arrange tomatoes, eggplants, zucchini, mushrooms, peppers and onion on two baking sheets lined with parchment paper. Drizzle with olive oil and sprinkle with salt and pepper. Cut top quarter off garlic heads and wrap garlic in foil. Place on baking sheet.

2. Roast vegetables in a preheated 400°F/200°C oven for 45 minutes, or until browned.

3. Meanwhile, cook pasta in boiling water until tender. Drain and rinse with cold water.

4. In a large bowl, combine noodles with roasted vegetables. Squeeze in garlic. Add pureed tomatoes, ricotta, basil, oregano and mozzarella. Taste and adjust seasonings.

5. Transfer mixture to a 13 x 9-inch/3.5 L baking dish and sprinkle with Parmesan. Cover and bake in a preheated 350°F/180°C for 30 minutes. Uncover and cook for 20 to 30 minutes longer, or until lightly browned. Allow to rest for 10 minutes before serving.

PER SERVING

Calories	408
Protein	21.2 g
Fat	11.6 g
Saturates	4.9 g
Cholesterol	25 mg
Carbohydrate	57.7 g
Fibre	7.9 g
Sodium	242 mg
Potassium	1005 mg

Excellent: Vitamin A; Vitamin C; Thiamine; Niacin; Vitamin B$_6$; Folacin; Calcium; Zinc
Good: Riboflavin; Vitamin B$_{12}$; Iron

VEGETARIAN DIET

A vegetarian diet can be extremely healthy, as long as it is followed with care and knowledge. Becoming a successful vegetarian means learning which foods are required for a balanced diet. The plus side is a diet high in fibre and complex carbohydrates and possibly low in saturated fat. But you should also make sure you are getting the key nutrients such as protein, iron, zinc, vitamin D, vitamin B_{12} and calcium. The more you eliminate from your diet, the more attention you must pay to ensuring adequate nutrition.

A lacto-ovo vegetarian (one who eats dairy products and eggs) generally has no trouble meeting nutritional requirements. A strict vegan (one who totally avoids animal products) must be more vigilant.

Calcium: Calcium is not an issue for vegetarians who consume calcium-rich milk, cheese or other dairy products. There is also calcium in tofu (make sure you buy the kind made with calcium), fortified soy beverages, dark green leafy vegetables (e.g., broccoli, kale and bok choy), and nuts and seeds (e.g., almonds and sesame seeds).

Iron: Non-meat sources of iron include lentils, kidney beans, chickpeas, pinto and white beans, dried fruits, egg yolks and iron-enriched cereals and pastas. The iron in vegetables and grains isn't as well absorbed as the iron in meat. But if you eat these foods with a food containing vitamin C, such as oranges, strawberries or peppers, it will be absorbed more easily. Also, tea can interfere with iron absorption, so it's better to drink juice, water or milk with meals.

Protein: If you are eating dairy products and eggs or properly combining grains, nuts and legumes, you will get ample protein. Soy protein has been shown to be equal in nutritional value to animal protein. You don't have to consciously combine foods at each meal for adequate protein intake. Many vegetarian meals naturally combine complementary protein.

Here are some healthy combinations:
- legumes + grains (e.g., peanut butter and bread, split pea soup and bread, rice and tofu, rice and red beans, falafel and pita bread)
- grains + nuts or seeds (e.g., granola with nuts, pasta with pine nuts)
- legumes or any grain + dairy products (e.g., macaroni and cheese)

Vitamin B_{12}: A strict vegan should eat B_{12} fortified foods such as fortified soy beverages, fortified nutritional yeast and fortified textured vegetable protein products, or consider supplements.

Vitamin D: Besides milk and some fortified soy beverages, vitamin D is found in egg yolk and fortified margarine. Vitamin D is also produced when your body is directly exposed to sunlight. If you are not eating food sources of vitamin D and decide to take a supplement, do it carefully, as excessive doses can be toxic. The recommended intake is 200 to 600 IU per day.

Zinc: Dairy products and eggs are good sources of zinc for lacto-ovo vegetarians. Non-animal sources include soy products such as tempeh, miso and tofu, legumes, wheat germ, peanut butter, nuts and grains.

FRITTATA BURGERS

Frittata burgers make a great vegetarian dinner. Instead of cooking them on top of the stove, you can bake the egg mixture in an 8-inch/1.5 L baking dish in the oven at 350°F/180°C until set. Cut into squares.

Makes 6 servings

SERVING SUGGESTIONS
• Serve with oven-baked fries and coleslaw.
• Serve with salsa (page 136) or hummos (page 34).

MAKE AHEAD
• These can be made ahead and served warm or cold.

2 tbsp	olive oil, divided	25 mL
3	onions, thinly sliced	3
1 tbsp	balsamic vinegar	15 mL
½ tsp	salt	2 mL
¼ tsp	pepper	1 mL
4	eggs	4
4	egg whites	4
¼ cup	water	50 mL
½ tsp	salt	2 mL
6	thin slices Fontina cheese, optional	6
6	hamburger buns, toasted	6
4	sweet red peppers, roasted (page 49), peeled and sliced	4
6	large leaves arugula	6

1. Heat 1 tbsp/15 mL oil in a 10-inch/25 cm non-stick ovenproof skillet on medium-high heat. Add onions but do not stir until onions begin to brown. Stir, and cook again without stirring for another few minutes. Continue to cook, stirring, for 10 to 15 minutes.

2. Add balsamic vinegar and cook until onions are very brown. Season with salt and pepper. Transfer to a bowl and cool.

3. In a large bowl, whisk eggs with egg whites, water and salt. Add cooled onion mixture.

4. Add remaining 1 tbsp/15 mL oil to skillet and heat on medium-high. Make 4-inch/10 cm burgers by spooning egg mixture into hot pan. You may have to do two or three at a time. Cook until bottom is set. Flip using a large spatula. Cook second side. If you are using cheese, place one slice on each frittata and allow it to melt slightly while cooking second side.

5. Place one burger on the bottom of each bun. Top with roasted red pepper, arugula and remaining half of bun.

PER SERVING

Calories	325
Protein	12.8 g
Fat	11.5 g
Saturates	2.5 g
Cholesterol	143 mg
Carbohydrate	43.1 g
Fibre	3.2 g
Sodium	768 mg
Potassium	343 mg

Excellent: Vitamin A; Vitamin C; Folacin
Good: Thiamine; Riboflavin; Niacin; Vitamin B$_6$; Vitamin B$_{12}$; Iron

SCRAMBLED TOFU
WITH ONIONS AND MUSHROOMS

*Most of my favourite tofu recipes are Asian, so I was really surprised that I liked this —
a take-off on scrambled eggs. The recipe comes from my friends Mitchell and Leslie
Davis. When they told me it was their favourite tofu recipe, I had to try it because
I really trust their taste. If you are looking for a way to love tofu, this may be it.*

Makes 2 to 3 servings

SERVING SUGGESTION
• Serve with bagels and/or
smoked salmon.

1½ lb	low-fat or regular tofu	750 g
2 tsp	vegetable oil	10 mL
1	onion, chopped	1
½ lb	mushrooms, sliced	250 g
2 tbsp	soy sauce	25 mL
	Pepper to taste	
2 tbsp	chopped green onions or chives	25 mL

1. Drain tofu and break into chunks in a bowl. Place in a strainer and discard any liquid that drains off.

2. Heat oil in a large non-stick skillet on high heat. Add onion and cook, stirring, until well browned, about 8 to 10 minutes. Add mushrooms and cook until pan is dry, about 5 minutes. Remove mushrooms and onion from pan and reserve.

3. Add tofu to pan. Cook, stirring, until tofu releases its liquid and liquid evaporates. This will take about 10 to 15 minutes. Tofu will resemble scrambled eggs.

4. Return onion and mushrooms to pan and sprinkle with soy sauce. Cook for about 5 minutes longer until pan is dry and tofu is coloured. Taste and add pepper if necessary. Sprinkle with green onions.

PER SERVING

Calories	222
Protein	27.8 g
Fat	7.8 g
Saturates	0.4 g
Cholesterol	0 mg
Carbohydrate	13.2 g
Fibre	2.8 g
Sodium	1297 mg
Potassium	607 mg

Good: Riboflavin; Niacin

NASI GORENG WITH TOFU

Nasi goreng is Indonesian fried rice. Leftovers can be made into a frittata (page 269) or salad.

Makes 4 to 6 servings

SERVING SUGGESTION
- This makes a great side dish as well as a light lunch or dinner.

MAKE AHEAD
- You can make this ahead and keep it warm in the oven or reheat. Add the garnishes just before serving.

½ lb	extra-firm tofu	250 g
¼ cup	soy sauce, divided	50 mL
2 tbsp	rice vinegar (page 132)	25 mL
1 tbsp	brown sugar	15 mL
1	egg	1
1 tbsp	water	15 mL
1 tbsp	vegetable oil, divided	15 mL
1	large onion or 4 shallots, chopped	1
3	cloves garlic, chopped	3
1 tbsp	finely chopped fresh ginger root	15 mL
1 tbsp	curry powder, or more to taste	15 mL
5 cups	cooked rice	1.25 L
½	English cucumber, thinly sliced	½
¼ cup	chopped fresh cilantro	50 mL
4	green onions, chopped	4
1 cup	yogurt cheese (page 303) or thick yogurt	250 mL

PER SERVING

Calories	472
Protein	20.7 g
Fat	10.8 g
Saturates	2.4 g
Cholesterol	60 mg
Carbohydrate	73.8 g
Fibre	3.1 g
Sodium	1118 mg
Potassium	615 mg

Excellent: Niacin; Folacin; Vitamin B$_{12}$; Calcium; Zinc
Good: Riboflavin; Iron

1. Cut tofu into 1-inch/2.5 cm slices. Drain well. Place in a shallow dish. In a small bowl, combine 2 tbsp/25 mL soy sauce with vinegar and sugar. Pour over tofu and turn to coat. Marinate for 10 minutes or up to a few hours in refrigerator.

2. In a small bowl, beat egg with water. Heat 1 tsp/5 mL oil in a large non-stick skillet on medium-high heat and add egg. Cook like a flat pancake, lifting edges so that uncooked egg can spread underneath and cook. Flip and cook second side. Remove from pan, roll up and slice into thin ribbons.

3. Heat 1 tsp/5 mL oil in the same skillet. Drain tofu, pat dry and cook until browned on both sides. Remove from pan and dice.

4. In a food processor or bowl, combine onion, garlic, ginger and curry powder. Heat remaining 1 tsp/5 mL oil in skillet. Add paste from food processor and cook until fragrant, about 2 to 3 minutes. Add rice and cook until rice is thoroughly heated. Add tofu and stir in remaining 2 tbsp/25 mL soy sauce. Taste and adjust seasonings.

5. Transfer rice to a serving bowl and garnish with egg strips, cucumber, cilantro and green onions. Serve yogurt on the side for guests to stir in themselves.

Nasi Goreng with Tofu and Shrimp
Add 1 to 2 cups/250 to 500 mL diced cooked shrimp and/or barbecued pork to the toppings.

CALCIUM

Calcium is an important mineral for bone health. Low intake is associated with increased risk of osteoporosis, a disease that causes bones to become brittle and more likely to break. Research suggests that calcium may also play a role in controlling blood pressure and may help lower the risk of colon cancer.

Recently, experts concluded that many North Americans aren't getting enough calcium, and in 1997, new recommendations were released. Teenagers need 1300 mg per day, adults aged 19 to 50 need 1000 mg per day, and adults over 50 need 1200 mg per day.

Calcium Content in Food

1 cup/250 mL 2 percent milk	313 mg
1 oz/30 g Cheddar cheese	212 mg
1 oz/30 g part-skim mozzarella	218 mg
¾ cup/175 mL yogurt	230 mg
2 cups/500 mL baked beans	283 mg
4 oz/125 g tinned salmon (with bones)	266 mg
7 sardines	336 mg
3 cups/750 mL cooked broccoli*	297 mg
⅔ cup/150 mL tofu (made with calcium)	300 mg
1 cup/250 mL soy beverage (fortified with calcium)	300 mg
¾ cup/175 mL almonds	288 mg

*Calcium is also present in kale, Swiss chard and other greens.

A heart-healthy diet includes choosing lower-fat dairy products. When you remove the fat from dairy products, you remove only the fat; all the other nutrients, including calcium, remain intact. For example, 1 cup/250 mL homogenized milk contains 308 mg calcium and 159 calories; 1 cup/250 mL 2 percent milk contains 313 mg calcium and 128 calories; 1 cup/250 mL skim milk contains 320 mg calcium and 90 calories.

Milk is our main source of vitamin D, a crucial nutrient for calcium absorption. Adults are advised to drink at least one cup of milk a day.

STIR-FRIED TOFU AND BROCCOLI WITH SWEET AND SOUR SAUCE

SERVING SUGGESTION
• Serve on a large platter with rice or noodles.

MAKE AHEAD
• You can marinate and cook the tofu ahead, as well as preparing the sauce and cornstarch mixture.

This recipe may sound too healthy to be delicious, but it has converted a lot of people over to tofu. Tofu is so good for us that people want to love it, but just need to be shown the way. This dish, full of health-giving ingredients, is popular in the food-as-medicine classes I conduct with Fran Berkoff.

The tofu can be added uncooked at the end, but it does enhance the colour and texture to cook it separately. It could also be grilled in large pieces and then diced. If you are introducing people to tofu, try substituting chicken or shrimp for half the tofu.

This is perfect to serve for a family dinner or as part of a Chinese banquet-style meal. It is also perfect for a spa menu. Use leftovers in fried rice (page 139) or as a filling for wraps.

Makes 4 to 6 servings.

2 tbsp	hoisin sauce	25 mL
2 tbsp	rice wine	25 mL
1 tsp	hot chili paste, or 1 tbsp/15 mL Thai hot sweet sauce (page 94)	5 mL
¾ lb	extra-firm tofu, cut in 2-inch/5 cm pieces	375 g
1½ cups	chopped or pureed tomatoes, canned or fresh	375 mL
¼ cup	ketchup	50 mL
2 tbsp	rice vinegar (page 132) or cider vinegar	25 mL
2 tbsp	honey	25 mL
2 tbsp	soy sauce	25 mL
¼ tsp	five-spice powder, optional	1 mL
2 tbsp	cornstarch	25 mL
2 tbsp	cold water	25 mL
1 tsp	sesame oil	5 mL

PER SERVING

Calories	287
Protein	15.2 g
Fat	11 g
Saturates	1.3 g
Cholesterol	0 mg
Carbohydrate	37.7 g
Fibre	6 g
Sodium	905 mg
Potassium	917 mg

Excellent: Vitamin A; Vitamin C; Folacin; Iron
Good: Thiamine; Riboflavin; Niacin; Vitamin B$_6$; Calcium; Zinc

1 tbsp	vegetable oil	15 mL
3	cloves garlic, finely chopped	3
1 tbsp	finely chopped fresh ginger root	15 mL
3	green onions, chopped	3
½ lb	fresh shiitake mushrooms, stemmed and sliced	250 g
1	sweet red pepper, thinly sliced	1
1	bunch broccoli, trimmed and cut in 1-inch/2.5 cm pieces	1
¼ cup	chopped fresh cilantro, basil or parsley	50 mL

1. In a medium bowl, combine hoisin sauce, rice wine and chili paste. Add tofu and turn to coat well. Marinate for up to 20 minutes.

2. In a large bowl, combine tomatoes, ketchup, vinegar, honey, soy sauce and five-spice powder (if using).

3. In a small bowl, combine cornstarch, cold water and sesame oil until smooth.

4. To cook, heat vegetable oil in a large non-stick skillet or wok on medium-high heat. Add tofu and cook for a few minutes until lightly browned. Remove from pan and reserve. There should still be a teaspoon or two of oil in pan; add oil if necessary.

5. Add garlic, ginger and green onions. Stir-fry for 30 seconds. Add mushrooms and red pepper. Cook for 2 minutes. Add broccoli and tofu.

6. Add tomato mixture and bring to a boil. Cook for 3 minutes. Stir up cornstarch mixture, add half to skillet and cook for 30 seconds. If sauce is not thick enough, add a bit more. Transfer to a platter and sprinkle with cilantro.

Tofu

Tofu is like a cheese made from soy milk. There are two types.

Japanese silken tofu is often sold in tubs or Tetrapaks. It can be soft or firm but is more fragile than Chinese tofu. It is used in pureed dishes and salad dressings and must be handled gently. Pat it dry with paper towels but do not weight it down as it breaks up easily.

Chinese tofu is more chewy and meaty than Japanese tofu. It can also be purchased in different degrees of firmness. It is used in stir-fried and grilled dishes. To make it less watery, place on a plate lined with paper towels, cover with more towels and weight down with a kitchen brick, frying pan or cans of tomatoes for about 30 minutes.

SUSHI SALAD WITH GRILLED TOFU

SERVING SUGGESTIONS
- Serve in bowls.
- Wrap salad in lettuce leaves.
- Make sushi rolls (page 36) or balls (page 108).

Rice Vinegars
Rice vinegar is very mild. If you don't have it, use cider vinegar, although the taste will be a little more acidic. Seasoned rice vinegar (sushi su) contains salt and sugar; it is used to flavour sushi rice but is also delicious sprinkled on regular salads and steamed rice.

Sushi salad is a terrific way to use up leftovers, whether from a sushi party or just things in your refrigerator that are too delicious to waste. The salad is fresh and clean-tasting, and every bite offers delectable textures and tastes. Make up your own versions (carrots, corn or peas can be used instead of the asparagus). Pickled ginger and nori are available at most supermarkets or specialty stores.

Makes 8 servings

1½ cups	sushi rice (page 37)	375 mL
1¾ cups	cold water	425 mL
⅓ cup	seasoned rice vinegar	75 mL
½ lb	extra-firm tofu	250 g
½ lb	shiitake mushrooms, stems removed	250 g
2 tbsp	teriyaki sauce (page 194)	25 mL
2	eggs	2
1 tbsp	rice wine	15 mL
1 tsp	granulated sugar	5 mL
½ lb	asparagus or green beans, trimmed, cooked and diced	250 g
1 cup	diced English cucumber	250 mL
¼ cup	chopped pickled ginger	50 mL
2 tbsp	chopped fresh chives or green onions	25 mL
2 tbsp	chopped fresh dill	25 mL
1	sheet toasted nori, cut in thin strips	1

1. Rinse rice in cold water until water runs clear. Drain well. Place rice in a medium saucepan and add cold water. Cover and bring to a boil. Boil for 1 minute. Reduce heat to low and cook for 10 minutes. Remove from heat and allow rice to rest, covered, for 10 minutes longer.

PER SERVING

Calories	226
Protein	8.5 g
Fat	3.5 g
Saturates	0.7 g
Cholesterol	54 mg
Carbohydrate	39.8 g
Fibre	2 g
Sodium	503 mg
Potassium	246 mg

Good: Folacin

2. Turn rice into a large bowl and toss while sprinkling with the vinegar. Taste. If rice tastes perfect, add a bit more vinegar, as flavour will dull as rice sits.

3. Meanwhile, brush tofu and mushrooms with teriyaki sauce. Grill tofu and mushrooms on both sides until browned. Cut tofu into 1-inch/2.5 cm chunks and slice mushrooms thinly. Add to rice.

4. Heat a lightly oiled 10-inch/25 cm non-stick pan on medium-high heat. In a medium bowl, beat eggs with rice wine and sugar. Pour one-quarter of egg mixture into pan and allow to set. Flip and cook second side. Repeat until 4 egg crêpes are made. Stack and cut into strips. Add to rice. (Eggs can also be scrambled and chopped.)

5. Add asparagus, cucumber, ginger, chives, dill and nori to rice and toss together. Taste and adjust seasonings if necessary.

Wheat Berry Sushi Salad with Grilled Chicken
Use cooked wheat berries (page 149) or couscous instead of sushi rice. Use grilled chicken breasts instead of the tofu.

SOY
Soy protein is high-quality vegetable protein found in soy bean products. It can play an important role in the diets of people who have given up or reduced their intake of animal products.

Soybeans are rich sources of isoflavones — naturally occurring plant chemicals linked to lowering disease risk. Research has shown that consuming soy products may help to reduce levels of LDL-cholesterol and may also help strengthen bone density and lower risk of osteoporosis. Other studies have shown that these plant chemicals may relieve some of the symptoms of menopause. Current research is also exploring the role of soy in lowering the risk of some cancers.

The most common sources of soy protein are tofu, tempeh and soy beverages. You can also find soy protein in veggie burgers, veggie hot dogs and other meat substitutes. Soy products with the least amount of processing have the highest isoflavone content.

A glass of soy beverage has the same amount of protein as a glass of cow's milk. Soy beverage is lactose free, making it a good choice for people who are lactose intolerant. You can now buy soy beverages that contain calcium and vitamin D. Read labels carefully; not all beverages are fortified.

Fresh Soybeans (Edamame)
You can buy fresh soybeans frozen in the pod. Cook for 5 minutes in boiling water and drain well. Season with salt. Eat with your fingers as an appetizer by popping the beans out of the shells. You can also buy them shelled; serve as a vegetable or in a vegetable melange (such as succotash).

PINEAPPLE UPSIDE-DOWN FRENCH TOAST

It's hard for me to find something that everyone in my family loves, but this recipe pleases us all. A cross between French toast and pineapple upside-down cake, it is sure to be a big hit wherever it is served. Other kinds of fruit can also be used.

Makes 8 servings

8	thick (about ¾ inch/2 cm) slices egg bread, crusts removed	8
3	eggs	3
4	egg whites	4
1½ cups	milk	375 mL
¼ cup	granulated sugar	50 mL
1 tsp	vanilla	5 mL
¼ tsp	cinnamon	1 mL
1 tbsp	soft non-hydrogenated margarine	15 mL
¾ cup	brown sugar	175 mL
8	round slices canned pineapple (14-oz/398 mL can)	8

1. Place slices of bread in a large, shallow pan.

2. In a large bowl, beat eggs and egg whites with milk, granulated sugar, vanilla and cinnamon. Strain mixture over bread. Turn bread over and allow to soak for at least 10 minutes (up to overnight in refrigerator).

3. Brush margarine over the bottom of a 13 x 9-inch/3.5 L baking dish. Sprinkle bottom evenly with brown sugar, pressing sugar into bottom of pan. Arrange slices of pineapple on sugar in a single layer. Place a piece of soaked bread over each.

4. Bake in a preheated 350°F/180°C oven for 30 to 40 minutes, or until bread is puffed and browned. Remove from oven and cool for 5 minutes.

5. To serve, cut around each slice of bread and serve each piece upside down with a slice of pineapple and some juices on top. (Or, invert the whole thing onto a large platter and cut into squares.)

MAKE AHEAD

• Soak the bread in the egg mixture overnight in the refrigerator. Have the pan with the sugar and pineapple ready to go into the oven as soon as you lay the bread on top.

PER SERVING

Calories	276
Protein	8.6 g
Fat	5.6 g
Saturates	1.5 g
Cholesterol	97 mg
Carbohydrate	48.4 g
Fibre	1.1 g
Sodium	245 mg
Potassium	265 mg

Good: Riboflavin; Vitamin B$_{12}$

BROCCOLI AND GORGONZOLA QUICHE

The mashed potato crust is great for those who are nervous about making pastry or want to avoid high-calorie crusts, or for those who just love mashed potatoes.

Makes 6 servings

Crust

1 lb	baking potatoes or Yukon Gold potatoes (about 2), peeled and cut in 1-inch/2.5 cm chunks	500 g
¼ cup	milk	50 mL
½ tsp	salt	2 mL
1 tbsp	olive oil	15 mL

Filling

2 cups	coarsely chopped cooked broccoli,	500 mL
½ cup	crumbled Gorgonzola or grated Cheddar cheese	125 mL
3	eggs	3
1 cup	milk	250 mL
½ tsp	salt	2 mL
½ tsp	pepper	2 mL
pinch	grated nutmeg	pinch
2	green onions, chopped	2

1. Place potatoes in a saucepan and cover with water. Bring to a boil and cook until tender, about 20 minutes. Drain well. Mash with milk and salt.

2. Brush a 9-inch/23 cm deep pie dish with a little of the olive oil. Press in mashed potatoes. Brush with remaining oil. Bake in a preheated 375°F/190°C oven for 30 to 35 minutes. Reduce oven temperature to 350°F/180°C. Arrange broccoli and cheese over potato crust.

3. In a medium bowl, whisk together eggs, milk, salt, pepper and nutmeg. Pour over broccoli and cheese. Sprinkle with green onions. Bake for 35 to 45 minutes until slightly puffed, browned and just set in the centre. Allow to cool for 10 minutes before serving. If crust is browning too much before filling has set, simply cover it with foil for the last 5 to 10 minutes.

MAKE AHEAD

- Make this ahead and serve at room temperature or cold.

PER SERVING

Calories	182
Protein	9.4 g
Fat	8.9 g
Saturates	3.6 g
Cholesterol	119 mg
Carbohydrate	17.1 g
Fibre	2.2 g
Sodium	625 mg
Potassium	467 mg

Excellent: Vitamin C
Good: Vitamin A; Riboflavin; Vitamin B_6; Folacin; Vitamin B_{12}; Calcium

VEGETARIAN BURGERS WITH TOMATO SALSA

A good veggie burger is hard to find, but look no further. Top these with lettuce, sliced tomatoes and/or onions, coleslaw, salad, hummos, caramelized onion dip (page 35) or any of the spreads in this book. Tomato sauce (page 177) can also be spread on the top. If you are vegan, do not include the egg in the mixture — the recipe will still work well.

Makes 6 servings

SERVING SUGGESTIONS
- Serve with a salad.
- Serve the burgers in pitas instead of buns.
- Make a topping for burgers by combining 2 tbsp/ 25 mL mayonnaise, 2 tbsp/25 mL yogurt cheese (page 303) and 2 tbsp/25 mL finely chopped cilantro.

MAKE AHEAD
- The patties can be assembled a day ahead and cooked just before serving. They can also be frozen.

PER SERVING

Calories	800
Protein	17.7 g
Fat	11.4 g
Saturates	1.9 g
Cholesterol	2 mg
Carbohydrate	160.1 g
Fibre	12.9 g
Sodium	880 mg
Potassium	764 mg

Excellent: Vitamin A; Thiamine; Riboflavin; Niacin; Vitamin B$_6$; Folacin; Iron; Zinc
Good: Vitamin C

4 cups	barley	1 L
1 tbsp	olive oil	15 mL
1	small onion, finely chopped	1
2	cloves garlic, finely chopped	2
1	small carrot, finely chopped	1
1	stalk celery, finely chopped	1
½ lb	mushrooms, trimmed and chopped	250 g
2 tbsp	chopped fresh parsley	25 mL
1 tsp	chopped fresh rosemary, or pinch dried	5 mL
1 tsp	grated lemon peel	5 mL
1 tsp	salt	5 mL
½ tsp	pepper	2 mL
dash	hot red pepper sauce	dash
2 cups	fresh breadcrumbs, divided	500 mL
1	egg, optional	1

Tomato Salsa

4	tomatoes, seeded and chopped	4
1	jalapeño, seeded and chopped	1
¼ cup	chopped fresh cilantro	50 mL
2 tbsp	chopped fresh chives or green onions	25 mL
1	clove garlic, minced	1
2 tbsp	olive oil, approx.	25 mL
6	kaiser buns	6

1. Cook barley in a large pot of boiling water until very tender — about 50 to 60 minutes. Drain well. Spread in a large bowl or shallow dish to cool.

2. Meanwhile, heat oil in a non-stick skillet on medium heat. Add onion and garlic and cook gently for a few minutes until tender. Add carrot and celery and cook for a few minutes longer. Add mushrooms, raise the heat and cook until any liquid evaporates. Add parsley, rosemary, lemon peel, salt, pepper and hot pepper sauce.

3. Combine vegetable mixture with barley. Taste and adjust seasonings if necessary. Stir in ½ cup/125 mL breadcrumbs and egg (if using).

4. Place mixture in a food processor and process on/off 16 to 20 times so that mixture holds together well but you can still see just a little of the barley. Shape mixture into 6 patties.

5. Place remaining 1½ cups/375 mL breadcrumbs in a flat dish and dip patties lightly into crumbs. You will probably have breadcrumbs left over but it is always easier to have a little more than you need. Refrigerate patties until ready to cook.

6. Meanwhile, to make salsa, in a medium bowl, combine tomatoes, jalapeño, cilantro, chives and garlic.

7. Cook burgers by heating about 1 tbsp/15 mL oil in a large non-stick skillet on medium-high heat. Add more oil if necessary. Cook burgers for about 5 minutes per side until browned and crisp. (You could also place burgers on a rack set over a baking sheet. Spray or drizzle with oil and bake in a preheated 400°F/200°C oven for 40 to 45 minutes or until crisp and lightly browned.)

8. Top burgers with salsa and serve in buns.

ROESTI POTATO PIZZA

MAKE AHEAD
• The potato crust can be baked a few hours ahead. Add toppings and bake for final 15 minutes at 375°F/190°C just before serving.

When you are in the food business it is hard to turn your culinary imagination off even when you are on holiday. Potato-crusted pizza was an idea I got from a restaurant called The Bistro in Banff. Use the suggested toppings, or try roasted tomatoes with or without pesto, or roasted or grilled fennel, zucchini or eggplant. Serve as an appetizer or light main course or brunch dish. If you prefer a thicker crust, add an extra potato.

Makes 8 servings

3	large Yukon Gold or baking potatoes, peeled and grated (about 4 cups/1 L grated)	3
1 tsp	salt	5 mL
2 tbsp	olive oil	25 mL
½ cup	tomato sauce (page 177)	125 mL
½ cup	grated part-skim mozzarella or smoked mozzarella cheese	125 mL
½	sweet green or red pepper, thinly sliced in rounds	½
1	head roasted garlic, squeezed out (page 41)	1
¼ cup	crumbled chèvre (goat cheese)	50 mL
½ cup	shredded fresh basil, divided	125 mL

1. Pat potatoes dry with a tea towel or paper towels. Place in a large bowl and toss with salt.

2. Brush a 12-inch/30 cm metal pizza pan with a little of the oil. Press potatoes into pan and brush with remaining oil. Bake in a preheated 425°F/220°C oven for 30 minutes, or until potatoes are cooked and crusty.

3. Spread tomato sauce over potatoes. Sprinkle with grated cheese. Arrange pepper and garlic on top and sprinkle with goat cheese and ¼ cup/50 mL basil.

4. Reduce oven to 375°F/190°C and bake for 15 minutes until hot and bubbling and cheese is melted. Sprinkle with remaining basil.

PER SERVING

Calories	131
Protein	4.5 g
Fat	5.7 g
Saturates	1.9 g
Cholesterol	6 mg
Carbohydrate	16.3 g
Fibre	1.4 g
Sodium	437 mg
Potassium	317 mg

Good: Vitamin B$_6$

LEFTOVER FRIED RICE

Make this with leftover cooked rice or any cooked grains. The method for adding the eggs comes from Jenny Burke who did the wonderful illustrations for this book. Always use cold cooked rice to make great fried rice. You can leave out the vinegar, juice and sesame oil (many children prefer it that way).

Makes 4 to 6 servings

MAKE AHEAD
• This tastes best when made just before serving, but everything can be assembled and the vegetables cooked up until it is time to add the rice.

1	egg	1
2	egg whites	2
½ tsp	salt	2 mL
¼ tsp	pepper	1 mL
2 tbsp	rice vinegar	25 mL
2 tbsp	orange juice	25 mL
2 tbsp	soy sauce	25 mL
1 tsp	sesame oil	5 mL
1 tbsp	vegetable oil	15 mL
1	clove garlic, finely chopped	1
1	small onion, sliced	1
1 tbsp	chopped fresh ginger root	15 mL
1	sweet red pepper, diced	1
1 cup	peas	250 mL
6 cups	cold cooked rice	1.5 L
3	green onions, thinly sliced on the diagonal	3
¼ cup	chopped fresh cilantro or basil	50 mL

1. In a small bowl, beat egg with egg whites, salt and pepper.

2. For sauce, in another bowl, combine vinegar, orange juice, soy sauce and sesame oil.

3. Heat vegetable oil in a wok or large non-stick skillet on medium-high heat. Add garlic, onion and ginger. Cook, stirring constantly, for 1 to 2 minutes until onion is lightly browned. Add red pepper and cook for 2 minutes longer. Add peas and rice, breaking rice up with a wooden spoon. Stir sauce into rice and combine well.

4. Make a hole in centre of rice all the way down to surface of pan. Add eggs, allowing some to set on bottom so that some of the eggs scramble and some coat rice. Stir in green onions and cilantro and cook for 1 minute longer.

PER SERVING

Calories	521
Protein	14.6 g
Fat	6.9 g
Saturates	1.1 g
Cholesterol	54 mg
Carbohydrate	98 g
Fibre	3.8 g
Sodium	886 mg
Potassium	370 mg

Excellent: Vitamin C; Vitamin B$_6$
Good: Vitamin A; Thiamine; Niacin; Folacin; Zinc

BEET RISOTTO

The vibrant colour of this risotto makes it perfect for a romantic dinner, especially if you cook it with your partner! If you have any leftovers, add an egg and shape the rice into patties. Pan-fry in a little olive oil until crusty on both sides and hot in the middle.

Makes 4 to 6 servings

- Serve risotto in pasta bowls or on plates. It is usually served as a first course or vegetarian main course.

MAKE AHEAD

- Risotto should be cooked just before serving, but the beets can be roasted ahead, and the onion, garlic and rice can be cooked up to the point of adding the stock.

1 lb	red beets, trimmed but not peeled	500 g
1 tbsp	olive oil	15 mL
1	large onion, chopped	1
2	cloves garlic, finely chopped	2
2 cups	short-grain Italian rice (page 141)	500 mL
5 cups	homemade vegetable stock (page 69)	1.25 L
	Salt and pepper to taste	
2 tbsp	chopped fresh parsley	25 mL
½ cup	crumbled chèvre (goat cheese)	125 mL

1. Wrap beets in foil in a single layer. Place in a preheated 400°F/200°C oven and roast until beets are tender when pierced with a knife. This should take at least 1 hour if beets are large. Unwrap, cool for 5 minutes and rub off peels. Dice.

2. Heat oil in a deep, medium skillet or Dutch oven on medium heat. Add onion and garlic and cook gently for a few minutes. Add rice and coat with onion and oil.

3. Meanwhile, heat stock in a saucepan just until simmering.

4. Add ½ cup/125 mL stock to rice. Stirring constantly, cook until all liquid has been absorbed or has evaporated. Then, still stirring, add ½ cup/125 mL stock at a time, waiting until pan is almost dry before adding next batch. It should take about 15 to 20 minutes to add all the liquid, cooking on medium to medium-high heat. Add more liquid if necessary or stop adding liquid if rice is tender before all liquid is used. Rice should be just barely tender.

5. Stir in beets when rice is almost done. Add salt and pepper. Sprinkle with parsley and chèvre.

Beet Risotto with Rapini

Add 2 cups/500 mL partially cooked chopped rapini, broccoli or Swiss chard to the risotto 5 minutes before the end of the cooking time.

PER SERVING

Calories	539
Protein	18 g
Fat	9.6 g
Saturates	3.7 g
Cholesterol	10 mg
Carbohydrate	93 g
Fibre	3.5 g
Sodium	173 mg
Potassium	658 mg

Excellent: Niacin; Folacin
Good: Riboflavin; Vitamin B_6; Vitamin B_{12}; Iron; Zinc

WILD MUSHROOM RISOTTO

The dried mushrooms in this recipe provide an intense mushroom taste, while the fresh mushrooms add a meaty texture. Leftovers can be cooked as patties or patted into a pie dish to make a savoury crust.

Makes 6 servings

½ oz	dried wild mushrooms	15 g
1½ cups	warm water	375 mL
1 tbsp	olive oil	15 mL
1	onion, chopped	1
2	cloves garlic, finely chopped	2
½ lb	portobello or other wild mushrooms, trimmed and sliced (or regular mushrooms)	250 g
2 cups	short-grain Italian rice	500 mL
6 cups	homemade vegetable stock (page 69)	1.5 L
	Salt and pepper to taste	
1 tbsp	white truffle oil, optional	15 mL
2 tbsp	chopped fresh parsley	25 mL
¼ cup	grated Parmesan cheese	50 mL

1. Place dried mushrooms in a medium bowl and cover with warm water. Allow to rest for about 20 minutes until mushrooms have softened. Pour through a strainer lined with cheesecloth, reserving liquid. Rinse mushrooms well and chop.

2. In a large, deep skillet or Dutch oven, heat oil on medium heat. Add onion and garlic. Cook for a few minutes until tender. Add fresh mushrooms and cook until any liquid has evaporated. Add chopped wild mushrooms and cook for a few minutes. Stir in rice and cook for 2 to 3 minutes.

3. Meanwhile, bring stock and reserved mushroom liquid to a simmer. Add ½ cup/ 125 mL stock to rice. Cook over medium to medium-high heat, stirring constantly, until liquid evaporates or has been absorbed. Continue adding liquid about ½ cup/ 125 mL at a time, stirring constantly, until rice is tender. This should take about 15 to 18 minutes once you start adding the liquid. Do not worry if you do not need all the liquid, or if you need more liquid. Rice should be just barely tender. Season with salt, pepper and truffle oil (if using). Add parsley and sprinkle with cheese.

MAKE AHEAD

• Risotto does not like to be made ahead, as it gets very sticky, although the onion, garlic and mushrooms can be cooked in advance.

Risotto Rices
Risotto is made with a special short-grain Italian rice such as Vialone Nano, Carnaroli and Arborio. When cooked in the risotto method, the rice should be a creamy mass, but each grain should be separate.

PER SERVING

Calories	338
Protein	12 g
Fat	5.4 g
Saturates	1.6 g
Cholesterol	4 mg
Carbohydrate	58.7 g
Fibre	1.9 g
Sodium	111 mg
Potassium	391 mg

Excellent: Niacin
Good: Vitamin B$_{12}$; Zinc

VEGETARIAN FEAST

Sesame-seared Tofu Salad Rolls

Black Bean and Corn Hummos

Roasted Squash and Garlic Soup
with Beet Splash

Mediterranean Vegetable Strudel

Green Salad with Tomato
Soy Dressing (page 116)

Carrot Cake with
Marshmallow Frosting

*Even meat-eaters are aware of the benefits of a vegetarian diet, and most will be happy
to eat a vegetarian menu on occasion — especially one like this.*

WORK PLAN

MAKE AHEAD

• The hummos can be made a few days ahead.

• Make the soup and beet splash up to two days ahead.

• The strudel and charmoula can be assembled a day
ahead.

• The cake (without frosting) can be made up to one
month ahead and frozen.

• The salad dressing can be made a day ahead.

SAME DAY

• Make the salad rolls in the morning and reheat or
serve at room temperature.

• Make the salad and toss with the dressing just before
serving.

• Defrost the cake (if frozen). Make the frosting and ice
the cake.

• Bake the strudel and reheat the soup just before
serving.

PRESENTATION IDEAS

- Use fruits and vegetables, nuts and dried fruits as a centrepiece.

- Arrange fall leaves and pine cones on the table.

- Decorate the table with wheat sheaves arranged in small vases.

- Hollow out small pumpkins or squashes to use as soup bowls. An ice cream scoop works well for this.

MATCHING FOOD WITH WINE*

If you want to serve wine: An off-dry Riesling (Ontario, British Columbia, New York State, Germany) would complement both the Asian spices of the spring rolls and the strudel.

* See Alcohol (page 274).

SESAME-SEARED TOFU SALAD ROLLS

If you have any leftover rolls, chop them up, combine with the dip and serve as a salad. The dip is also great with sushi, shrimp or chicken satays.

Makes 30 to 36 pieces

1 lb	extra-firm tofu	500 g
2 tsp	sesame oil	10 mL
1 tbsp	coarsely ground black pepper	15 mL
1 tbsp	sesame seeds	15 mL
½ tsp	coarse salt	2 mL
6	rice paper wrappers (about 6 inches/15 cm)	6
1 tbsp	wasabi (page 109) or Russian-style mustard	15 mL
2 tbsp	water	25 mL
2 cups	watercress sprigs or other greens	500 mL
¼ cup	thinly sliced pickled ginger	50 mL

Wasabi Dipping Sauce

½ cup	soy sauce	125 mL
1½ tbsp	wasabi	20 mL
1 tsp	sesame oil	5 mL
2 tbsp	rice wine	25 mL
½ tsp	hot chili paste	2 mL

1. Cut tofu into 6 sticks about 1 inch/2.5 cm wide and 4 to 5 inches/10 to 12 cm long. Rub with sesame oil.

2. In a small dish, combine pepper, sesame seeds and salt. Pat into tofu.

3. Grill tofu for about 2 to 3 minutes until brown, rotating to cook all sides (tofu can also be cooked in a lightly oiled non-stick skillet).

4. Partially fill a large bowl with very hot or boiling water. Immerse each rice paper wrapper in water for about 10 seconds or until softened. Arrange them on a damp tea towel in a single layer.

5. In a small bowl, combine wasabi and water. With a pastry brush, brush mixture in the centre part of the wrappers. Arrange half the watercress down the centre and place tofu on top. Place 1 tbsp/15 mL pickled ginger on tofu and top with remaining watercress. Roll up tightly. Wrap in plastic wrap and cover with a damp tea towel until ready to serve.

6. To prepare dipping sauce, in a small bowl, combine soy sauce, wasabi, sesame oil, rice wine and chili paste.

7. Just before serving, trim off any excess wrapper at the ends. Slice each roll into 4 or 5 pieces slightly on the diagonal. Skewer them from edge to edge so the wrapper and filling stay together. Use one 4-inch/10 cm skewer for each piece. Arrange on a platter cut side up. Serve with sauce.

Grilled Tuna Salad Rolls
Instead of the tofu, use 1 lb/500 g very fresh tuna steak, cut about 1 inch/2.5 cm thick. Cut the tuna into four sticks about 5 to 6 inches/12 to 15 cm long. Grill on all sides until cooked but still very rare inside. You can also use sirloin steak, shrimp (cooked on skewers to keep them straight — page 37) or strips of chicken breast.

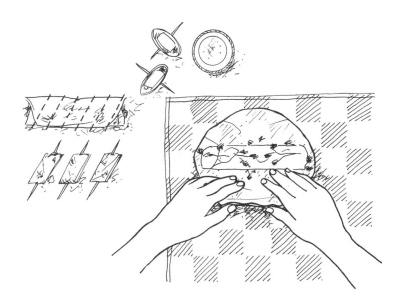

BLACK BEAN AND CORN HUMMOS

MAKE AHEAD
• This can be made a
few days ahead and
refrigerated.

There's always another hummos recipe around the corner and this is a great one. Use any leftovers as a sandwich spread.

Makes about 2 to 2½ cups/500 to 625 mL

1	19-oz/540 mL can black beans, drained and rinsed	1
2 tsp	ground cumin	10 mL
2 tbsp	olive oil	25 mL
2 tbsp	lemon juice	25 mL
1 tbsp	chipotle (page 73), pureed, or 1 jalapeño, finely chopped	15 mL
2 tbsp	yogurt cheese (page 303) or mayonnaise	25 mL
1 cup	cooked corn niblets	250 mL
¼ cup	chopped fresh cilantro, divided	50 mL
	Salt and pepper to taste	
8	10-inch/25 cm flour tortillas	8

1. In a food processor or blender, combine beans, cumin, olive oil, lemon juice, chipotle and yogurt cheese. Blend until smooth or slightly chunky, as you wish.

2. Partially blend or stir in corn and half the cilantro. Taste and add salt and pepper if necessary.

3. Make tortilla chips by barbecuing the tortillas on both sides until lightly browned. Cut into chunks. The tortillas can also be baked (page 34).

4. Sprinkle dip with remaining cilantro and serve with grilled tortilla chips.

Black Bean and Corn Hummos with Roasted Garlic
Add one or two heads of roasted garlic (page 41) to dip.

PER TABLESPOON WITH
CHIPS

Calories	75
Protein	2.5 g
Fat	2 g
Saturates	0.3 g
Cholesterol	0 mg
Carbohydrate	11.9 g
Fibre	1.3 g
Sodium	97 mg
Potassium	74 mg

ROASTED SQUASH AND GARLIC SOUP WITH BEET SPLASH

Roasting the garlic and squash adds a fabulous flavour to this soup. With the beet splash, it looks stunning, too. (Wrap the unpeeled beet in foil and roast with the other vegetables, though it may take a bit longer to cook.) This recipe can also be halved. If your squash is not bright orange inside, bake a sweet potato with the other vegetables, peel, and add to squash and onions in the soup.

Makes 10 to 12 servings

4	heads garlic	4
2	large butternut squash (at least 2 lb/1 kg each)	2
2	onions, peeled	2
8 cups	homemade vegetable stock (page 69)	2 L
1 tsp	salt	5 mL
1 tsp	pepper	5 mL

Beet Splash

| 1 | large beet (about 8 oz/250 g), or 2 smaller beets, roasted | 1 |
| 1 cup | yogurt cheese (page 303) or thick yogurt | 250 mL |

1. Cut top quarter off heads of garlic and wrap garlic in foil. Cut squash in half lengthwise and discard pulp and seeds. Place squash, cut side down, on baking sheet lined with parchment paper. Cut onion into quarters and place beside squash.

2. Roast garlic and vegetables in a preheated 350°F/180°C oven for 45 to 60 minutes, or until very tender.

3. Squeeze garlic into food processor. Scrape out squash flesh and add to processor with onions. Puree, adding a bit of stock if necessary.

4. Transfer vegetable puree to a saucepan and add stock. Bring to a boil and simmer gently for 10 minutes. Add salt and pepper. Taste and adjust seasonings.

5. Peel beet, cut into chunks and add to food processor. Puree. Add yogurt and puree until smooth. Add milk, yogurt or water if mixture is too thick.

6. Serve soup in wide bowls with some beet puree "splashed" on top (page 23).

SERVING SUGGESTION
• Use red chile paint (page 73) or plain yogurt instead of the beet splash.

MAKE AHEAD
• The soup can be made a day ahead. It also freezes well.

PER SERVING

Calories	143
Protein	5.8 g
Fat	1.5 g
Saturates	0.5 g
Cholesterol	2 mg
Carbohydrate	30 g
Fibre	3.8 g
Sodium	304 mg
Potassium	738 mg

Excellent: Vitamin A; Vitamin C; Folacin
Good: Vitamin B$_6$; Calcium

MEDITERRANEAN VEGETABLE STRUDEL

This makes a spectacular vegetarian main course, but it can also be served as an appetizer or as a side dish. Serve warm or at room temperature with charmoula (page 52) or tomato sauce. All kinds of vegetables and different grains can be used, so you can invent your own variations.

Makes 8 to 10 servings

MAKE AHEAD
• This can all be made ahead and frozen or refrigerated baked or unbaked.

2	heads garlic	2
1	onion, cut in ½-inch/1 cm cubes	1
2	carrots, cut in ½-inch/1 cm cubes	2
1	sweet red pepper, diced	1
½ lb	celeriac, peeled and diced	250 g
2	plum tomatoes, seeded and diced	2
1 tbsp	olive oil	15 mL
1 tsp	salt	5 mL
½ tsp	pepper	2 mL
1 tbsp	chopped fresh rosemary, or ½ tsp/2 mL dried	15 mL
1 tbsp	chopped fresh thyme, or ½ tsp/2 mL dried	15 mL
2 cups	cooked wheat berries (page 149) or rice	500 mL
½ cup	crumbled chèvre (goat cheese)	125 mL
¼ cup	chopped fresh basil	50 mL

Phyllo

10	sheets phyllo pastry	10
3 tbsp	olive oil	45 mL
3 tbsp	water	45 mL
½ cup	dry breadcrumbs	125 mL

PER SERVING

Calories	301
Protein	8 g
Fat	11.3 g
Saturates	2.6 g
Cholesterol	4 mg
Carbohydrate	43.8 g
Fibre	4.7 g
Sodium	557 mg
Potassium	327 mg

Excellent: Vitamin A; Vitamin C
Good: Thiamine; Niacin; Vitamin B$_6$; Iron

1. Cut top quarter off each head of garlic. Wrap garlic in foil. Place onion, carrots, red pepper, celeriac and tomatoes in a large bowl. Toss with olive oil, salt, pepper, rosemary and thyme. Spread on a large baking sheet lined with parchment paper.

2. Roast garlic and vegetables in a preheated 400°F/200°C oven for 30 to 40 minutes, or until garlic is very tender when squeezed and vegetables are brown and tender. Toss vegetables occasionally during cooking.

3. Place vegetables in a large bowl. Cool. Squeeze in garlic. Add wheat berries, goat cheese and basil. Taste and adjust seasonings if necessary.

4. Arrange 2 tea towels in a single layer on work surface. Place a piece of phyllo on each. Combine olive oil with water and brush pastry lightly. Dust with breadcrumbs. Repeat until you have 5 layers in each stack.

5. Place filling along long edge of each stack. Roll up lengthwise, using tea towel to help. Transfer to a baking sheet. Slash through top layers of phyllo on the diagonal in serving-sized pieces and brush with any remaining oil mixture.

6. Bake in a preheated 400°F/200°C oven for 40 minutes, or until well browned and crisp.

Cooking Wheat Berries
To cook wheat berries, place in a large saucepan and cover with plenty of cold water (berries should be covered by about 4 inches/10 cm). Bring to a boil and simmer gently for 1 to 1½ hours, or until tender but still chewy. (1 cup uncooked berries equals 3 cups/750mL cooked approximately.) Drain well.

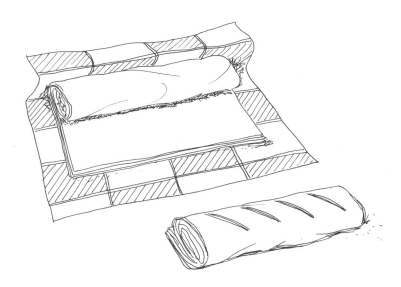

CARROT CAKE WITH MARSHMALLOW FROSTING

MAKE AHEAD
• This cake (without the frosting) freezes well. Defrost before icing.

Carrot cake never seems to go out of style. Serve it with or without the marshmallow frosting — an old-fashioned icing that is a great alternative to the traditional cream cheese frosting, and it has no fat. You can use pasteurized egg whites in the frosting.

Makes 12 servings

4	eggs	4
¾ cup	honey	175 mL
¾ cup	brown sugar	175 mL
½ cup	vegetable oil	125 mL
1	14-oz/398 mL can crushed pineapple, well-drained (about ¾ cup/175 mL)	1
1 cup	all-purpose flour	250 mL
1 cup	whole wheat flour	250 mL
2 tsp	baking powder	10 mL
½ tsp	baking soda	2 mL
1 tbsp	cinnamon	15 mL
¼ tsp	grated nutmeg	1 mL
pinch	allspice	pinch
3 cups	finely grated carrots	750 mL
¾ cup	raisins	175 mL
⅓ cup	chopped candied ginger	75 mL

Marshmallow Frosting

1 cup	granulated sugar	250 mL
⅓ cup	water	75 mL
pinch	cream of tartar	pinch
pinch	salt	pinch
2	egg whites	2
1 tsp	vanilla	5 mL

PER SERVING

Calories	435
Protein	5.9 g
Fat	11.2 g
Saturates	1.2 g
Cholesterol	72 mg
Carbohydrate	81.9 g
Fibre	3.1 g
Sodium	149 mg
Potassium	430 mg

Excellent: Vitamin A
Good: Iron

1. Line a 13 x 9-inch/3.5 L baking dish with parchment paper. Have paper hanging over two longer sides and covering bottom; lightly oil other two sides.

2. Beat eggs in a large bowl with an electric mixer until light. Slowly beat in honey and sugar. Beat in oil. Stir in pineapple.

3. In a separate large bowl, combine or sift flours with baking powder, baking soda, cinnamon, nutmeg and allspice. Stir flour mixture into egg mixture just until combined. Stir in carrots, raisins and ginger.

4. Spoon batter into baking dish. Bake in a preheated 325°F/160°C oven for 35 to 40 minutes, or until cake springs back when gently pressed in centre. Cool for 10 minutes on wire rack.

5. Meanwhile, to make frosting, combine sugar, water, cream of tartar and salt in a medium saucepan. Bring to a boil, stir to dissolve sugar and continue to cook, without stirring, until mixture reaches soft ball stage of 240°F/115°C.

6. Place egg whites in a bowl and beat with an electric mixer until white and frothy. Continue to beat, adding sugar mixture very slowly until very light and fluffy. Beat in vanilla.

7. Remove cake from pan. Cool completely before icing.

SERVING SUGGESTIONS
- For a round cake, bake in two 8-inch/20 cm round cake pans or, one 10 inch/25 cm pan. Bake 30 to 35 minutes.
- Make little marzipan carrots for decorations. Knead some orange food colouring into about ½ cup/125 mL marzipan and shape into tiny carrots, making horizontal lines on the carrots with a toothpick. Knead some green food colouring into about 2 tbsp/25 mL marzipan and shape into leaves.
- Omit the frosting and dust cake with sifted icing sugar.
- Ice the cake with a cream cheese frosting. Beat 4 oz/125 g light cream cheese with about 2½ cups/625 mL sifted icing sugar, 1 tsp/5 mL vanilla and 1 tbsp/15 mL grated orange peel. Add more icing sugar if necessary until you have a spreadable consistency.

ANTIOXIDANTS

Recent research suggests that antioxidants in food may protect us against heart disease, some cancers and some aging processes.

Antioxidants help deactivate harmful elements in our bodies called free radicals. Free radicals are highly reactive molecules that can damage cell structures, making them more susceptible to cardiovascular disease and certain cancers. Free radicals also unite with oxygen to form compounds that lead to the build-up of LDL-cholesterol.

Key antioxidants are vitamin C, vitamin E and carotenoids, including beta-carotene and lycopene. How antioxidants work with the fibre and total make-up of food is not yet clear. Scientists agree, however, that they are best taken in their natural state — in food rather than as supplements.

More than five hundred carotenoids are found in food. Beta-carotene and lycopene are two of the most common. Lycopene, found in tomatoes, is one of the most powerful antioxidants, and is associated with lower risk of prostate cancer and heart disease. Beta-carotene, which becomes vitamin A in the body, is found in deep yellow, orange or green vegetables and fruits. As a general rule, the richer the colour of the vegetable, the more beta-carotene it contains.

Vitamin E is found in some higher-fat foods such as oils, salad dressings and nuts. If you are following a low-fat diet, you may want to speak to a dietitian or doctor to determine whether you need a vitamin E supplement.

Eating a balanced diet, including a variety of fruits, vegetables and grains, has always been an important step in staying healthy.

Foods rich in vitamin C: citrus fruits, broccoli, Brussels sprouts, strawberries, peppers, cabbage, tomatoes, cantaloupe, cauliflower, kiwi, mangoes, papayas

Foods rich in vitamin E: vegetable oils, margarine, wheat germ, sunflower seeds, peanuts, asparagus

Foods rich in beta-carotene: apricots, cantaloupe, carrots, arugula, collard greens, kale, dandelion greens, mustard greens, Swiss chard, mangoes, red peppers, pumpkins, spinach, squash and sweet potatoes

Foods rich in lycopene: tomatoes, tomato sauce, tomato paste, red grapefruit

SEAFOOD AND POULTRY

ROASTED HALIBUT WITH
FENNEL AND ARTICHOKES

SERVING SUGGESTION
• Serve fish on a bed of greens as a salad.

MAKE AHEAD
• The fennel can be roasted ahead.
• This is also delicious served cold or at room temperature.

David Forestell, a chef who prides himself on working with the best ingredients, cooked this for me in Kelowna. He used fresh halibut that his friends had caught, and it was sensational. When you know where your food comes from and you trust your suppliers, food has the extra flavour of a heart and soul.

Salmon, sea bass, cod or red snapper would also be good in this.

Makes 4 servings

4	halibut fillets, skin removed, about 4 oz/125 g each	4
3 tbsp	olive oil, divided	45 mL
1 tbsp	lemon juice	15 mL
1 tsp	grated lemon peel	5 mL
1 tbsp	capers	15 mL
1 tbsp	chopped fresh rosemary, or ½ tsp/2 mL dried	15 mL
1 tsp	crushed fennel seed, optional	5 mL
2	bulbs fennel, trimmed and thinly sliced	2
2 lb	baby potatoes, cleaned	1 kg
1	14-oz/540 mL can artichoke hearts, drained and halved	1
¼ tsp	salt	1 mL
¼ tsp	pepper	1 mL

1. Place halibut in a shallow dish and sprinkle with 2 tbsp/25 mL olive oil, lemon juice, peel, capers, rosemary and fennel seed (if using). Marinate for 15 minutes at room temperature.

2. Spread thinly sliced fennel in bottom of a baking dish. Sprinkle with remaining 1 tbsp/15 mL oil and bake in a preheated 450°F/230°C oven for 10 to 15 minutes, or until it starts to browned.

3. Spoon artichokes over fennel and combine gently. Arrange fish in a single layer on top. Sprinkle with salt and pepper. Roast for 15 to 20 minutes or just until fish is cooked through and lightly brown.

4. Meanwhile, cook potatoes in boiling water until tender — 20 to 25 minutes. Drain well. Serve fish with potatoes.

PER SERVING

Calories	375
Protein	30.9 g
Fat	5.7 g
Saturates	0.8 g
Cholesterol	36 mg
Carbohydrate	53 g
Fibre	10.1 g
Sodium	485 mg
Potassium	1931 mg

Excellent: Vitamin C; Niacin; Vitamin B$_6$; Folacin; Vitamin B$_{12}$
Good: Thiamine; Iron; Zinc

FISH AND SHELLFISH

Fish is an excellent source of protein, niacin, vitamin B_{12}, iron, selenium, zinc and more. Most fish contains fewer calories and less fat per serving than many cuts of meat. Research shows that people who regularly consume fish have lower rates of heart disease. While some meats are high in saturated fats, fish contains mostly polyunsaturated fats, in particular, omega-3 fatty acids, which help reduce the thickness of blood so the heart doesn't have to work as hard to push the blood through the blood vessels. Omega-3 fatty acids also reduce the stickiness of blood platelets that clump together to form clots. They are also associated with lower triglyceride levels, which can decrease the risk of heart disease.

The best sources of omega-3 fats are fish from deep, cold water. These include mackerel, herring, salmon, sardines, anchovies and trout. The second-best sources include halibut, bluefish, ocean perch, bass, red snapper and smelts.

Lean fish such as sole or flounder are low in fat and high in protein. Mixing fish high in omega-3 fats with leaner fish varieties lets you add the special oils to the diet and keep your total fat intake low at the same time.

Shellfish is a rich source of protein as well as important vitamins and minerals. Shellfish is also low in fat — a 3-oz/90 g serving of scallops, for example, has less than 1 gram of fat. Shrimp and squid are higher in cholesterol, but research indicates that it is excess fat (especially saturated fat), not cholesterol, that has the biggest impact on your cholesterol levels. If your cholesterol is elevated, you should eat these foods in moderation. Lobster, crab and scallops are low in fat and calories as long as they are not dipped in butter or cooked in a rich, creamy sauce.

If you buy canned fish, pick the water-packed rather than the oil-packed products. This will omit extra fat and calories. And be careful with the mayo. If you use canned salmon, be sure to mash in the bones. They are a good source of calcium.

When you are eating out in the fast-food outlets, go easy on the fish sandwiches. The breading and frying make them higher in fat than a burger. In fact, a fish sandwich contains about 400 calories and 19 grams of fat, compared with a plain burger at 260 calories and 9 grams of fat.

CILANTRO-ROASTED SEA BASS

I made this on my WTN show, "Bonnie Stern Entertains," and the crew couldn't believe how much they loved it. Salmon, shrimp or halibut would work equally well. Use the cilantro stems and roots as well as the leaves for a more intense flavour.

Makes 6 to 8 servings

SERVING SUGGESTION
• Serve with pad Thai (page 120) or steamed rice.

MAKE AHEAD
• This can be marinated ahead and cooked just before serving, or it can be cooked ahead and served at room temperature.

1	clove garlic, chopped	1
1½ cups	fresh cilantro leaves, stems and roots	375 mL
2 tbsp	hoisin sauce	25 mL
1 tbsp	Thai fish sauce (page 105) or soy sauce	15 mL
1 tbsp	lime juice or lemon juice	15 mL
1 tbsp	rice vinegar	15 mL
½ tsp	hot chili paste	2 mL
2 lb	sea bass, in one piece (about 2 inches/5 cm thick), skin removed	1 kg

Asian Sesame Salad

2 tbsp	rice vinegar (page 132)	25 mL
1 tsp	Russian-style mustard	5 mL
1 tbsp	olive oil	15 mL
½ tsp	sesame oil	2 mL
½ tsp	hot chili paste	2 mL
8 cups	mixed salad greens	2 L

PER SERVING

Calories	194
Protein	29.4 g
Fat	6.1 g
Saturates	1.2 g
Cholesterol	63 mg
Carbohydrate	4.6 g
Fibre	1.3 g
Sodium	372 mg
Potassium	633 mg

Excellent: Niacin; Vitamin B_6; Folacin
Good: Vitamin A; Thiamine; Riboflavin; Vitamin B_{12}

1. In a food processor or blender, chop garlic and cilantro. Add hoisin sauce, fish sauce, lime juice, rice vinegar and chili paste. Process to form a paste.

2. Place sea bass in a shallow dish and smear marinade over fish, turning to coat well. Refrigerate for 30 minutes.

3. Place fish on a baking sheet lined with parchment paper. Roast in a preheated 425°F/220°C oven for 30 to 35 minutes, or until cooked through.

4. Meanwhile, prepare salad dressing by combining vinegar, mustard, olive oil, sesame oil and hot chili paste.

5. Toss greens with dressing. Serve fish on a bed of greens.

ROASTED SEA BASS WITH BALSAMIC VINEGAR

I demonstrated this recipe in my roasting class, and you could hear the oohs and aahs when the fish came out of the oven. ("Look at that fish!" one person actually yelled.) It is rare that you get a reaction like that over fish! This is a winner.

In this recipe, the fish is roasted a little like a chunk of meat. You can also cook individual fillets or steaks, but a whole piece is juicier and makes a fabulous presentation. Ask the person in the fish store for 2 lb/1 kg (or more) in one piece; it should be about 2 to 3 inches/5 to 7.5 cm thick (if your fish isn't this thick, reduce the cooking time slightly).

Instead of sea bass, you could also use halibut, salmon or cod. Use any leftovers in salads or sandwiches.

Makes 6 to 8 servings

2 tbsp	balsamic vinegar	25 mL
2 tbsp	brown sugar	25 mL
1 tbsp	olive oil	15 mL
1	clove garlic, minced	1
1 tbsp	chopped fresh rosemary, or ½ tsp/2 mL dried	15 mL
½ tsp	pepper	2 mL
2 lb	sea bass, in one piece, skin removed	1 kg
½ tsp	salt	2 mL

1. In a small bowl, combine vinegar, brown sugar, olive oil, garlic, rosemary and pepper. Place fish in a shallow dish and gently rub marinade into fish. Allow to marinate at room temperature for 30 minutes or up to 2 hours in the refrigerator.

2. Place fish on a baking sheet lined with parchment paper. Sprinkle with salt. Roast in a preheated 425°F/220°C oven for 30 to 40 minutes, depending on thickness of the fish. When it is cooked, it should flake apart when prodded. Transfer fish to a serving platter with a large spatula (the bottom of a removable-bottomed tart pan will work if you do not have a large enough spatula).

SERVING SUGGESTIONS
- Place fish on a serving platter lined with sprigs of fresh rosemary.
- Serve the fish in irregular pieces using two large spoons, or carve it into equal-sized pieces.
- Serve fish on a bed of arugula tossed with roasted garlic dressing (page 58).

MAKE AHEAD
- Marinate fish ahead but cook just before serving; or you could cook the fish ahead and serve it at room temperature.

PER SERVING

Calories	179
Protein	27.9 g
Fat	4.7 g
Saturates	1 g
Cholesterol	63 mg
Carbohydrate	4.5 g
Fibre	0 g
Sodium	295 mg
Potassium	402 mg

Excellent: Niacin; Vitamin B_6
Good: Vitamin B_{12}

Tandoori Salmon

This salmon is very tender and flavourful. Serve leftovers in a wrap along with rice and raita (page 117), or break up the fish and add to salads.

You can also use boneless, skinless chicken breasts or shrimp.

Makes 6 servings

SERVING SUGGESTIONS
• Serve the salmon on a bed of mixed greens or arugula.
• Cut the salmon into 1-inch/2.5 cm chunks or strips. Cook and serve on skewers as an appetizer.
• Serve with a rice pilaf (page 245).

6	salmon fillets (4 oz/125 g each), skin removed	6
⅓ cup	yogurt cheese (page 303) or thick yogurt	75 mL
1 tbsp	finely chopped fresh ginger root	15 mL
1	clove garlic, minced	1
1	jalapeño, seeded and finely chopped	1
1 tbsp	ground cumin	15 mL
1 tbsp	paprika	15 mL
½ tsp	salt	2 mL
1 tsp	pepper	5 mL
¼ tsp	ground cloves	1 mL
¼ tsp	ground cardamom	1 mL

1. Pat salmon dry and place in a shallow baking dish.

2. In a small bowl, combine yogurt cheese, ginger, garlic, jalapeño, cumin, paprika, salt, pepper, cloves and cardamom.

3. Spoon yogurt mixture over salmon and gently rub into fish. Marinate in refrigerator for 20 minutes or up to 2 hours.

4. Place salmon on a baking sheet lined with parchment paper. Roast in a preheated 450°F/230°C oven for 10 to 12 minutes (for fillets that are just under 1 inch/2.5 cm thick), or until salmon is just cooked through.

PER SERVING

Calories	204
Protein	21.4 g
Fat	11.9 g
Saturates	2.5 g
Cholesterol	59 mg
Carbohydrate	1.6 g
Fibre	0.2 g
Sodium	167 mg
Potassium	55 mg

Excellent: Thiamine; Niacin; Vitamin B$_6$; Vitamin B$_{12}$
Good: Folacin

SWEET AND SOUR PICKLED SALMON APPETIZER

If you like pickled foods, this dish cannot be beat. The salmon pieces are arranged in a dish and covered with hot pickling liquid so that the fish cooks in the liquid and becomes very tender and juicy. The pickling flavour cuts the richness of the salmon perfectly. Serve it as an appetizer, brunch or light dinner. Leftovers on rye or pumpernickel make great sandwiches.

Makes 12 small servings

1½ cups	red wine vinegar or sherry vinegar	375 mL
1 cup	rice vinegar	250 mL
2 cups	water	500 mL
½ cup	granulated sugar	125 mL
2 tsp	salt	10 mL
2	cloves garlic, slivered	2
2 tbsp	slivered fresh ginger root	25 mL
1	large onion, thinly sliced	1
2 lb	salmon fillet, skin removed	1 kg
6 cups	baby spinach leaves	1.5 L
2 cups	cherry tomatoes	500 mL

1. Place vinegars, water, sugar, salt, garlic, ginger and onion in a saucepan and bring to a boil. Cook for about 5 minutes.

2. Meanwhile, cut salmon fillets into 12 thin slices on the diagonal. Arrange in a single layer in bottom of a deep glass or ceramic baking dish.

3. Pour vinegar mixture over salmon (fish should be generously covered). Cover baking dish with foil. Allow to rest for 30 minutes at room temperature.

4. Refrigerate salmon overnight or up to 4 days.

5. To serve, arrange spinach leaves on individual plates and place a piece of salmon on top with some juices and onions. Garnish with a few cherry tomatoes. Serve cold.

SERVING SUGGESTION
• Serve with black bread.

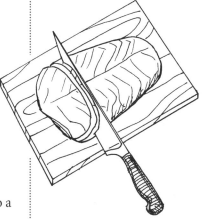

PER SMALL SERVING

Calories	164
Protein	14.9 g
Fat	7.8 g
Saturates	1.6 g
Cholesterol	39 mg
Carbohydrate	9 g
Fibre	1.2 g
Sodium	253 mg
Potassium	246 mg

Excellent: Niacin; Vitamin B_6; Folacin; Vitamin B_{12}
Good: Vitamin A; Thiamine

SMOKED SALMON SOUFFLÉ ROLL

SERVING SUGGESTIONS
• Bring the soufflé to the table on a long platter or large wooden cutting board, or slice ahead of time and serve as individual servings.
• Cut the roll into small pieces and serve as hors d'oeuvres.
• Garnish soufflé with pieces of smoked salmon rolled into little roses and arranged with watercress leaves to look like flowers.

MAKE AHEAD
• This can all be made ahead and refrigerated overnight. Place on a baking sheet and warm at 350°F/180°C for 15 minutes.
• This can also be made ahead and served at room temperature.

This looks stunning, and it's a sure way to turn you into a culinary star! You can use prosciutto or thinly sliced ham instead of the salmon, or even fill the roll with chicken, tuna or salmon salad.

Makes 10 to 12 servings

2 cups	cold milk	500 mL
½ cup	all-purpose flour	125 mL
½ tsp	salt	2 mL
½ tsp	pepper	2 mL
pinch	grated nutmeg	pinch
¼ tsp	hot red pepper sauce	1 mL
2 tbsp	chopped fresh dill, chives or green onions	25 mL
4	egg yolks	4
7	egg whites (about 1 cup/250 mL)	7
½ tsp	cream of tartar	2 mL
¼ cup	grated Parmesan cheese	50 mL
1½ cups	yogurt cheese (page 303) or light sour cream	375 mL
1 tbsp	Russian-style mustard	15 mL
8 oz	smoked salmon, thinly sliced	250 g
3 tbsp	chopped fresh chives or green onions	45 mL

1. Lightly oil a 12 x 18 inch/30 x 45 cm baking sheet. Line with parchment paper. Lightly oil paper.

2. In a large saucepan, whisk milk with flour until smooth. Bring mixture to a boil slowly, stirring often. Remove from heat and stir in salt, pepper, nutmeg, hot pepper sauce and dill.

3. Beat egg yolks in a small bowl. Add a little hot milk mixture and then beat eggs back into saucepan.

PER SERVING

Calories	155
Protein	14.6 g
Fat	5.5 g
Saturates	2.3 g
Cholesterol	101 mg
Carbohydrate	11 g
Fibre	0.2 g
Sodium	456 mg
Potassium	282 mg

Excellent: Vitamin B$_{12}$
Good: Riboflavin; Niacin; Calcium

4. Place egg whites in a large bowl. Add cream of tartar and beat until opaque and firm. Stir one-quarter of the whites into sauce to lighten. Then fold remaining whites into sauce lightly. Fold in Parmesan.

5. Spread mixture over prepared baking sheet and bake in a preheated 400°F/200°C oven for 15 to 18 minutes until firm but not overbaked. Cool for 10 minutes.

6. Meanwhile, in a medium bowl, combine yogurt cheese with mustard. Taste and add more mustard if you wish.

7. Invert soufflé onto a clean tea towel. Carefully lift off paper. Spread yogurt cheese mixture over soufflé. Arrange smoked salmon on yogurt cheese in a single layer. Do not worry if it doesn't completely cover cheese. Sprinkle with chives.

8. Gently, using the tea towel to help you, roll up lengthwise. Carefully transfer to a long serving tray.

Smoked Salmon and Spinach Soufflé Roll
Add ¾ cup/175 mL chopped cooked spinach to the soufflé and fill with 2 cups/500 mL chopped cooked broccoli and ½ cup/125 mL grated Cheddar cheese.

Homemade Fish Stock
Place 3 lb/1.5 kg fish bones, tails and heads in a large pot (use only lean, white-fleshed fish). Add 2 onions, 2 carrots, 2 stalks celery and 1 leek (all cut in chunks). Add a handful of fresh parsley, 1 bay leaf, ½ tsp/2 mL dried thyme, 6 whole peppercorns and 1 cup/250 mL cold water. Bring to a boil and skim off scum. Reduce heat and simmer gently for 30 minutes. Strain and freeze. Makes about 3 qt/3 L.

SWORDFISH SICILIAN

When I was teaching a class on Baffin Island, I made this recipe with very fresh Arctic char, and it was a huge hit. But this is also a great way to cook veal or lamb chops.

Makes 6 servings

1 tbsp	olive oil, divided	15 mL
1	large onion, chopped	1
1	clove garlic, finely chopped	1
1 cup	fresh breadcrumbs	250 mL
2 tbsp	pine nuts, toasted	25 mL
2 tbsp	currants (soaked in boiling water for 5 minutes if hard)	25 mL
2 tbsp	chopped fresh parsley	25 mL
2 tbsp	grated Parmesan cheese	25 mL
2 tbsp	capers	25 mL
6	swordfish steaks, about 4 oz/125 g each, ¾ inch/2 cm thick	6
½ tsp	salt	2 mL
¼ tsp	pepper	1 mL

1. Heat 1½ tsp/7 mL oil in a large non-stick skillet on medium heat. Add onion and garlic and cook until tender, about 5 minutes. If onion begins to stick, add a few spoonfuls of water and cook until it evaporates.

2. Add onion mixture to a bowl with breadcrumbs, pine nuts, currants, parsley, cheese and capers.

3. Brush swordfish with remaining 1½ tsp/7 mL olive oil and sprinkle with salt and pepper. Cook for 2 to 3 minutes per side on a barbecue, under broiler, or in a hot non-stick pan or grill pan. Transfer fish to a baking sheet. Pat breadcrumb mixture evenly over top.

4. Just before serving, broil fish for 2 to 3 minutes, or until crisp and golden. Watch closely, as it can burn easily.

SERVING SUGGESTIONS
- You can serve this on a bed of salad greens or roasted vegetables.
- Garnish each serving with a wedge of lemon.

MAKE AHEAD
- The fish can be cooked ahead and broiled just before serving.
- The whole dish can be cooked ahead and served cold or at room temperature.

Toasting Pine Nuts
Spread pine nuts on a baking sheet and bake in a preheated 350°F/180°C oven for 3 to 5 minutes until lightly browned.

PER SERVING

Calories	224
Protein	25.3 g
Fat	9.5 g
Saturates	2.3 g
Cholesterol	46 mg
Carbohydrate	9.1 g
Fibre	1.3 g
Sodium	419 mg
Potassium	430 mg

Excellent: Niacin; Vitamin B$_{12}$
Good: Vitamin B$_6$; Zinc

ROASTED RED SNAPPER
WITH TOMATO AND HERB SALSA

A fish does look important and impressive when it is brought to the table with its head and tail intact. You can use one large fish, two smaller fish or even fish fillets or steaks in this recipe. You can also use striped bass or trout.

Makes 8 servings

2	3-lb/1.5 kg whole red snappers, cleaned, or 2½ lb/1.25 kg fish fillets, cut in 8 pieces	2
8	plum tomatoes (about 2 lb/1 kg), seeded and diced	8
4	shallots, peeled (page 173) and thinly sliced	4
¼ cup	pitted and halved green and/or black olives	50 mL
1	lemon, quartered and thinly sliced	1
1 tbsp	chopped fresh rosemary, or ½ tsp/2 mL dried	15 mL
1 tbsp	chopped fresh thyme, or ½ tsp/2 mL dried	15 mL
1 tsp	salt	5 mL
1 tsp	pepper	5 mL
2 tbsp	olive oil	25 mL
¼ cup	chopped fresh parsley, divided	50 mL

1. Line a roasting pan (large enough to hold fish in a single layer) with parchment paper or foil. Brush lightly with oil. Arrange fish on paper. Cut slashes in top of fish about ½ inch/1 cm deep.

2. In a large bowl, combine tomatoes, shallots, olives, lemon, rosemary, thyme, salt, pepper, olive oil and 2 tbsp/25 mL parsley.

3. Spoon some salsa inside fish cavity and spread remainder over top. If you are using fillets, place salsa over and under fillets.

4. Cover fish loosely with foil or parchment paper and bake in a preheated 425°F/220°C oven for 45 to 50 minutes. Check fish and cook just until it flakes (this could take as long as 60 minutes, depending on thickness of fish; fillets should take only 15 to 20 minutes in total).

5. Sprinkle fish with remaining 2 tbsp/25 mL parsley. For carving and boning instructions, see page 29.

MAKE AHEAD
- The fish and salsa can be prepared ahead and then baked just before serving.
- This dish can also be baked ahead and served at room temperature.

PER SERVING

Calories	205
Protein	30.4 g
Fat	6.2 g
Saturates	1 g
Cholesterol	52 mg
Carbohydrate	7.2 g
Fibre	2.5 g
Sodium	498 mg
Potassium	860 mg

Excellent: Niacin; Vitamin B_{12}
Good: Vitamin A; Vitamin C; Vitamin B_6

GEFILTE FISH LOAF

SERVING SUGGESTIONS
- Serve a slice of loaf on a lettuce leaf, garnished with cherry tomatoes and red horseradish.
- Cut the loaf into thick slices and then into little squares and serve on matzo or bread as an appetizer.

MAKE AHEAD
- This can be made a few days ahead. Keep it refrigerated; the loaf becomes watery if it is frozen.

Homemade Horseradish
Peel a 6-inch/15 cm piece of horseradish root, cut it into pieces and chop it finely in a food processor (or grate with a rasp) with a small, peeled raw red beet. Add a few spoonfuls of vinegar and puree.

PER SERVING

Calories	188
Protein	23.9 g
Fat	7.2 g
Saturates	1.3 g
Cholesterol	131 mg
Carbohydrate	5.5 g
Fibre	0.4 g
Sodium	844 mg
Potassium	371 mg

Excellent: Niacin; Vitamin B$_{12}$
Good: Vitamin A; Thiamine; Vitamin B$_6$

Gefilte fish is a traditional Jewish holiday food that is generally served as part of the Passover Seder dinner and on Rosh Hashanah. Every Jewish cook makes it his or her own way, varying the types and quantities of the fish, how it is cooked, whether it is sweet or salty, peppery or mild. In our family my mother used to place the bones, heads and tails of the fish in the bottom of the pot along with onions and sliced carrots as a base, and the fish mixture was shaped into balls which were then poached on top of the vegetables and bones. An easier method is simply to cook the mixture in a loaf pan. We also used to grind the fish ourselves, but now most fish stores will grind the fish for you (be sure to use the freshest fish possible).

Makes 12 to 16 servings

3 lb	mixed ground fish (e.g., 1½ lb/750 g whitefish, 1 lb/500 g pickerel and ½ lb/250 g salmon)	1.5 kg
3	eggs	3
1 cup	cold water	250 mL
⅓ cup	matzo meal (page 78)	75 mL
4 tsp	salt	20 mL
1 tsp	pepper	5 mL
1 tbsp	granulated sugar	15 mL
1	small onion, grated (¼ to ⅓ cup/50 to 75 mL)	1
1	carrot, grated and chopped (about 1 cup/250 mL)	1

1. Place fish in a large bowl. Add eggs, water, matzo meal, salt, pepper, sugar, onion and carrot. Gently combine ingredients together.

2. Place mixture in a 9 x 5-inch/2 L loaf pan lined with parchment paper. Cover with foil. Place a roasting pan in a preheated 350°F/180°C oven and half fill pan with hot or boiling water. Gently place pan of fish in water bath. Bake for 1 hour. Uncover pan and bake for 30 minutes longer.

3. Cool fish and then refrigerate for a few hours or overnight. Remove from pan and slice.

MUSSELS PROVENÇALE

Mussels are the kind of thing that people eat in restaurants a lot but don't think to make for themselves. Yet they are actually easy to prepare. If you are serving them for dinner, count on 1 lb/500 g per person; if you are serving them as an appetizer, count on ½ lb/ 250 g per person. Provide bowls on the table for the empty shells.

Some people prefer the taste of wild mussels rather than cultivated ones; they are usually less expensive but are harder to clean.

Makes 8 servings as an appetizer; 4 as a main course

4 lb	cultivated mussels (about 90 to 100)	2 kg
1 tbsp	olive oil	15 mL
1	shallot, chopped	1
4	cloves garlic, chopped	4
1	28-oz/796 mL can plum tomatoes, drained and chopped (about 1½ cups/375 mL), or 1½ lb/ 750 g fresh tomatoes, peeled, seeded and diced	1
1 cup	dry white wine, stock or water	250 mL
1 tbsp	chopped fresh tarragon, or 1 tsp/5 mL dried	15 mL
¼ tsp	salt	1 mL
pinch	pepper	pinch
3 tbsp	chopped fresh parsley	45 mL
2	French sticks, sliced	2

1. Rinse mussels and pull off any beards. Discard any mussels that seem very heavy or that have cracked shells.

2. Heat oil in a large Dutch oven or wok on medium-high heat. Add shallot and garlic. Cook until fragrant and tender but do not brown. Add tomatoes and bring to a boil.

3. Add mussels and turn to coat well. Add wine and bring to a boil. Sprinkle with tarragon, salt and pepper. Cover and cook mussels for 5 minutes until all mussels open. Discard any that do not open after another minute or 2 of cooking.

4. Transfer mussels to large bowls. Sprinkle with parsley and serve with lots of bread to soak up juices.

SERVING SUGGESTIONS
- Serve the mussels and sauce on pasta or rice.
- Remove the mussels from their shells and serve the sauce, juices and shelled mussels as a soup.

MAKE AHEAD
- This dish only takes 5 to 8 minutes to cook, but you could cook the shallots, garlic and tomatoes ahead and then add the mussels shortly before serving.

PER APPETIZER

Calories	318
Protein	15.5 g
Fat	5.6 g
Saturates	1 g
Cholesterol	18 mg
Carbohydrate	47.9 g
Fibre	2 g
Sodium	739 mg
Potassium	345 mg

Excellent: Thiamine; Niacin; Folacin; Vitamin B_{12}; Iron
Good: Riboflavin; Zinc

THAI SHRIMP WRAP

This is a great idea for a casual meal. You can "build a wrap" with so many different foods. The wrapper can be any kind of tortilla or crêpe (page 284). The filling can be something grilled, stir-fried, left over or storebought, and the rice can be replaced by mashed potatoes, couscous, wheat berries or any cooked grain. You can also omit the tortillas and simply serve the shrimp mixture as a stir-fry over rice.

Instead of the shrimp, you can use extra-firm tofu (use about ¾ lb/375 g) or boneless, skinless chicken breasts cut in strips.

Makes 8 servings

1½ cups	basmati, Thai-scented or sticky rice	375 mL
1¾ cups	cold water	425 mL
2 tbsp	peanut butter	25 mL
2 tbsp	soy sauce or Thai fish sauce	25 mL
2 tbsp	rice vinegar (page 132)	25 mL
1 tbsp	honey	15 mL
1 tbsp	sesame oil	15 mL
½ tsp	hot chili paste	2 mL
⅓ cup	water	75 mL
1 tbsp	vegetable oil	15 mL
1½ lb	shrimp, cleaned (page 249)	750 g
2	cloves garlic, finely chopped	2
1 tbsp	chopped fresh ginger root	15 mL
1	large carrot, grated or cut in very thin sticks	1
1	stalk celery, cut in very thin sticks	1
1	sweet red pepper, cut in very thin sticks	1
3	green onions, sliced on the diagonal	3
⅓ cup	chopped fresh cilantro	75 mL
8	10-inch/25 cm flour tortillas	8

SERVING SUGGESTIONS

- If guests are going to be eating these casually while they are walking around (a backyard party or buffet), I like to wrap them in foil so nothing will drip or drop out the bottom. If guests are seated at the table, the wraps look nice cut in half on the diagonal.
- Serve the tortillas and filling separately and let guests assemble their own wraps.
- Grill the wraps after assembling them, or to reheat them.

PER SERVING

Calories	472
Protein	23.5 g
Fat	11 g
Saturates	1.7 g
Cholesterol	107 mg
Carbohydrate	68.6 g
Fibre	3.2 g
Sodium	670 mg
Potassium	314 mg

Excellent: Vitamin A; Thiamine; Niacin; Vitamin B$_{12}$; Iron
Good: Vitamin C; Zinc

1. To cook rice, rinse with lots of cold water until water runs clear. Place rice with 1¾ cups/425 mL cold water in a medium saucepan and bring to a boil. Cook, uncovered, on medium heat until all surface water disappears. Reduce heat to the lowest setting, cover and steam for 5 to 10 minutes. Remove from heat and allow to rest for 10 minutes. Fluff with a fork. Cool slightly.

2. Meanwhile, blend peanut butter, soy sauce, vinegar, honey, sesame oil and chili paste in a bowl, blender or food processor. Add water and blend until smooth.

3. Heat oil in a wok or large non-stick skillet on medium-high heat. Add shrimp, garlic and ginger. Cook for 1 minute. Add carrot, celery and red pepper. Cook for 1 more minute. Add peanut sauce and bring to a boil. Add green onions and cilantro. Shrimp should be cooked and vegetables should be slightly wilted.

4. Just before assembling, wrap tortillas in foil and place in a preheated 350°F/180°C oven for about 10 minutes. Place a tortilla on work surface. Shape about ½ cup/125 mL rice in a "brick" shape and place in centre of lower third of tortilla. Spoon about ¾ cup/175 mL filling and sauce on top. Fold up bottom, fold in sides and roll up.

MAKE AHEAD
- These can be made ahead, wrapped in foil and kept warm in a 250°F/125°C oven.
- The rice can be cooked ahead on the day of serving; the shrimp mixture can be cooked the day before.

CILANTRO-GRILLED CHICKEN BREASTS

SERVING SUGGESTIONS
- Serve with pad Thai (page 120) or steamed rice.
- Cut cooked chicken into 1-inch/2.5 cm by 4-inch/ 10 cm strips and skewer to serve as an appetizer.

MAKE AHEAD
- This can be cooked ahead and served at room temperature, or it can be marinated ahead and cooked just before serving.

Cilantro is sometimes called fresh coriander or Chinese parsley. By any name I think it is delicious, with a clean, fresh citrus taste. But not everyone loves it as much as I do. Some people think it tastes so clean that it's soapy (Ken Beatty, host of WTN's "Get Growing," advised me once that young plants will have a milder taste). I always say people should get used to it because it is very hard to avoid these days, but the advantage of cooking at home is that you can substitute other herbs. In this dish I would use a combination of basil, mint and chives.

If you have any leftover chicken, dice it and add it to fried rice (page 139) or use it in sandwiches. You can make wraps filled with the chicken, steamed rice and peanut sauce (page 102).

Makes 8 servings

4	cloves garlic, chopped	4
1	small onion, chopped	1
1 cup	fresh cilantro, including stems and roots	250 mL
2 tbsp	Thai fish sauce or soy sauce	25 mL
3 tbsp	lime juice	45 mL
2 tbsp	rice vinegar	25 mL
2 tbsp	hoisin sauce	25 mL
½ tsp	hot chili paste	2 mL
8	boneless, skinless single chicken breasts (about 5 oz/150 g each)	8

1. In a food processor or blender, chop garlic, onion and cilantro. Add fish sauce, lime juice, rice vinegar, hoisin sauce and chili paste. Process to form a paste.

2. Pound chicken breasts until thin (this step is optional, but it will help the chicken cook more evenly). Place in a shallow dish. Pour marinade over chicken and turn to coat well. Refrigerate for 30 minutes or up to a few hours.

3. Grill, broil or saute chicken in a lightly oiled non-stick skillet for about 3 to 4 minutes per side, depending on thickness.

Cilantro-grilled Shrimp
Use 2 lb/1 kg cleaned shrimp instead of chicken. Grill or saute for about 5 minutes.

PER SERVING

Calories	170
Protein	32.7 g
Fat	2.2 g
Saturates	0.6 g
Cholesterol	84 mg
Carbohydrate	2.9 g
Fibre	0.2 g
Sodium	387 mg
Potassium	434 mg

Excellent: Niacin; Vitamin B$_6$
Good: Vitamin B$_{12}$

CHICKEN TAGINE WITH HONEYED TOMATOES AND COUSCOUS *(page 170)*

TASTE OF SUMMER MENU

Double-wrapped Shrimp Salad Rolls

Asparagus Soup
with Fresh Tarragon

Cedar-planked Salmon

Potato and Arugula Salad
with Mustard and Roasted Garlic

Bumbleberry Cobbler

(see recipes starting page 248)

SHOWN HERE:
DOUBLE-WRAPPED SHRIMP SALAD ROLLS, CEDAR-PLANKED SALMON
POTATO AND ARUGULA SALAD WITH MUSTARD AND ROASTED GARLIC

CELEBRATION DINNER

Buckwheat Blini with Smoked Trout

Smoked Salmon Napoleons

Roast Cornish Hens with Herbs

Polenta with Wild Mushrooms

Fennel, Endive and
Red Pepper Salad

Frozen Lemon Meringue Cake

(see recipes starting page 184)

FROZEN LEMON MERINGUE CAKE

ROAST CORNISH HENS WITH HERBS
(page 187)

COSY WINTER DINNER MENU

Hot Apple Cranberry Drink
French Onion Soup
Pot Roast of Beef with Root Vegetables
Succotash
Apple Crisp Strudel

(see recipes starting page 84)

SHOWN HERE:
FRENCH ONION SOUP
MIXED GREENS WITH TOMATO SOY DRESSING *(page 116)*

SUSHI PIZZA *(page 42)*

SPAGHETTI WITH CHICKEN MEATBALLS

Everybody loves this dish. You can add grilled or roasted vegetables (page 96) and/or hot sauce. You can also use ground beef, turkey, or veal for the meatballs.
Serve this with a salad and you are set. Leftover meatballs make great sandwiches.

Makes 6 servings

1 tbsp	olive oil	15 mL
1	onion, chopped	1
2	cloves garlic, finely chopped	2
pinch	hot red pepper flakes	pinch
1	carrot, finely chopped	1
1	stalk celery, finely chopped	1
1	28-oz/796 mL can plum tomatoes, pureed with juices	1
1 lb	ground lean chicken breast	500 g
1	egg, beaten	1
¾ cup	fresh breadcrumbs	175 mL
1 tsp	salt	5 mL
¼ tsp	pepper	1 mL
1 lb	spaghetti	500 g
3 tbsp	chopped fresh parsley	45 mL

1. Heat oil in a large, deep skillet on medium-high heat. Add onion, garlic, hot pepper flakes, carrot and celery. Cook for about 5 minutes until tender. Add tomatoes and bring to a boil. Cook gently, uncovered, for about 10 minutes.

2. Meanwhile, to make meatballs, combine chicken, egg, breadcrumbs, salt and pepper in a large bowl. Shape into about 24 small meatballs and place on a baking sheet lined with waxed paper. Add meatballs to sauce. Spoon some sauce over meatballs. Cook for about 20 minutes over low heat, covered, and then uncovered for about 10 minutes. Taste and adjust seasonings.

3. Meanwhile, bring a large pot of water to a boil. Add pasta and cook until tender. Serve sauce over pasta and sprinkle with parsley.

SERVING SUGGESTIONS
- Use your family's favourite pasta shape instead of spaghetti.
- Make tiny mini meatballs or simply brown meat with the garlic and onions and incorporate into the sauce.

MAKE AHEAD
- The sauce and meatballs can be made ahead, but cook the spaghetti just before serving and combine at the last minute. The sauce and meatballs can also be made ahead and frozen. Add a little extra water when reheating.

PER SERVING

Calories	455
Protein	30 g
Fat	6.2 g
Saturates	1.2 g
Cholesterol	80 mg
Carbohydrate	68.6 g
Fibre	5.4 g
Sodium	699 mg
Potassium	676 mg

Excellent: Vitamin A; Thiamine; Niacin; Vitamin B_6; Folacin
Good: Vitamin B_{12}; Iron; Zinc

CHICKEN TAGINE WITH HONEYED TOMATOES AND COUSCOUS

SERVING SUGGESTIONS
• Serve the chicken in a tagine (a traditional Moroccan cooking vessel with a conical lid) and the couscous in a separate bowl.
• Serve in individual pasta bowls.
• Serve with charmoula (page 52) or harissa (page 206) if you like hot and spicy food.

MAKE AHEAD
• The chicken can be made a day ahead and reheated; it can also be made a few weeks in advance and frozen.

PER SERVING

Calories	485
Protein	40.8 g
Fat	5.3 g
Saturates	1 g
Cholesterol	77 mg
Carbohydrate	66.9 g
Fibre	4.5 g
Sodium	396 mg
Potassium	792 mg

Excellent: Niacin; Vitamin B$_6$
Good: Thiamine; Folacin; Vitamin B$_{12}$; Iron; Zinc

This recipe was inspired by one of my favourite guest instructors, Joanne Weir. She is a prolific cookbook author and the host of her own television series. If you want to serve this for a buffet, use boneless chicken breasts cut in 2-inch/5 cm chunks, brown at the start and then add to the sauce, but only cook for 10 to 15 minutes. You can also use chicken thighs.

Makes 8 servings

1 tbsp	olive oil	15 mL
8	chicken breasts, skin removed but bone in	8
½ tsp	salt	2 mL
¼ tsp	pepper	1 mL
1	onion, finely chopped	1
3	cloves garlic, finely chopped	3
1 tbsp	chopped fresh ginger root	15 mL
1 tsp	ground cumin (page 227)	5 mL
1 tsp	cinnamon	5 mL
¼ tsp	cayenne	1 mL
½ tsp	saffron threads, crushed and dissolved in 2 tbsp/25 mL boiling water	2 mL
1	28-oz/796 mL can plum tomatoes, crushed with juices	1
3 tbsp	honey	45 mL
1 tbsp	lemon juice	15 mL
3 cups	Israeli couscous (page 243)	750 mL
1 tbsp	sesame seeds, toasted (page 245)	15 mL
¼ cup	chopped fresh cilantro	50 mL

1. Heat oil in a large, deep non-stick skillet on high heat. Season chicken with salt and pepper. Brown well on both sides. Remove chicken from pan.

2. Discard all but a teaspoon of oil from pan and add onion, garlic and ginger. Cook for a few minutes until tender. Add cumin, cinnamon and cayenne. Cook for 30 seconds. Add saffron and tomatoes. Bring to a boil.

3. Return chicken to pan. Cover and simmer gently for 20 to 30 minutes, or just until chicken is cooked. Remove chicken from pan and keep warm. If sauce is oily on surface, skim it off with a large spoon or dab with paper towels.

4. Add honey and lemon juice to sauce. Bring to a boil. If sauce is not thick enough, cook, uncovered, until liquid has reduced. Taste and adjust seasonings if necessary. Combine sauce with chicken.

5. Meanwhile, cook Israeli couscous in a large pot of boiling water. Place in a large serving bowl and pour chicken and sauce on top. Sprinkle with sesame seeds and cilantro.

HOISIN-GLAZED CHICKEN SATAYS

This is a great recipe for summer entertaining. If you grill the chicken breasts whole, cut them into strips and then thread them on skewers, they look clean and neat and the wooden skewers don't burn!

Makes 20 to 24 appetizers

1 lb	boneless, skinless chicken breasts	500 g
¼ cup	hoisin sauce	50 mL
2 tbsp	soy sauce	25 mL
2 tbsp	orange juice	25 mL
2 tbsp	honey	25 mL
2 tbsp	ketchup	25 mL
½ tsp	hot chili paste	2 mL

1. Pat chicken dry. Remove "filets" and reserve.

2. In a large bowl, combine hoisin, soy sauce, orange juice, honey, ketchup and chili paste. Add all chicken and marinate for 10 minutes at room temperature or up to overnight in refrigerator.

3. Heat grill. Barbecue filets for about 2 minutes per side and large pieces for 4 to 6 minutes per side until just cooked through (cooking time will depend on thickness of pieces).

4. Cut large chicken pieces crosswise into about 5 strips and thread lengthwise on skewers. Skewer filets as well (you should have 20 to 24 skewers).

SERVING SUGGESTIONS
- Serve with peanut dip (page 102) as an appetizer.
- Serve whole breasts with rice as a main course.

Skewering Tips
- If you are using wooden skewers, soak them in cold water for 30 minutes before using.
- Keep soaked skewers in a bag in the freezer, so you always have some on hand.
- Skewer food after cooking, so the skewers don't burn.
- If you are cooking chunks of food, insert two skewers side by side to stop the food from slipping. Or thread skewers through strips of food instead of chunks.

PER APPETIZER

Calories	38
Protein	5.3 g
Fat	0.4 g
Saturates	0.1 g
Cholesterol	13 mg
Carbohydrate	2.9 g
Fibre	0.1 g
Sodium	144 mg
Potassium	78 mg

Excellent: Vitamin B$_6$

COQ AU VIN

SERVING SUGGESTION
• Serve with mashed or roasted potatoes, rice, pasta, polenta or couscous.

MAKE AHEAD
• This can all be made ahead. Reheat in a casserole dish at 350°F/180°C for 30 minutes or until hot. You can also freeze the chicken and reheat from the frozen state or defrost overnight in the refrigerator.

Coq au vin is one of those delicious dishes that is making a big comeback. It is quick to make and can also be made ahead and reheated, which makes it great for entertaining. It is traditionally made with white and dark meat, but you can use just the breasts — do not overcook them.

If you prefer, you can use a combination of cultivated and wild mushrooms to reduce the expense. Slice them if they are large.

If you have any leftovers, remove the chicken from the bones and add it to soups, or combine with pasta or rice to make a casserole. Recipe can be halved.

Makes 8 servings

2	3-lb/1.5 kg chickens, cut in 4 pieces each, skin removed	2
½ cup	all-purpose flour	125 mL
½ tsp	salt	2 mL
¼ tsp	pepper	1 mL
1 tbsp	olive oil, or 2 slices bacon, cut in 1-inch/2.5 cm pieces	15 mL
¼ cup	brandy, optional	50 mL
24	pearl onions or shallots, peeled (page 173)	24
24	whole cloves garlic, peeled	24
1 lb	wild mushrooms, trimmed	500 g
4	large carrots, sliced on the diagonal in ¾-inch/2 cm pieces	4
1 cup	dry red wine (preferably Burgundy) or stock	250 mL
2 cups	homemade beef stock (page 86) or chicken stock (page 79)	500 mL
1	bay leaf	1
1 tbsp	chopped fresh thyme, or pinch dried	15 mL
1 tbsp	chopped fresh rosemary, or pinch dried	15 mL
1 tbsp	chopped fresh tarragon, or pinch dried	15 mL
¼ cup	coarsely chopped fresh parsley	50 mL

PER SERVING

Calories	342
Protein	47.8 g
Fat	8.8 g
Saturates	2 g
Cholesterol	144 mg
Carbohydrate	15.1 g
Fibre	2.7 g
Sodium	279 mg
Potassium	869 mg

Excellent: Vitamin A; Riboflavin; Niacin; Vitamin B_6; Vitamin B_{12}; Iron; Zinc
Good: Thiamine; Folacin

1. Pat chicken dry. In a shallow dish, combine flour, salt and pepper. Coat chicken pieces with mixture, dusting off any excess. (You'll have to discard the excess flour, but it is much easier to work with more than you need.)

2. Heat olive oil in a large, deep skillet or Dutch oven on high heat. Brown chicken pieces on both sides, in batches if necessary. (If you are using bacon, brown bacon pieces. Remove bacon and reserve. Discard fat, but do not wash pan. Brown chicken in same pan.) Return all chicken to pan and sprinkle with brandy if using. Flambé (page 284); once flames subside, remove chicken (do not worry if the flambé doesn't work — when the sauce comes to a boil, the alcohol will evaporate).

3. Add onions, garlic, mushrooms and carrots to pan. Brown for about 8 minutes.

4. Add wine and bring to a boil. Scrape up browned bits from bottom of pan. Add stock, bay leaf, thyme, rosemary and tarragon. Add chicken. Bring to a boil. Cook gently, covered, for about 45 minutes.

5. Remove chicken and vegetables to a serving platter. Cover to keep warm. Discard bay leaf. Place a paper towel on surface of pan juices for a couple of seconds to remove any fat. Repeat if necessary.

6. Bring juices to a simmer and cook, uncovered, until thickened. Pour sauce over chicken (discard any juices that have accumulated on platter or incorporate them into sauce if the sauce is a little thick). Sprinkle with parsley.

Boeuf Bourguignon
Use stewing beef instead of chicken. Cut 2 lb/1 kg stewing beef into chunks and cook with vegetables for 2 hours, or until beef is very tender.

Peeling Pearl Onions
To peel pearl onions or shallots more easily, trim and immerse in boiling water for 1 minute. Cool under cold water and peel.

THAI MANGO CHICKEN STIR-FRY

This is a different and delicious stir-fry to serve over noodles or rice. If you are using coconut milk, freeze the unused portion for another time, as it is highly perishable.

Use leftovers in wraps (page 166) or chop and use as a filling for spring rolls (page 60) or salad rolls (page 248).

Makes 4 to 6 servings

SERVING SUGGESTIONS
- Serve in hollowed-out pineapple boats.
- Place rice on a platter in a ring and serve chicken in the centre.
- Mound rice on a platter and serve chicken around it.
- Garnish with edible flowers (page 22).

MAKE AHEAD
- This is best cooked at the last minute, but the ingredients and sauces can be prepared ahead.

¼ cup	hoisin sauce	50 mL
2 tbsp	Thai fish sauce (page 105) or soy sauce	25 mL
2 tbsp	mango nectar or low-fat coconut milk	25 mL
2 tbsp	orange juice	25 mL
1 tbsp	peanut butter, or 1 tsp/5 mL sesame oil	15 mL
½ tsp	hot chili paste	2 mL
1 lb	boneless, skinless chicken breasts, cut in 1-inch/2.5 cm chunks	500 g
1 tbsp	cornstarch	15 mL
1 tbsp	cold water	15 mL
1 tbsp	vegetable oil	15 mL
1 tbsp	chopped fresh ginger root	15 mL
2	cloves garlic, chopped	2
4	green onions, chopped	4
1	1-inch/2.5 cm piece lemongrass, tender part only, smashed and finely chopped (about 2 tsp/10 mL), optional	1
1	onion, cut in 1-inch/2.5 cm chunks	1
2	sweet red peppers, cut in 1-inch/2.5 cm chunks	2
¼ lb	mushrooms, stemmed and thickly sliced	125 g
2	mangoes (not too ripe), peeled and cut in 1-inch/2.5 cm chunks	2
¼ cup	coarsely chopped fresh cilantro, Thai basil, basil or mint, or a combination	50 mL
6 cups	steamed jasmine or sticky rice	1.5 L

PER SERVING

Calories	744
Protein	37.4 g
Fat	9 g
Saturates	1.5 g
Cholesterol	66 mg
Carbohydrate	127.5 g
Fibre	6.2 g
Sodium	1053 mg
Potassium	923 mg

Excellent: Vitamin A; Vitamin C; Niacin; Vitamin B$_6$; Zinc
Good: Thiamine; Riboflavin; Folacin; Vitamin B$_{12}$; Iron

1. In a small bowl, whisk together hoisin, fish sauce, mango nectar, orange juice, peanut butter and chili paste.

2. In a large bowl, toss chicken with cornstarch and water to coat.

3. Heat oil in a wok or large non-stick skillet on high heat. Add chicken and stir-fry until chicken is about three-quarters cooked through.

4. Add ginger, garlic, green onions and lemongrass (if using) to pan and stir-fry until fragrant, about 30 seconds. Add onion and red peppers. Cook until softened, about 2 minutes. Add mushrooms and cook for 1 minute.

5. Add mangoes and sauce. Bring to a boil and cook for 2 minutes. Add cilantro and remove from heat. Serve with rice.

Thai Papaya Chicken Stir-fry
Use about 2 cups/500 mL diced papaya or pineapple instead of mangoes.

FLAX

Flaxseed is one of the newer players in the diet and health arena. Traditionally known as linseed, it's a great source of soluble fibre and omega-3 fatty acids, both of which may reduce the risk of heart disease. Studies have shown that flax can significantly lower the cholesterol of healthy people and also help reduce the body's blood-clotting tendency. Omega-3 fatty acids help lower levels of triglycerides — blood fats that in excess can raise the risk of heart disease. These omega-3 fats are abundant in fatty fish such as salmon, mackerel, herring and sardines. Experts recommend we include more of these fish in our diets. But if you're allergic to fish or just don't like it, flaxseed provides a good alternative source of these healthy fats. Flax also contains phytochemicals — naturally occurring plant chemicals that are being studied for their cancer-fighting properties.

The chemicals in flax are called lignans. They act as antioxidants (page 152) and also appear to counter some of the harmful effects of estrogen. Studies are currently looking at the role flax may play in lowering the risk of breast and colon cancer.

You can buy flaxseed whole at health food stores, but ground flax releases more of the healthy ingredients. You can grind the seeds yourself with a coffee grinder or ask the store to do it for you. Keep ground flaxseed in a tightly sealed container in the freezer or fridge. Sprinkle it on cereal, mix it with yogurt, juice or applesauce or add it to muffins, breads or pancakes.

Be careful when adding any new fibre to your diet. Too much too quickly can cause unnecessary intestinal discomfort, and you'll probably stop using it before it has a chance to do its important work. Aim towards 1 to 2 tablespoons per day.

You can also buy flaxseed oil. This will give you the omega-3 fatty acids but won't provide the fibre of the seeds.

RED CURRY CHICKEN

SERVING SUGGESTION
• Serve chicken over couscous or rice noodles instead of rice.

MAKE AHEAD
• This can all be made a day ahead; it can also be frozen.

Thai curry has a very different taste from West Indian or East Indian curry. Red and green curry pastes are now easy to find in supermarkets and specialty stores.

You can also make this using six to eight skinless chicken breasts. Leftover chicken can be used with rice to fill wraps (page 166). Or you can dice the chicken and vegetables and add stock to serve as a soup.

If you are using coconut milk, freeze any extra to use another time. Often used in Asian cooking, coconut milk is high in fat. Use the suggested substitutes; low-fat coconut milk is available at health food stores and specialty shops.

Makes 6 servings

1	large (4-lb/2 kg) chicken, cut in 8 pieces, skin removed	1
2 tsp	vegetable oil	10 mL
1	¾-oz/50 g package red curry paste	1
1	large onion, thickly sliced	1
2	carrots, thickly sliced	2
2	cloves garlic, chopped	2
2	potatoes, peeled and cut in 2-inch/5 cm chunks (about 1 lb/500 g)	2
1	sweet red pepper, cut in chunks	1
3	whole jalapeños (page 73)	3
½ lb	mushrooms, trimmed	250 g
1	stalk lemongrass, cut in 2-inch/5 cm pieces, smashed	1
2 cups	homemade chicken stock (page 79) or water	500 mL
2 tbsp	Thai fish sauce (page 105) or soy sauce	25 mL
½ cup	tomato puree, tomato sauce or low-fat coconut milk	125 mL
6 cups	cooked Thai-scented rice	1.5 L
¼ cup	chopped fresh cilantro	50 mL

PER SERVING

Calories	572
Protein	40.8 g
Fat	9.1 g
Saturates	1.7 g
Cholesterol	103 mg
Carbohydrate	79.2 g
Fibre	4 g
Sodium	595 mg
Potassium	881 mg

Excellent: Vitamin A; Vitamin C; Niacin; Vitamin B$_6$; Vitamin B$_{12}$; Zinc
Good: Thiamine; Riboflavin; Folacin; Iron

1. Trim any fat from chicken pieces and pat dry. Heat oil in a large, deep skillet or Dutch oven on high heat. Brown chicken pieces on both sides. Remove chicken and reserve.

2. Discard all but a thin film of fat from pan. Add curry paste and cook for 30 to 60 seconds. Add onion, carrots, garlic, potatoes, red pepper, jalapeños, mushrooms and lemongrass. Cook for about 1 minute. (If pan is very hot, add ¼ cup/50 mL of the stock now.)

3. Add stock and fish sauce. Bring to a boil. Add chicken pieces. Reduce heat, cover and simmer for 40 minutes, or until chicken is cooked through.

4. Remove chicken from pot. Lift out vegetables and add to chicken. Cover and keep warm. Return pot with juices to heat. Bring to a boil and cook, uncovered, until about 1 to 1½ cups/250 to 375 mL stock is left — about 10 minutes. Add tomato puree and cook, uncovered, for 5 minutes, until thickened.

5. Place rice on a large platter. Make an indentation for chicken. Place chicken and sauce on rice. Sprinkle with cilantro.

Red Curry Lamb
Instead of chicken, cut 2 lb/1 kg stewing lamb into 2-inch/5 cm chunks. Cook for 1 to 1½ hours or until lamb is very tender.

Homemade Tomato Sauce
In a large skillet, heat 2 tsp/10 mL olive oil. Add 2 chopped cloves garlic, pinch hot red pepper flakes and 1 chopped onion. Cook until tender. Add 1 28-oz/796 mL can plum tomatoes, crushed with juices. Bring to a boil and cook on medium heat for 10 minutes until thick. Add salt and pepper to taste. Makes about 1½ to 2 cups/375 to 500 mL.

OLD-FASHIONED ROAST TURKEY

SERVING SUGGESTION
• Serve with cranberry sauce (page 260) and stuffing (page 240).

After trying hundreds of this-is-the-only-way-to-cook-a-turkey recipes, I have found that the real secret is to buy a fresh, preferably organic turkey and don't overcook it.

Even though the skin is high in fat, I like to roast the turkey with the skin on and then remove it before serving. The skin keeps the turkey moist as it cooks. I also like to bake the stuffing on the side (page 240) rather than in the bird. That stops the fat from being absorbed into the stuffing and also enables me to take the turkey out at 165°F/75°C (if the turkey is stuffed, it should be cooked until the stuffing reaches about 165°F/75°C and the turkey is 180°F/90°C, which means the meat is on the verge of drying out).

If you are cooking a smaller turkey (14 lb/6.5 Kg or less), cook it breast side down for the first half hour, then turn it over. Although it is hard to turn the turkey when it is hot in the pan, the breast meat stays very juicy. You can use folded tea towels, extra pot holders, oven mitts or large spoons to turn it over.

This recipe will make sixteen servings, though I usually make it for twelve so I can enjoy the leftovers. Use leftovers in sandwiches or turkey pot pie, tacos, wraps or fried rice (page 139).

Makes 16 servings

1	15-lb/7 kg fresh turkey (preferably free range or organic)	1
1 tbsp	olive oil	15 mL
½ tsp	salt	2 mL
¼ tsp	pepper	1 mL
1	orange, quartered	1
1	lemon, quartered	1
1	onion, quartered	1
3	sprigs fresh rosemary	3
3	sprigs fresh sage	3
1	large onion, sliced	1
1 cup	Port or water	250 mL

Stock and Gravy

	Turkey neck and giblets	
1	onion, chopped	1
1	carrot, chopped	1
1	stalk celery, chopped	1

PER SERVING

Calories	414
Protein	62.9 g
Fat	14 g
Saturates	4.1 g
Cholesterol	161 mg
Carbohydrate	2.8 g
Fibre	0.1 g
Sodium	303 mg
Potassium	692 mg

Excellent: Riboflavin; Niacin; Vitamin B_6; Vitamin B_{12}; Iron; Zinc

1 cup	dry white wine or water	250 mL
3 cups	water	750 mL
½ cup	Port or water	125 mL
2 tbsp	olive oil	25 mL
¼ cup	all-purpose flour	50 mL
1 tbsp	soy sauce	15 mL
1 tbsp	Worcestershire sauce	15 mL
½ tsp	hot red pepper sauce	2 mL
	Salt and pepper to taste	

1. Rinse turkey inside and out and pat dry with paper towels. Reserve neck and giblets. Rub turkey with olive oil and sprinkle with salt and pepper. Fill cavity with orange, lemon, onion, rosemary and sage. Tie legs together to close cavity.

2. Line roasting pan with parchment paper. Scatter onions in pan. Add turkey and roast in a preheated 400°F/200°C oven for 30 minutes. Add Port.

3. Reduce heat to 350°F/180°C and continue to roast for 2 hours, or until a thermometer inserted into thigh reads 165°F/75°C. Baste every 20 to 30 minutes. If turkey becomes too brown, cover loosely with foil.

4. Meanwhile, make stock by putting neck and giblets in a large saucepan with onion, carrot and celery. Cook on medium-high heat until lightly browned. Add wine and bring to a boil. Cook until wine is reduced by about half. Add water and bring to a boil. Simmer for about 1 hour. Strain. You should have about 2½ cups/625 mL.

5. When turkey is ready, remove to a serving platter or carving board. Remove orange, lemon, onion and herbs from inside and discard. Place foil over turkey and allow to rest while making gravy.

6. For gravy, strain pan juices and place in a large measuring cup. Add Port to roasting pan. Place on heat and scrape bottom. Add to pan juices. Spoon off any fat from surface of juices. You should have about 1 cup/250 mL pan juices. Add enough turkey stock to make 3 cups/750 mL liquid.

7. Heat olive oil in a saucepan. Add flour and cook for a few minutes until lightly browned. Add turkey stock mixture and bring to a boil. Add soy sauce, Worcestershire and hot pepper sauce. Cook for 5 minutes. Taste and adjust seasonings with salt and pepper.

8. Carve turkey (page 28) and drizzle with gravy. Pass remaining gravy at table.

Turkey Pastrami-style

Turkey pastrami is a great substitute for bacon or fatty cold cuts. Use it in sandwiches, salads, soups or pasta sauces. You can also serve it sliced like ham or chicken.

Makes 12 servings

1 tsp	salt	5 mL
2 tbsp	brown sugar	25 mL
4 cups	water	1 L
1	2-lb/1 kg turkey breast	1
2 tbsp	coarsely cracked black pepper	25 mL
2 tbsp	coarsely cracked coriander seeds	25 mL
2 tbsp	paprika	25 mL
2	cloves garlic, minced	2
1 tbsp	olive oil	15 mL

1. In a medium bowl or large measuring cup, combine salt, brown sugar and water and stir until dissolved. Poke holes in the turkey breast to allow brine to penetrate. Place turkey in a 13 x 9-inch/3.5 L glass baking dish or in a zipper bag. Pour salt/sugar water over turkey to cover. Refrigerate for 8 to 24 hours.

2. In a small bowl, combine pepper, coriander, paprika and garlic.

3. Drain turkey and pat dry. Rub with seasoning mixture.

4. Heat oil in a large, heavy ovenproof skillet on high heat. Brown turkey for about 5 minutes on each side. Transfer skillet to oven (or transfer turkey to a baking sheet lined with parchment paper).

5. Roast turkey in a preheated 325°F/160°C oven for 40 to 45 minutes, or until a meat thermometer inserted into thickest part of turkey reads 165°F/75°C. Turn off heat and allow turkey to rest in oven (or covered with foil on counter) for another 30 minutes. Cool. Slice thinly as needed.

Chicken Pastrami-style

Use chicken breast instead of turkey, but roast for only 20 minutes.

SERVING SUGGESTIONS
- Serve with cabbage and mashed potatoes.
- Fast-fry thin slices in a non-stick skillet and serve instead of bacon.

MAKE AHEAD
- This can be made up to one week ahead and refrigerated. It can also be frozen, though it may dry out a bit.

PER SERVING

Calories	109
Protein	18 g
Fat	2.6 g
Saturates	0.6 g
Cholesterol	41 mg
Carbohydrate	3 g
Fibre	0.4 g
Sodium	135 mg
Potassium	236 mg

Excellent: Niacin
Good: Vitamin B$_6$

ITALIAN TURKEY MEATLOAF

Meatloaf is becoming very elegant. If you cannot find lean ground turkey, use lean ground chicken.

Makes 6 to 8 servings

1 lb	baking potatoes or Yukon Gold potatoes	500 g
1	egg	1
2 tsp	salt	10 mL
1 tsp	pepper	5 mL
½ tsp	grated lemon peel	2 mL
½ cup	fresh breadcrumbs	125 mL
2 tbsp	chopped fresh parsley	25 mL
2 tsp	chopped fresh rosemary, or ½ tsp/2 mL dried	10 mL
2 tsp	chopped fresh oregano, or ½ tsp/2 mL dried	10 mL
1 lb	lean ground turkey breast	500 g
1 tbsp	olive oil	15 mL
½ cup	dry white wine or homemade chicken stock (page 79)	125 mL
1	28-oz/796 mL can plum tomatoes, pureed with juices	1

1. Peel and quarter potatoes and place in a large pot of water to cover. Bring to a boil and simmer gently until tender, about 20 minutes. Drain well and cool.

2. Mash potatoes with egg, salt, pepper, lemon peel, breadcrumbs, parsley, rosemary and oregano. Add turkey and combine well. Shape mixture into a flattened ball about 8 inches/20 cm in diameter and about 2 inches/5 cm thick.

3. Heat oil in a 10-inch/25 cm non-stick ovenproof skillet on high heat. Gently add meatloaf and cook for a few minutes until browned on bottom. Carefully turn over (the bottom of a removable-bottomed flan pan makes a fabulous big turner) and cook for a few minutes longer.

4. Add wine and spoon tomatoes over and around meat.

5. Cover and bake in a preheated 350°F/180°C oven for 30 minutes. Uncover and bake for 30 minutes longer, basting with tomatoes. Cut into wedges or slices to serve. Spoon tomato sauce over top.

SERVING SUGGESETIONS
- This is fabulous over polenta (page 213) or mashed potatoes.
- Serve with red pepper "ketchup" (page 261).

MAKE AHEAD
- This can be made ahead and reheated or served cold (it is delicious in sandwiches).

PER SERVING

Calories	209
Protein	21.4 g
Fat	4.8 g
Saturates	1 g
Cholesterol	81 mg
Carbohydrate	19.3 g
Fibre	2.3 g
Sodium	1064 mg
Potassium	744 mg

Excellent: Niacin; Vitamin B_6
Good: Vitamin B_{12}; Iron; Zinc

CELEBRATION DINNER

Buckwheat Blini
with Smoked Trout

Smoked Salmon Napoleons

Roast Cornish Hens with Herbs

Polenta with Wild Mushrooms

Fennel, Endive and
Red Pepper Salad

Frozen Lemon Meringue Cake

There is always a reason to celebrate — New Year's, birthdays, anniversaries, weddings, promotions, to name just a few — and here's a menu that you can adapt depending on the number of guests, length of the party and amount of food you want to serve.

WORK PLAN

MAKE AHEAD

• Make the cake a few weeks in advance and freeze.

• Make the blini, smoked trout topping, polenta and mushrooms a day ahead.

• Assemble the salad except for the endive. Make the salad dressing.

• The phyllo for the Napoleons can be baked and frozen in containers

SAME DAY

• Make the Napoleons early on the same day.

• Before serving, reheat the mushrooms and polenta.

• Prepare the garnishes for the cake.

• Just before serving, add the endive and dressing to the salad. Warm the blini and add the topping.

• Remove the cake from the freezer about 30 minutes before serving. Garnish with the frozen grapes just before serving.

PRESENTATION IDEAS

- Make tuxedo napkin folds (page 26).

- Have plenty of sparklers and candles on hand. Put sparklers in the cake.

- If you are having a New Year's Eve party, invite people to come a bit later (e.g., 8:30 instead of 6:30) so the evening doesn't run too long before midnight.

- On New Year's Eve, have something prepared to serve at 2 A.M. (or for an early breakfast) in case guests are having too good a time to leave. Try a potato-crusted pizza, French toast (page 134) or crêpes (page 284).

- Garnish the cake with frozen grapes. Cut green grapes into small bunches and place in the freezer for a few hours before serving. Remove grapes from the freezer just before serving and place around cake.

- Tuck placecards into herb bouquets.

MATCHING FOOD WITH WINE*

If you want to serve wine: The crisp acidity, fresh fruit and creamy mousse of a Vintage Champagne (France) will balance the richness of the blini and smoked fish. Pinot Noir (Burgundy or New World) is generally lower in tannins than other red wines, and its earthiness and ripe berries will complement the wild mushrooms without overpowering the Cornish hens. The luscious tropical fruit and naturally high sweetness of Icewine (Ontario) will match perfectly with the citrus dessert.

See Alcohol (page 274).

BUCKWHEAT BLINI WITH SMOKED TROUT

There are many ways to make blini, but this easy method has always been my favourite. You can top them with caviar or smoked salmon, but this version is delicious and a bit different.

You can serve these as a first course by making small blinis, or make larger blinis and cut them into wedges. You can also make thin crêpes by using 1¼ cups/300 mL milk in the batter and cooking the crêpes in an omelette or crêpe pan. Add filling and bring up the sides to form a little "beggar's purse" that you tie with a chive or blanched green onion.

Leftover blini can be served as pancakes with maple syrup for breakfast. Leftover topping can be used as a spread on bruschetta, in sandwiches or as a garnish for soup.

Makes about 24 2-inch/5 cm pancakes

2	baking potatoes or Yukon Gold potatoes, peeled, quartered and cooked (1 lb/500 g)	2
3	eggs	3
½ cup	all-purpose flour	125 mL
⅓ cup	buckwheat flour	75 mL
½ tsp	salt	2 mL
½ tsp	pepper	2 mL
1 tbsp	vegetable oil	15 mL
¾ cup	milk	175 mL

Smoked Trout Topping

8 oz	smoked trout, bones and skin removed	250 g
1	stalk celery, finely chopped	1
2 tbsp	chopped fresh chives	25 mL
2 tbsp	chopped fresh dill	25 mL
2 tbsp	mayonnaise	25 mL
2 tbsp	yogurt cheese (page 303) or thick yogurt	25 mL
¼ tsp	pepper	1 mL
1 tsp	lemon juice	5 mL

1. Mash potatoes in a large bowl. (You will have about 2 cups/500 mL.)

2. Beat in eggs, flours, salt, pepper, oil and milk. Batter should be the consistency of thick yogurt. If not, add a bit more milk.

3. Brush a large non-stick pan with oil and heat on medium-high heat. Add batter by the tablespoon to make 2-inch/5 cm pancakes. Cook for a few minutes on each side. Arrange in a single layer on a serving platter or on baking sheets if you are doing this ahead.

4. To make topping, in a medium bowl, mash trout, celery, chives, dill, mayonnaise, yogurt cheese, pepper and lemon juice. Taste and adjust seasonings if necessary. Place a spoonful of topping on each blini.

SMOKED SALMON NAPOLEONS

This is spectacular served as a first course or with a salad as a lunch or light dinner.

Makes 8 servings

SERVING SUGGESTION
• Garnish each serving with
a little caviar.
• You can make mini
napoleons with only two
layers for bite-size appetizers.

MAKE AHEAD
• Serve within one hour of
assembling or pastry will
become soggy.

3 tbsp	unsalted butter, melted	45 mL
1 tbsp	water	15 mL
8	sheets phyllo pastry	8
⅓ cup	dry breadcrumbs	75 mL
1 tsp	pepper	5 mL

Filling

2 cups	thick yogurt cheese (page 303) or light sour cream	500 mL
2 tbsp	horseradish	25 mL
2 tbsp	chopped shallots or green onions	25 mL
2 tbsp	chopped fresh dill	25 mL
2 tbsp	chopped fresh chives	25 mL
1 tbsp	pepper, or to taste	15 mL
	Salt to taste	
1 lb	smoked salmon, thinly sliced	500 g
1	bunch fresh dill or chives	1

1. In a small bowl, combine melted butter and water.

2. Place one sheet of phyllo on work surface. Brush with butter mixture and sprinkle with about 1 tbsp/15 mL breadcrumbs and a little pepper. Repeat until you have 4 layers. Cut phyllo into 4-inch/10 cm squares and place on baking sheets of parchment paper. Repeat with remaining 4 sheets of phyllo, ending with butter. Cut into squares (you should have at least 24 squares in total).

3. Bake in a preheated 400°F/200°C oven for 5 to 8 minutes, or until crisp and lightly browned. Cool.

4. Meanwhile, in a medium bowl, combine yogurt cheese, horseradish, shallots, dill, chives and 1 tbsp/15 mL pepper. Taste and add salt if necessary.

5. Arrange one square of phyllo on each plate. Place a large spoonful of yogurt mixture on top. Top with a curled slice of salmon. Top with another layer of phyllo, yogurt cheese and salmon. Repeat with last layer, a curl of salmon and a sprig of dill.

PER SERVING

Calories	263
Protein	18.9 g
Fat	10.2 g
Saturates	4.6 g
Cholesterol	31 mg
Carbohydrate	23.3 g
Fibre	1 g
Sodium	654 mg
Potassium	356 mg

Excellent: Niacin; Vitamin B₁₂
Good: Thiamine; Riboflavin;
Calcium; Zinc

ROAST CORNISH HENS WITH HERBS

This looks sophisticated yet comforting. Cooking with the skin keeps the bird juicy but adds no fat if you remove it. If you can only find larger Cornish hens, serve half a bird per person.

Makes 8 servings

16	cloves garlic, peeled	16
16	lemon wedges	16
8	small Cornish hens (about 1 lb/500 g each)	8
2 tbsp	olive oil	25 mL
3	cloves garlic, minced	3
2 tbsp	chopped fresh rosemary, or 1 tsp/5 mL dried	25 mL
2 tbsp	chopped fresh sage, or 1 tsp/5 mL dried	25 mL
2 tbsp	chopped fresh tarragon, or 1 tsp/5 mL dried	25 mL
2 tbsp	chopped fresh thyme, or 1 tsp/5 mL dried	25 mL
1 tsp	salt	5 mL
½ tsp	pepper	2 mL
2 cups	homemade chicken stock (page 79)	500 mL
2 tbsp	soy sauce	25 mL
2 tbsp	Worcestershire sauce	25 mL
2 tbsp	all-purpose flour	25 mL
1 tbsp	soft non-hydrogenated margarine	15 mL

1. Place 2 whole cloves garlic and 2 lemon wedges in each hen.

2. In small bowl, combine oil, minced garlic, rosemary, sage, tarragon, thyme, salt and pepper. Gently separate skin from breast and thigh of each hen. Rub meat with herb mixture. Rub extra over skin. Arrange birds on parchment-lined baking sheets.

3. Roast birds in a preheated 400°F/200°C oven for 45 minutes or until well browned and cooked through. Baste occasionally. Place birds on a platter and transfer pan juices to a measuring cup.

4. To make sauce, spoon off fat from pan juices. Place juices in a saucepan with stock, soy sauce and Worcestershire and bring to a boil. Cook for a few minutes.

5. In a small bowl, combine flour and margarine. Stir into sauce and cook until just slightly thickened. Adjust seasonings. Serve hens with sauce on the side.

SERVING SUGGESTION
- Bring the birds to the table on a large platter. Serve on a bed of fresh sage or bay leaves and garnish with lemon slices. Fresh figs also make a lovely garnish.

MAKE AHEAD
- Assemble everything ahead of time but roast just before serving.

PER SERVING (WITHOUT SKIN)

Calories	322
Protein	42.3 g
Fat	13.4 g
Saturates	2.9 g
Cholesterol	182 mg
Carbohydrate	6 g
Fibre	0.3 g
Sodium	727 mg
Potassium	549 mg

Excellent: Riboflavin; Niacin; Vitamin B_6; Vitamin B_{12}; Zinc
Good: Iron

POLENTA WITH WILD MUSHROOMS

- This makes a great vegetarian entree.
- Cut into small squares and serve as an appetizer.

MAKE AHEAD
- This can all be made ahead and reheated.

White Truffle Oil
White truffle oil is olive oil infused with white truffles. White (and black) truffles are incredibly aromatic fungi found buried at the roots of trees such as oaks and poplars in Italy and France. You can buy the oil in specialty stores.

PER SERVING

Calories	300
Protein	13.9 g
Fat	7.4 g
Saturates	2.6 g
Cholesterol	12 mg
Carbohydrate	44.6 g
Fibre	2.8 g
Sodium	729 mg
Potassium	672 mg

Excellent: Riboflavin; Calcium
Good: Vitamin A; Niacin; Folacin; Vitamin B$_{12}$; Zinc

Polenta can be served in many different ways. It can be served creamy style, but most people prefer it firm like this the first couple of times they have it, as the texture is more familiar. After the polenta firms up you can grill it, broil it, roast it, fry it or just warm it up.

I use the quick-cooking cornmeal for polenta. Otherwise use regular cornmeal but cook the polenta slowly, stirring often, until tender, about 20 to 30 minutes.

Leftover polenta can be cut up and used as croutons in salads, or you can add pizza toppings and reheat. It is also delicious cold.

Makes 8 servings

10 cups	milk or water, or a combination	2.5 L
2 tsp	salt	10 mL
½ tsp	pepper	2 mL
2 cups	quick-cooking cornmeal	500 mL
1 tbsp	white truffle oil, optional	15 mL
2 tbsp	olive oil	25 mL
1	onion, thinly sliced	1
3	cloves garlic, finely chopped	3
1 lb	portobello mushrooms, trimmed and sliced	500 g
	Salt and pepper to taste	
¼ cup	fresh parsley leaves	50 mL

1. Place milk in a large, deep saucepan. Bring to a boil. Add salt and pepper. Whisk in cornmeal slowly. Reduce heat to medium low. Cook for about 5 minutes stirring with a wooden spoon. Stir in truffle oil (if using). Taste and adjust seasonings if necessary. Pour polenta into two 8- or 9-inch/1.5 or 2 L round baking dishes lined with parchment paper on the bottom. Cool.

2. Brush polenta with a little of the olive oil and reheat in a preheated 400°F/200°C oven for 20 to 30 minutes. You could also remove polenta from pans, cut into wedges and barbecue or cook in a grill pan or non-stick skillet until browned and crisp.

3. Meanwhile, heat remaining olive oil in a large skillet on medium-high heat. Add onion and garlic. Cook until wilted. Add mushrooms and cook until any liquid evaporates. Season with salt and pepper. Spoon mushrooms over polenta and garnish with parsley.

FENNEL, ENDIVE AND RED PEPPER SALAD

This salad is light and delicate. Use leftovers as a sandwich topping.

Makes 8 servings

2	bulbs fennel (about 1 lb/500 g each)	2
4	Belgian endives (about 4 oz/125 g each)	4
1	sweet red pepper	1
3 tbsp	rice vinegar (page 132)	45 mL
1 tbsp	olive oil	15 mL
	Salt and pepper to taste	
2	green onions, thinly sliced on the diagonal	2

1. Cut tops off fennel. Cut in half lengthwise and remove cores. Slice lengthwise into thin strips. Place in a large bowl.

2. Trim endives. Cut in half lengthwise. Slice into thin strips and add to fennel.

3. Cut red pepper in half. Remove ribs and seeds. Slice into thin strips. Combine with fennel and endives.

4. In a small bowl, combine vinegar, oil, salt and pepper. Toss with salad. Sprinkle with green onions.

Grilled Fennel, Endive and Red Pepper Salad

Slice the endive and fennel into wedges and grill (the endive will only take a minute). Cut the peppers in half, remove the ribs and seeds and grill skin side down until blackened. Peel and then cut into strips. Serve with the dressing above or with tomato soy dressing (page 116).

MAKE AHEAD
• This can be made up to a day ahead without the endive. Add endive just before serving.

PER SERVING

Calories	62
Protein	2 g
Fat	2 g
Saturates	0.2 g
Cholesterol	0 mg
Carbohydrate	10.9 g
Fibre	4 g
Sodium	60 mg
Potassium	572 mg

Excellent: Vitamin C; Folacin

FROZEN LEMON MERINGUE CAKE

This looks spectacular garnished with frozen grapes. When frozen, the grapes take on a frosted, glazed look. They have about 15 minutes of fame and then start to defrost, so remove the grapes from the freezer just before serving.

Makes 10 to 12 servings

1½ cups	granulated sugar, divided	375 mL
2 tbsp	cornstarch	25 mL
6	egg whites (about ¾ cup/175 mL)	6
¼ tsp	cream of tartar	1 mL
1 tsp	vanilla	5 mL

Filling

⅓ cup	cornstarch	75 mL
1¼ cups	granulated sugar	300 mL
2	eggs	2
1 cup	lemon juice	250 mL
⅔ cup	orange juice	150 mL
2 tbsp	grated lemon peel	25 mL
2 cups	light ricotta cheese, pureed until smooth	500 mL
	Icing sugar	

1. Trace four 8-inch/20 cm circles on two baking sheets lined with parchment paper.

2. Prepare meringues by combining ¾ cup/175 mL sugar with cornstarch in a small bowl. Reserve.

3. Place egg whites in a large stainless-steel or glass bowl. Add cream of tartar. With an electric mixer, whip egg whites until they start to turn opaque. Beat in remaining ¾ cup/175 mL sugar until white, opaque and firm. Beat in vanilla. Fold in cornstarch/sugar mixture.

SERVING SUGGESTIONS

- For New Year's, a birthday or any celebration, put sparklers or tall candles in the cake and light them as you bring it to the table.
- Serve on a pedestal platter.
- Garnish with sprigs of fresh mint.
- Serve with raspberry sauce (page 296) or chocolate sauce (page 272).

MAKE AHEAD

- This can all be made ahead and then frozen. Be sure to defrost the cake for about 30 minutes before serving. If you are using frozen grapes, remove them from the freezer just before serving.

PER SERVING

Calories	330
Protein	9.2 g
Fat	3.5 g
Saturates	1.8 g
Cholesterol	58 mg
Carbohydrate	67 g
Fibre	0.3 g
Sodium	108 mg
Potassium	166 mg

Good: Vitamin B$_{12}$

4. Spoon or pipe meringue onto baking sheet to fill circles. Smooth tops to make meringues level. Bake in a preheated 300°F/150°C oven for 1 hour until dry. Cool completely.

5. Meanwhile, for filling, in a large saucepan, combine cornstarch and sugar and mix well. Whisk in eggs, lemon juice, orange juice and lemon peel. Bring to a boil and cook gently, stirring, until thick. Transfer to a large bowl and cool. (If you put custard over a large bowl filled with ice and water, it will chill more quickly.) Fold in pureed ricotta.

6. To assemble, place one meringue in a 9-inch/23 cm springform pan. (Trim it to fit if necessary — sometimes the meringues expand when baked.) Spread with one-third of the filling. Place another meringue on top, spread with another one-third of the filling. Top with third meringue and spread with the remaining filling. Take the fourth meringue (the least nice-looking one), break it into pieces and sprinkle over the top. Dust with icing sugar. Freeze for at least a few hours.

7. Remove cake from springform and place on a cake stand about 30 minutes before serving.

DIABETES

Diabetes, a condition in which one lacks or is resistant to the hormone insulin, affects more than one million Canadians. The result is an inability to convert sugar to energy for the body to use. Left untreated, diabetes can increase the risk of heart disease, kidney disease and other problems of circulation.

The most common form of diabetes is Type 2. Many people with Type 2 diabetes are overweight, physically inactive and/or have high blood pressure. The treatment is generally lifestyle modification — a healthy diet balanced with exercise, and medication if required.

Type 1 diabetes typically appears before the age of thirty. The treatment includes diet and exercise as well as daily injections of insulin.

Healthy eating for diabetes involves a balanced, low-fat eating plan that includes whole grain breads and cereals, fresh fruits and vegetables, lean proteins such as lean meat or meat alternates, chicken without the skin, fish and low-fat dairy products. You should eat at least three well-balanced meals per day with portion sizes that help you achieve and maintain a healthy weight. This well-balanced diet will help control blood sugar levels and so lower your risk of developing complications. Refer to the Canadian Diabetes Association Food Choice Values (pages 305-311) to help with meal planning.

MEAT

TERIYAKI NOODLES WITH BEEF   *194*

GRILLED FLANK STEAK AND VEGETABLE SALAD   *196*

STRIPLOIN ROAST WITH WILD MUSHROOMS   *198*

SOUTHWESTERN BARBECUED BRISKET   *200*

GRILLED STEAK SANDWICHES WITH MELTED ONIONS   *202*

POT ROAST OF LAMB WITH TOMATOES AND ORZO   *204*

MOROCCAN-SPICED LAMB SHANKS   *206*

MISO-GLAZED LAMB CHOPS WITH CARAMELIZED SOY DRIZZLE   *208*

RACK OF LAMB WITH HONEY CRUST   *209*

CROWN ROAST OF PORK   *210*

BONELESS "SPARERIB" ROAST WITH POLENTA   *212*

MORE MEAT DISHES

POT ROAST OF BEEF WITH ROOT VEGETABLES   *86*

LAMB BIRYANI   *112*

BALSAMIC MAPLE-GLAZED LAMB CHOPS WITH SWEET POTATOES   *218*

TERIYAKI NOODLES WITH BEEF

MAKE AHEAD
- Make ahead and serve at room temperature. Or cook beef and pasta ahead and toss together to reheat before serving.

Teriyaki Sauce
Combine 3 tbsp/45 mL soy sauce, 3 tbsp/45 mL water, 3 tbsp/45 mL rice wine, 3 tbsp/45 mL granulated sugar, 1 peeled and smashed clove garlic, 1-inch/2.5 cm piece smashed fresh ginger root and 1-inch/2.5 cm piece lemon peel in a small saucepan. Bring to a boil and cook until mixture is reduced by half. Cool and remove garlic, ginger and lemon peel. Makes about ⅓ cup/75 mL.

PER SERVING

Calories	443
Protein	25.5 g
Fat	11.3 g
Saturates	2.9 g
Cholesterol	31 mg
Carbohydrate	58 g
Fibre	4.2 g
Sodium	488 mg
Potassium	607 mg

Excellent: Vitamin A; Vitamin C; Thiamine; Niacin; Folacin; Vitamin B$_{12}$; Zinc
Good: Riboflavin; Vitamin B$_{12}$; Iron

This is a recipe that everyone in the family will love. You can also use soba or udon noodles (you should have about 6 cups/1.5 L cooked noodles) and you can substitute chicken for the beef. You can also add 1 cup/250 mL of bean sprouts at the end of step 6.

Makes 6 servings

1 lb	flank steak, partially frozen	500 g
⅓ cup	teriyaki sauce, divided	75 mL
¾ lb	penne, fusilli or spaghetti	375 g
2 tbsp	vegetable oil, divided	25 mL
1	onion, thinly sliced	1
1	carrot, thinly sliced	1
1	sweet red pepper, thinly sliced	1
1	stalk celery, thinly sliced	1
3	shiitake mushrooms, stems removed, sliced	3
1½ cups	sliced broccoli florets and stems	375 mL
⅔ cup	boiling water	150 mL
4	green onions, sliced on the diagonal	4

1. Slice flank steak as thinly as possible, on the diagonal against the grain. Cut each slice into thirds crosswise.

2. Place steak in a bowl and toss with 1 tbsp/15 mL teriyaki sauce. Marinate for about 10 minutes or up to a few hours in refrigerator.

3. Bring a large pot of water to a boil. Add pasta and cook until almost tender. Drain well.

4. Meanwhile, heat 1 tbsp/15 mL oil in a large, deep skillet or wok. Add steak and cook for about 2 minutes or until meat loses its raw appearance. Remove meat from pan and reserve. Clean wok if necessary and return to heat.

5. Heat remaining 1 tbsp/15 mL oil in wok. Add onion, carrot, red pepper, celery, mushrooms and broccoli. Stir-fry for 3 to 4 minutes, or until vegetables are brightly coloured and beginning to become tender.

6. Add steak to vegetables. Add remaining 5 tbsp/60 mL teriyaki sauce and boiling water. Bring to a boil and simmer for about 2 minutes. Add pasta to wok. Cook for a few minutes, tossing, until pasta absorbs juices but is still moist. Sprinkle with green onions before serving.

IRON

Iron is necessary for producing haemoglobin, the part of red blood cells that carries oxygen through the body. Iron-deficiency anaemia is one of the most common nutritional deficiencies in North America. It is especially a problem for many women in their childbearing years, people on calorie-restricted diets, teenagers and children.

There are two kinds of iron in our food: heme and non-heme. Heme iron is found in red meat, fish and poultry and is better absorbed than the non-heme iron found in enriched cereals, some dark green vegetables and certain fruits, such as raisins. To enhance the absorption of non-heme iron, eat the iron-rich food with something that contains vitamin C. For example, if you eat a bowl of iron-enriched cereal (such as bran flakes) with a glass of orange juice, you will better absorb the iron from the cereal. It has been shown that the tannins in tea interfere with iron absorption, so it is a good idea to save your cup of tea until after you have eaten your meal.

If you are iron deficient, discuss your diet and the possibility of supplementation with your doctor and dietitian.

Recommended Nutrient Intake of Iron: 8 to 14 mg per day

3 oz/90 g cooked beef	3.0 mg
1 cup/250 mL chili with beans	4.5 mg
¼ cup/50 mL sunflower seeds	2.5 mg
½ cup/125 mL cooked kidney beans	2.4 mg
½ cup/125 mL prune juice	1.6 mg
½ cup/125 mL raisins	1.8 mg
½ cup/125 mL cooked spinach	3.4 mg
½ cup/125 mL cooked enriched cream of wheat	7.9 mg
¾ cup/175 mL enriched bran flakes	5.3 mg

GRILLED FLANK STEAK AND VEGETABLE SALAD

SERVING SUGGESTION
• Serve on a long oval platter for a different look.

MAKE AHEAD
• You can make this ahead and serve at room temperature.

People are always amazed that flank steak can be so delicious. It is lean and inexpensive. Just be sure to cook it rare and slice it thinly against the grain.

If you wish, you can remove the gills from the mushrooms with a small spoon before grilling (see diagram).

Makes 6 servings

1 tbsp	Dijon mustard	15 mL
1 tbsp	brown sugar	15 mL
1	clove garlic, minced	1
1 tbsp	balsamic or sherry vinegar	15 mL
1 tsp	pepper	5 mL
1 tsp	ground cumin	5 mL
1	1¼-lb/625 g flank steak, well trimmed	1
2	sweet red peppers, halved and seeded	2
2	sweet yellow peppers, halved and seeded	2
2	medium zucchini, cut in ½-inch/1 cm slices on the diagonal	2
2	thin eggplants, cut in ½-inch/1 cm slices on the diagonal	2
2	portobello mushrooms, stems removed	2
1	large sweet onion, cut in ½-inch/2 cm slices	1

Mustard Horseradish Vinaigrette Dressing

2	cloves garlic, minced	2
1 tbsp	finely grated white horseradish	15 mL
1 tsp	Dijon mustard	5 mL
¼ cup	balsamic vinegar	50 mL
¼ cup	olive oil	50 mL
¼ cup	fresh basil leaves, torn in ½-inch/1 cm pieces	50 mL

PER SERVING

Calories	341
Protein	24.3 g
Fat	16.7 g
Saturates	4.3 g
Cholesterol	36 mg
Carbohydrate	25.4 g
Fibre	5.5 g
Sodium	101 mg
Potassium	937 mg

Excellent: Vitamin A; Vitamin C; Niacin; Vitamin B_6; Vitamin B_{12}; Zinc
Good: Thiamine; Riboflavin; Folacin; Iron

1. In a small bowl, combine mustard, brown sugar, garlic, vinegar, pepper and cumin. Rub into steak and marinate for 1 to 12 hours in refrigerator.

2. Grill steak on medium-high for 3 to 4 minutes per side for rare. Allow to rest for 5 to 30 minutes before carving.

3. Meanwhile, grill peppers, skin side down, until blackened. Cool and peel. Cut into 1-inch/2.5 cm slices.

4. Grill zucchini, eggplants, mushrooms and onion on both sides until brown and cooked through. Slice mushrooms and onions.

5. Cut steak on the diagonal, against the grain, into thin slices. Combine with grilled vegetables in a large bowl and toss.

6. In a small bowl, combine garlic, horseradish, mustard, vinegar and oil. Toss with salad. Sprinkle with basil.

How to Tell When a Steak Is Done

When you order a medium-rare steak in a restaurant, it never arrives at the table with little slits in it so the chef could peek to see whether it was ready! An experienced grill chef can tell by pressing down on the meat how well done it is. You can do this, too. Relax your forearm on a table and feel the muscle in your upper arm; that's what a rare steak feels like when you press it. Now raise your forearm off the table but don't make a muscle; that's medium. Now make a hard muscle; that's well done. (This method does vary slightly, depending on how much resistance training you have had!)

STRIPLOIN ROAST WITH WILD MUSHROOMS

SERVING SUGGESTION
• Serve with polenta
(page 213), mashed or
roasted potatoes, roasted
vegetables (page 96) or
risotto patties (page 140).

MAKE AHEAD
• You can brown the meat a
few hours ahead, but roast
just before serving.
• The shallots and mush-
rooms can be cooked
ahead and reheated.

A striploin roast is amazingly tender with great flavour. If your butcher does not have one, use a boneless rib roast of the same size and weight. Or you can use a filet roast, but reduce the cooking to only 40 minutes in total for medium-rare (start checking with a meat thermometer after about 30 minutes, depending on the thickness of the roast). You can also use a flank steak — cook for 3 to 4 minutes per side in a grill pan or on the barbecue.

Leftover beef can be sliced very thinly and wrapped around breadsticks or barely cooked asparagus spears for appetizers. You can also use it in sandwiches or serve cold with potato salad (page 90).

Makes 10 to 12 servings

1 tbsp	Dijon mustard	15 mL
2	cloves garlic, minced	2
1 tbsp	pepper	15 mL
1 tbsp	Worcestershire sauce	15 mL
1 tbsp	chopped fresh rosemary, or ½ tsp/2 mL dried	15 mL
4 lb	striploin roast, well trimmed and tied (about 2½ inches/6 cm thick)	2 kg
1 tsp	salt	5 mL
1 tsp	olive oil	5 mL
1 lb	shallots (about 12), peeled (page 173) and quartered	500 g
2 tbsp	balsamic vinegar	25 mL
2 cups	dry red wine	500 mL
1 lb	wild mushrooms (portobello, shiitake, oyster, or a combination), trimmed and cut in ½-inch/1 cm slices	500 g
⅓ cup	oyster sauce	75 mL
2 tbsp	coarsely chopped fresh parsley	25 mL

PER SERVING

Calories	341
Protein	39.5 g
Fat	13.3 g
Saturates	5.0 g
Cholesterol	80 mg
Carbohydrate	11.9 g
Fibre	2.1 g
Sodium	584 mg
Potassium	808 mg

Excellent: Niacin; Vitamin B$_6$;
Vitamin B$_{12}$; Iron; Zinc
Good: Riboflavin

1. In a small bowl, combine mustard, garlic, pepper, Worcestershire and rosemary. Pat roast dry and rub mustard mixture into roast. Marinate for 30 minutes at room temperature or longer in refrigerator. Just before cooking, sprinkle roast with salt.

2. Heat oil in a large non-stick skillet on high heat. Brown roast well on all sides — this should take about 10 minutes. Transfer roast to a baking sheet lined with parchment paper. Discard all but 1 tbsp/15 mL fat from skillet.

3. Roast meat in a preheated 375°F/190°C oven for 45 minutes, or until a meat thermometer inserted in thickest part of meat registers 130°F/55°C for medium-rare. Allow roast to rest for 10 to 20 minutes before carving.

4. Meanwhile, return skillet to heat. Add shallots and vinegar. Cook, stirring, until vinegar evaporates and shallots begin to brown. Add wine. Cook on medium-high heat, scraping pan, until wine reduces to about ½ cup/125 mL and shallots are tender.

5. Add mushrooms to pan and cook until wilted and browned. Add oyster sauce and cook for 5 minutes. Add parsley and taste and adjust seasonings if necessary.

6. Remove string from roast and carve into slices. Top with mushrooms, shallots and juices.

Butterflied Leg of Lamb with Wild Mushrooms
Use a butterflied leg of lamb instead of beef. Cook for about 30 minutes for rare (test with a meat thermometer).

SOUTHWESTERN BARBECUED BRISKET

SERVING SUGGESTIONS
• Serve slices of brisket draped over mashed potatoes or diamond-shaped slices of polenta.
• Serve in oversized pasta bowls.
• Serve brisket with a spoonful of guacamole and/or a drizzle of goat cheese thinned with milk and warmed.

MAKE AHEAD
• Brisket can be made ahead and reheated. It can also be frozen.

Brisket was something I had often growing up in a Jewish household, but we never had brisket even remotely this daring! (For a more traditional version, see the variation.) One of the best things about this dish is the leftovers, which you can make into a shepherd's pie, burritos (top with yogurt cheese and lots of fresh cilantro) or quesadillas (add smoked mozzarella). I like to make this the day before serving; I can then chill it so it will slice better, and I can easily defat the juices.

Makes 16 servings

4 lb	beef brisket, trimmed of excess fat	2 kg
1 tsp	salt	5 mL
1 tsp	pepper	5 mL
1 tbsp	paprika	15 mL
1 tsp	ground cumin	5 mL
½ tsp	cayenne	2 mL
3	large onions, sliced	3
2	carrots, sliced	2
1	head garlic, separated in cloves (about 12), peeled	1
1 cup	ketchup	250 mL
1 cup	commercial or homemade chili sauce	250 mL
1	chipotle or jalapeño, minced	1
2 tbsp	Dijon mustard	25 mL
2 tbsp	brown sugar	25 mL
2 tbsp	red wine vinegar or sherry vinegar	25 mL
1½ cups	beer or beef stock (page 86) or water	375 mL

1. Pat brisket dry. In a small bowl, combine salt, pepper, paprika, cumin and cayenne. Rub on brisket. Allow to marinate for 5 minutes or up to overnight in refrigerator.

2. Place onions, carrots and garlic cloves in bottom of a large roasting pan. Place brisket on top of vegetables.

3. In a large measuring cup, combine ketchup, chili sauce, chipotle, mustard, sugar, vinegar and beer. Pour over brisket. Cover tightly. Roast in a preheated 350°F/180°C oven for 4 hours, checking every 45 minutes to make sure there is always about 2 cups/500 mL liquid in pot. Add water if necessary. Uncover and roast for 30 minutes longer.

PER SERVING

Calories	216
Protein	18.8 g
Fat	8.6 g
Saturates	3.1 g
Cholesterol	45 mg
Carbohydrate	16.2 g
Fibre	2.1 g
Sodium	648 mg
Potassium	413 mg

Excellent: Vitamin A; Niacin; Vitamin B$_{12}$; Zinc
Good: Vitamin B$_6$; Iron

4. Transfer roast to a carving board. Skim fat from juices (or blot off quickly using paper towels). Carve roast and serve with juices. If you are not serving immediately, cool and then chill meat and vegetables. Put juices in a bowl and chill as well. Before reheating, slice brisket against grain into thin slices. Place in a baking dish with vegetables. Remove and discard any fat from top of juices (it will have come to surface and solidified). Spoon juices on top of meat. Cover and heat in a 350°F/180°C oven for approximately 45 minutes.

Friday Night Brisket

Add 3 more carrots to the onions and garlic. Omit cumin and cayenne from the rub. Omit chipotles from the sauce and use water or gingerale instead of beer.

Shepherd's Pie

Combine about 3 cups/750 mL cubed leftover brisket or pot roast (page 86) with 3 cups/750 mL leftover cooked vegetables. Chop finely by hand or in a food processor. Spoon mixture into a deep 10-inch/25 cm pie dish or 9-inch/2 L square baking dish. Beat 3 cups/750 mL cooked mashed potatoes (or mashed sweet potatoes or other root vegetable) until spreadable and spoon in a layer on top of meat and vegetables. Dust with paprika. Bake at 350°F/180°C for 30 to 45 minutes, or until hot. Makes 8 servings .

GRILLED STEAK SANDWICHES WITH MELTED ONIONS

Garlic Mayonnaise
Squeeze pulp from 4 heads roasted garlic (page 41). Blend with 2 tbsp/25 mL mayonnaise and 2 tbsp/ 25 mL yogurt cheese (page 303). Makes about ½ cup/125 mL.

These sandwiches are perfect for a casual barbecue, but for a fancier dinner just serve the steak sliced over mashed potatoes or polenta with the onions on top. Either way it is delicious.

When you grill a whole steak rather than small individual ones, the results are often juicier and the thin slices look like more. You can also make this with flank steak (you may need two, as they are about 1 lb/500 g each). Add 2 tbsp/25 mL balsamic vinegar to the marinade and marinate the steak overnight.

Use diced leftover steak in salads, stir-fries, wraps, burritos or tacos. Leftover onions can be used in omelettes, frittatas, quiches, soups, crostini or bruschetta.

Makes 8 servings

1 tbsp	brown sugar	15 mL
2	cloves garlic, minced	2
1 tsp	coarsely ground pepper	5 mL
1 tsp	coarse salt	5 mL
1 tsp	olive oil	5 mL
2 lb	sirloin steak, about 1½ inches/4 cm thick, trimmed	1 kg

Melted Onions

2 tbsp	olive oil	25 mL
4	large sweet onions, thinly sliced	4
1 tbsp	brown sugar	15 mL
¼ cup	balsamic vinegar	50 mL
	Salt and pepper to taste	
2	French sticks (each about 16 inches/40 cm long)	2
1	bunch arugula	1

1. In a small bowl, combine brown sugar, garlic, pepper and salt. Pat steak dry, brush with oil and rub with sugar mixture. Marinate for 1 hour at room temperature or up to overnight in refrigerator.

PER SERVING

Calories	488
Protein	30.7 g
Fat	11.4 g
Saturates	2.9 g
Cholesterol	51 mg
Carbohydrate	65.6 g
Fibre	4.4 g
Sodium	774 mg
Potassium	712 mg

Excellent: Thiamine; Riboflavin; Niacin; Vitamin B$_6$; Folacin; Vitamin B$_{12}$; Iron; Zinc

2. To prepare onions, heat 2 tbsp/25 mL oil in a large, deep skillet on medium-high heat. Add onions. Cook for 10 minutes, without stirring, until onions begin to brown. Reduce heat to medium and cook, stirring occasionally, for 30 minutes. Onions should be very brown. Add sugar and vinegar and cook gently, adding water if necessary, until onions are very tender and "melted." Keep warm or reheat before serving.

3. Cut each French stick into four pieces and then cut each piece in half horizontally.

4. Grill steak for 4 to 6 minutes per side for medium. Let steak rest on a carving board for at least 5 minutes and then slice thinly on the diagonal.

5. Drape slices of steak on bread and smear with onions. Top with arugula.

Grilled Lamb Sandwiches
Use a boneless, butterflied leg of lamb instead of steak. Double the marinade. Cook lamb for about 10 to 15 minutes per side for rare. (Check temperature with a meat thermometer; the internal temperature should be 130°F/55°C.)

Grilled Turkey Sandwiches
Use a boneless, skinless turkey breast instead of steak. Grill for about 15 to 20 minutes per side, making sure it is cooked through (165°F/75°C).

SERVING SUGGESTIONS
• Serve with garlic mayonnaise (page 202).
• Serve sandwiches in shallow wicker baskets lined with brightly coloured napkins.
• Arrange ingredients like a buffet and let guests assemble their own sandwiches.
• Serve as an appetizer by using rounds of French stick spread with garlic mayonnaise, a slice of steak and a spoonful of onions.
• Serve sliced steak over salad greens with balsamic dressing (page 96).
• Use as a topping on potato crostini (page 58).

MAKE AHEAD
• The onions can be made weeks ahead and frozen or a few days ahead and refrigerated. The steak can be marinated a day ahead.
• The sandwiches can be made ahead and served at room temperature.

POT ROAST OF LAMB
WITH TOMATOES AND ORZO

MAKE AHEAD
- This is a perfect make-ahead dish. Slice when cold and reheat in reserved sauce. Reheat orzo or cook orzo fresh.

This recipe is always a big hit. It has a Greek influence and tastes wonderfully hearty and robust. You could also make it with a beef pot roast instead of lamb.

Orzo is rice-shaped pasta, but you can use any small pasta in this, or you could use rice (precook it for 10 minutes and then finish cooking in the sauce until tender). You can also omit the pasta, reduce the sauce until it is thicker and serve this over mashed potatoes or polenta. Use leftovers in wraps or chop and serve as a stew. You could also grind the meat and use the orzo as a different topping for shepherd's pie (page 201).

Makes 10 to 12 servings

4 lb	boneless leg or shoulder of lamb, well trimmed, rolled and tied	2 kg
1 tsp	salt	5 mL
¼ tsp	pepper	1 mL
1 tbsp	olive oil	15 mL
3	onions, coarsely chopped	3
20	cloves garlic, peeled	20
2 tbsp	ground cumin	25 mL
1 tbsp	dried oregano	15 mL
1	28-oz/796 mL can plum tomatoes with juices	1
1 cup	dry white or red wine, homemade chicken stock (page 79) or water	250 mL
1 lb	orzo or other small pasta (3 cups/750 mL)	500 g
	Bunch of fresh parsley	

PER SERVING

Calories	447
Protein	45.3 g
Fat	9.6 g
Saturates	3.3 g
Cholesterol	132 mg
Carbohydrate	43 g
Fibre	3.5 g
Sodium	447 mg
Potassium	655 mg

Excellent: Riboflavin; Niacin; Iron; Zinc
Good: Vitamin B$_6$; Folacin

1. Pat roast dry and season with salt and pepper.

2. Heat oil in a heavy Dutch oven on high heat. Add lamb and brown well on all sides. Remove roast from pan. Discard all but 1 tbsp/15 mL fat from pan.

3. Add onions and garlic to pan. Reduce heat to medium and cook for a few minutes. Add cumin and oregano and cook for 1 to 2 minutes. Add tomatoes and wine and bring to a boil. Break up tomatoes with a spoon. Add roast, spooning some tomato mixture on top.

4. Cover and cook in a preheated 350°F/180°C oven for 3 to 4 hours, or until meat is very tender. Check every 30 minutes or so to be sure there are always a few cups of liquid in pan.

5. Meanwhile, cook orzo in a large pot of boiling water for 5 minutes. Drain, rinse with cold water and drain again.

6. Remove roast from pan to a carving board. Skim any fat from surface of the sauce and discard. Place pan on heat and bring to a boil. Cook over medium-high heat until you have about 5 cups/1.25 L sauce (if there isn't enough sauce, add some stock or water).

7. Reserve about 1 cup/250 mL sauce. Add orzo to remaining 4 cups/1 L liquid in pan and cook for 5 minutes or until very tender. Taste and adjust seasonings if necessary.

8. Slice roast, place in a large, deep serving dish and moisten with reserved sauce. Spoon orzo around lamb and garnish with parsley.

CHOLESTEROL

Cholesterol is a waxy, fatlike substance produced by the body. It helps produce hormones, enables the brain to function properly and maintains the body's nerve structure.

Cholesterol is transported to and from cells in the form of lipoproteins. The two main lipoproteins are HDL (High Density Lipoprotein) and LDL (Low Density Lipoprotein). HDL is commonly called "good" cholesterol because it carries excess blood cholesterol back to the liver to be excreted from the body. LDL is called "bad" cholesterol because it is the kind of cholesterol that builds up on artery walls. A high level of LDL-cholesterol in the blood is associated with an increased risk of heart disease. Ideally, you should have high levels of HDL-cholesterol and low levels of LDL-cholesterol.

The body produces cholesterol regardless of what you eat. In fact, most of the cholesterol in your blood is made by the liver. To lower levels of LDL-cholesterol, reduce your intake of fat, especially saturated fats and trans-fatty acids (page 222). Include some unsaturated fat in your diet and increase your intake of soluble fibre. To raise your HDL-cholesterol levels, exercise regularly and maintain a healthy weight.

The cholesterol in food has less impact on blood cholesterol than the saturated fat in food. So the best defense is a low-fat diet. However, for some people, too many cholesterol- containing foods can raise blood cholesterol. The foods that contain cholesterol are animal products such as egg yolks, liver, shrimp, squid and fatty meats. If your blood cholesterol is elevated, you should moderate your intake of these foods.

MOROCCAN-SPICED LAMB SHANKS

This recipe is roughly based on one created by talented chef Craig Domville of Le Paradis bistro in Toronto. Lamb shanks look very large served whole, so I like to remove the meat from the bones and serve it like a stew. Leftovers can be shredded and used to fill wraps.

Makes 8 servings

SERVING SUGGESTIONS
- This looks very impressive brought to the table on a large platter with the cous-cous spooned around the lamb.
- Serve with harissa.

MAKE AHEAD
- This is a perfect dish to make ahead because it reheats so well, and all the fat can be removed when the sauce is cold.

Harissa
Harissa is a spicy condiment traditionally used in Moroccan food. You can find it in Middle Eastern stores, but it is also easy to make yourself. Combine 3 tbsp/45 mL paprika, 2 tsp/ 10 mL cayenne, 1 tsp/5 mL ground cumin, 1 tsp/5 mL salt and ⅓ cup/75 mL olive oil. Use in small quantities.

PER SERVING

Calories	662
Protein	45.6 g
Fat	15.3 g
Saturates	4.8 g
Cholesterol	106 mg
Carbohydrate	83.4 g
Fibre	6.1 g
Sodium	788 mg
Potassium	1013 mg

Excellent: Thiamine; Niacin; Vitamin B$_6$; Folacin; Vitamin B$_{12}$; Iron; Zinc
Good: Riboflavin

6	lamb shanks (about 12 oz/375 g each)	6
1 tsp	dried thyme	5 mL
1 tsp	dried rosemary	5 mL
1½ cups	dry red wine	375 mL
1 tbsp	olive oil	15 mL
2 tsp	ground coriander	10 mL
2 tsp	ground cumin	10 mL
1 tsp	cinnamon	5 mL
1 tsp	turmeric	5 mL
1 tsp	fennel seed, or ½ tsp/2 mL ground fennel	5 mL
½ tsp	hot red pepper flakes	2 mL
2	onions, chopped	2
3	cloves garlic, finely chopped	3
1 tbsp	chopped fresh ginger root	15 mL
2	28-oz/796 mL cans plum tomatoes, drained and chopped (about 4 cups/1 L)	2
1 tbsp	tomato paste	15 mL
3 cups	homemade beef stock (page 86) or water	750 mL
4 cups	quick-cooking couscous	1 L
4 cups	boiling water or homemade stock	1 L
1 tsp	salt	5 mL
¼ tsp	pepper	1 mL
¼ cup	fresh cilantro leaves	50 mL

1. Trim any fat from lamb and discard. Place lamb shanks in a large dish and sprinkle with thyme and rosemary. Pour wine over lamb. Marinate for a few hours or overnight in refrigerator. Remove lamb from marinade and pat dry. Reserve marinade.

2. Heat oil in a large, deep skillet or Dutch oven on high heat. Add lamb and brown well. Remove. Discard all but 1 tbsp/15 mL fat from pan.

3. In a small bowl, combine coriander, cumin, cinnamon, turmeric, fennel and hot pepper flakes. Add to skillet. Cook for 30 to 60 seconds until fragrant. Reduce heat to medium and add onions, garlic and ginger. Cook gently until very aromatic. Add tomatoes, tomato paste, stock and reserved marinade and bring to a boil. Add lamb shanks and salt and pepper if stock is unseasoned. Cover tightly and simmer for about 2½ hours, or until lamb is very tender. (You could also transfer to a baking dish and cook in the oven at 350°F/180°C for 2½ hours.)

4. Remove lamb from pan. If sauce is very thin, cook, uncovered, on medium-high heat until juices reduce and sauce thickens. You should have about 6 cups/1.5 L sauce.

5. Meanwhile, remove lamb meat from bones in large pieces. Return to sauce.

6. Place couscous in a 13 x 9-inch/3.5 L baking dish and add boiling water. Cover tightly with foil and allow to rest for 10 to 30 minutes. Fluff with a fork and season with salt and pepper. Serve with lamb and sprinkle with cilantro leaves.

Moroccan-spiced Chicken

Use a 2 to 4 lb/1 to 2 kg chicken, cut in pieces, instead of lamb. Cook for 45 minutes.

Carrot and Orange Salad
Cook 2 lb/1 kg thinly sliced carrots in boiling water for 4 minutes. Rinse with cold water and drain. In a large bowl, combine carrots, 2 tbsp/25 mL halved and pitted black olives and 4 peeled and segmented oranges. In a small bowl, combine ¼ cup/50 mL orange juice, ¼ cup/50 mL lemon juice, 2 tbsp/25 mL honey, pinch of cinnamon, 1 minced clove garlic and ½ tsp/2 mL salt. Combine with salad. Sprinkle with 2 tbsp/25 mL chopped fresh cilantro, 2 tbsp/25 mL chopped fresh mint and 2 chopped green onions. *Makes 8 servings.*

MISO-GLAZED LAMB CHOPS WITH CARAMELIZED SOY DRIZZLE

SERVING SUGGESTION
• Serve with green beans
and bean sprouts
(page 238).

MAKE AHEAD
• Marinate the lamb ahead
and cook just before serving; you can also cook the
lamb ahead and serve at
room temperature.

The miso glaze can also be used on a butterflied leg of lamb, pork chops, salmon or a sirloin steak. This drizzle is an idea from Mark McEwan, the creative chef/owner of North 44° in Toronto.

Leftovers can be sliced and added to a sushi salad (page 245).

Makes 6 servings

3 tbsp	light miso (page 226)	45 mL
1 tbsp	Dijon or Russian-style mustard	15 mL
1 tbsp	rice wine	15 mL
1 tbsp	brown sugar	15 mL
1 tsp	sesame oil	5 mL
12	thin rib lamb chops, well trimmed (about 3 oz/90 g each)	12

Caramelized Soy Drizzle

3 tbsp	granulated sugar	45 mL
3 tbsp	water	45 mL
¼ cup	soy sauce or balsamic vinegar	50 mL
¼ cup	water	50 mL
1 tbsp	chopped fresh ginger root	15 mL

1. In a small bowl, combine miso, mustard, rice wine, brown sugar and oil. Mix until smooth. If very thick, thin with 1 tbsp/15 mL water.

2. Place lamb in a shallow dish. Rub miso mixture into lamb. Marinate for up to 30 minutes at room temperature or overnight in refrigerator.

3. Meanwhile, to prepare drizzle, combine sugar and water in a medium saucepan on high heat. Bring to a boil and then, without stirring, cook until just golden brown. Standing back, add soy sauce, water and ginger. Cook for a few minutes until thick (it will thicken much more when it cools to room temperature). Add more water if mixture becomes too thick or too salty.

4. Just before serving, grill lamb chops for 2½ to 3 minutes per side for rare. Drizzle with soy mixture.

PER SERVING

Calories	181
Protein	15.7 g
Fat	7.3 g
Saturates	2.7 g
Cholesterol	54 mg
Carbohydrate	12.3 g
Fibre	0.8 g
Sodium	1064 mg
Potassium	141 mg

Excellent: Niacin; Vitamin B$_{12}$; Zinc

RACK OF LAMB WITH HONEY CRUST

Rack of lamb is a great dish to serve at a special dinner. I usually count on serving two chops per person with a couple of extra just in case someone really wants more! Have the butcher trim the racks, trim between the bones and remove the chine bone so that you can carve the rack easily.

Makes 6 servings

2	racks of lamb (with 7 ribs each), trimmed (about 1 lb/500 g each)	2
2 tbsp	balsamic vinegar	25 mL
2 tbsp	chopped fresh rosemary, or ½ tsp/2 mL dried	25 mL
2 tbsp	chopped fresh thyme, or ½ tsp/2 mL dried	25 mL
1 tsp	pepper	5 mL
2	cloves garlic, minced	2
½ tsp	salt	2 mL
½ tsp	olive oil	2 mL
2 tbsp	Dijon mustard	25 mL
2 tbsp	honey	25 mL
1 cup	fresh breadcrumbs	250 mL

1. Remove any visible fat from lamb.

2. In a small bowl, combine vinegar, rosemary, thyme, pepper and garlic. Rub on lamb and marinate for 30 minutes at room temperature or up to overnight in refrigerator.

3. Just before cooking, pat lamb dry. Season with salt.

4. Heat oil in a heavy non-stick skillet on high heat. Brown lamb for 2 to 3 minutes.

5. In a small bowl, combine mustard and honey. Smear on lamb. Place lamb on baking sheet and roast in a preheated 400°F/200°C oven for 15 minutes.

6. Remove lamb from oven. Pat breadcrumbs into top side of lamb. Return to baking sheet. Roast again for about 10 minutes, or until a meat thermometer registers 130 to 140°F/55 to 60°C (for rare) when inserted into muscle of meat. Allow racks to rest for 5 to 10 minutes before carving by slicing between bones.

Rack of Lamb with Honey Nut Crust

Use chopped toasted hazelnuts or pecans in place of half the breadcrumbs.

SERVING SUGGESTIONS
• Serve on a bed of roasted vegetables (page 96), rice or potatoes.
• Serve with caramelized soy drizzle (page 208) or teriyaki sauce (page 194).

MAKE AHEAD
• You can roast the racks for the first 15 minutes ahead of time. Then bread them and roast for 20 minutes longer just before serving. Use a meat thermometer to determine whether or not they are done.

PER SERVING

Calories	155
Protein	13.4 g
Fat	6.1 g
Saturates	2.4 g
Cholesterol	48 mg
Carbohydrate	11.3 g
Fibre	0.2 g
Sodium	321 mg
Potassium	98 mg

Excellent: Niacin; Vitamin B$_{12}$
Good: Zinc

CROWN ROAST OF PORK

This recipe from master chef Hubert Aumeier is easier than it looks, and very impressive.

Makes 10 servings

SERVING SUGGESTIONS

- Bring the whole roast to the table for maximum effect.
- Instead of the stuffing, fill the centre of the crown with brightly coloured cooked vegetables just before serving.
- Serve roast on a platter surrounded by fresh bay leaves, fresh figs, orange slices and cherry tomatoes.

MAKE AHEAD
- This roast should rest for about 20 minutes before carving, so it can be made slightly ahead. The stuffing can be made ahead as well.

4½ lb	crown roast of pork (with 10 ribs)	2 kg
1 tbsp	olive oil	15 mL
1 tsp	salt	5 mL
2 tsp	coarsely cracked black pepper	10 mL
3	cloves garlic, coarsely chopped	3
1 tbsp	chopped fresh rosemary, or ½ tsp/2 mL dried	15 mL
1 tbsp	chopped fresh thyme, or ½ tsp/2 mL dried	15 mL
½ tsp	olive oil	2 mL
20	cloves garlic, peeled	20
1	onion, diced	1
1	carrot, diced	1
1 tbsp	crumbled dried porcini mushrooms, optional	15 mL

Dried Winter Fruit Stuffing

16 cups	cubed day-old Italian or French bread (about 1 loaf)	4 L
3 cups	homemade chicken stock (page 79), or water, hot	750 mL
½ cup	dried cranberries	125 mL
12	dried figs, diced	12
12	prunes, diced	12
3 cups	hot strong tea	750 mL
2 tbsp	soft non-hydrogenated margarine or olive oil	25 mL
4	onions, sliced	4
6	cooking apples, peeled and diced	6
2 tsp	chopped fresh thyme, or ¼ tsp/1 mL dried	10 mL
	Grated peel of 2 lemons (about 2 tbsp/25 mL)	
	Salt and pepper to taste	
2	eggs, beaten	2
½ cup	chopped fresh parsley	125 mL

PER SERVING

Calories	535
Protein	35.6 g
Fat	16.6 g
Saturates	5.1 g
Cholesterol	110 mg
Carbohydrate	61.4 g
Fibre	6.3 g
Sodium	619 mg
Potassium	891 mg

Excellent: Vitamin A; Thiamine; Riboflavin; Niacin; Vitamin B$_6$; Folacin; Vitamin B$_{12}$; Iron; Zinc

1. Pat roast dry. In a small bowl, combine 1 tbsp/15 mL olive oil, salt, pepper, chopped garlic, rosemary and thyme. Rub paste into roast.

2. Heat ½ tsp/2 mL olive oil in a heavy ovenproof skillet on high heat. Add roast with bones up and brown for a few minutes. Transfer to a 425°F/220°C oven for 20 minutes. Reduce heat to 350°F/180°C. Scatter whole garlic cloves, onion, carrot and mushrooms (if using) around roast. Add 1 cup/250 mL water. Roast for 1 hour, checking every 15 minutes and adding about ½ cup/125 mL water as liquid in pan evaporates.

3. Meanwhile, place bread in a large bowl. Pour hot stock over bread and stir.

4. In a separate bowl, combine cranberries, figs and prunes. Cover with hot tea. Allow to steep for about 30 minutes.

5. Heat margarine in a large, deep skillet on medium-high heat and cook onions and apples until tender. Stir in thyme, lemon peel, salt and pepper.

6. Squeeze any liquid out of bread and combine with onion/apple mixture, fruits and eggs.

7. Place stuffing in an oiled 13 x 9-inch/3.5 L baking dish. Cover and bake in a 325°F/160°C oven with roast for 15 minutes. Uncover and bake for 15 minutes longer.

8. When roast is cooked, transfer it to a baking sheet. Fill cavity with as much stuffing as it will take (leave remaining stuffing in baking dish) and keep roast and stuffing in turned-off oven for 20 minutes before carving.

9. Place skillet on stove on high heat and place a piece of paper towel quickly on surface of juices to remove top layer of fat. Scrape bottom of pan to release any caramelized pork juices from roast and simmer juices until you have about ¾ to 1 cup/175 to 250 mL. Taste and adjust seasonings.

10. When pork has rested for 20 minutes, transfer to a serving platter. Scatter parsley leaves over stuffing and roast.

11. To serve, remove stuffing and carve between bones. Serve stuffing and meat with juice spooned over each serving. See page 29 for carving instructions.

Ordering a Crown Roast
When ordering a crown roast from your butcher be sure to order the rack by the number of ribs you need. I usually order one pork chop per person. Make sure the butcher removes the chine bone (see page 29).

Boneless "Sparerib" Roast with Polenta

Serving Suggestions
- Serve with mashed potatoes, rice or pasta instead of polenta.
- Try shredding the meat instead of slicing it — a great version of Southern-style pulled pork!
- Serve in large shallow bowls to catch all the juices.

Make Ahead
- This can be made a few days ahead and reheated. It can also be frozen.

Per Serving

Calories	384
Protein	38.7 g
Fat	10.4 g
Saturates	3.4 g
Cholesterol	96 mg
Carbohydrate	31.8 g
Fibre	3.8 g
Sodium	731 mg
Potassium	647 mg

Excellent: Vitamin A; Thiamine; Niacin; Vitamin B$_6$; Vitamin B$_{12}$; Zinc
Good: Iron; Riboflavin

Pot roasts sound and smell like home. And they are great for entertaining because you can make them ahead and they taste even better reheated. Defat the sauce when it is cold; it will rise to the surface and solidify, making it easy to remove.

This roast tastes like barbecued spareribs, but with less fat. The sauce is also excellent with chicken or a boneless crossrib roast of beef. You can add potatoes and carrots along with the other vegetables.

Leftovers can be cut up and served as a stew, or shredded or ground and used as a filling for tacos or shepherd's pie (page 201). You could also add beans and serve over rice as a chili. Or cut leftover meat and vegetables into bits, add stock and serve as a soup.

Makes 10 to 12 servings

4 lb	boneless pork loin roast, tied	2 kg
½ tsp	salt	2 mL
¼ tsp	pepper	1 mL
2 tsp	olive oil	10 mL
1 cup	barbecue sauce	250 mL
2 tbsp	Dijon mustard	25 mL
2 tbsp	brown sugar	25 mL
2 tbsp	Worcestershire sauce	25 mL
2 tbsp	red wine vinegar	25 mL
2	chipotles (page 73) or jalapeños, chopped, optional	2
1 cup	water	250 mL
2	onions, cut in chunks	2
2	carrots, cut in chunks on the diagonal	2
2	stalks celery, cut in 2-inch/5 cm pieces	2

Polenta

10 cups	water or milk, or a combination	2.5 L
1 tsp	ground cumin	5 mL
1 tsp	salt	5 mL
½ tsp	pepper	2 mL
2 cups	quick-cooking cornmeal for polenta	500 mL
	Sprigs of fresh parsley	

1. Pat roast dry and season with salt and pepper.

2. Heat oil in a heavy Dutch oven on high heat. Brown meat well on all sides. Discard any fat from pan.

3. Meanwhile, in a large measuring cup or medium bowl, combine barbecue sauce, mustard, brown sugar, Worcestershire, vinegar, chipotles (if using) and water. Pour over roast. Cover tightly and cook in preheated 350°F/180°C oven for 1½ hours.

4. Place onions, carrots and celery around roast, cover and cook for 1½ hours longer, or until meat is tender.

5. Remove meat to a carving board. Skim any fat from surface of sauce. If sauce is thin, place on medium-high heat and cook, uncovered, until liquid reduces. You should have about 2 cups/500 mL sauce. Keep warm if not serving immediately.

6. Meanwhile, in a medium saucepan, heat water with cumin, salt and pepper. Whisk in cornmeal slowly and then, stirring constantly, cook gently for about 5 minutes. Taste and adjust seasonings if necessary. Keep warm if not serving immediately.

7. Slice meat into thick pieces. Transfer polenta to a large serving platter and arrange pork, vegetables and sauce over top. Garnish with parsley.

BACKYARD BARBECUE

Cranberry Orange "Sangria"

Spicy Thai Shrimp

Balsamic Maple-glazed Lamb Chops
with Sweet Potatoes

Wheat Berry and Grilled
Corn Salad

Grilled Tomato Salad

Raspberry Upside-down Cake

*Entertaining changes in the summer, becoming casual and spontaneous.
You can invite people at the last minute, you don't have to dress up, and it doesn't have
to cost a bundle! Don't forget that you can have a barbecue in the winter,
too — bring the decoration ideas inside, serve summery foods and use lots of fresh herbs
to make your food taste as if the sun is shining on it.*

WORK PLAN

MAKE AHEAD

• Marinate shrimp the night before.

• Make wheat berry salad a day ahead.

• Peel and cut up sweet potatoes and soak in cold water
overnight.

SAME DAY

• Make punch.

• Make cake.

• Make tomato salad earlier in the day.

• Wrap sweet potatoes in foil and put on barbecue
when guests arrive; they will stay warm in the foil
while you cook the chops.

• Cook lamb while guests are enjoying the appetizer.

PRESENTATION IDEAS

- Use a large throw blanket or car blanket for a tablecloth.
- Use a fold-up picnic table indoors.
- Use benches instead of chairs.
- Cover fold-up chairs with throws, or decorate the backs with herbs or flowers.
- As a centrepiece, use a basket of perennials, a vase filled with fresh herbs instead of flowers, or a large pot of herbs.
- Arrange branches, twigs or cedar branches on the table and set dishes on top; in late summer, decorate the table with pine cones.
- Light a citronella candle and lots of votives.
- Use vines or herbs as napkin rings.
- Garnish food with lots of fresh herbs and edible flowers (page 22).

MATCHING FOOD WITH WINE*

The "Sangria" will go well with both the shrimp and lamb, but if you want to serve wine, try a spicy, floral Gewürztraminer (Alsace, France, Ontario, British Columbia) — the mild sweetness of the wine will match the Asian flavours and sweet ingredients of the food. A Shiraz (Australia) will also deliver the full-bodied, ripe fruit flavours needed to balance the sweetness of the lamb.

See Alcohol (page 274).

CRANBERRY ORANGE "SANGRIA"

- Serve in a large pitcher or punch bowl.
- Use your largest wine glasses or tall glasses.
- Make flavoured ice cubes with fruit juices.

MAKE AHEAD
- This can be mostly made the night before. Just add the ginger ale and ice cubes before serving.

Fruit Sugar

Fruit sugar is also called instant blending sugar, castor sugar, bar sugar and finely granulated sugar. You can buy it or make it yourself by processing regular granulated sugar in a food processor or blender for about 1 minute. Measure after processing.

For a spirited version, use 3 cups/750 mL red, white or rosé wine (I like to use a reasonably priced Spanish red) instead of the cranberry juice, and add ¼ cup/50 mL brandy or Cognac and/or ¼ cup/50 mL orange liqueur instead of the orange juice. Use soda water instead of ginger ale.

Leftover sangria can be used to marinate fruit salad, or cook with other fruit to make a fruit compote. Or you can make a jellied dessert by using one envelope unflavoured gelatin for every 2 cups/500 mL sangria — follow the package directions.

Makes 8 servings

½ cup	orange juice	125 mL
⅓ cup	fruit sugar or granulated sugar	75 mL
3 cups	cranberry juice	750 mL
1	orange, sliced	1
1	lemon, sliced	1
1½ cups	ginger ale	375 mL
	Lots of ice	

1. Pour orange juice into a large pitcher. Add sugar and stir until dissolved.

2. Add cranberry juice and orange and lemon slices. Stir well. Cover and marinate in refrigerator until ready to serve.

3. Just before serving, stir in ginger ale and ice cubes.

PER SERVING

Calories	119
Protein	0.4 g
Fat	0.1 g
Saturates	0 g
Cholesterol	0 mg
Carbohydrate	30.5 g
Fibre	0.5 g
Sodium	7 mg
Potassium	92 mg

Excellent: Vitamin C

SPICY THAI SHRIMP

This is a version of a recipe I learned when I attended classes at the fabulous cooking school at the Oriental Hotel in Bangkok. Spearing the shrimp right through from head to tail prevents them from rolling around on the skewers when you try to turn them. This method also works well with chicken fingers and strips of salmon.

In North America we tend to use only the leaves of fresh cilantro, but many Asian recipes call for the stems and roots, adding a tremendous amount of flavour.

Leftovers are great for up to two days, or they can be frozen. Chop them up and use in a salad, stir-fry or as a filling for wraps (page 166) with rice and peanut sauce.

Makes 32 appetizers

2 lb	extra-large shrimp (about 32), cleaned (page 249)	1 kg
3	cloves garlic	3
1	1-inch/2.5 cm piece fresh ginger root, peeled	1
1	hot chile, seeded and deribbed	1
¼ cup	fresh cilantro leaves, stems and roots	50 mL
2 tbsp	hoisin sauce	25 mL
1 tbsp	Thai fish sauce or soy sauce	15 mL
1 tbsp	lime juice or lemon juice	15 mL
1 tbsp	honey	15 mL
1 tbsp	rice vinegar	15 mL
1 tsp	sesame oil	5 mL
½ cup	Thai hot sweet sauce (page 94)	125 mL

1. Pat shrimp dry and place in a large bowl.

2. In a food processor or blender, combine garlic, ginger, chile and cilantro and blend into a paste. Blend in hoisin sauce, fish sauce, lime juice, honey, vinegar and sesame oil.

3. Combine marinade with shrimp and marinate for at least 30 minutes in refrigerator.

4. If you are using wooden skewers, soak in cold water for 30 minutes before using.

5. Thread shrimp on skewers from head to tail so shrimp are relatively straight. (Make sure shrimp is pushed right to the point of skewers so wooden tips don't burn.)

6. Grill or broil shrimp for a few minutes on each side or until pink and opaque. Place dipping sauce in a small bowl and place in middle of serving platter. Arrange shrimp around sauce.

SERVING SUGGESTIONS
- Line the serving platter with banana leaves, available fresh or frozen in Asian markets (wash them well so they look fresh), or garnish with sprigs of fresh cilantro or edible flowers (page 22).
- Serve the sauce in a seashell or rice bowl.
- Serve shrimp over rice as a main dish. Use smaller (less expensive) shrimp if you prefer and thread two on each skewer (or use shorter skewers).
- Use rosemary branches as skewers.

MAKE AHEAD
- Marinate the shrimp overnight or cook ahead and serve cold or at room temperature.

PER APPETIZER SERVING

Calories	38
Protein	4.4 g
Fat	0.5 g
Saturates	0.1 g
Cholesterol	32 mg
Carbohydrate	3.8 g
Fibre	0 g
Sodium	139 mg
Potassium	37 mg

BALSAMIC MAPLE-GLAZED LAMB CHOPS WITH SWEET POTATOES

This is a great way to use a less-expensive balsamic vinegar, as it becomes sweeter when it is reduced. I save my better-quality vinegar for salads.

You can use teriyaki sauce (page 194) instead of the balsamic glaze. Leftover lamb can be used in salads and as filling for dumplings or phyllo pastries (page 46).

Makes 8 servings

1 tbsp	olive oil	15 mL
3 lb	sweet potatoes (4 large), peeled and thickly sliced	1.5 kg
8	shallots, peeled (page 173) and halved	8
1 tbsp	chopped fresh rosemary, or ½ tsp/2 mL dried	15 mL
1 tsp	salt, divided	5 mL
¼ tsp	pepper	1 mL
2 cups	balsamic vinegar	500 mL
3 tbsp	maple syrup	45 mL
1 tsp	Dijon mustard	5 mL
1	1-inch/2.5 cm piece orange peel	1
16	thin rib lamb chops, trimmed (about 2½ to 3 oz/75 to 90 g each)	16

1. Brush a large sheet of heavy-duty foil with oil. Arrange sweet potato slices on foil, overlapping slightly. Arrange shallots on sweet potatoes. Sprinkle with rosemary, ½ tsp/2 mL salt and pepper. Wrap and place in or on barbecue. Cook for about 35 minutes, turning package once or twice. (Sweet potatoes can also be baked in a 400°F/200°C oven for about 35 minutes or until tender.)

2. In a medium saucepan, combine vinegar, maple syrup, mustard, orange peel and remaining ½ tsp/2 mL salt. Bring to a boil. Reduce heat and simmer, uncovered, until mixture is syrupy — 10 to 15 minutes. You should have about 1 cup/250 mL glaze. Discard peel.

3. Rub ½ cup/125 mL glaze into chops generously. (Freeze the remaining glaze.) Grill lamb for 2 minutes. Brush again, turn and cook for 2 minutes longer. Lamb should be medium rare. Cook longer if desired.

4. Serve chops on a bed of sweet potatoes.

WHEAT BERRY AND GRILLED CORN SALAD

This is a perfect pot luck dish because everybody loves it — it has a wonderful flavour and is very healthful. It's great served as a vegetarian main course or as a side salad.

If you don't have wheat berries, use rice; if you don't have time to grill the corn, use frozen corn. Just make it — it's so good!

Makes 8 to 10 servings

2 cups	uncooked wheat berries	500 mL
4	ears corn, husked	4
2	sweet red peppers	2
1 lb	asparagus or green beans, trimmed	500 g
½ cup	rice vinegar	125 mL
2	cloves garlic, minced	2
2 tbsp	orange juice concentrate	25 mL
1 tbsp	minced chipotle (page 73) or jalapeño, optional	15 mL
1 tsp	salt	5 mL
½ tsp	pepper	2 mL
3 tbsp	olive oil	45 mL
½ cup	chopped fresh cilantro or basil	125 mL
¼ cup	chopped fresh chives	50 mL

1. Rinse wheat berries. Place in a large saucepan with 4 qt/4 L cold water. Bring to a boil and simmer gently for 1 to 1½ hours, or until tender. Rinse with cold water, drain well and place in a large bowl.

2. Meanwhile, grill corn until lightly browned. Cool. Cut corn in half, place cut side on cutting board and cut niblets off cob from top to bottom. Add corn to wheat berries.

3. Grill peppers on all sides until blackened. Cool. Remove skin, ribs and seeds. Dice peppers and add to wheat berries and corn.

4. Grill asparagus until barely cooked. Dice. Add to wheat berries.

5. In a small bowl, combine vinegar, garlic, orange juice concentrate, chipotle (if using), salt and pepper. Whisk in olive oil. Toss with wheat berries and add cilantro and chives. Taste and adjust seasonings if necessary.

SERVING SUGGESTIONS
- I like to mound this on a platter, but you can also serve it in individual moulds.
- You can fill hollowed-out tomato halves with the salad.

MAKE AHEAD
- This can be made a day ahead. Vegetables such as asparagus and green beans may discolour, so add them just before serving.

PER SERVING

Calories	277
Protein	7.9 g
Fat	6.7 g
Saturates	1 g
Cholesterol	0 mg
Carbohydrate	52.7 g
Fibre	8.9 g
Sodium	304 mg
Potassium	473 mg

Excellent: Vitamin C; Thiamine; Folacin
Good: Vitamin A; Niacin; Vitamin B_6; Iron; Zinc

GRILLED TOMATO SALAD

This salad is spectacular when tomatoes are in season. It is worth using a good-quality balsamic vinegar as you will require less oil. Instead of barbecuing, you could grill the tomatoes and onions in a grill pan or under the broiler.

Use leftovers as a pasta sauce, sandwich filling or bruschetta topping, or as a sauce on grilled foods. You could even puree the salad, add stock and turn it into a soup.

Makes 8 servings

6	large tomatoes (about 3 lb/1.5 kg), cut in 1-inch/2.5 slices	6
2	large onions, cut in ½-inch/1 cm slices	2
2 tbsp	olive oil, divided	25 mL
1 cup	fresh basil leaves, torn in pieces	250 mL
¼ cup	balsamic vinegar	50 mL
1	clove garlic, minced	1
	Salt and pepper to taste	

1. Brush tomatoes and onions with some of the olive oil. Grill tomatoes briefly on each side just until warm with grill marks. Grill onions until tender and browned. (They will take longer than the tomatoes.)

2. Combine tomatoes and onions in a serving bowl either whole or cut up. Add basil leaves.

3. In a small bowl, combine vinegar, garlic, remaining oil and salt and pepper to taste. Combine with tomatoes. Taste and adjust seasonings if necessary.

Grilled Tomato Salad with Fennel
Add 1 lb/500 g grilled fennel (or eggplant) to the salad.

PER SERVING

Calories	86
Protein	2.1 g
Fat	3.8 g
Saturates	0.5 g
Cholesterol	0 mg
Carbohydrate	12.8 g
Fibre	2.8 g
Sodium	15 mg
Potassium	424 mg

Good: Vitamin A; Vitamin C

RASPBERRY UPSIDE-DOWN CAKE

You can make upside-down cakes with many different fruits, but berries say summer best. Use raspberries, blackberries, blueberries or a combination. In winter, use individually quick-frozen berries.

Makes 8 servings

2 tbsp	unsalted butter	25 mL
⅔ cup	brown sugar	150 mL
2 cups	fresh raspberries	500 mL
⅓ cup	vegetable oil or unsalted butter	75 mL
¾ cup	granulated sugar	175 mL
1	egg	1
2	egg whites	2
1 tsp	vanilla	5 mL
1 tbsp	grated orange peel	15 mL
1½ cups	all-purpose flour	375 mL
1½ tsp	baking powder	7 mL
½ tsp	baking soda	2 mL
¾ cup	buttermilk or unflavoured low-fat yogurt	175 mL

1. Place butter in an 8-inch/1.5 L baking dish and place in a preheated 350°F/180°C oven for 3 to 5 minutes, or until melted. Sprinkle butter with brown sugar and pat down. Sprinkle berries over sugar.

2. Beat oil with granulated sugar in a large bowl or mixer. Add egg, egg whites, vanilla and orange peel.

3. In a separate bowl, combine or sift together flour, baking powder and baking soda.

4. Stir flour mixture into egg mixture alternately with buttermilk just until combined.

5. Spoon batter over berries and spread evenly. Bake for 35 to 40 minutes, or until cake springs back when lightly touched in centre. Cool on a wire rack for 5 minutes. Invert onto serving plate.

PER SERVING

Calories	373
Protein	5.1 g
Fat	13.2 g
Saturates	2.8 g
Cholesterol	35 mg
Carbohydrate	59.6 g
Fibre	2.4 g
Sodium	174 mg
Potassium	188 mg

Good: Folacin

FATS

There are several different kinds of fat. They fall into two main categories — saturated fat and unsaturated fat — each of which has different effects on heart health. Unsaturated fats can help lower LDL-cholesterol levels when they replace saturated fat in the diet.

Saturated fat is solid at room temperature and generally comes from animal sources such as meat, poultry, eggs and dairy. Plant sources of saturated fats are coconut oil, palm oil and palm kernel oil. Saturated fats can raise blood cholesterol levels. Therefore, reducing saturated fats is an important step in lowering heart-disease risk. This can be achieved by choosing lean meats, removing the skin from chicken and using lower-fat dairy products. In addition, any cooking method that allows fat to drain off (e.g., broiling, barbecuing, roasting on a rack) further helps reduce saturated fat intake.

There are two types of unsaturated fats: monounsaturated and polyunsaturated.

Monounsaturated fats have been found to lower LDL-cholesterol levels. They are found mainly in olive and canola oils and some soft non-hydrogenated margarines.

There are two kinds of polyunsaturated fats: omega-3 and omega-6. Omega-3 fats are found in fatty fish such as salmon, mackerel, herring and sardines as well as in flax and some newer products such as omega-3 eggs. These fats help prevent blood from sticking and clotting. They also help lower triglycerides, decreasing your risk for heart disease.

Omega-6 fats are found in foods that come from plant sources and are liquid at room temperature — safflower, sunflower and corn oils. They are also found in some soft non-hydrogenated margarines and in some nuts and seeds such as almonds, pecans, brazil nuts, sunflower seeds and sesame seeds. These fats help lower harmful blood cholesterol but should be eaten in moderation since they will still contribute to your total calorie intake.

Trans-fatty acids are created when an unsaturated fat is processed or hydrogenated. Like saturated fats, trans-fatty acids raise LDL-cholesterol levels. They are found in partially hydrogenated vegetables oils and some margarines, as well as in many crackers, cookies and commercially baked products. You should limit them in your diet. Trans-fatty acids may not appear on food labels. Look also for the words "hydrogenated" or "partially hydrogenated."

VEGETABLES AND SIDE DISHES

GLAZED FENNEL WITH BALSAMIC VINEGAR

SERVING SUGGESTION
- Delicious with roast chicken or turkey, grilled veal chops or salmon.

MAKE AHEAD
- Serve at room temperature or reheat.

Fennel is great raw or cooked. When it is raw it has a wonderful crunch and licorice/anise flavour. It is good used for dipping and in salads. Cooked fennel is very tender and has a more gentle flavour.

Makes 4 to 6 servings

2	bulbs fennel (about 2 lb/1 kg)	2
1 tbsp	olive oil	15 mL
3 tbsp	honey, brown sugar or maple syrup	45 mL
⅓ cup	balsamic vinegar	75 mL
½ tsp	salt	2 mL
½ cup	water	125 mL

1. Trim fennel. Cut in half vertically. Cut into wedges through the core so the wedges stay together.

2. Heat oil in a large non-stick skillet on high heat. Add fennel and cook for a few minutes, without stirring, until it is lightly browned. Turn and brown again.

3. Add honey and vinegar. Coat fennel well. Sprinkle with salt and add water.

4. Bring to a boil, reduce heat to medium and cook, stirring occasionally, until liquid evaporates and fennel is glazed — about 25 minutes. (If liquid evaporates before fennel is tender, add a bit more water.)

PER SERVING

Calories	146
Protein	1.9 g
Fat	3.7 g
Saturates	0.5 g
Cholesterol	0 mg
Carbohydrate	29.3 g
Fibre	4.7 g
Sodium	367 mg
Potassium	637 mg

TIAN OF EGGPLANT AND ZUCCHINI

Linda Stephen developed a recipe like this for one of her popular Provence classes at my school. This casserole actually tastes like the south of France. Serve it as an appetizer, as a side dish with steaks or chops, or as a vegetarian main course. I used to fry the eggplant slices, but grilling or broiling them works well and reduces the calorie count considerably.
Leftovers are delicious in sandwiches or combined with eggs to make a frittata (page 269).

Makes 8 servings

(page 269)

2	eggplants (about 1½ lb/750 g total)	2
1 tsp	salt	5 mL
2	onions, cut in rings	2
2	zucchini (about 1 lb/500 g total), sliced on the diagonal in ¼-inch/5 mm slices	2
2 tbsp	olive oil	25 mL
2	cloves garlic, minced	2
2 tbsp	chopped fresh basil or parsley	25 mL
1 tbsp	chopped fresh thyme, or ½ tsp/2 mL dried	15 mL
½ tsp	salt	2 mL
½ tsp	pepper	2 mL
1	19-oz/540 mL can chickpeas, drained and rinsed	1
4	plum tomatoes, thinly sliced	4

1. Cut eggplant into slices ½ inch/1 cm thick. Sprinkle with salt and allow to drain in a colander for about 30 minutes. Rinse eggplant and pat dry.

2. Spray or brush eggplant, onions and zucchini with oil. Barbecue, grill in a grill pan or broil until browned on both sides.

3. In a small bowl, combine garlic, basil, thyme, salt and pepper.

4. Brush a 13 x 9-inch/3.5 L baking dish with oil. Spread half the onions, eggplant, zucchini, chickpeas and tomatoes over pan. Sprinkle with herb mixture. Layer again, ending with tomatoes and herbs (bury the chickpeas if you don't want them to become a little crunchy). Sprinkle with any remaining olive oil.

5. Cook, uncovered, in a preheated 375°F/190°C oven for 50 to 60 minutes, or until any liquid evaporates.

SERVING SUGGESTION
• This can also be layered in a loaf pan and served as a terrine.

MAKE AHEAD
• This can be baked ahead and reheated.

PER SERVING

Calories	140
Protein	5 g
Fat	4.5 g
Saturates	0.6 g
Cholesterol	0 mg
Carbohydrate	22.1 g
Fibre	5.1 g
Sodium	253 mg
Potassium	490 mg

Good: Vitamin B$_6$; Folacin

STIR-FRIED EGGPLANT WITH MISO

Once you start using miso to flavour your food, you will find all kinds of ways to use it! Experiment with different vegetables and different kinds of miso.

Serve this with a Japanese or Asian meal or with something barbecued. Leftovers can be combined with rice and stir-fried.

Makes 6 to 8 servings

1 tbsp	vegetable oil	15 mL
1 tbsp	finely chopped fresh ginger root	15 mL
4	shallots, thinly sliced (or 1 small onion, sliced)	4
1 lb	thin eggplant, cut in 1-inch/2.5 cm chunks	500 g
2 tbsp	light miso	25 mL
1½ tbsp	granulated sugar	20 mL
1 tbsp	rice wine	15 mL
1 tsp	hot chili paste	5 mL
⅓ cup	water	75 mL
4	green onions, sliced	4
	Salt and pepper to taste	

1. Heat oil in a large non-stick pan or wok on medium-high heat. Add ginger and shallots. Cook for 3 to 5 minutes. Add eggplant and stir-fry until it is lightly browned and beginning to wilt, about 8 to 10 minutes. If pan is too dry, add 2 tbsp/25 mL water.

2. In a small bowl, combine miso, sugar, rice wine, hot chili paste and water. Add to eggplant and stir-fry until eggplant is tender, about 3 minutes. If sauce is too thick, add about ¼ cup/50 mL more water. Sauce should coat eggplant but not be too sticky.

3. Add green onions, salt and pepper. Cook for 1 minute longer.

MAKE AHEAD
- This can be made ahead and reheated. If it is too thick when reheated, just add some water.

Miso
Miso is a fermented soybean product that has become very popular with the increased interest in Japanese food and soy products. It is available in different flavours, but the light/yellow version is the mildest and most popular.

PER SERVING

Calories	77
Protein	1.7 g
Fat	2.9 g
Saturates	0.3 g
Cholesterol	0 mg
Carbohydrate	11.9 g
Fibre	2.8 g
Sodium	220 mg
Potassium	253 mg

DAL WITH SPICED YOGURT

If you make this very thick, you can serve it as a side vegetable or main course. If you make it thinner, serve it as a soup. It is delicious as part of an East Indian meal or vegetarian dinner, but also tastes great with anything barbecued or roasted.

Makes 8 servings

1½ cups	dried red or yellow lentils, or split peas	375 mL
1 tbsp	vegetable oil	15 mL
3	cloves garlic, finely chopped	3
1 tbsp	finely chopped fresh ginger root	15 mL
1	large onion, thinly sliced or chopped	1
1 tbsp	curry powder	15 mL
4 cups	homemade vegetable stock (page 69) or water	1 L
1 tbsp	lemon juice	15 mL
	Salt and pepper to taste	
¼ cup	chopped fresh cilantro	50 mL

Spiced Yogurt

1 tsp	vegetable oil	5 mL
1 tsp	cumin seeds	5 mL
1 cup	yogurt cheese (page 303) or thick yogurt	250 mL

1. Rinse lentils, pick over and discard any stones.

2. Heat 1 tbsp/15 mL oil in a large saucepan or Dutch oven on medium heat. Add garlic, ginger and onion and cook gently until tender and fragrant. Add curry powder and cook until fragrant, about 30 seconds.

3. Add rinsed lentils and stir. Add stock and bring to a boil. Reduce heat and simmer gently for 30 to 45 minutes, or until lentils are very tender and mixture is thick. Stir in lemon juice, salt and pepper.

4. Meanwhile, to make spiced yogurt, heat 1 tsp/5 mL oil in a non-stick skillet on medium-high heat. Add cumin seeds. Cook until they start to "pop," but do not let them burn. Cool. Stir into yogurt cheese.

5. Adjust thickness of soup with stock or water. Taste and adjust seasonings if necessary. Serve with spiced yogurt swirled on puree and garnish with cilantro.

SERVING SUGGESTIONS
• Serve as a base for a curried dish.
• Serve in a mould or mound as a side dish.

MAKE AHEAD
• This can be made ahead and reheated.

Cumin Seeds
For the most flavourful cumin, always buy cumin seeds rather than ground cumin. Toast the seeds in a dry skillet over medium heat until the cumin turns slightly reddish and very aromatic. Cool, then grind the seeds in a spice grinder or with a mortar and pestle.

PER SERVING

Calories	194
Protein	13.1 g
Fat	4.1 g
Saturates	0.8 g
Cholesterol	3 mg
Carbohydrate	27.7 g
Fibre	4.9 g
Sodium	50 mg
Potassium	562 mg

Excellent: Folacin; Iron
Good: Thiamine; Vitamin B$_{12}$; Zinc

PUREED CARROTS AND GINGER

SERVING SUGGESTION
• Pipe the puree onto plates, or use an ice cream scoop or spoon to serve in mounds. You can also use the puree as a filling in tart shells.

MAKE AHEAD
• This can be made ahead and spooned into a casserole dish. Cover and reheat at 375°F/190°C for 20 minutes.

Pureed carrots have a very intense flavour and are beautiful to look at. The ginger adds an exotic taste. Cooked parsnips, squash, sweet potatoes, celeriac, turnip or Jerusalem artichokes could be used instead of the carrots or in combination with them.

This dish goes well with a turkey dinner, harvest dinner or celebration meal. If you have any leftovers, serve as a dip or spread, or add stock and serve as a soup. The recipe also halves easily.

Makes 8 to 10 servings

4 lb	carrots, sliced	2 kg
1 tbsp	olive oil	15 mL
1 tbsp	finely chopped fresh ginger root	15 mL
1	clove garlic, finely chopped	1
½ cup	homemade vegetable stock (page 69), chicken stock (page 79) or water	125 mL
2 tbsp	lemon juice	25 mL
2 tbsp	honey or brown sugar	25 mL
	Salt and pepper to taste	

1. Cook carrots in boiling water until tender, about 25 minutes. Drain well.

2. Meanwhile, heat oil in a saucepan or skillet on medium heat. Add ginger and garlic and cook gently until fragrant, about 30 seconds. Add stock. Bring to a boil and cook for a few minutes. Add lemon juice.

3. Puree carrots with ginger/garlic mixture and honey and season with salt and pepper.

PER SERVING

Calories	124
Protein	2.3 g
Fat	2.1 g
Saturates	0.3 g
Cholesterol	0 mg
Carbohydrate	26.1 g
Fibre	5.5 g
Sodium	137 mg
Potassium	476 mg

Excellent: Vitamin A; Vitamin B$_6$

GRATED SQUASH WITH PEARS AND CRANBERRIES

Sweet and tangy, this unusual and delicious dish is lovely to look at as well as to eat. It makes a great side dish for a big harvest-style dinner. Any kind of winter squash works well, but butternut is the smoothest — and you can often buy it already peeled! If you do not have a food processor and it is too difficult to grate the squash, just dice it, but it may take a little longer to cook.

Leftovers can be tossed with a salad dressing and served cold or at room temperature.

Makes 8 servings

MAKE AHEAD
• This can be made ahead and reheated, but be careful not to overcook the squash.

1 tbsp	olive oil	15 mL
1	shallot or small onion, thinly sliced	1
3 lb	butternut squash, peeled and grated	1.5 kg
2	pears, peeled and diced	2
½ cup	homemade chicken stock (page 79) or vegetable stock (page 69), or water	125 mL
3 tbsp	dried cranberries	45 mL
2 tbsp	maple syrup or honey	25 mL
	Salt and pepper to taste	
2 tbsp	chopped fresh mint or chives	25 mL

1. Heat oil in a large, deep skillet on medium-high heat. Add shallot and cook for 1 to 2 minutes. Add squash and pears and cook, stirring, for about 2 minutes.

2. Add stock, cranberries and maple syrup. Combine well. Stirring often, cook, uncovered, for about 10 minutes, or until squash is tender. Season with salt and pepper. Sprinkle with mint.

Grated Carrots with Apples and Cherries

Use carrots, apples and dried cherries instead of squash, pears and cranberries.

PER SERVING

Calories	123
Protein	1.9 g
Fat	2.1 g
Saturates	0.3 g
Cholesterol	0 mg
Carbohydrate	27.5 g
Fibre	3.7 g
Sodium	9 mg
Potassium	523 mg

Excellent: Vitamin A
Good: Vitamin C; Folacin

DOUBLE ROASTED SMASHED POTATOES

SERVING SUGGESTION
• Serve as a side dish, or use as vegetables for dipping.

MAKE AHEAD
• You can make ahead and serve at room temperature.

If you are in a hurry, you can simply omit the second roasting of the potatoes, but it does make them extra crispy and delicious. Use mini Yukon Golds.

Makes 4 to 6 servings

2 lb	baby potatoes	1 kg
4 tsp	olive oil, divided	20 mL
½ tsp	salt	2 mL
¼ tsp	pepper	1 mL
1 tbsp	chopped fresh rosemary, or ½ tsp/2 mL dried	15 mL

1. In a large bowl, toss potatoes with 1 tbsp/15 mL olive oil, salt, pepper and rosemary. Spread on a baking sheet lined with parchment paper and roast in a preheated 375°F/190°C oven for 45 to 60 minutes until browned and very tender.

2. Cut larger potatoes in half and flatten each individual potato or potato half gently with a meat pounder. Brush or spray with remaining 1 tsp/5 mL oil. Roast for 30 to 45 minutes longer, turning once or twice during cooking time, until browned and crisp.

FRUITS AND VEGETABLES

Fruits and vegetables are delicious, versatile and brimming with top-quality nutrition. Most are excellent sources of vitamins C and A, fibre, folic acid, potassium and other nutrients that may provide protection from disease. As an added bonus, they're low in fat and usually low in calories.

Fruits and vegetables are rich in compounds called phytochemicals ("phyto" is Greek for plant). Unlike vitamins and minerals, phytochemicals have no known nutritional value but act in a variety of ways that may protect you from many kinds of diseases.

Many phytochemicals give colour and flavour to fruits and vegetables. Red tomatoes, for example, get their colour from a powerful antioxidant called lycopene, which may lower heart-disease risk. Studies also show that regular intake of tomatoes and tomato-based products may reduce your risk of prostate cancer.

Most fruits and vegetables have more than one benefit. Red peppers, for example, contain beta-carotene, vitamin C, folic acid and fibre as well as important phytochemicals, all for only 35 calories per pepper.

It's still unclear exactly how all these substances act together in our bodies, but we do know that eating five to ten servings of fruits and vegetables every day will pay off in the long run. If you could make just one positive health step, add an extra serving of fruits and vegetables to your diet.

PER SERVING

Calories	204
Protein	3.5 g
Fat	4.7 g
Saturates	0.7 g
Cholesterol	0 mg
Carbohydrate	37.9 g
Fibre	3.4 g
Sodium	299 mg
Potassium	628 mg

Excellent: Vitamin B$_6$
Good: Vitamin C; Niacin; Iron

STUFFED BAKED POTATOES

These potatoes can be served as a side dish with roasts, steaks, chops or turkey, or as a vegetarian main course. Chopped dill, parsley or chives can be used instead of the green onions. The potato shells can also be stuffed with mashed root vegetables.

Makes 6 servings

3	large baking potatoes (about 9 oz/280 g each)	3
1 tsp	ground cumin	5 mL
½ cup	low-fat yogurt or light sour cream	125 mL
½ cup	grated old Cheddar or crumbled blue cheese	125 mL
3	green onions, chopped	3
½ tsp	salt	2 mL
½ tsp	pepper	2 mL

1. Scrub potatoes. Place on a baking sheet and bake in a preheated 400°F/200°C oven for 1 to 1½ hours, or until potatoes are very tender.

2. Cut potatoes in half lengthwise and gently scoop out flesh, leaving a shell ¼–½ inch/ 5 mm–1 cm thick.

3. Mash potato flesh with cumin, yogurt, cheese, green onions, salt and pepper. Taste and adjust seasonings if necessary. Spoon potatoes back into potato shells.

4. Arrange potatoes in a single layer on baking sheet. Reheat at 400°F/200°C for 20 minutes, or until thoroughly heated.

MAKE AHEAD
• This can be assembled a day ahead to the end of step 3. Bake the potatoes just before serving.

PER SERVING

Calories	147
Protein	5.6 g
Fat	3.6 g
Saturates	2.2 g
Cholesterol	11 mg
Carbohydrate	23.6 g
Fibre	2.1 g
Sodium	273 mg
Potassium	438 mg

Good: Vitamin B_6

LYNN'S LEMON POTATOES

SERVING SUGGESTION
• Garnish with sprigs of fresh rosemary.

MAKE AHEAD
• This can be made a few hours ahead and served at room temperature.

One of my very best friends, Lynn Saunders, was so excited to give me a recipe for a change. Use ½ cup/125 mL lemon juice if you like things really lemony. You can also use thyme instead of rosemary, a combination of chicken stock and milk instead of just chicken stock, or use half potatoes and half sweet potatoes, celeriac or turnip.

Serve this with roast chicken, lamb or smoked turkey. Leftover potatoes can be cut up, tossed with dressing and served as potato salad, or you can mix with beaten eggs and bake in a frittata (page 269).

Makes 8 servings

3 lb	baking potatoes or Yukon gold potatoes	1.5 kg
2 tbsp	chopped fresh rosemary, or ½ tsp/2 mL dried	25 mL
½ tsp	salt	2 mL
¼ tsp	pepper	1 mL
1½ cups	homemade chicken stock (page 79) or water	375 mL
⅓ cup	lemon juice	75 mL

1. Peel or scrub potatoes. Cut into 2-inch/5 cm chunks. Place in a 13 x 9-inch/3.5 L baking dish and sprinkle with rosemary, salt and pepper.

2. Combine stock and lemon juice and pour over potatoes. Bake in a preheated 400°F/200°C oven for 1½ to 2 hours, stirring occasionally, until potatoes are tender, tops are crispy and brown and almost all liquid has evaporated.

PER SERVING

Calories	117
Protein	3.1 g
Fat	0.4 g
Saturates	0.1 g
Cholesterol	0 mg
Carbohydrate	25.8 g
Fibre	1.8 g
Sodium	158 mg
Potassium	457 mg

Good: Vitamin B$_6$

CELERIAC AND POTATO MASH

Of the many root vegetables you can add to mashed potatoes, celeriac (celery root) is one of my favourites (you can also use rutabaga, turnips or parsnips). Many people cannot identify it in the finished dish, but they know that something special is in there! Celeriac is quite odd-looking — very knobby and hairy. To peel it, cut a flat piece off the top and bottom, place it on a cutting board on one flat end and cut off the peel from top to bottom all the way around. It is delicious raw and grated in a mustard mayonnaise sauce, or it can be roasted like potatoes.

The celeriac takes a little longer to cook than the potatoes; cut it into slightly smaller chunks so they are ready at the same time.

This is delicious served with salmon. Leftovers can be formed into patties and cooked in a lightly oiled non-stick pan (add bits of leftover diced fish or poultry if you wish). The recipe also halves easily.

Makes 8 to 10 servings

SERVING SUGGESTION
• Serve as a base for stews or pot roasts.

MAKE AHEAD
• This can be made a few hours ahead and held, covered, in a 200°F/ 100°C oven.

3 lb	Yukon gold or baking potatoes (about 6 large), peeled and cut in chunks	1.5 kg
1½ lb	celeriac, peeled and cut in chunks	750 g
20	whole cloves garlic, peeled	20
1 tbsp	olive oil	15 mL
¾ cup	vegetable cooking liquid or milk, hot	175 mL
	Salt and pepper to taste	
1	bunch chives, cut in 2-inch/5 cm lengths	1

1. Place potatoes, celeriac and garlic in a large pot of water. Bring to a boil and simmer gently for 20 to 25 minutes, or until vegetables are very tender.

2. Drain vegetables, reserving about 1 cup/250 mL cooking liquid. Mash with a potato masher, whisk or press through a food mill, adding olive oil and as much hot cooking liquid as necessary to achieve a creamy consistency. Add salt and pepper to taste.

3. Chop about three-quarters of the chives and stir into mash mixture. Sprinkle remaining chives on top.

PER SERVING

Calories	162
Protein	3.8 g
Fat	2.1 g
Saturates	0.3 g
Cholesterol	0 mg
Carbohydrate	34.2 g
Fibre	3.4 g
Sodium	78 mg
Potassium	643 mg

Excellent: Vitamin B$_6$
Good: Vitamin C

CARAMELIZED ROASTED ROOT VEGETABLES

MAKE AHEAD
• This dish can be made ahead and reheated or served at room temperature.

This recipe is an adaptation of one given to me by David Forestell, a talented young chef at Amphora Bistro (Hainle Vineyards) in Peachland, British Columbia. David loves cooking with local foods in season (he is also the inspiration behind the recipe on page 154).

Leftovers can be mashed and reheated or moulded into patties and pan-fried in a non-stick skillet brushed with a little oil.

Makes 8 servings

1 lb	carrots, cut in 1-inch/2.5 cm slices on the diagonal	500 g
1 lb	parsnips, peeled and cut in 1-inch/2.5 cm slices on the diagonal	500 g
1 lb	turnips, peeled and cut in 1-inch/2.5 cm wedges	500 g
1 lb	rutabaga, peeled and cut in 1-inch/2.5 cm chunks	500 g
1 cup	homemade chicken stock (page 79) or vegetable stock (page 69), or water	250 mL
1 tbsp	olive oil	15 mL
1½ tbsp	honey or maple syrup	20 mL
1 tsp	salt	5 mL
½ tsp	pepper	2 mL
1 tbsp	chopped fresh rosemary or oregano, or ½ tsp/2 mL dried	15 mL
1 tbsp	chopped fresh thyme or marjoram, or ½ tsp/2 mL dried	15 mL
2 tbsp	parsley leaves, optional	25 mL

1. Arrange carrots, parsnips, turnips and rutabaga in a single layer in a 13 x 9-inch/3.5 L roasting pan lined with parchment paper. Pour stock into the pan. Drizzle vegetables with olive oil and honey. Sprinkle with salt, pepper, rosemary and thyme.

2. Cover pan tightly with foil. Roast in a preheated 400°F/200°C for 30 minutes. Remove cover and roast for 20 to 30 minutes longer, or until vegetables are nicely glazed and browned and liquid has evaporated. Toss a few times during cooking.

3. Transfer vegetables to a serving bowl and scatter parsley leaves (if using) over the top.

PER SERVING

Calories	123
Protein	2.8 g
Fat	2.3 g
Saturates	0.3 g
Cholesterol	0 mg
Carbohydrate	24.8 g
Fibre	4.8 g
Sodium	368 mg
Potassium	542 mg

Excellent: Vitamin A
Good: Vitamin C; Folacin

SAUTEED PEPPERS WITH GARLIC AND BALSAMIC VINEGAR

This gorgeous mix of peppers is great on its own, in frittatas (page 269), as a sauce for pastas or pasta salads, served on top of grilled chicken or chops, chopped and used as a topping for bruschetta or pizzas or stirred into risottos. It can also be pureed and used as a spread.

To peel peppers easily, use a vegetable peeler and buy peppers that are squarish (you don't have to peel the peppers, but they will be sweeter if you do). Use multi-coloured peppers or all one kind. The peppers could also be grilled or roasted (page 49) and then peeled — if you use grilled or roasted peppers, shorten the cooking time. You don't have to peel the peppers but they're much sweeter if you do.

Makes 8 servings

2 tsp	olive oil	10 mL
3	cloves garlic, finely chopped	3
1	hot banana pepper or jalapeño, seeded and chopped, optional	1
3	sweet red peppers, peeled, seeded and cut in 1-inch/2.5 cm chunks	3
3	sweet yellow peppers, peeled, seeded and cut in 1-inch/2.5 cm chunks	3
3	sweet green peppers, peeled, seeded and cut in 1-inch/2.5 cm chunks	3
2 tbsp	balsamic vinegar	25 mL
	Salt and pepper to taste	
⅓ cup	shredded fresh basil	75 mL

1. Heat oil in a large, deep non-stick skillet on medium-high heat. Add garlic and banana pepper (if using) and cook for 1 to 2 minutes.

2. Add sweet peppers and combine well. Cook for 5 minutes until peppers begin to wilt. Cover and cook for 10 to 15 minutes until peppers are very tender. Add a few spoon-fuls of water if pan becomes too dry. Uncover and cook until any liquid in pan has evaporated.

3. Add balsamic vinegar. Bring to a boil and cook for a few minutes. Add salt and pepper. Stir in basil.

MAKE AHEAD
• This can be made ahead and reheated or served at room temperature. It is also delicious served cold as a relish.

PER SERVING

Calories	52
Protein	1.4 g
Fat	1.4 g
Saturates	0.2 g
Cholesterol	0 mg
Carbohydrate	10 g
Fibre	2.2 g
Sodium	3 mg
Potassium	250 mg

Excellent: Vitamin A; Vitamin C
Good: Vitamin B$_6$

VEGETABLE STIR-FRY

MAKE AHEAD
• The ingredients can be assembled and prepared ahead of time, but stir-frying should be done at the last minute.

This is an easy vegetable dish that you can make with any vegetables you have on hand. Letty Lastima and Dely Balagtas, who work at the cooking school, often make this for staff lunches; they like to use oyster sauce as the flavouring.

This can be served as a side dish or with rice as a vegetarian main course. Leftovers can be reheated, served cold, or tossed with a dressing and turned into a salad.

Makes 6 to 8 servings

2 tsp	vegetable oil	10 mL
2	cloves garlic, finely chopped	2
1 tbsp	finely chopped fresh ginger root	15 mL
3	green onions, sliced	3
1	onion, sliced	1
2	carrots, sliced on the diagonal	2
1	zucchini, sliced on the diagonal	1
1	sweet red, green or yellow pepper, sliced	1
1 cup	green beans, trimmed and sliced on the diagonal	250 mL
8	shiitake mushrooms, stemmed and sliced	8
1	small head broccoli, trimmed, with stems sliced and florets broken into pieces	1
¼ cup	homemade vegetable stock (page 69) or water	50 mL
1 cup	snow peas, trimmed	250 mL
2 tbsp	hoisin sauce, teriyaki sauce (page 194), soy sauce or oyster sauce	25 mL
½ tsp	sesame oil	2 mL

1. Heat vegetable oil in a wok or large, deep non-stick skillet on medium-high heat. Add garlic, ginger and green onions. Cook for 30 seconds but do not burn.

2. Add onion, carrots, zucchini and pepper. Stir-fry for 2 to 3 minutes.

3. Add green beans, mushrooms, broccoli and stock. Cook for 2 to 3 minutes. Cook, covered, for 1 more minute if necessary to help cook broccoli.

4. Add snowpeas and hoisin sauce and bring to a boil. Cook for 1 minute. Stir in sesame oil. Serve immediately.

PER SERVING

Calories	101
Protein	4 g
Fat	2.6 g
Saturates	0.3 g
Cholesterol	0 mg
Carbohydrate	18.3 g
Fibre	4.6 g
Sodium	125 mg
Potassium	497 mg

Excellent: Vitamin A; Vitamin C; Folacin
Good: Vitamin B$_6$

SAUTEED BRUSSELS SPROUT LEAVES

This is a very whimsical way to cook Brussels sprouts. People who don't normally like Brussels sprouts often love them cooked this way! Serve them as a bed for chops or roasted meats. You can also simply cut the sprouts into quarters and cook them a little longer — about 10 minutes. Leftovers can be stirred into mashed potatoes or rice.

Makes 8 servings

MAKE AHEAD
• Be careful not to overcook, and then reheat quickly.

2 tsp	olive oil	10 mL
1	clove garlic, finely chopped	1
2 lb	large Brussels sprouts, halved and broken apart into leaves	1 kg
¼ cup	water	50 mL
2 tbsp	tiny capers, rinsed and drained	25 mL
2 tbsp	chopped fresh parsley	25 mL
1 tbsp	lemon juice or balsamic vinegar	15 mL
	Salt and pepper to taste	

1. Heat oil in a wok or large, deep non-stick skillet on medium-high heat. Add garlic and cook gently until fragrant — about 1 minute.

2. Add sprout leaves and cook for about 1 minute. Add water and bring to a boil. Cook, stirring, for 2 to 3 minutes, or until water evaporates.

3. Stir in capers, parsley and lemon juice. Add salt and pepper to taste.

PER SERVING

Calories	55
Protein	2.9 g
Fat	1.7 g
Saturates	0.3 g
Cholesterol	0 mg
Carbohydrate	10.1 g
Fibre	4.9 g
Sodium	60 mg
Potassium	365 mg

Excellent: Vitamin C; Folacin

SAUTEED GREEN BEANS WITH BEAN SPROUTS AND GREEN ONIONS

MAKE AHEAD
- You can make this ahead and serve it at room temperature.

Serve this under lamb chops, salmon or thinly sliced steak. Leftovers can be added to a salad or to clear broth and served as a soup.

If you can't find really fresh bean sprouts, omit them. (In Asia at the markets you can buy cleaned bean sprouts that have had the ends removed. You can do this, too; it's time-consuming, but the sprouts end up looking like translucent jewels.)

Enoki mushrooms come in little shrink-wrapped packages. You cut off the stems and cut open the package at the same time.

Makes 6 to 8 servings

2 tsp	vegetable oil	10 mL
¾ lb	green beans, thinly sliced on the diagonal	375 g
1½ tbsp	soy sauce	20 mL
½ lb	bean sprouts, cleaned	250 g
1	package enoki mushrooms (3½ oz/100 g)	1
4	green onions, thinly sliced on the diagonal	4

1. Heat oil in a large, non-stick skillet or wok on medium-high heat. Add green beans and stir-fry for 1 minute.

2. Add soy sauce and bring to a boil. Add bean sprouts and saute for 30 seconds.

3. Stir in enoki mushrooms and green onions. Cook for 20 to 30 seconds.

Sauteed Asparagus with Enoki Mushrooms
Use asparagus instead of green beans. Omit the bean sprouts. Use twice as many enoki mushrooms.

PER SERVING

Calories	50
Protein	2.9 g
Fat	1.8 g
Saturates	0.2 g
Cholesterol	0 mg
Carbohydrate	7.8 g
Fibre	2.1 g
Sodium	265 mg
Potassium	279 mg

Good: Vitamin B$_6$; Folacin

BRAISED RED CABBAGE AND APPLES

Red cabbage is a wonderful vegetable that is often overlooked. It can be served raw in a slaw or salad or used as a garnish. Cooked, it is mild and sweet tasting. Use an apple like Golden Delicious, which won't completely fall apart when cooked.

Leftovers can be chopped and added to mashed potatoes or used as a filling in phyllo pastries (page 46).

Makes 8 servings

2 tsp	olive oil	10 mL
2	onions, thinly sliced	2
2	apples, peeled and thinly sliced	2
1	red cabbage, shredded (about 2 lb/1 kg or 8 cups/2 L)	1
2 tbsp	cider vinegar or red wine vinegar	25 mL
2 tbsp	maple syrup	25 mL
1 cup	apple juice or cider	250 mL
	Salt and pepper to taste	
2 tbsp	chopped fresh parsley	25 mL

1. In a Dutch oven or large, deep non-stick skillet, heat oil on medium-high heat. Add onions and apples. Cook for 5 minutes, or until tender.

2. Add cabbage, vinegar, maple syrup and apple juice. Bring to a boil. Cook, covered, over medium heat until tender, about 25 minutes. Season with salt and pepper and stir in parsley.

MAKE AHEAD
• This can be made a day ahead and reheated.

PER SERVING

Calories	89
Protein	1.6 g
Fat	1.5 g
Saturates	0.2 g
Cholesterol	0 mg
Carbohydrate	19.3 g
Fibre	3.8 g
Sodium	11 mg
Potassium	279 mg

Excellent: Vitamin C

BREAD STUFFING WITH HERBS

SERVING SUGGESTIONS
• The stuffing can be baked
  in muffin pans for easy
  serving.
• Chop all ingredients
  finely and use bread-
  crumbs instead of bread
  cubes. Shape the stuffing
  into balls (a small ice
  cream scoop works well)
  and bake on a baking
  sheet at 350°F/180°C
  for about 30 minutes.
  Makes about 48
  1½-inch/4 cm balls.

MAKE AHEAD
• This can be made ahead
  and baked while the
  turkey is roasting.

I like to bake stuffing beside the turkey. That way the stuffing does not draw moisture from the bird and you do not have to overcook the turkey (page 178) to ensure the stuffing is fully cooked. If you want more turkey flavour in the stuffing, simply spoon a few tablespoons of defatted turkey juice over the stuffing before serving. You can also add two heads of roasted garlic; squeeze the garlic out of the cloves and add along with the bread cubes.

Maria Armstrong, the producer of "Bonnie Stern Entertains," gave me a fabulous idea for serving stuffing in cute balls (see Serving Suggestions).

Any leftover stuffing can be used in frittatas (page 269), turkey sandwiches, or as an omelette filling.

Makes 12 servings

1 tbsp	olive oil	15 mL
2	onions, chopped	2
4	cloves garlic, finely chopped	4
4	stalks celery, chopped	4
4	leeks, trimmed and chopped	4
1½ lb	mushrooms (mixture of wild and cultivated), trimmed and sliced	750 g
1 lb	crusty bread, cut in 1-inch/2.5 cm cubes (about 6 cups/1.5 L)	500 g
4 cups	homemade chicken or turkey stock (page 79)	1 L
½ cup	chopped fresh parsley	125 mL
½ cup	chopped fresh sage, or 1 tbsp/15 mL dried	125 mL
2 tbsp	chopped fresh thyme, or 1 tsp/5 mL dried	25 mL
	Salt and pepper to taste	

1. Heat oil in a large, deep skillet or Dutch oven on medium-high heat. Add onions and garlic and cook for a few minutes until fragrant. Add celery and leeks. Cook for 5 minutes or until softened.

2. Add mushrooms and cook until any liquid evaporates. Add bread cubes and combine well. Add chicken stock, parsley, sage, thyme, salt and pepper.

3. Place stuffing in an oiled 13 x 9-inch/3.5 L baking dish (if you want the top crusty, leave uncovered; if you want it moist, cover with foil). Bake in a preheated 325°F/160°C oven for 30 to 40 minutes, or until heated thoroughly.

PER SERVING

Calories	162
Protein	6.7 g
Fat	2.2 g
Saturates	0.4 g
Cholesterol	1 mg
Carbohydrate	29.4 g
Fibre	3 g
Sodium	249 mg
Potassium	346 mg

Good: Niacin; Folacin; Iron

BUCKWHEAT BLINI
WITH SMOKED TROUT
(page 184)

BACKYARD BARBECUE MENU

Cranberry Orange "Sangria"

Spicy Thai Shrimp

Balsamic Maple-glazed Lamb
with Sweet Potatoes

Wheat Berry and Grilled
Corn Salad

Grilled Tomato Salad

Raspberry Upside-down Cake

(see recipes starting page 216)

SHOWN HERE:
CRANBERRY ORANGE "SANGRIA"
BALSAMIC MAPLE-GLAZED LAMB WITH SWEET POTATOES
WHEAT BERRY AND GRILLED CORN SALAD
GRILLED TOMATO SALAD

TEA IN THE AFTERNOON MENU

Potato Currant Scones

Chopped Salad Niçoise

Lime Chiffon Mousse
with Caramel and Fresh Fruit

Strawberries with Spiced Sugar
and Yogurt Cream

(see recipes starting page 300)

VEGETARIAN FEAST MENU

Sesame-seared Tofu Salad Rolls

Black Bean and Corn Hummos

Roasted Squash and Garlic Soup
with Beet Splash

Mediterranean Vegetable Strudel

Green Salad with
Tomato Soy Dressing *(page 116)*

Carrot Cake with
Marshmallow Frosting

(see recipes starting page 144)

SHOWN HERE:

MEDITERRANEAN VEGETABLE STRUDEL

ROASTED SQUASH AND GARLIC SOUP WITH BEET SPLASH

CARAMELIZED PEARS WITH TIRAMISU CREAM
(page 118)

MEDITERRANEAN DIET

People of the Mediterranean have long been known for robust good health. Recent nutritional research suggests that this may be partly due to diet. The Mediterranean diet contains lots of fruits, vegetables, legumes and grains with olive oil as the main source of fat. Fish, poultry, eggs and dairy (mostly cheese and yogurt) are eaten a few times per week and red meat only a few times per month.

Because this diet concentrates on complex carbohydrates in the form of breads, grain, pasta, beans, fruits and vegetables, it is high in fibre, lower in fat than the North American diet, often low in calories, and includes lots of important vitamins and minerals. The Mediterranean diet has also been associated with lowered risk of heart disease.

Olive oil, a basic ingredient of traditional Mediterranean cuisine, is rich in monounsaturated fats associated with lower levels of "bad" LDL-cholesterol while maintaining the level of "good" HDL-cholesterol. Lowering LDL-cholesterol is a key step in our fight against heart disease, and olive oil is a healthy oil when it replaces highly saturated fats in everyday cooking. Olive oil is also a source of vitamin E, which is being explored for its antioxidant role (page 152). However, while olive oil is a healthy oil, it still contains about 100 calories per tablespoon just like any other oil. If you eat it in large quantities, you may gain weight and offset the benefits of the healthy Mediterranean diet.

The lifestyle and culture of the people of the Mediterranean also play a part in their good health. They take time to relax with meals — a great stress reliever. And they tend to be more physically active, which is another factor in lowering heart-disease risk. Still to come is the verdict on red wine, but some research points to its benefits in moderate consumption. Most likely it is the combination of diet and lifestyle that makes the Mediterranean eating style so heart healthy.

SLICED WILD MUSHROOMS AND SHALLOTS

MAKE AHEAD
• This can be made ahead and served at room temperature.

At the teppanyaki bar in the Four Seasons Hotel in Tokyo, I watched the chef prepare all sorts of delicious vegetable dishes, including the green bean recipe on page 238 and this simple preparation of mushrooms. He cooked the whole mushrooms on a big grill, but I just use the barbecue or grill pan. Use leftovers in sandwiches, add to clear soups or chop and spoon on top of crackers or bread. You can also use regular (white button) mushrooms or cremini (brown button) in this recipe.

Makes 6 to 8 servings

1 lb	fresh wild mushrooms (shiitake or portobello or a combination)	500 g
1 tbsp	vegetable oil, divided	15 mL
2	shallots, thinly sliced	2
2 tbsp	soy sauce	25 mL
	Salt and pepper to taste	

1. Clean mushrooms well. Remove stems (save to use in homemade stocks). If you are using portobellos, gently scrape off gills if you wish (page 197).

2. Brush mushrooms with 1½ tsp/7 mL oil. Grill until lightly browned. Slice mushrooms.

3. Heat remaining 1½ tsp/7 mL oil in a non-stick skillet. Add shallots and cook gently for a few minutes until tender. Raise heat to medium-high and add mushrooms and soy sauce. Combine well with shallots. Cook for a few minutes until pan is dry. Season with salt and pepper.

PER SERVING

Calories	36
Protein	1.2 g
Fat	2.5 g
Saturates	0.2 g
Cholesterol	0 mg
Carbohydrate	3 g
Fibre	1 g
Sodium	347 mg
Potassium	161 mg

COUSCOUS WITH VEGETABLES

Everyone loves couscous, and you can make it plain or fancy. Whether you are using regular or whole wheat, make sure you buy quick-cooking couscous; if you use quick-cooking whole wheat couscous, increase the liquid to 4½ cups/1.125 L.

Leftovers can be tossed with a dressing and served as a salad.

Makes 8 servings

3 cups	boiling water or stock	750 mL
½ tsp	cinnamon	2 mL
½ tsp	ground cumin	2 mL
1 tbsp	honey	15 mL
1 tbsp	lemon juice	15 mL
3 cups	quick-cooking couscous	750 mL
2 tsp	olive oil	10 mL
1	small onion, finely chopped	1
1	small carrot, finely chopped	1
½	sweet red pepper, finely chopped	½
1	small zucchini, finely chopped	1
⅓ cup	currants or raisins	75 mL
	Salt and pepper to taste	
3 tbsp	finely chopped fresh cilantro or basil	45 mL

1. In a saucepan or large measuring cup, combine boiling water with cinnamon, cumin, honey and lemon juice.

2. Place couscous in large, shallow baking dish. Pour boiling water mixture over couscous. Cover tightly with foil. Allow to rest for at least 10 minutes.

3. Meanwhile, in a large, deep non-stick skillet or Dutch oven, heat oil on medium heat. Add onion, carrot, red pepper, zucchini and currants and cook gently for 5 to 10 minutes until very tender.

4. Fluff couscous with a fork. Combine with vegetables. Season with salt and pepper. Stir in cilantro.

SERVING SUGGESTIONS
- Serve on a large platter with chicken, lamb shanks or a stew on top.
- Mound couscous to a point on a large platter.

MAKE AHEAD
- Make ahead and keep warm or cover tightly and reheat. If the couscous becomes dry, stir in some thick yogurt, yogurt cheese (page 303) or a liquid such as orange juice.

Israeli Couscous
Israeli couscous is different from traditional couscous. It is more like little pearl pasta, and must be cooked in boiling water rather than simply being reconstituted.

PER SERVING
Calories	305
Protein	9.4 g
Fat	1.6 g
Saturates	0.2 g
Cholesterol	0 mg
Carbohydrate	62.9 g
Fibre	4.1 g
Sodium	21 mg
Potassium	272 mg

Good: Vitamin A; Niacin; Folacin

FRAGRANT RICE WITH AROMATIC SPICES

MAKE AHEAD
- The rice can be rinsed and soaked ahead. Or you could make the whole dish a few hours ahead, cover and keep warm in a 200°F/100°C oven.

This rice was inspired by Madhur Jaffrey, who is a fantastic cook as well as an accomplished actress. There is no end to her talents, yet she and her recipes are always friendly and approachable.

Serve this as part of an East Indian meal or with any spicy dish. If you have any leftovers, add dressing and serve cold as a salad.

Makes 8 servings

2 cups	fragrant or basmati rice	500 mL
2 tsp	vegetable oil	10 mL
3	whole cardamom pods, crushed	3
1	2-inch/5 cm cinnamon stick	1
4	whole cloves	4
1	onion, thinly sliced	1
2	carrots, grated in long pieces	2
2½ cups	homemade chicken stock (page 79) or vegetable stock (page 69) or water	625 mL
1 cup	peas	250 mL
	Salt to taste	

1. Rinse rice well. Place in a bowl and cover with cold water. Allow to soak for 30 minutes or up to a few hours.

2. Heat oil in a large saucepan on medium-high heat. Add cardamom, cinnamon and cloves. Cook for 1 or 2 minutes until fragrant. Add onion and cook until browned. Add carrots and combine well.

3. Drain rice well and stir into onion mixture. Cook until rice is slightly translucent, about 2 minutes. Add stock. Bring to a boil. Reduce heat to medium-low, cover and cook for 12 minutes.

4. Add peas, cover and cook for 4 or 5 minutes longer. Stir gently to combine and season with salt to taste. Remove whole spices or warn guests not to eat them.

PER SERVING

Calories	215
Protein	6.2 g
Fat	2 g
Saturates	0.3 g
Cholesterol	0 mg
Carbohydrate	41.8 g
Fibre	1.9 g
Sodium	39 mg
Potassium	201 mg

Excellent: Vitamin A

SUSHI RICE "PILAF"

Soaking the rice isn't essential, but it does result in a better texture. This can also be made with brown rice.

Sushi-flavoured rice is so delicious that you don't want to wait to make sushi to have it. Be sure to wash the rice in plenty of cold water before using.

Makes 6 to 8 servings

2 cups	sushi rice (page 37)	500 mL
2½ cups	cold water	625 mL
¼ cup	seasoned rice vinegar (page 132)	50 mL
2 tbsp	chopped pickled ginger, optional	25 mL
2 tbsp	sesame seeds, toasted (page 245)	25 mL
2 tbsp	finely chopped fresh cilantro or parsley	25 mL

1. Rinse rice by placing in a large bowl and covering with cold water. Swish rice and water and then drain well. Repeat until you can clearly see rice through the water.

2. Place rice in a medium saucepan. Add 2½ cups/625 mL cold water, cover and allow to soak for 30 minutes.

3. Place saucepan on high heat, cover and bring to a boil. Cook for 1 minute. Reduce heat to low and cook for 10 minutes. Remove from heat and allow rice to rest for 10 minutes or more. Do not remove cover at any time during cooking!

4. Gently fluff rice and toss with vinegar, pickled ginger (if using), sesame seeds and cilantro.

Sushi Salad

This homestyle sushi dish is called "chirasi" (meaning scattered), and it is very popular in Japanese households. Simply combine any leftovers or other additions with the rice — chopped pickled ginger, peas, diced cucumber, diced cooked asparagus or green beans, diced mushrooms, grilled tofu, meat, poultry or fish. Use a little more rice vinegar for the dressing.

MAKE AHEAD
• This can all be prepared ahead. Serve at room temperature or reheat.

Toasting Sesame Seeds
Toasting gives sesame seeds twice as much flavour. Place them in a dry skillet and shake over medium-high heat until lightly toasted. Or spread on a baking sheet and bake at 350°F/180°C for a couple of minutes. Watch them carefully, as they can burn quickly!

PER SERVING

Calories	274
Protein	5.2 g
Fat	2.1 g
Saturates	0.3 g
Cholesterol	0 mg
Carbohydrate	57.1 g
Fibre	0.9 g
Sodium	357 mg
Potassium	62 mg

TASTE OF SUMMER

Double-wrapped Shrimp Salad Rolls

Asparagus Soup
with Fresh Tarragon

Cedar-planked Salmon

Potato and Arugula Salad
with Mustard and Roasted Garlic

Bumbleberry Cobbler

*Summer is a time for serving dishes that highlight local fresh produce and fresh herbs.
Eat outdoors or bring this menu inside and create a relaxed outdoor feeling by decorating
the table with lots of fresh flowers, candles and lanterns.*

WORK PLAN

MAKE AHEAD

• Make the soup a day ahead or make a few weeks ahead and freeze. It is also delicious served cold.

• Make the salad a day ahead and refrigerate, but do not add the arugula.

SAME DAY

• Make the cobbler the same day and serve warm or at room temperature.

• Make the shrimp rolls earlier in the day.

• Marinate the salmon earlier in the day.

• Soak the cedar plank in a tub of water for a few hours before using.

• Reheat soup or serve cold.

• Add arugula to salad just before serving.

PRESENTATION IDEAS

- Put twinkle lights under the table and use a gauzy tablecloth that allows the lights to glow through.
- Use glasses filled with a little water as candle holders.
- Use a watermelon as a centrepiece.
- Tuck napkins in small flower pots and place at each setting. Use plant markers as place cards.
- Bring outdoor table and chairs inside.
- Decorate chair backs with fresh or dried flowers.

MATCHING FOOD WITH WINE*

If you want to serve wine: A dry or off-dry Riesling (Ontario, British Columbia, New York State, Germany) would go well with the salad rolls; its fruity flavours will complement the sweetness of the shrimp and mango. The red-berry fruit of a Pinot Noir (Oregon or Burgundy) would be a perfect foil for the barbecued salmon.

* See Alcohol (page 274).

DOUBLE-WRAPPED SHRIMP SALAD ROLLS

SERVING SUGGESTIONS
• Make tiny salad rolls and
serve as mini appetizers.
• Serve rolls on a platter
lined with banana leaves.

MAKE AHEAD
• You can make these a few
hours ahead. Arrange in a
single layer on a baking
sheet lined with a damp
tea towel. Cover with
another damp tea towel

These rolls can be made with thinly sliced rare grilled steak, smoked salmon or strips of grilled tofu. The raw shrimp can also be brushed with extra marinade and grilled or broiled for 2 to 3 minutes per side instead of simmered. Sometimes rice vermicelli noodles are put inside, too. And crab would be terrific!

These rolls are also a great way to use up leftover Asian salads or stir-fries.

Makes 20 rolls

Thai Dipping Sauce

¼ cup	rice vinegar (page 132)	50 mL
2 tbsp	Thai fish sauce (page 105) or soy sauce	25 mL
2 tbsp	lime juice	25 mL
2 tbsp	granulated sugar	25 mL
½ tsp	hot chili paste	2 mL

Filling

20	extra-large shrimp, cleaned (page 249) and skewered straight through from head to tail	20
20	rice paper wrappers, approx.	20
1	ripe mango, peeled and cut in very thin strips	1
1	carrot, cut in very thin strips and blanched in boiling water for 30 seconds	1
1	sweet red pepper, cut in very thin strips	1
1 cup	bean sprouts	250 mL
20	large leaves fresh cilantro	20
20	leaves fresh mint	20
20	pieces Boston lettuce (about ¼ leaf each)	20
20	fresh chives, approx.	20

PER ROLL

Calories	57
Protein	5.1 g
Fat	0.5 g
Saturates	0.1 g
Cholesterol	32 mg
Carbohydrate	8.3 g
Fibre	0.5 g
Sodium	176 mg
Potassium	87 mg

Good: Vitamin A

1. To make dipping sauce, in a small bowl, combine vinegar, fish sauce, lime juice, sugar and chili paste. Reserve.

2. Place skewered shrimp in a deep skillet of boiling water. Cook for a few minutes just until shrimp turn pink and opaque. Cool. Remove shrimp from skewers.

3. Working with 2 or 3 wrappers at a time, soften rice paper wrappers in a large bowl of very warm water for about 20 seconds. Arrange on damp tea towels in a single layer.

4. Arrange one shrimp on the bottom third of the wrapper. Arrange a strip of mango, carrot, pepper, a few bean sprouts and a leaf of cilantro and mint on top. Fold up bottom, fold in both sides and roll up snuggly. Wrap each roll in a piece of lettuce and tie it on with a chive. (You could also put lettuce inside the rice paper wrapper.)

5. Serve salad rolls with dipping sauce.

Buying and Cleaning Shrimp

I like to buy shrimp frozen in the shell because it is less expensive and the shells protect the shrimp from freezer burn. I usually buy 4 to 5 pounds at a time and defrost what I need by holding a portion of the shrimp block under cold water until I can break it off and defrost it in a bowl of cold water or in the refrigerator overnight. The rest of the shrimp can be returned to the freezer.

To clean shrimp, peel the shells off with your fingers and wiggle the tail piece off gently. Clean the shrimp by running a knife about ¼ inch/5 mm deep along the top side of the shrimp. If the intestinal tract is black and full of sand, remove and discard it.

You can also buy shimp already cleaned and frozen, in or out of the shell. Most "fresh" shrimp that you see in stores has been previously frozen and defrosted, as fresh shrimp is highly perishable.

ASPARAGUS SOUP
WITH FRESH TARRAGON

- Lay one whole asparagus spear, barely cooked, across bowl as a garnish.
- Garnish soup with a skewered shrimp or chicken strip.

MAKE AHEAD
- This soup can be made a day ahead and refrigerated, or make a few weeks ahead and freeze. Reheat quickly so the soup does not overcook and discolour.

I love asparagus and this soup has an especially intense taste. The soup can be completely or partially pureed.

Makes 6 to 8 servings

2 lb	asparagus	1 kg
1 tbsp	olive oil	15 mL
1	onion, chopped	1
2	cloves garlic, chopped	2
1	large Yukon Gold or baking potato, peeled and diced	1
4 cups	homemade chicken stock (page 79) or vegetable stock (page 69)	1 L
½ cup	dry white wine (preferably Chardonnay), additional stock or water	125 mL
2 tbsp	chopped fresh tarragon	25 mL
	Salt and pepper to taste	
¼ cup	crumbled chèvre (goat cheese) or mild blue cheese	50 mL
1	bunch chives, cut in 2-inch/5 cm lengths	1

1. Trim asparagus and peel about 1 inch/2.5 cm up stalks. Bring a large skillet of water to a boil and cook asparagus for about 2 minutes. Drain well. Cut off tips and reserve for garnish. Dice remaining asparagus.

2. Heat olive oil in a large saucepan or Dutch oven on medium-high heat. Add onion and garlic. Cook for a few minutes until tender and fragrant.

3. Add potato, stock and wine. Bring to a boil, reduce heat, cover and simmer gently for 15 minutes, or until potato is very tender.

4. Add asparagus stalks to saucepan and cook for a few minutes. Puree all or half the soup in a food mill, food processor or blender. Add tarragon, salt and pepper. Heat just until hot and serve garnished with cheese, asparagus tips and chives.

PER SERVING

Calories	127
Protein	8.1 g
Fat	4.9 g
Saturates	1.5 g
Cholesterol	4 mg
Carbohydrate	13.2 g
Fibre	2.6 g
Sodium	58 mg
Potassium	458 mg

Excellent: Folacin
Good: Vitamin C; Niacin; Vitamin B$_6$

CEDAR-PLANKED SALMON

This is fun and delicious. "Planked" foods are a native tradition but have become extremely fashionable. Get a few planks of untreated cedar from a lumber yard — sometimes you can use the same one a few times until it gets too charred. You may also want to save one board just for presentation (the one that the fish has been cooked on usually looks a bit worn).

If you do not want to barbecue this, place the soaked plank on a rimmed baking sheet, lay the marinated fish on top and cover loosely with foil. Roast in a preheated 450°F/ 230°C oven for about 20 minutes, or until fish barely flakes. Remove foil for the last 5 minutes of the cooking time.

You can also use this marinade and simply roast, grill or barbecue the fish. Use leftover fish in sandwiches or salads, or puree with a little yogurt cheese, mayonnaise or cream cheese to make a smoky spread.

Makes 6 to 8 servings

2 lb	salmon fillet, with skin	1 kg
2 tsp	sesame oil	10 mL
1	clove garlic, minced	1
1 tbsp	minced fresh ginger root	15 mL
3 tbsp	brown sugar	45 mL
1 tsp	salt	5 mL
½ tsp	pepper	2 mL
1 tsp	ground cumin	5 mL

1. Soak 12 x 8-inch/30 x 20 cm cedar plank in a tub of cold water for a few hours.

2. With salmon skin side down, score fish in about 2-inch/5 cm strips, but do not cut through skin.

3. In a small bowl, combine sesame oil, garlic and ginger. Rub into salmon. In another small bowl, combine sugar, salt, pepper and cumin. Rub into slits in fish. Allow salmon to marinate for 10 to 20 minutes.

4. Place salmon on soaked plank. Place plank on rack of barbecue. Close lid or cover with foil and barbecue for 15 to 25 minutes, or until salmon is cooked through. Remove cover for last 5 minutes of cooking. Do not turn fish during cooking.

5. Lift salmon off and serve without skin.

SERVING SUGGESTIONS
- Serve the salmon on a clean plank decorated with fresh herbs.
- Use individual clean planks as plates. Vegetables can go on side plates or right on the planks if there is room.

MAKE AHEAD
- This is also delicious served at room temperature.

PER SERVING

Calories	287
Protein	27.5 g
Fat	16.5 g
Saturates	3.3 g
Cholesterol	78 mg
Carbohydrate	5.5 g
Fibre	0.1 g
Sodium	364 mg
Potassium	33 mg

Excellent: Thiamine; Niacin; Vitamin B$_6$; Vitamin B$_{12}$
Good: Folacin

POTATO AND ARUGULA SALAD WITH MUSTARD AND ROASTED GARLIC

This is a wonderful summer potato salad, perfect for barbecues and al fresco dinners. For a one-dish meal add grilled chicken or steak. Be sure to use a good-quality vinegar in the dressing.

Makes 6 to 8 servings

2 lb	small potatoes	1 kg
½ cup	red wine vinegar	125 mL
½ tsp	salt	2 mL
1	bunch arugula, trimmed	1

Sherry Vinegar and Shallot Dressing

2	heads roasted garlic (page 41)	2
3 tbsp	sherry vinegar or red wine vinegar	45 mL
1	shallot, finely chopped, soaked in ice water for 30 minutes and drained	1
2 tsp	Dijon mustard	10 mL
½ tsp	salt	2 mL
½ tsp	pepper	2 mL
3 tbsp	olive oil	45 mL

1. Scrub potatoes well or peel if they are very dirty. Cut in half if necessary (potatoes should be about 1½ inches/4 cm in diameter). Place in a large pot of water with vinegar and salt. Bring to a boil and cook for 20 minutes, or until tender. Drain well.

2. Meanwhile, to prepare dressing, squeeze garlic out of cloves into food processor. Add vinegar, shallot, mustard, salt, pepper and olive oil and blend together. Taste and adjust seasonings if necessary.

3. Combine dressing with hot potatoes. Cool for about 5 minutes.

4. Arrange arugula in a shallow bowl and spoon potatoes and dressing on top. Toss lightly. Serve warm or at room temperature.

PER SERVING

Calories	198
Protein	4 g
Fat	7.2 g
Saturates	1 g
Cholesterol	0 mg
Carbohydrate	31.8 g
Fibre	2.7 g
Sodium	420 mg
Potassium	651 mg

Excellent: Vitamin B$_6$
Good: Vitamin C; Folacin

BUMBLEBERRY COBBLER

I first heard about "bumbleberry" when I was in Prince Edward Island and had a bumbleberry pie. Bumbleberry, it seems, is not actually a fruit but a mix of fantasy fruits that does not seem to be terribly consistent.

You can use fresh or frozen fruit in this. (In winter make it with cranberries, apples and pears.) Chop up any leftover fruit and pastry, mix with plain yogurt and serve like a trifle or in long glasses like a parfait.

Makes 8 to 10 servings

1 lb	rhubarb, diced (about 4 cups/1 L)	500 g
2	apples, peeled, cored and diced (3 cups/750 mL)	2
1 cup	raspberries	250 mL
1 cup	blueberries	250 mL
½ cup	granulated sugar	125 mL
3 tbsp	all-purpose flour	45 mL

Biscuit Topping

1 cup	all-purpose flour	250 mL
½ cup	whole wheat flour	125 mL
3 tbsp	granulated sugar	45 mL
2 tsp	baking powder	10 mL
⅓ cup	soft non-hydrogenated margarine, cold, cut in bits	75 mL
1	egg	1
¾ cup	buttermilk	175 mL
2 tbsp	icing sugar, sifted	25 mL

1. In a large bowl, combine rhubarb, apples, raspberries, blueberries, sugar and flour. Spoon into a 12 x 8-inch/2.5 L baking dish.

2. To make topping, in a large bowl, combine flours with sugar and baking powder. Cut in margarine with a pastry blender or fingertips (or use a food processor).

3. In a medium bowl, whisk egg with buttermilk. Stir into flour mixture until a soft dough is formed. Spoon batter on top of fruit in 8 large spoonfuls, leaving room for fruit to bubble up on sides.

4. Bake in a preheated 375°F/190°C oven for 45 to 50 minutes, or until topping is browned and fruit bubbles. Sprinkle with icing sugar before serving.

SERVING SUGGESTIONS
- Spoon a biscuit on each dessert plate or in a wide, shallow bowl. Top and surround with fruit. Dust with more icing sugar.
- Serve with a spoonful of sweetened yogurt cheese (page 303).
- Serve with frozen yogurt or sorbet.
- Sprinkle with edible flowers (page 22).
- Serve with raspberry sauce (page 296).
- Have bowls of fresh berries on the table to garnish the cobbler.

MAKE AHEAD
- This can be made ahead and served at room temperature or reheated in a preheated 350°F/ 180°C oven for about 30 minutes or until warm.

PER SERVING

Calories	300
Protein	5.4 g
Fat	9 g
Saturates	1.4 g
Cholesterol	28 mg
Carbohydrate	51.5 g
Fibre	4.5 g
Sodium	202 mg
Potassium	315 mg

BREAKFAST

Breakfast is called the most important meal of the day for good reason. After not eating for 12 to 14 hours, your blood sugar is low, you're hungry, and your brain, as well as the rest of your body, needs refueling. Breakfast enhances learning and physical performance. Studies show that children who skip breakfast don't do as well on tests of learning, memory, concentration and language.

Breakfast stimulates the metabolism after a night of fasting, so it gets the whole system going. This is good news for people trying to control their weight, blood sugar and/or cholesterol. If you think you'll lose weight by skipping breakfast, think again. Most breakfast skippers more than make up the calories of their morning meal later in the day. But they rarely make up the nutrients, especially calcium, fibre, vitamin D, iron and zinc.

An ideal breakfast should include some carbohydrate (cereal, bread and/or fruit) and some protein (milk, yogurt, cottage cheese, peanut butter, cheese or an egg). A breakfast of only carbohydrates (toast and juice, for example) is burned up quickly and can result in hungry moments later in the morning. Adding a bit of protein provides longer-lasting energy. Your breakfast is digested more slowly and your blood sugar rises more steadily.

If time is an issue, plan the night before and make something portable that you can eat in the car, on the bus or at your desk: a muffin with a small amount of peanut butter or cheese, a sandwich, cheese and crackers, yogurt plus cereal in a zip-lock bag. If you're not hungry first thing in the morning, take something for your morning break.

If you want your kids to eat breakfast, eat it with them. Have a leisurely breakfast on the weekends so the family gets used to enjoying a morning meal. Breakfast cereal with milk and fresh fruit is quick and easy and can provide a good portion of your daily fibre, calcium, vitamin D, iron and B vitamin requirements. Try whole-grain varieties or hot cereal (one minute in the microwave). Look for cereals with at least 2 grams of fibre per serving. These (as well as whole wheat bread or bagels, bran muffins or oatmeal with raisins) will go a long way to meeting your daily fibre needs. If you prefer lower-fibre cereals, add a banana, dried fruit or berries.

Let your kids choose their favourite cereal. Don't worry if it is higher in sugar. The B-vitamins, iron, zinc and other nutrients are still there in abundance, and it's better to have them eat a breakfast they enjoy than no breakfast at all. Let them make a breakfast shake of milk or yogurt with fruits and/or grains. Or go with the non-traditional — leftovers, a tuna melt, pizza, grilled cheese sandwich, banana bread, bread pretzels or a cereal bar.

BREADS, CONDIMENTS AND BEVERAGES

ASIAGO DROP BISCUITS

These delicious little drop biscuits are great for brunch, tea time or a snack. Leftovers can be diced and baked as croutons.

Makes 16 biscuits

MAKE AHEAD
• These are best baked just before serving, but the ingredients up to the end of step 2 can be mixed together, covered tightly and refrigerated up to one day ahead. Stir in the buttermilk just before baking.

2 cups	all-purpose flour	500 mL
1 cup	whole wheat flour	250 mL
2 tbsp	granulated sugar	25 mL
1 tbsp	baking powder	15 mL
1 tsp	baking soda	5 mL
⅓ cup	soft non-hydrogenated margarine, cold	75 mL
⅔ cup	grated Asiago, Cheddar or smoked mozzarella cheese	150 mL
1¾ cups	buttermilk	425 mL

1. In a large bowl, combine all-purpose flour, whole wheat flour, sugar, baking powder and baking soda. Stir together well. (If baking powder or baking soda are lumpy, sift ingredients together.)

2. Cut margarine into flour mixture until it is in tiny bits. Stir in grated cheese.

3. Pour buttermilk over flour mixture and stir until a rough batter is formed.

4. Drop batter in 16 mounds on a baking sheet lined with parchment paper. Bake in a preheated 425°F/220°C oven for 12 to 15 minutes, or until lightly browned.

Herbed Asiago Biscuits

To the flour mixture, add 2 tbsp/25 mL chopped fresh herbs (e.g., rosemary, thyme or sage) or 1 tsp/5 mL spices (e.g., pepper or crushed cumin, caraway or fennel seeds).

PER BISCUIT

Calories	151
Protein	4.5 g
Fat	5.7 g
Saturates	1.6 g
Cholesterol	5 mg
Carbohydrate	20.7 g
Fibre	1.4 g
Sodium	240 mg
Potassium	91 mg

FIVE-GRAIN MUFFINS

These muffins almost sound too good for you to be so delicious. You can buy different kinds of five- and seven-grain cereals, and as long as they are fairly fine (e.g., five-minute oats), they should work well in this recipe. The mix that I have contains cracked wheat, cracked rye, rolled oats, cornmeal and flax seeds. You could also make your own multi-grain mix (page 287).

Serve these for breakfast or brunch. Leftovers can be broken up and dried in a 350°F/180°C oven. Layer with yogurt and fresh berries for a breakfast parfait.

Makes 12 medium muffins

1 cup	five-grain cereal mix or rolled oats	250 mL
1 cup	boiling water	250 mL
1	egg	1
½ cup	brown sugar	125 mL
¼ cup	vegetable oil	50 mL
½ cup	buttermilk or low-fat yogurt	125 mL
1 cup	all-purpose flour	250 mL
2 tsp	baking powder	10 mL
1 tsp	baking soda	5 mL
¼ tsp	salt	1 mL
¼ tsp	cinnamon	1 mL
½ cup	chopped dates, raisins or dried apricots	125 mL

1. Place five-grain cereal mix in a large bowl. Pour boiling water over top. Allow to rest for 15 minutes.

2. Meanwhile, in a separate bowl, beat together egg, brown sugar, oil and buttermilk.

3. In a separate bowl, sift or mix together flour, baking powder, baking soda, salt and cinnamon.

4. When cereal has softened, stir in egg mixture and then quickly blend in flour mixture. Stir in dates.

5. Spoon batter into non-stick, lightly oiled or paper-lined muffin cups (an ice cream scoop works well). Bake in a preheated 400°F/200°C oven for 22 to 25 minutes, or until muffins are slightly puffed and firm to the touch. Remove from pan and cool on a rack.

PER MUFFIN

Calories	188
Protein	3.9 g
Fat	5.5 g
Saturates	0.5 g
Cholesterol	18 mg
Carbohydrate	31.9 g
Fibre	2.3 g
Sodium	212 mg
Potassium	113 mg

CHUNKY BANANA MUFFINS

Use homemade or low-fat storebought granola in this recipe. You can add ½ cup/125 mL diced apricots, prunes or dates. You can make these into mini muffins but bake for 15 to 20 minutes. These muffins freeze well.

Makes 12 large muffins

Granola

In a large bowl, combine 4 cups/1 L rolled oats, 1 cup/250 mL sliced almonds, ½ cup/125 mL unsweetened coconut, ½ cup/125 mL sunflower seeds, ½ cup/125 mL wheat bran and ½ tsp/2 mL cinnamon.

In a saucepan, combine ½ cup/125 mL brown sugar and ⅓ cup/75 mL honey or maple syrup. Bring to a boil. Toss with oat mixture.

Place granola on a large baking sheet lined with parchment paper. Bake in a preheated 325°F/160°C oven for 35 to 40 minutes, or until lightly toasted. Turn and bake for 10 to 15 minutes longer. Break up granola and cool. Stir in 1 cup/250 mL chopped dried fruit. Store in an airtight container. Makes about 6 cups/1.5 L.

1½ cups	all-purpose flour	375 mL
1 cup	whole wheat flour	250 mL
½ cup	wheat bran	125 mL
¾ cup	brown sugar	175 mL
1½ tsp	baking powder	7 mL
¾ tsp	baking soda	4 mL
¼ tsp	salt	1 mL
½ cup	vegetable oil	125 mL
2	eggs	2
½ cup	buttermilk	125 mL
1 tsp	vanilla	5 mL
1 cup	mashed ripe bananas	250 mL
1 cup	diced bananas	250 mL
¾ cup	granola, plus 2 tbsp/25 mL for topping	175 mL

1. In a large bowl, combine flours, bran, sugar, baking powder, baking soda and salt.

2. In a separate bowl, combine oil, eggs, buttermilk and vanilla. Stir in mashed bananas.

3. Add wet ingredients to dry ingredients and stir just until combined. Stir in diced bananas and granola.

4. Spoon batter into 12 large lightly oiled non-stick muffin cups. Bake in a preheated 350°F/180°C oven for 25 to 30 minutes, or until brown and firm to the touch.

PER LARGE MUFFIN

Calories	319
Protein	6.3 g
Fat	12.3 g
Saturates	1.6 g
Cholesterol	36 mg
Carbohydrate	49.2 g
Fibre	4.3 g
Sodium	181 mg
Potassium	336 mg

Good: Vitamin B$_6$; Folacin; Iron

SOUTHWEST CORNMEAL SCONES

This is a great savoury biscuit. Serve it as a snack, with a soup or with a Southwest-theme dinner.

Leftovers can be crumbled and used in stuffings, as a breading for chicken or as a topping for casseroles.

Makes 12 scones

2 cups	all-purpose flour	500 mL
3 tbsp	cornmeal	45 mL
1 tbsp	baking powder	15 mL
1 tbsp	granulated sugar	15 mL
1 tsp	ground cumin	5 mL
½ tsp	salt	2 mL
½ tsp	pepper	2 mL
¼ cup	soft non-hydrogenated margarine, cold	50 mL
½ cup	grated smoked mozzarella, Monterey Jack or Cheddar cheese	125 mL
1	jalapeño or chipotle (page 73), finely chopped	1
1 cup	buttermilk, divided	250 mL
1 tbsp	cumin or caraway seeds	15 mL

1. In a large bowl, combine flour, cornmeal, baking powder, sugar, ground cumin, salt and pepper. With a pastry blender or your fingertips, cut in margarine until it is in tiny bits.

2. Stir in cheese and jalapeño. Pour ⅞ cup/225 mL buttermilk over mixture. Work the dough with your fingers until it becomes soft and manageable.

3. Gently press dough into a non-stick or lightly oiled 8-inch/20 cm round baking pan and score top to make 12 wedges. Brush surface with remaining 2 tbsp/25 mL buttermilk and sprinkle with cumin seeds.

4. Bake in a preheated 425°F/220°C oven for 20 to 25 minutes, or until golden and cooked through. Remove from pan and cool on a wire rack. Cut into wedges.

SERVING SUGGESTION

• Form dough into 12 individual scones. Place on a parchment-lined baking sheet and bake for 12 to 15 minutes until golden. Cut in half horizontally and serve with a goat cheese spread (page 58) as an appetizer.

MAKE AHEAD

• These taste best when freshly baked, but you can combine the dry ingredients in advance, cover well and refrigerate overnight. Just before serving, combine everything, bake and serve.

PER SCONE

Calories	147
Protein	4.5 g
Fat	5.2 g
Saturates	1.2 g
Cholesterol	3 mg
Carbohydrate	20.5 g
Fibre	0.9 g
Sodium	259 mg
Potassium	82 mg

FRESH CILANTRO AND MINT CHUTNEY

This is delicious with lamb or with any East Indian meal. It also makes a great dressing for a potato salad, or it can be used to season soups or salad dressings.

Makes ¾ cup/175 mL

2 cups	fresh cilantro (leaves, stems and roots)	500 mL
1 cup	fresh mint leaves	250 mL
1	jalapeño, halved	1
3 tbsp	boiling water	45 mL
3 tbsp	rice vinegar (page 132)	45 mL
	Salt and pepper to taste	

1. Place cilantro, mint and jalapeño in a food processor or blender and chop finely. Add boiling water and puree. Add vinegar and season with salt and pepper.

CARAMELIZED CRANBERRY SAUCE

This cranberry sauce is wonderful with roast turkey or in turkey sandwiches. If you do not want to caramelize the sugar, simply put everything in a pot and cook until the cranberries pop and the sauce thickens. Add one chopped jalapeño if you like things spicy.

Makes about 2 cups/500 mL

1 cup	granulated sugar	250 mL
¼ cup	cold water	50 mL
1 cup	apple, orange or cranberry juice	250 mL
¾ lb	frozen or fresh cranberries	375 g
¼ cup	chopped candied ginger, optional	50 mL

1. Combine sugar and water in a large, heavy saucepan. On high heat, bring mixture to a boil, stirring. Without stirring, cook until mixture turns golden. (If mixture crystallizes, don't worry; sugar should melt again when sauce cooks.)

2. Standing back, add juice. Mixture will bubble up furiously. Add cranberries and ginger (if using). Bring to a boil. Reduce heat and cook gently for 10 minutes, or until cranberries pop and mixture thickens. Sauce will become thicker when cool.

PER TABLESPOON

Calories	4
Protein	0.2 g
Fat	0.1 g
Saturates	0 g
Cholesterol	0 mg
Carbohydrate	0.9 g
Fibre	0.3 g
Sodium	2 mg
Potassium	38 mg

MAKE AHEAD

• This can be made a few days in advance. Serve warm, cold or at room temperature.

PER TABLESPOON

Calories	33
Protein	0 g
Fat	0 g
Saturates	0 g
Cholesterol	0 mg
Carbohydrate	8.5 g
Fibre	0.5 g
Sodium	0 mg
Potassium	17 mg

SPICY RED PEPPER "KETCHUP"

Try this with meatloaf, sandwiches or any roasted or grilled food.

Makes about 4 cups/1 L

1	28-oz/796 mL can plum tomatoes with juices, broken up	1
3	sweet red peppers, raw or roasted (page 49), peeled and cut in pieces	3
1	small red onion, chopped	1
⅓ cup	honey or brown sugar	75 mL
¼ cup	rice vinegar (page 132)	50 mL
1 tsp	ground cumin	5 mL
½ tsp	ground fennel, anise or five-spice powder, optional	2 mL
1 tsp	pureed chipotles (page 73) or finely chopped jalapeño	5 mL
2	cloves garlic, chopped	2
1 tbsp	chopped fresh ginger root	15 mL
½ tsp	salt	2 mL

1. Place tomatoes, peppers, onion, honey, vinegar, cumin, fennel, chipotles, garlic, ginger and salt in a large saucepan and bring to a boil. Reduce heat and simmer gently, uncovered, until thick — 30 to 40 minutes.

2. In a food processor or blender, puree mixture until smooth or leave slightly chunky. Taste and adjust seasonings if necessary.

PER TABLESPOON

Calories	12
Protein	0.2 g
Fat	0.1 g
Saturates	0 g
Cholesterol	0 mg
Carbohydrate	2.9 g
Fibre	0.3 g
Sodium	40 mg
Potassium	47 mg

Strawberry Lemonade

This refreshing drink can be made with fresh or frozen berries. Blueberries, blackberries and raspberries also work well. Use freshly squeezed lemon juice.

Makes 6 to 8 servings

2 cups	strawberries	500 mL
1 cup	granulated sugar	250 mL
1 cup	lemon juice	250 mL
3 cups	sparkling mineral water	750 mL
2 cups	ice cubes	500 mL

1. In a medium saucepan, combine strawberries and sugar. Bring to a boil and cook gently for 5 minutes. Strain through a strainer, pushing through as much pulp as possible. Cool.

2. Add lemon juice to puree and place in a pitcher with sparkling water and ice.

MAKE AHEAD

- The strawberry/lemon puree can be made ahead and water added as you use it. Use ¼ to ⅓ cup/50 to 75 mL puree for every ½ cup/125 mL water.

PER SERVING

Calories	149
Protein	0.4 g
Fat	0.1 g
Saturates	0 g
Cholesterol	0 mg
Carbohydrate	39.2 g
Fibre	0.9 g
Sodium	3 mg
Potassium	107 mg

Good: Vitamin C

Hot Spiced Apple Cider

Greet your guests with warm apple cider and they will be yours forever. If you want to make this alcoholic, add ⅓ cup/75 mL dark rum, brandy or apple brandy to the cider before serving.

Makes 6 to 8 servings

4 cups	unsweetened apple cider	1 L
1	cinnamon stick, broken in half	1
3	whole cloves	3
5	whole allspice	5
4	whole black peppercorns	4
¼ tsp	grated nutmeg	1 mL
2 tbsp	honey	25 mL

1. Place cider in a large saucepan with cinnamon, cloves, allspice, peppercorns, nutmeg and honey. Heat gently for about 10 minutes.

2. Taste and adjust seasonings, adding more honey if necessary.

SERVING SUGGESTION

- Serve in mugs with cinnamon sticks as stirrers.

PER SERVING

Calories	104
Protein	0.2 g
Fat	0 g
Saturates	0 g
Cholesterol	0 mg
Carbohydrate	28.7 g
Fibre	0 g
Sodium	5 mg
Potassium	201 mg

SPICED CHAI

I first heard of chai on a trip out west. It was served to me as a warm welcome at an Indian restaurant (Vij's) in Vancouver and then as a trendy new beverage at a coffee house in Seattle. Some coffee shops serve chai lattes, and you can also buy chai tea bags and syrups, but I love this homemade version the best. I also like to use the seasonings in custards, French toast, scones, cookies and rice pudding (page 292).

To make a chai latte, use 3 cups/750 mL boiling water and do not add the milk to the tea mixture. Froth milk and add to each serving (even if you don't have a cappuccino machine, there are all kinds of frothers available these days, or you can always whip milk in a blender and then heat it). Dust the top with a little cinnamon and nutmeg.

Makes 8 servings

4	Darjeeling tea bags, or 4 tsp/20 mL loose tea	4
10	whole cloves	10
10	whole cardamom pods, bruised	10
2	cinnamon sticks, broken	2
1	star anise	1
2 tbsp	honey	25 mL
2 cups	boiling water	500 mL
2 cups	milk	500 mL

1. Place tea, cloves, cardamom, cinnamon, star anise, honey and water in a large saucepan. Bring to a boil. Cook gently for 5 minutes.

2. Add milk and heat thoroughly but do not boil. Strain mixture and serve in mugs.

PER SERVING

Calories	49
Protein	2 g
Fat	1.2 g
Saturates	0.7 g
Cholesterol	5 mg
Carbohydrate	7.9 g
Fibre	0 g
Sodium	38 mg
Potassium	184 mg

MINT TEA

SERVING SUGGESTION
• This looks especially
  beautiful served in a glass
  tea pot.

Mint tea is soothing and refreshing at the same time. In fact, it is easy to drink all day long! Allow it to steep 3 to 4 minutes, then strain into tea cups, or into another teapot if not serving right away.

Warm the pot before making any tea. Simply pour hot or boiling water into the pot and allow it to rest for a few minutes. Discard the water and then make tea.

Makes 8 servings

PER SERVING

Calories	13	
Protein	0 g	
Fat	0 g	
Saturates	0 g	
Cholesterol	0 mg	
Carbohydrate	3.4 g	
Fibre	0 g	
Sodium	2 mg	
Potassium	27 mg	

4 tsp	Chinese green tea (e.g., gunpowder)	20 mL
2 tbsp	granulated sugar	25 mL
1	small bunch fresh mint	1
4 cups	boiling water	1 L

1. Place tea, sugar and mint in a warmed tea pot.

2. Pour boiling water into pot. Cover. Allow to rest for 3 minutes before serving.

LEMON ROSEMARY HERBAL REMEDY

Whenever anyone gets a sore throat, has a cough or has laryngitis, I make them this special remedy. It tastes wonderful, soothes your throat and contains lots of vitamin C. Sometimes I drink it when I feel fine — and then I feel even better.

Makes 3 to 4 servings

1	lemon	1
2	sprigs fresh rosemary, or 1 tbsp/15 mL dried	2
¼ cup	honey	50 mL
3 cups	water	750 mL

PER SERVING

Calories	89	
Protein	0.1 g	
Fat	0 g	
Saturates	0 g	
Cholesterol	0 mg	
Carbohydrate	24.4 g	
Fibre	0.1 g	
Sodium	8 mg	
Potassium	33 mg	

1. Roll lemon on counter to soften it so that more juice will be released. Cut lemon in half and squeeze out juice. Save juice and put two halves of lemon in a medium saucepan.

2. Add rosemary, honey and water to saucepan. Bring to a boil and simmer gently for 10 minutes.

3. Strain, discarding lemon peels and rosemary. Add lemon juice. Taste and add more honey if necessary.

GINGER AND HONEY TEA

On a recent trip to Asia, I was astounded to discover that everyone I spoke with, whether they were in the food business or not, knew why they ate the foods they ate. People were very aware of the medicinal effects of foods.

There was a reason our mothers told us to drink ginger ale when we didn't feel well. Ginger has many anti-nausea properties; it also improves digestion and acts as an anti-inflammatory.

Enjoy this tea hot or iced. When I have it cold, I sometimes add a little cranberry juice. You can add 2 tbsp/25 mL green tea leaves or 2 green tea bags as well.

Makes 8 servings

2 tbsp	grated fresh ginger root (see below)	25 mL
2 tbsp	honey	25 mL
4 cups	boiling water	1 L

1. Grate peeled ginger root using a large-holed grater. Place in a tea pot with honey.

2. Pour boiling water over ginger and honey. Cover and allow to steep for 3 to 5 minutes before serving.

TEA

Tea is one of the world's most popular beverages. And it has more than just a refreshing taste. The tea plant contains natural chemicals that act as antioxidants (page 152). These chemicals, called polyphenols, are being studied for their role in lowering the risk of heart disease.

Black, green and oolong tea all come from the same plant but are processed differently. It appears that they all have similar health properties.

Herbal teas are not made from tea leaves so they don't have the same antioxidant properties, but they are caffeine free. However, some herbal teas contain medicinal ingredients that can interact with medications you are taking. If you have any concerns, check with your dietitian or pharmacist.

PER SERVING

Calories	18
Protein	0.1 g
Fat	0 g
Saturates	0 g
Cholesterol	0 mg
Carbohydrate	4.8 g
Fibre	0.1 g
Sodium	4 mg
Potassium	15 mg

SPRING BRUNCH

Sparkling Orange Juice Jelly

Southwest Frittata
or
Roasted Salmon Salad Niçoise

Phyllo Baskets with
Mango Ice

Dried Cherry and
Hazelnut Biscotti

*Brunch is a wonderful way to entertain. Everyone is fresh and well rested. It can be
as casual as you like — we have even had surprise birthday brunches where
guests came in pyjamas! The menu can be simple. And, after the guests have gone home,
there's still plenty of time to do the dishes.*

WORK PLAN

MAKE AHEAD

- Make the biscotti up to a month ahead and freeze.

- Make the phyllo cups up to a week ahead and freeze in a container to prevent breakage.

- Prepare the jelly a day ahead.

- Prepare vegetables and marinate salmon the night before.

SAME DAY

- Scoop ice and place in phyllo cups in the freezer. Serve directly from the freezer.

- Make the salad and serve warm or at room temperature.

PRESENTATION IDEAS

- Place a runner of grass down the centre of the table. It looks stunning. Lay out the grass a day or two in advance so that it has time to fluff out.
- Arrange little flowers in the grass to look as if they were growing there.
- Use flat rocks to make multi levels for platters.
- Use egg cups as vases for tiny flower arrangements at each place setting.
- For a casual brunch, use a quilt or satin bedspread as a tablecloth.
- Tie a pillow to the back of each chair.
- Use bagels as napkin holders.
- Use old milk jugs as vases.

MATCHING FOOD WITH WINE*

If you want to serve wine: The acid in the tomatoes and the vinegar in the salmon salad would be echoed in a rosé Champagne (France); the fruit and tannin in the wine would balance the sweet richness of the salmon.

See Alcohol (page 274).

SPARKLING ORANGE JUICE JELLY

- This looks great served in little ramekins or in fluted Champagne glasses or cocktail glasses.
- Make jelly in a loaf pan that has been lined with plastic wrap. Refrigerate for 3 to 4 hours, or until firm. Unmould and slice.

MAKE AHEAD
- This can be made a day ahead.

This is such a nice welcome for guests at brunch. It also makes a fabulous no-fat dessert that tastes very special. Unmould onto a dessert plate and surround with diced fruit. Try using different kinds of fruit juices. The mixture can also be whipped when it is half set.

You can use powdered gelatin or buy sheets of gelatin, which are preferred by professional cooks. You can find them at specialty shops and at bakery suppliers. Use six to eight sheets of gelatin for every envelope, depending how set the mixture needs to be. If the dessert is being unmoulded, it should hold very well, but if you are eating this out of a glass, the jelly can be a little softer. To use sheet gelatin, place in a bowl and cover generously with cold water to soften. Squeeze out water, add gelatin to warm juice and stir until dissolved.

For a spirited version, use Champagne or other sparkling white wine instead of the ginger ale.

Makes 8 servings

2	envelopes unflavoured gelatin	2
¼ cup	cold water	50 mL
2 cups	orange juice, divided	500 mL
⅓ cup	granulated sugar	75 mL
2 cups	ginger ale	500 mL
4	oranges, peeled, sectioned and diced	4
8	strawberries, hulled and thinly sliced	8
8	sprigs fresh mint	8

1. Sprinkle gelatin over cold water in a small saucepan. Allow to soften for 5 minutes and then heat gently until gelatin has dissolved. Add ½ cup/125 mL orange juice and sugar. Warm gently until sugar dissolves. Do not overheat.

2. Place remaining 1½ cups/375 mL orange juice and ginger ale in a large bowl and whisk in gelatin.

3. Place some oranges and berries in bottom of serving bowls or glasses. Spoon about ½ cup/125 mL gelatin mixture into each glass. Allow to set in refrigerator for a few hours. Garnish with remaining strawberry slices and sprigs of fresh mint.

PER SERVING

Calories	121
Protein	2.6 g
Fat	0.2 g
Saturates	0 g
Cholesterol	0 mg
Carbohydrate	28.8 g
Fibre	1.7 g
Sodium	7 mg
Potassium	259 mg

Excellent: Vitamin C
Good: Folacin

SOUTHWEST FRITTATA

A frittata is a cross between an open-faced omelette and a quiche without a crust. I like to start a frittata on top of the stove and finish it in the oven. If you do not have an ovenproof skillet, just pour the egg/vegetable mixture into an 8-inch/1.5 L buttered baking dish and bake at 350°F/180°C for 30 to 40 minutes. Use leftovers in sandwiches, or dice and use as a garnish for soups or salads.

Makes 6 servings

4 tsp	olive oil, divided	20 mL
1	onion, diced	1
1	jalapeño or chipotle (page 73), finely chopped, optional	1
1	baking potato, peeled and diced	1
1 cup	corn niblets	250 mL
⅓ cup	chopped fresh cilantro, basil, chives or dill, divided	75 mL
4	eggs	4
4	egg whites	4
¼ cup	water	50 mL
1 tsp	salt	5 mL
2	tomatoes, seeded and chopped	2
1 cup	chopped red cabbage	250 mL
½ cup	crumbled chèvre (goat cheese) or feta	125 mL

1. Heat 2 tsp/10 mL oil in a 10-inch/25 cm non-stick ovenproof skillet on medium-high heat. Add onion, jalapeño and potato. Cook for 10 to 15 minutes until potato is just cooked. Add corn and ¼ cup/50 mL cilantro. Transfer to a bowl. Wipe out pan.

2. In a large bowl, whisk eggs with egg whites, water and salt. Stir in vegetable mixture.

3. Add remaining 2 tsp/10 mL oil to skillet. Heat on medium-high heat. Add egg mixture. Cook until bottom is set. Transfer to a preheated 350°F/180°C oven for 15 to 20 minutes, or until bottom is lightly browned. Eggs should be set.

4. Frittata can be served from pan or loosen edges and gently slide onto a large round serving platter. Sprinkle with tomatoes, cabbage, cheese and remaining 2 tbsp/25 mL cilantro. Serve in wedges.

SERVING SUGGESTION
• Sprinkle the garnishes on the frittata in concentric circles, in spokes or just randomly.

MAKE AHEAD
• This is great served at room temperature or even cold.

Frittatas
A frittata is a great way to use up various kinds of leftovers. Combine eggs (6 whole eggs; 4 whole eggs plus 4 egg whites; or 12 egg whites) with 2 to 3 cups/ 500 to 750 mL diced cooked vegetables, pasta, or meat and up to 1 cup/250 mL grated cheese. Pour into a buttered baking dish and bake at 350°F/180°C for 30 to 40 minutes or just until set.

PER SERVING

Calories	181
Protein	10.6 g
Fat	9.1 g
Saturates	3.2 g
Cholesterol	148 mg
Carbohydrate	15.4 g
Fibre	1.9 g
Sodium	512 mg
Potassium	336 mg

Good: Vitamin A; Riboflavin; Folacin; Vitamin B$_{12}$

ROASTED SALMON SALAD NIÇOISE

SERVING SUGGESTION
• Serve on a large platter
  or arrange salad on
  individual plates.

MAKE AHEAD
• This can all be made
  ahead and served warm
  or at room temperature.

This salad really looks like springtime. Instead of salmon you could use sea bass or halibut. Roasted broccoli, green beans or red and/or yellow peppers could be substituted for the asparagus.

Leftovers make a great sandwich filling.

Makes 8 servings

4 tbsp	olive oil, divided	50 mL
1 tbsp	chopped fresh rosemary, or ½ tsp/2 mL dried	15 mL
½ tsp	salt	2 mL
½ tsp	pepper	2 mL
2 lb	baby potatoes, cleaned and halved (about 1-inch/2.5 cm pieces)	1 kg
6	plum tomatoes, cut in wedges	6
2	heads garlic	2
1 lb	asparagus, trimmed and peeled about 1 inch/2.5 cm up stems	500 g
2 lb	salmon fillet in one piece, skin removed	1 kg
⅓ cup	balsamic vinegar	75 mL
	Salt and pepper to taste	
2 cups	cooked wheat berries (page 149), rice or barley	500 mL
8 cups	mixed greens	2 L
2 tbsp	chopped fresh tarragon or basil, or ½ tsp/2 mL dried	25 mL
1	small bunch chives	1

PER SERVING

Calories	441
Protein	27.2 g
Fat	19 g
Saturates	3.4 g
Cholesterol	59 mg
Carbohydrate	42.3 g
Fibre	6.2 g
Sodium	230 mg
Potassium	810 mg

Excellent: Vitamin A; Vitamin C; Thiamine; Niacin; Vitamin B$_6$; Folacin; Vitamin B$_{12}$
Good: Riboflavin; Iron; Zinc

1. In a small bowl, combine 2 tbsp/25 mL olive oil, rosemary, salt and pepper. Toss potatoes with half of this mixture.

2. In a single layer, arrange tomato wedges skin side down on a parchment-lined baking sheet along with potatoes. Cut top quarter off heads of garlic and wrap garlic in foil.

3. Roast potatoes, tomatoes and garlic in a preheated 400°F/200°C oven for 40 minutes. Remove baking sheet from oven and scatter asparagus over potatoes and tomatoes. Roast vegetables for 10 to 15 minutes longer, until potatoes and garlic are tender and asparagus is bright green.

4. Meanwhile, coat salmon with remaining oil/rosemary marinade. Place salmon on another baking sheet lined with parchment. About 20 minutes before vegetables are ready, place salmon in oven and roast for 18 to 20 minutes, or just until cooked through.

5. For dressing, in a medium bowl, whisk vinegar with salt and pepper. Squeeze roasted garlic into dressing. Whisk in remaining 2 tbsp/25 mL oil. (If you want dressing to be completely smooth, puree in a food processor or blender and add a little stock or water if it is too thick.)

6. Combine a few tablespoons of dressing with wheat berries.

7. Arrange greens on bottom of a large platter. Top with wheat berries. Arrange potatoes down centre and tomatoes and asparagus along sides. With a large spatula, place salmon on top of potatoes. Drizzle remaining dressing over salad. Sprinkle with tarragon. Cut chives into 2-inch/5 cm lengths and sprinkle over top.

PHYLLO BASKETS WITH MANGO ICE

This is very easy to make but looks beautiful and decadent. The baskets can also be filled with fruit salad, rice pudding (page 292) or other sorbets. Dely Balagtas, who works in my test kitchen, cuts the phyllo with a crinkled pastry cutter — it looks fabulous.

Makes 8 servings

SERVING SUGGESTION
• Drizzle with chocolate sauce and garnish with mint.

Chocolate Sauce
Combine 4 oz/125 g chopped bittersweet or semisweet chocolate, 2 tbsp/25 mL cocoa, 2 tbsp/25 mL corn syrup and ⅓ cup/75 mL milk in a saucepan. Heat, stirring constantly, until smooth. Remove from heat. Stir in ½ tsp/2 mL vanilla. Makes about 1 cup/250 mL.

8	sheets phyllo pastry	8
3 tbsp	unsalted butter, melted	45 mL
3 tbsp	water	45 mL
½ cup	dry breadcrumbs	125 mL
2 tbsp	granulated sugar	25 mL
8	scoops mango ice	8
¼ cup	sifted icing sugar	50 mL
8	fresh strawberries	8

1. Place phyllo sheets in a stack and cover with a sheet of plastic wrap. Cover plastic with a damp tea towel.

2. In a small bowl, combine melted butter and water. Combine breadcrumbs and sugar in a separate small bowl.

3. Arrange one sheet of phyllo on work surface. Brush with butter mixture and sprinkle with crumbs.

4. Cut phyllo in half lengthwise and then crosswise into thirds to make 6 pieces. Stack them on top of each other at odd angles. Press into bottom of a muffin cup so that bottom and sides are flat but edges poke up and look a little wild. Repeat with remaining phyllo.

5. Bake in a preheated 375°F/190°C oven for 8 to 12 minutes, or until golden brown and crisp. Cool and remove from muffin pans. Use immediately or freeze in sturdy containers.

6. Place a scoop of mango ice in each cup, dust with icing sugar and garnish with a strawberry.

PER SERVING

Calories	225
Protein	2.8 g
Fat	6.2 g
Saturates	3 g
Cholesterol	12 mg
Carbohydrate	40.1 g
Fibre	0.9 g
Sodium	171 mg
Potassium	75 mg

Dried Cherry and Hazelnut Biscotti

Here's the latest version of my favourite biscotti, with hazelnuts, dried cherries and chocolate. The egg whites make the cookies more chewy. Although it is not necessary, the biscotti will be more flavourful if you use toasted nuts (page 295). You can also use almonds instead of hazelnuts.

Makes 50 to 60

MAKE AHEAD
• These can be made ahead and frozen for up to a few months.

2 cups	all-purpose flour	500 mL
¾ cup	granulated sugar	175 mL
¾ cup	hazelnuts, finely ground	175 mL
½ tsp	cinnamon	2 mL
½ tsp	baking powder	2 mL
½ tsp	baking soda	2 mL
½ cup	coarsely chopped hazelnuts	125 mL
⅓ cup	chopped semisweet or bittersweet chocolate	75 mL
½ cup	dried cherries, cranberries or raisins	125 mL
⅓ cup	honey	75 mL
⅓ cup	orange juice or coffee	75 mL
2	egg whites	2

1. In a large bowl, combine flour, sugar, ground nuts, cinnamon, baking powder and baking soda. Mix in chopped nuts, chocolate and cherries. Combine very well.

2. In a small bowl, combine honey, orange juice and egg whites. Add liquid to flour mixture and knead until a dough is formed.

3. Divide dough in half and roll each half into a strip about 12 inches/30 cm long. Arrange strips on a baking sheet lined with parchment paper and set in another baking sheet to help prevent burning.

4. Bake in a preheated 350°F/180°C oven for 30 to 40 minutes, or until fully baked and puffed. Cool slightly.

5. Place logs on a cutting board and cut into ½-inch/1 cm slices on the diagonal. Turn cookies cut side up on baking sheet and rebake (biscotti means twice cooked) for 15 minutes longer, until cookies are dry and slightly brown.

PER BISCOTTI

Calories	63
Protein	1.1 g
Fat	1.9 g
Saturates	0.4 g
Cholesterol	0 mg
Carbohydrate	11 g
Fibre	0.5 g
Sodium	17 mg
Potassium	41 mg

Alcohol

Chances are you have heard a lot about how alcohol may protect your heart. You also know of the many personal and social problems linked to alcohol and the dangers of excessive alcohol use. So where does that leave you?

Excess alcohol is associated with elevated triglycerides (a fatty acid in the blood) and high blood pressure, both risks for heart disease and stroke. It is also associated with some cancers, including breast cancer, as well as liver disease and other medical problems.

However, there is some evidence that drinking moderate amounts of alcohol may lower the overall risk of heart disease and stroke. There are a number of theories about the reasons including alcohol's ability to raise HDL (the good cholesterol) levels and to reduce the formation of potentially harmful blood clots. It appears that any alcohol — red wine, white wine, spirits or beer — may have this effect, but some researchers believe it to be particularly true for red wine. They attribute this to polyphenols — compounds with antioxidant properties, thought to prevent plaque build-up on the artery walls.

Most experts suggest that one drink a day (12 oz/350 mL beer, 5 oz/150 mL wine or 1½ oz/50 mL spirits) will do little harm even though the benefits may still be the subject of debate. More is definitely not better and if you don't drink now, this is no reason to start. The general consensus is that the protective effects, if any, disappear with increased intake. And, it doesn't mean saving your one drink a day and having a week's worth at the company party.

You must take into consideration your personal history and other risk factors when deciding whether it's better to abstain. Pregnant women should definitely abstain. Use sensible judgement when hosting your friends. Offer alternate beverages so your guests can make a choice. And, if necessary, make sure there is a designated driver or be sure to provide a taxi.

DESSERTS

Oatmeal and Ginger Florentines *276*
Cranberry Oatmeal Cookies *278*
Nick Malgieri's Fudge Brownies *279*
Chewy Chocolate Oatmeal Cookies *280*
Chocolate-coated Strawberries *281*
Caramelized Pineapple and Bananas *282*
Fruit Salad "Margarita" *283*
Crêpes with Orange Marmalade *284*
Amaretti Pear Crisp *285*
Cranapple Crisp *286*
Phyllo Nests with Caramelized Winter Fruits *288*
Poached Meringues in Rhubarb Strawberry Sauce *290*
Chai-spiced Rice Pudding Brûlée *292*
Strawberry Shortcake Napoleons *293*
Almond Angel Cake with Cinnamon Apricots *294*
Angel Berry Shortcake with Raspberry Sauce *296*

MORE DESSERTS

Chewy Spice Cookies *63*
Apple Crisp Strudel *88*
Caramelized Pears with Tiramisu Cream *118*
Carrot Cake with Marshmallow Frosting *150*
Frozen Lemon Meringue Cake *190*
Raspberry Upside-down Cake *221*
Bumbleberry Cobbler *253*
Phyllo Baskets with Mango Ice *272*
Dried Cherry and Hazelnut Biscotti *273*
Lime Chiffon Mousse with Caramel and Fresh Fruit *302*
Strawberries with Spiced Sugar and Yogurt Cream *304*

OATMEAL AND GINGER FLORENTINES

SERVING SUGGESTIONS
• Use milk chocolate and/or white chocolate for the drizzle.
• Sandwich two cookies together with a bit of chocolate.

MAKE AHEAD
• Freeze these if you are making them more than two days ahead.

These cookies have been adapted from a recipe by dessert and chocolate expert Alice Medrich, author of Cocolat: Extraordinary Chocolate Desserts *and* Chocolate and the Art of Low Fat Desserts. *I love them with or without the chocolate drizzle. Leftover cookies can be broken into small pieces and used as a garnish on cakes or on top of sorbets.*

They are perfect take-home gifts in packages of three wrapped in clear cellophane and tied with different coloured ribbons.

Makes 72 to 84 cookies

3	eggs	3
¾ cup	granulated sugar	175 mL
¾ cup	brown sugar	175 mL
¾ tsp	vanilla	4 mL
	Finely grated peel of 1 orange	
2 tbsp	unsalted butter, melted	25 mL
4 tsp	baking powder	20 mL
3½ cups	old-fashioned rolled oats (not quick-cooking)	875 mL
½ cup	diced candied orange peel	125 mL
¼ cup	diced candied ginger	50 mL
2 oz	bittersweet or semisweet chocolate, melted, optional	60 g

1. In a medium bowl, beat eggs with granulated sugar, brown sugar, vanilla and orange peel. Beat until very thick and light, about 3 minutes. Beat in melted butter.

2. Add baking powder (strain or sift if it is lumpy) and beat just until mixed. Stir in rolled oats, candied orange peel and candied ginger.

3. Drop batter by level teaspoon onto baking sheets lined with parchment paper or foil. Cookies should be about 2 inches/5 cm apart. Bake in a preheated 350°F/180°C oven for 8 to 10 minutes, or until nicely browned. Rotate position of baking pans halfway through baking.

PER COOKIE

Calories	44
Protein	0.9 g
Fat	0.8 g
Saturates	0.3 g
Cholesterol	10 mg
Carbohydrate	8.6 g
Fibre	0.5 g
Sodium	18 mg
Potassium	41 mg

4. Slide cookies and paper off baking sheet onto counter to cool for a few minutes. Cookies will then peel off paper easily. Cool completely on racks.

5. Place melted chocolate (if using) in a small plastic zipper bag. Twist bag so chocolate is in one corner. Cut off the tip of corner so that there is a tiny opening and drizzle a little chocolate back and forth over cookies (or just drizzle using a small spoon). Allow chocolate to set.

WEIGHT

Being overweight increases your risk of high cholesterol (page 205), diabetes (page 192) and high blood pressure (page 64). But losing weight is a complex issue. A healthy weight is more than just a number. It's a weight you can maintain without starving by eating foods that you enjoy and that are good for you.

Losing weight and eating healthier meals requires a commitment. Do it because you're ready to make changes that are healthier for you, not because it's a new year or you think it will change other areas of your life. Be patient. It took time to gain weight and it will take time to lose it. A loss of ½ to 2 lb/.25 to 1 kg a week is healthy and realistic.

Start slowly. Putting spread on only one slice of bread in your sandwich, using mustard instead of mayonnaise, taking the skin off your chicken, buying 1 percent yogurt instead of 4 percent, frying in a non-stick pan or using an herb vinegar instead of oil on your salad are all simple ways to get started. Losing weight isn't as hard as keeping it off; small, realistic changes will help you keep off unwanted pounds.

If you think you eat for reasons other than hunger, start to explore this. Look for activities and strategies that help curb the urge to overeat. Learn your hunger patterns and hunger triggers (stress, boredom, a hard day at the office or a fight with your partner). Rearrange your eating schedule so you eat to avoid intense hunger and find different ways to deal with other triggers to overeat.

Identify your good habits — perhaps you already eat lots of fruits and vegetables, or you already eat a good breakfast every morning. Strengthen these habits and add new ones to the list.

Active living is an excellent partner in a weight-loss routine. Find an activity you enjoy. It doesn't have to be aerobics or working out at the gym. Consider walking the dog, dancing, cross-country skiing, skating, or even taking a break at the office and walking briskly around the building. Try to increase the number of times or the length of time that you're physically active. Exercise helps you feel better physically and mentally. For more information on appropriate activities, refer to Canada's Physical Activity Guide to Healthy Active Living available from your local Heart and Stroke Foundation office.

CRANBERRY OATMEAL COOKIES

At my friend Evelyn Zabloski's wonderful coffee shops in Banff (Evelyn's and Evelyn's Too), these are one of her best-selling cookies. They are sure to become your favourite, too. You can use raisins or chopped dried apricots instead of the cranberries.

Leftover cookies can be crumbled over yogurt for breakfast or crumbled and used in toppings for fruit crisps.

Makes 16 large cookies

¾ cup	all-purpose flour (or half whole wheat and half all-purpose flour)	175 mL
1 tsp	cinnamon	5 mL
¼ tsp	baking powder	1 mL
¼ tsp	ground allspice	1 mL
¼ tsp	ground ginger	1 mL
½ cup	soft non-hydrogenated margarine	125 mL
½ cup	brown sugar	125 mL
⅓ cup	granulated sugar	75 mL
1	egg	1
½ tsp	vanilla	2 mL
1½ cups	rolled oats	375 mL
¾ cup	dried cranberries	175 mL

1. In a medium bowl, combine well or sift together flour, cinnamon, baking powder, allspice and ginger.

2. In a large bowl, cream together margarine, brown sugar and granulated sugar. Beat in egg and vanilla. Stir in flour mixture just until blended. Stir in rolled oats and cranberries.

3. Shape mixture into 16 balls and flatten slightly on baking sheets lined with parchment paper.

4. Bake in a preheated 350°F/180°C oven for 12 to 15 minutes, or until cookies are lightly browned and hold their shape. Cool on racks.

SERVING SUGGESTIONS
- Shape mixture into ½-inch/1 cm balls to make tiny cookies. Check cookies after 9 minutes of baking time and remove from oven when they are lightly browned.
- Pat cookie dough into a 13 x 9-inch/3.5 L baking dish lined with parchment paper. Bake for 15 to 20 minutes and cut into squares.

MAKE AHEAD
- These freeze well. Wrap well or store in a sealed container.

Ice Cream Sandwiches
Make large flat cookies. Place a layer of ice cream between two cookies and freeze.

PER LARGE COOKIE
Calories	164
Protein	2.3 g
Fat	6.5 g
Saturates	1 g
Cholesterol	13 mg
Carbohydrate	24.6 g
Fibre	1.5 g
Sodium	86 mg
Potassium	72 mg

NICK MALGIERI'S FUDGE BROWNIES

Nick Malgieri, author of Chocolate *and many other wonderful dessert cookbooks, has fabulous recipes. Although I have been known to say that if you want a brownie, just eat half of the real thing rather than a bunch of no-fat ones, these are truly satisfying. These freeze very well.*

Makes 16 squares

SERVING SUGGESTION
• Serve with a scoop of raspberry or mango sorbet with raspberry sauce (page 296) or chocolate sauce (page 272) drizzled on top.

½ cup	cocoa	125 mL
1 cup	all-purpose flour	250 mL
1 tsp	baking powder	5 mL
½ tsp	salt	2 mL
2 tbsp	unsalted butter, at room temperature	25 mL
1½ cups	granulated sugar	375 mL
2	egg whites	2
½ cup	unsweetened applesauce	125 mL
1 tsp	vanilla	5 mL

1. Sift cocoa, flour, baking powder and salt into a medium bowl.

2. In a large bowl, beat together butter and sugar. Whisk in egg whites, applesauce and vanilla.

3. Stir flour mixture into butter/applesauce mixture just until combined.

4. Line the bottom of an 8-inch/1.5 L square baking pan with parchment paper. Pour batter into pan. Bake in a preheated 350°F/180°C oven for 35 to 40 minutes, or until firm. Cool in pan. Cut into squares.

Fudge Brownies with Dried Cherries
Add ½ cup/125 mL dried cherries to the batter.

PER SQUARE

Calories	129
Protein	1.8 g
Fat	2.2 g
Saturates	1.3 g
Cholesterol	4 mg
Carbohydrate	27 g
Fibre	1.3 g
Sodium	116 mg
Potassium	40 mg

CHEWY CHOCOLATE OATMEAL COOKIES

MAKE AHEAD
- The dough can be prepared ahead and refrigerated or frozen.

These cookies taste much richer than they really are. You can process the oatmeal in a food processor or blender.

Makes about 34 cookies

½ cup	soft non-hydrogenated margarine	125 mL
½ cup	granulated sugar	125 mL
½ cup	brown sugar	125 mL
2	egg whites	2
½ tsp	vanilla	2 mL
½ cup	all-purpose flour	125 mL
½ cup	whole wheat flour	125 mL
1¼ cups	rolled oats, blended into a flour	300 mL
½ tsp	baking powder	2 mL
½ tsp	baking soda	2 mL
¾ cup	dried cherries or raisins	175 mL
½ cup	grated milk chocolate (about 2 oz/60 g)	125 mL

1. In a large bowl, cream margarine with sugars until light. Beat in egg whites and vanilla.

2. In a separate bowl, combine flours, oats, baking powder and baking soda. Stir together well.

3. Stir flour mixture into margarine mixture. Stir in cherries and chocolate.

4. Drop batter by the tablespoon onto parchment-lined baking sheets and press down. Bake in a preheated 325°F/160°C oven for 12 to 14 minutes, or until lightly browned. Cool on racks.

PER COOKIE

Calories	92
Protein	1.5 g
Fat	3.6 g
Saturates	0.8 g
Cholesterol	0 mg
Carbohydrate	14.3 g
Fibre	0.8 g
Sodium	62 mg
Potassium	76 mg

CHOOSING A HEALTHY MARGARINE
Different margarines contain different kinds of fats. Here are some guidelines to help you choose the healthiest variety.
- Choose a soft, spreadable margarine sold in a tub, not in stick or brick form.
- Look for margarines that are non-hydrogenated. This product will be lower in saturated fat and will not contain trans-fatty acids.
- Do not buy a margarine that does not include nutrition information on the label.

CHOCOLATE-COATED STRAWBERRIES

These seem very rich and decadent, but there is actually only a bit of chocolate on each berry, making this a great HeartSmart treat. Here are some pointers to make them easier to prepare:

- *Use only the very best strawberries; berries should be perfectly dry when they are dipped.*
- *If the greens on the berries are nice, leave them on to be used as little handles for dipping. If they aren't that nice, remove them and dip the fat end of the berries in the chocolate, leaving the points to be used as handles.*
- *Use the very best chocolate. I like Lindt and Callebaut.*
- *Chopped chocolate melts more evenly than large pieces. Place the melted chocolate in a deep rather than wide vessel to make dipping easier.*
- *Make sure your utensils and bowls are completely dry when you are handling or melting chocolate — the least bit of moisture can cause the chocolate to "seize," or become dull and hard. Don't be tempted to add a liqueur or any liquid flavouring to the chocolate. (Professional chocolate makers sometimes flavour chocolate with flavoured oils, which do not cause seizing.) Some people inject the berries with liqueur, but I like them plain, especially if you are using great chocolate! If your chocolate does seize, warm chocolate with 1 tbsp/15 mL vegetable oil and stir until smooth.*

Makes 20 berries

| 20 | medium strawberries, preferably with hulls (greens) | 20 |
| 8 oz | bittersweet or semisweet chocolate, chopped | 250 g |

1. Clean and dry berries.

2. Melt chocolate in a bowl set over gently simmering water or on medium power in the microwave. Remove chocolate from heat before it has completely melted and stir to finish the melting. This helps prevent the chocolate from burning.

3. Transfer chocolate to a 1 cup/250 mL measure to make dipping easier. Dip the strawberries part way into the chocolate and place on a waxed paper-lined baking sheet. Allow them to set in the refrigerator for about 30 minutes. You will have about half the chocolate left over — refrigerate it for another time (it will probably turn white and streaky, but the whiteness will disappear when the chocolate is melted).

SERVING SUGGESTIONS
- Arrange these like pastries on a pedestal platter or on a tiered serving dish.
- Use the berries to garnish cakes or other desserts.
- Drizzle a contrasting chocolate over the dipped berries.

MAKE AHEAD
- These cannot be made too far in advance, as the hulls tend to wilt and dry out and the bottoms become wet and soggy through the chocolate. Prepare a few hours before serving.

PER STRAWBERRY

Calories	32
Protein	0.5 g
Fat	2.3 g
Saturates	1.3 g
Cholesterol	0 mg
Carbohydrate	3.7 g
Fibre	0.7 g
Sodium	0 mg
Potassium	60 mg

CARAMELIZED PINEAPPLE AND BANANAS

SERVING SUGGESTIONS
- Instead of serving fruit in pineapple boats, serve in bowls over the sorbet.
- Garnish each serving with a sprig of fresh mint.
- Serve in crêpes (page 284) as a filling or on crêpes as a sauce.

MAKE AHEAD
- You can make this ahead up to the point of adding the bananas. Add the bananas when you reheat it (otherwise they tend to get mealy).

If you cannot find small pineapples, buy large ones and use them as serving "dishes," serving two or three people from one pineapple "boat." (Or you can buy the fresh pineapple already peeled and cored and simply cut it into sticks.) You can also use mangoes instead of pineapples.

In the summer I toss the fruit with the spiced sugar and grill the fruit on the barbecue until lightly browned and caramelized. Leftovers can be chopped and added to rice pudding (page 292) or used as a filling for phyllo pastries (page 288).

Makes 8 servings

4	small pineapples	4
½ cup	brown sugar	125 mL
½ tsp	cinnamon	2 mL
pinch	grated nutmeg	pinch
pinch	allspice	pinch
¾ cup	pineapple, mango or orange juice	175 mL
4	bananas, cut in half crosswise and then in half lengthwise	4
¼ cup	dark rum or orange liqueur, optional	50 mL
8	scoops mango sorbet	8

1. Cut pineapples in half lengthwise, including the "tops." Using a grapefruit knife and paring knife, remove pineapple flesh from shell, being careful not to cut through skin. Cut pineapple into large sticks. Pat shells dry and place upside down on a baking sheet lined with paper towels.

2. Place brown sugar, cinnamon, nutmeg and allspice in a large skillet. Heat gently. Add pineapple juice and bring to a boil. Add pineapple sticks and heat thoroughly for about 2 minutes. Add bananas and stir gently just to heat and combine with pineapple.

3. Pour rum (if using) over fruit and heat. If you want to flambé (page 284), light a long match and hold it carefully over fruit while it is heating (it will ignite just before liquid comes to a boil). If you are not flambéing, simply add rum and heat.

4. Spoon some fruit and sauce into each pineapple half. Place a scoop of sorbet on top.

PER SERVING

Calories	270
Protein	1.4 g
Fat	1.1 g
Saturates	0.2 g
Cholesterol	0 mg
Carbohydrate	68.8 g
Fibre	3.2 g
Sodium	8 mg
Potassium	529 mg

Good: Vitamin C; Vitamin B$_6$

FRUIT SALAD "MARGARITA"

For an alcoholic version of this delicious fruit salad, use tequila instead of ginger ale and orange liqueur instead of orange juice. You can also use other fruits such as raspberries or blueberries.

Leftovers can be pureed to make a great drink!

Makes 8 to 10 servings

3	oranges	3
4 cups	strawberries	1 L
2	kiwis	2
1	small pineapple	1
1	ripe mango	1
⅓ cup	limeade concentrate	75 mL
⅓ cup	orange juice	75 mL
⅓ cup	ginger ale	75 mL

1. Cut top and bottom off each orange. Holding orange in place on a cutting board, cut off peel from top to bottom, exposing segments. Cut out orange segments from between membranes (do this over a large bowl to catch the juices).

2. Remove hulls from strawberries and cut each berry in half or quarters depending on their size. Peel kiwis and cut each one into 6 to 8 chunks. Cut pineapple into chunks. Peel mango and cut into chunks. Toss all fruit together.

3. Combine limeade, orange juice and ginger ale in a small bowl. Pour over fruit and toss. Marinate for up to 1 hour at room temperature or longer in the refrigerator.

SERVING SUGGESTIONS
- Serve in cocktail glasses with rim wiped with a wedge of lime and then dipped in sugar. Garnish each glass with a sprig of fresh mint.
- Serve in tortillas that have been sprinkled with cinnamon sugar and baked on cookie sheets at 350°F/180°C for 10 minutes, or until crusty.
- Serve in crêpes (page 284).

MAKE AHEAD
- Make a few hours in advance (some fruits become soggy if this is made a day ahead).

PER SERVING

Calories	126
Protein	1.5 g
Fat	0.7 g
Saturates	0.1 g
Cholesterol	0 mg
Carbohydrate	31.7 g
Fibre	4.3 g
Sodium	3 mg
Potassium	392 mg

Excellent: Vitamin C
Good: Folacin

CRÊPES WITH ORANGE MARMALADE

Joso's, a somewhat crazy and eclectic Mediterranean restaurant in Toronto, serves some of the best fish I have ever tasted. And some of the best crêpes — something like these. They often use homemade quince jam — tart and sweet at the same time.
These wonderful pancakes are great for breakfast, brunch or dessert.

Makes 8 servings

Crêpes

2	eggs	2
⅔ cup	all-purpose flour	150 mL
⅔ cup	milk	150 mL
2 tbsp	granulated sugar	25 mL
1 tbsp	soft non-hydrogenated margarine, melted	15 mL

Filling and Sauce

¼ cup	orange marmalade or apricot jam	50 mL
¼ cup	granulated sugar	50 mL
½ cup	orange juice	125 mL
2 tbsp	orange liqueur, optional	25 mL
2 tbsp	icing sugar, sifted	25 mL

1. For the crêpes, whisk eggs in a medium bowl. Whisk in flour and then milk. Beat in sugar and melted margarine. Cover and allow batter to rest for at least 1 hour in refrigerator.

2. To cook crêpes, heat an 8-inch/20 cm non-stick pan on medium-high heat. Brush with a tiny amount of vegetable oil or margarine. Add ½ cup/125 mL batter and swirl in pan. Pour any batter that doesn't stick to pan back into bowl of batter. Cook crêpe until brown, flip and cook second side for about 30 seconds. (Second side will never look as attractive as the first side.) Repeat until all crêpes are cooked (you should have 8).

3. Place crêpes with less attractive side up. Spread half of each crêpe with marmalade. Fold over and then in half again to form quarters.

4. For the sauce, heat a large, deep, heavy skillet on medium-high heat and sprinkle with sugar. When sugar has melted and browns, add orange juice and bring to a boil. Add crêpes. When crêpes are hot, add liqueur (if using) and flambé (see sidebar).

5. Dust with icing sugar. Serve one crêpe per guest.

SERVING SUGGESTIONS
- Serve crêpes with mango sorbet or vanilla ice cream.
- Serve crêpes filled with marmalade but without sauce. Simply dust with icing sugar.
- To make a garnish for each crêpe, thinly slice an orange. Cut a slit in each slice from the centre to the rind. Twist. Add a sprig of fresh mint.

MAKE AHEAD
- These can be made a few hours in advance and rewarmed.

Flambé Tips
- Pull back long hair and roll up loose sleeves.
- Turn off smoke alarm.
- Heat the liqueur. Using a long match, ignite at the edge of the pan. The alcohol will ignite as it starts to evaporate.
- Wait for the flames to die down before serving.

PER SERVING

Calories	153
Protein	3.5 g
Fat	3 g
Saturates	0.7 g
Cholesterol	55 mg
Carbohydrate	28.7 g
Fibre	0.9 g
Sodium	47 mg
Potassium	91 mg

Amaretti Pear Crisp

Amaretti are delicious crisp Italian biscuits. They are available at most Italian delis and supermarkets. They come in various sizes and brands and are virtually fat-free. If you cannot find them, you can use honey Graham crackers, but they are very different in taste.

I like Bartlett or Bosc pears the best. Buy them a few days ahead, as pears are one of the few fruits (like bananas) that ripen after they are picked. If your pears are not ripe, use a bit more sugar and bake longer. You can also use apples, plums or peaches instead of the pears.

If you do not have the suggested liqueurs, use brandy, orange liqueur, Scotch or a Late Harvest Riesling or Icewine.

Makes 12 servings

3 lb	ripe pears (about 7 or 8)	1.5 kg
½ cup	chopped dried apricots	125 mL
¼ cup	granulated sugar	50 mL
¼ cup	dark rum, Amaretto or pear nectar	50 mL

Crisp

1 cup	crushed Amaretti cookies (about 40 1¼-inch/3 cm cookies)	250 mL
½ cup	all-purpose flour	125 mL
⅓ cup	brown sugar	75 mL
⅓ cup	granulated sugar	75 mL
⅓ cup	soft non-hydrogenated margarine, cold	75 mL

1. Peel pears, cut in half, remove cores and slice each half into 3 pieces.

2. In a large bowl, combine pears, apricots, sugar and rum. Arrange in a 13 x 9-inch/ 3.5 L baking dish.

3. In a medium bowl, combine Amaretti crumbs with flour, brown sugar and granulated sugar. Cut in margarine until it is in little bits. Sprinkle over pears.

4. Bake in preheated 350°F/180°C oven for 50 to 55 minutes, or until pears are really tender and topping is crisp. Serve warm.

Amaretti Rhubarb Crisp

Use rhubarb instead of pears. Increase the sugar in the topping to 1 cup/250 mL.

Serving Suggestions
- Serve old-fashioned style by spooning into a dessert bowl and dusting with icing sugar.
- Serve with a small scoop of vanilla ice cream or frozen yogurt on top.
- Garnish with sprigs of fresh mint.

Make Ahead
- This can be assembled ahead and baked just before the meal, or it can be baked ahead and reheated at 350°F/180°C for 30 minutes. It can also be served cold or at room temperature.

Per Serving

Calories	229
Protein	1.5 g
Fat	7.2 g
Saturates	1.5 g
Cholesterol	0 mg
Carbohydrate	41.5 g
Fibre	2.9 g
Sodium	72 mg
Potassium	244 mg

CRANAPPLE CRISP

SERVING SUGGESTIONS
• Serve with sweetened
yogurt cheese (page 303).
• Serve with a small scoop
of vanilla yogurt or
ice cream.
• Dust top with sifted
icing sugar.

MAKE AHEAD
• This can be made a day
ahead and warmed in a
350°F/180°C oven for
30 minutes before serving.
Or you can assemble it
ahead of time and bake
while you are eating din-
ner. (The crisp will fill the
house with a wonderful
aroma if it is in the oven
when your guests arrive;
this is a good dish to have
in the oven when you are
trying to sell your house!)

PER SERVING

Calories	364
Protein	3.6 g
Fat	9 g
Saturates	1.3 g
Cholesterol	0 mg
Carbohydrate	71.5 g
Fibre	6.8 g
Sodium	113 mg
Potassium	347 mg

Good: Iron

Cranberries are all the rage. They make this crisp tart-tasting and colourful — a real plus for a winter dessert. If you like sweet desserts, add a bit more brown sugar.

You can add ½ cup/125 mL dried cranberries to the fruit mixture for a more intense flavour. Use only all-purpose flour or all whole wheat flour in the topping if you wish.

Eat any leftovers with milk for breakfast.

Makes 8 to 10 servings

5	baking apples (Spy, Golden Delicious, Empire, Ida Reds), peeled, cored and sliced (about 6 cups/1.5 L)	5
1	12-oz/340 g package frozen cranberries, or 2½ cups/625 mL fresh	1
½ cup	brown sugar	125 mL

Topping

½ cup	all-purpose flour	125 mL
½ cup	whole wheat flour	125 mL
¾ cup	brown sugar	175 mL
1 tsp	cinnamon	5 mL
⅓ cup	soft non-hydrogenated margarine, cold	75 mL
¾ cup	oatmeal mix (page 287) or large flaked rolled oats	175 mL

1. In a large bowl, combine apples, cranberries and sugar. Place in a lightly oiled 13 x 9-inch/3.5 L baking dish.

2. To make topping, in a medium bowl, combine flours with sugar and cinnamon. Cut in margarine with your fingertips, two knives or a pastry blender until it is in tiny bits. (This can be done in a food processor.) Stir in oatmeal mix. Sprinkle mixture over fruit.

3. Bake in a preheated 350°F/180°C oven for 1 hour, or until apples are very tender and fruit is bubbling.

CAFFEINE

Caffeine is a natural part of coffee, tea and chocolate and is also found in cola beverages and certain over-the-counter drugs. Most healthy people do not increase their risk for heart disease or high blood pressure by consuming moderate amounts of caffeine, in the range of 400 to 450 mg per day (about four 6-oz cups of drip coffee or strong tea).

Caffeine acts as a stimulant. The stimulant effects vary from person to person and can include insomnia, headaches and irritability. Caffeine also acts as a diuretic. If you are caffeine sensitive, you should be aware of its sources. Read labels and moderate your consumption of caffeine-containing products.

Product	Milligrams of Caffeine
Coffee (per 6 oz/175 mL)	
Filter drip	106-180
Instant regular	60-90
Instant decaffeinated	less than 1
Tea (per 6 oz/175 mL)	
Weak	36-50
Strong	78-108
Decaffeinated	less than 1
Cola beverages (per 355 mL can)	28-64
Cocoa products	
Dark chocolate bar (about 2 oz/60 g)	40-50
Milk chocolate bar (about 2 oz/60 g)	3-20
Chocolate milk (8 oz/250 mL)	2-8
Medications (1 tablet or capsule)	
Cold remedies	15-30
Headache relievers	30-32

Homemade Oatmeal Mix
During one of my visits to Banff, my friend Ann Sharp found a delicious oatmeal mix in the supermarket. This mix is just an approximation, but it works well.

Combine 4 cups/1 L large flaked rolled oats, ⅓ cup/75 mL flax seed, ⅓ cup/75 mL wheat bran and ⅓ cup/75 mL oat bran. Store in a tightly closed container. Use in muffins, crisps and porridge. Makes about 5 cups/1.25 L. Use in muffins, crisps and recipes that call for oatmeal. I store it in the refrigerator.

Phyllo Nests with Caramelized Winter Fruits

This is a version of a recipe that I used for a Bon Appetit *magazine article about desserts created by North American cooking teachers. It looks amazing and tastes fabulous. You can serve the fruits warm or at room temperature.*

Leftover pastries can be crumbled and used as a crispy topping on other desserts. Leftover fruit can be served on its own or on oatmeal for breakfast. It can also be served as a condiment with roast pork or duck, or it can be pureed or chopped finely and used as a jam. The fruit can also be made into a crisp (page 286) or cobbler (page 253) or served on top of frozen yogurt, angel cake (page 294) or in phyllo cups (page 272).

Makes 8 servings

Phyllo Nests

8	sheets phyllo pastry	8
¼ cup	unsalted butter, melted	50 mL
¼ cup	water	50 mL
⅓ cup	dry breadcrumbs	75 mL
¼ cup	granulated sugar	50 mL

Caramelized Winter Fruits

1 cup	granulated sugar	250
2	apples, peeled, cored and sliced	2
2	pears, peeled, cored and sliced	2
1½ cups	dried fruits (mixture of apricots, prunes, figs, cherries, cranberries, etc.)	375 mL
2 tbsp	diced candied ginger	25 mL
1 cup	Port, sherry, sweet wine, orange juice or apple juice	250 mL
1 cup	strong tea (regular or herbal)	250 mL
2 tbsp	lemon juice	25 mL

Topping

½ cup	yogurt cheese (page 303) or thick yogurt	125 mL
1 tsp	vanilla, or 1 tbsp/15 mL dark rum or orange liqueur	5 mL

Serving Suggestions

- Serve on large plates.
- Drizzle plates with raspberry sauce (page 296).
- Dust dessert and plates with icing sugar and/or gold dust (page 289).
- Garnish with edible flowers (page 22).
- Fill nests with a scoop of sorbet and sprinkle with fresh berries.

Make Ahead

- The phyllo nests can be made ahead and frozen.
- The fruit mixture can be made ahead and refrigerated for one week or frozen for longer.

Per Serving

Calories	428
Protein	4.9 g
Fat	8.3 g
Saturates	4.2 g
Cholesterol	17 mg
Carbohydrate	83.9 g
Fibre	5 g
Sodium	175 mg
Potassium	477 mg

Good: Iron

1. To make phyllo nests, line a baking sheet with parchment paper. Unwrap phyllo pastry and cover with a sheet of heavy plastic (could be a clean plastic bag opened up). Cover that with a damp tea towel.

2. Combine melted butter with water in a small bowl. Combine breadcrumbs with sugar in a separate bowl.

3. Place one sheet of phyllo on work surface. Brush lightly with butter mixture. Dust with breadcrumbs and sugar. Fold in thirds lengthwise. Brush again with butter mixture and sprinkle with breadcrumbs.

4. To form nests, hold about one quarter of phyllo in place on a baking sheet to make a base. Wrap remaining strip around base to form a nest. It can look ragged and uneven. Repeat until you have made all the nests. (You'll need 2 baking sheets.)

5. Bake nests in a preheated 400°F/200°C oven for 8 minutes. Reduce heat to 350°F/180°C and bake for 5 to 8 minutes longer, or until crispy and browned. Cool.

6. Meanwhile, to make fruit mixture, place sugar in a large, deep, heavy skillet. Cook on medium-high heat, watching closely but not stirring until sugar starts to brown.

7. Add apples and pears. Cook for 5 to 8 minutes until juicy. Do not worry if caramel becomes sticky — it will melt. Add dried fruits, ginger, Port, tea and lemon juice. Bring to a boil. Simmer gently for 10 to 15 minutes or until fruit is tender. Juices should be thick.

8. To make topping, in a small bowl, combine yogurt cheese and vanilla.

9. To serve, drizzle a little of the juices from fruit onto a dessert plate, top with nest and spoon fruits into centre. Spoon a small amount of yogurt cheese on each serving.

Gold Dust
Glittery gold dust (or silver dust) looks gorgeous sprinkled lightly over or around desserts. It is sold in small vials in specialty food shops.

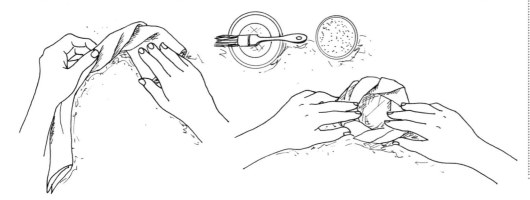

POACHED MERINGUES IN RHUBARB STRAWBERRY SAUCE

SERVING SUGGESTION
• Serve in wide pasta bowls. Garnish each serving with a whole strawberry and dust with sifted icing sugar.

MAKE AHEAD
• Meringues can be made a few hours ahead. Keep on paper towels to absorb excess moisture.
• Sauce can be made up to 2 days ahead and refrigerated. It could also be frozen.

This dessert is a fruit version of floating island — the old-fashioned nursery dessert of meringues on top of custard sauce. In the traditional recipe you poach the meringues in milk and then use the milk to make the sauce, but here the sauce is made with caramelized rhubarb and strawberries. You can poach the meringues in water, or you can save the milk (you will have at least 2½ cups/625 mL remaining) and use it when baking muffins, breads, cakes or scones.

Soft meringues do not keep well, but the leftover sauce can be served with sorbets or angel cake (page 294) or used as a filling in baked meringues or in phyllo cups or nests (page 288). It can also be eaten for dessert like applesauce or served with pork roast.

You can use raspberries instead of strawberries in the sauce. You could also puree the sauce before serving, or add 2 tbsp/25 mL orange liqueur.

Makes 8 servings

Rhubarb Strawberry Sauce

¾ cup	granulated sugar	175 mL
4 cups	diced rhubarb (about 1 lb/500 g)	1 L
4 cups	quartered strawberries (about 1 qt/1L)	1 L

Meringues

3 cups	milk or water	750 mL
4	egg whites	4
½ cup	granulated sugar	125 mL

1. For sauce, sprinkle sugar over bottom of a large, deep, heavy skillet. Cook on medium-high heat, watching closely but not stirring, until sugar melts and turns golden brown. Standing back, carefully add rhubarb. Mixture will bubble and splatter at first. Cook gently, stirring, for 5 to 6 minutes until rhubarb is tender.

2. Add strawberries and cook for 2 minutes. Remove from heat. (If strawberries cook longer they will disintegrate, which is fine, but sauce will not be "chunky.") Cool.

PER SERVING

Calories	202
Protein	5.7 g
Fat	1.4 g
Saturates	0.6 g
Cholesterol	4 mg
Carbohydrate	43.5 g
Fibre	2.7 g
Sodium	76 mg
Potassium	436 mg

Excellent: Vitamin C
Good: Riboflavin; Vitamin B$_6$; Calcium

3. For meringues, heat milk in a deep skillet or saucepan about 9 inches/23 cm wide. Bring to a simmer but do not boil.

4. Meanwhile, in a large bowl, beat egg whites until frothy and opaque. Beat in sugar slowly and continue to beat until egg whites hold a peak when beaters are removed.

5. Spoon egg whites into milk in eight mounds (you should do two or three at a time), leaving space between them. Cook for about 2 minutes on each side. The meringues should swell and then deflate. Remove to a plate lined with paper towels to absorb excess liquid. Cool.

6. To serve, spoon about ½ cup/125 mL sauce on each plate or bowl. Place a meringue on top.

Apple Rhubarb Sauce
Instead of the berries, peel and dice 2 apples and cook with rhubarb for about 10 minutes, or until tender.

CHAI-SPICED RICE PUDDING BRÛLÉE

This rice pudding is flavoured with chai (Indian spiced tea) seasonings. The top can be broiled into a crunchy sugar glaze. You can now buy special little blowtorches made just for brûlées. They have an automatic starter and a very focused flame.

Makes 8 servings

SERVING SUGGESTION
• This looks nicest served in small custard cups, but it can also be made in a larger dish and spooned onto individual plates.

MAKE AHEAD
• This can be made ahead, but the brûlée should be done just before serving.

½ cup	short-grain rice	125 mL
1 cup	boiling water	250 mL
⅓ cup	granulated sugar	75 mL
1 tsp	cornstarch	5 mL
5 cups	milk, divided	1.25 L
1	cinnamon stick, broken in half	1
10	whole cloves	10
10	white cardamom pods, bruised slightly	10
1	star anise	1
1 tsp	vanilla	5 mL

Topping (optional)

½ cup	granulated sugar	125 mL

1. Place rice and boiling water in a large saucepan. Bring to a boil. Reduce heat and cook gently, covered, for 10 minutes, or until rice has absorbed water.

2. Meanwhile, combine sugar and cornstarch in a small bowl. Whisk in 1 cup/250 mL milk.

3. Add cornstarch/sugar mixture to rice with remaining milk. Bring to a boil slowly. Add cinnamon, cloves, cardamom and star anise. Cook, covered, very gently for 45 to 60 minutes (or longer) until rice is very creamy and all liquid has been absorbed. Add vanilla. Try to remove all the spices (or warn guests to watch out for them).

4. If you are making brûlée topping, spoon pudding into 8 individual ovenproof ramekins. Refrigerate until cold — a few hours or overnight.

5. To brûlée, sprinkle top of each dessert with 1 tbsp/15 mL sugar. Place under broiler until sugar melts and browns. Allow to firm for a few minutes before serving.

Classic Rice Pudding

Omit the cinnamon, cloves, cardamom, star anise and brûlée topping. Sprinkle the pudding with ground cinnamon before serving.

PER SERVING

Calories	144
Protein	5.8 g
Fat	1.7 g
Saturates	1 g
Cholesterol	6 mg
Carbohydrate	26 g
Fibre	0.1 g
Sodium	77 mg
Potassium	247 mg

Good: Riboflavin; Calcium

STRAWBERRY SHORTCAKE NAPOLEONS

This is a light, romantic and lovely dessert that looks incredible and tastes like a dream. You can use raspberries, mangoes or other fruits.

Makes 8 servings

3 tbsp	unsalted butter, melted	45 mL
1 tbsp	water	15 mL
⅓ cup	dry breadcrumbs	75 mL
3 tbsp	finely chopped toasted walnuts	45 mL
¼ cup	granulated sugar	50 mL
8	sheets phyllo pastry	8

Filling

2 cups	thick yogurt cheese (page 303)	500 mL
3 tbsp	orange liqueur or orange juice concentrate, divided	45 mL
¼ cup	granulated sugar or spiced sugar (page 304), divided	50 mL
4 cups	sliced strawberries	1 L
	Sifted icing sugar for dusting	

1. In a small bowl, combine butter and water. In a separate bowl, combine breadcrumbs, nuts and sugar.

2. Place one sheet of phyllo on work surface. Keep remaining phyllo covered with plastic wrap and tea towel. Brush phyllo sheet with butter mixture and sprinkle with a little sugar mixture. Repeat with three more sheets of phyllo so you have four layers. End with a sprinkling of sugar mixture. Cut phyllo layers into 4-inch/10 cm squares. Repeat with remaining four sheets of phyllo (you should have at least 24 squares).

3. Place phyllo on baking sheets lined with parchment paper. Bake in a preheated 400°F/200°C oven for 5 to 8 minutes, or until crisp and lightly browned. Cool.

4. Meanwhile, in a medium bowl, combine yogurt cheese, 2 tbsp/25 mL liqueur and 2 tbsp/25 mL sugar.

5. In a separate bowl, combine strawberries with remaining liqueur and sugar.

6. Arrange eight squares of phyllo on individual plates. Place a large spoonful of yogurt mixture on top. Top with strawberries. Repeat with a second layer of phyllo, yogurt and berries. Top with a third square of phyllo. Dust with icing sugar.

SERVING SUGGESTION
• Garnish each serving with a sprig of fresh mint and dust with sifted icing sugar.

MAKE AHEAD
• The phyllo squares and filling can be prepared ahead of time. Serve within one hour of assembling or the pastry will become soggy.

PER SERVING

Calories	300
Protein	9 g
Fat	9.5 g
Saturates	4.2 g
Cholesterol	18 mg
Carbohydrate	42.5 g
Fibre	2.3 g
Sodium	206 mg
Potassium	349 mg

Excellent: Vitamin C; Vitamin B_{12}
Good: Thiamine; Riboflavin; Folacin; Calcium

ALMOND ANGEL CAKE
WITH CINNAMON APRICOTS

Angel cake is a mainstay of healthy eaters who love dessert. It is old-fashioned and comforting but low in fat and completely natural. This cake is made using a new technique that gives it a fluffy texture while using fewer egg whites. If you don't have a heavy-duty mixer, just use a hand mixer.

You can easily substitute other nuts for the almonds, or omit the nuts altogether. The cake can be served with winter fruits (page 288) instead of the apricots, and the apricots on their own can be served on top of sorbets, in phyllo containers (page 272) or with yogurt.

If you don't have an angel cake pan, use a 10-inch/25 cm springform pan. Leftover cake can be diced and used in trifles.

Makes 12 to 16 servings

1 cup	cake and pastry flour	250 mL
1½ cups	granulated sugar, divided	375 mL
¼ cup	finely chopped toasted almonds	50 mL
1½ cups	egg whites (about 11 or 12)	375 mL
1 tsp	cream of tartar	5 mL
pinch	salt	pinch
1 tsp	vanilla	5 mL
½ tsp	almond extract	2 mL
1 tsp	grated lemon peel	5 mL

Cinnamon Apricots

2 cups	water	500 mL
⅔ cup	honey or granulated sugar	150 mL
2	cinnamon sticks, broken up	2
¼ cup	Amaretto, orange liqueur or orange juice concentrate	50 mL
1½ cups	dried apricots (about 40)	375 mL
1 tbsp	lemon juice	15 mL

Yogurt Drizzle (optional)

½ cup	yogurt cheese (page 303) or thick yogurt	125 mL
1 tbsp	honey	15 mL
1 tbsp	Amaretto, orange liqueur or orange juice concentrate	15 mL

1. Sift flour and ¾ cup /175 mL sugar into a large bowl. Stir in almonds.

2. Place egg whites in large bowl of an electric mixer with cream of tartar and salt. In a medium saucepan, heat a few cups of water to a simmer and place bowl of egg whites over the water, stirring, until egg whites just feel warm. This takes 3 to 5 minutes. Immediately start beating egg whites with mixer until frothy and opaque. Gradually beat in remaining ¾ cup/175 mL sugar. Beat until soft peaks form. Beat in vanilla and almond extract.

3. Gently fold flour mixture into egg whites in three additions. Fold in lemon peel. Gently spoon into a 10-inch/3 L angel cake pan, preferably one with a removable bottom.

4. Bake in a preheated 350°F/180°C oven for 40 to 45 minutes, or until a cake tester comes out clean and dry and top of cake springs back when gently touched. Turn cake upside-down on a rack so that cake can cool in pan. To remove cake from pan, use a thin knife to loosen sides. Use a spatula or knife to loosen bottom (if pan has a removable bottom, remove sides and then loosen bottom with a knife).

5. Meanwhile, to prepare apricots, in a large saucepan, bring water, honey and cinnamon to a boil. Add liqueur and cook for 5 minutes. Add apricots and cook for 15 to 20 minutes or until soft and tender. Add lemon juice and cook for 1 minute longer. Remove cinnamon sticks or warn guests not to eat them (they do make a great-looking garnish). If syrup becomes too thick when it cools, just add a little hot water.

6. If preparing yogurt drizzle, combine yogurt cheese, honey and liqueur in a small bowl. If mixture is too thick to drizzle, thin with a little milk. (You can put yogurt in a squeeze bottle to drizzle or just use a spoon.) Serve cake with apricots, juices and yogurt drizzle.

Chocolate Chip Angel Cake
Add ¼ cup/50 mL chopped milk chocolate or dark chocolate to cake with almonds.

Toasting Nuts
Toasting nuts greatly intensifies their flavour. Place the nuts on a baking sheet and bake at 350°F/ 180°C for 5 to 10 minutes. Chop or grind nuts after toasting.

Angel Berry Shortcake
with Raspberry Sauce

Serving Suggestion
• Serve cake on a pedestal platter. Surround with edible flowers (page 22) and sprigs of fresh mint. For an old-fashioned look, make sure some of fruit is coming out of the sides.

Make Ahead
• Cake can be made a week or two ahead, wrapped well and frozen, although dessert should be assembled and filling should be made on the day of serving.

This cake can also be served completely plain, which is the way my daughter Anna loves it. But it is also a sensational dessert with layer upon layer of cake, "cream" and berries. For the cream, use light ricotta or thick yogurt cheese (page 303). Use one kind of berry or a mixture. You can also make an orange, chocolate or toasted almond angel cake (page 294) and serve with the filling and berries. Leftovers, even if a bit soggy, taste great. Or you can cut up the leftovers and serve trifle style.

Makes 12 to 16 servings

1½ cups	granulated sugar, divided	375 mL
1 cup	cake and pastry flour	250 mL
1½ cups	egg whites (about 11 or 12)	375 mL
1 tsp	cream of tartar	5 mL
pinch	salt	pinch
1 tsp	vanilla	5 mL
1 tbsp	grated lemon peel	15 mL

Ricotta Berry Filling

2 cups	light ricotta cheese, well drained	500 mL
¼ cup	honey	50 mL
3 tbsp	dark rum, or 1 tbsp/15 mL frozen orange juice concentrate	45 mL
3 cups	mixed fresh berries	750 mL

Raspberry Sauce

2	10-oz/300 g packages frozen raspberries, defrosted, drained and pureed	2
2 tbsp	granulated sugar	25 mL
2 tbsp	raspberry liqueur, dark rum or orange juice concentrate	25 mL

Per Serving

Calories	280
Protein	9.4 g
Fat	2.6 g
Saturates	1.3 g
Cholesterol	13 mg
Carbohydrate	53.1 g
Fibre	3.9 g
Sodium	103 mg
Potassium	233 mg

Good: Vitamin C; Riboflavin; Folacin

1. Into a medium bowl, sift ½ cup/125 mL sugar with flour.

2. Place egg whites in large bowl of an electric mixer with cream of tartar and salt. In a medium saucepan, heat a few cups of water to a simmer and place bowl of egg whites over water, stirring, just until egg whites feel a little warm. This takes 3 to 5 minutes. Immediately start beating egg whites with mixer and gradually beat in remaining 1 cup/250 mL sugar. Beat in vanilla and lemon peel.

3. Gently fold flour mixture into egg whites in three additions. Carefully spoon mixture into a 10-inch/3 L angel cake pan, preferably one with a removable bottom.

4. Bake in a preheated 350°F/180°C oven for 35 to 45 minutes or until cake tester comes out clean and dry and top of cake springs back when gently touched. Turn cake upside down on a rack so that cake can cool in pan. To remove cake from pan, use a thin knife to loosen sides. Remove tube and run a knife between top of cake and pan.

5. Chill cake or freeze for 30 minutes. When it is cold (or even partially frozen), cut into three layers. (Cut small notches in side of cake so that you will be able to line up layers after assembling.)

6. Meanwhile, in a medium bowl, stir ricotta until smooth and add honey and rum.

7. Place bottom layer of cake on plate. Smear one-third of ricotta on top. Scatter 1 cup/ 250 mL fresh berries on cheese. Repeat with remaining layers of cake, cheese and berries, ending with berries.

8. For sauce, combine raspberry puree with sugar and liqueur. Serve separately.

Chocolate Angel Cake
Add ⅓ cup/75 mL cocoa to flour mixture. Omit lemon peel.

TEA IN THE AFTERNOON

Potato Currant Scones

Chopped Salad Niçoise

Lime Chiffon Mousse
with Caramel and Fresh Fruit

Strawberries with Spiced Sugar
and Yogurt Cream

*What could be more sociable than a tea party? Everyone can use a pick-me-up in the
late afternoon, and you can make it as simple or as complicated as you wish.
Traditionally, afternoon tea includes little sandwiches, scones,
tiny tarts and other delicacies, whereas high tea is usually a "meal" at about 6 P.M.
with sausages and other heavier foods.
Tea itself is very popular right now because of the antioxidants
it contains (page 152). You might want to offer a number of choices
(e.g., black, green, herbal and fruit) to your guests.*

WORK PLAN

MAKE AHEAD
• The mousse, sauce and compote can be made a day
  ahead.
• Make the yogurt cream a day ahead.

SAME DAY
• The salad can be made early in the day. Serve the
  scones and salad separately or cut the scones in half
  and top each half with some salad like an open-faced
  sandwich.
• Scones are best made close to serving time.

PRESENTATION IDEAS

- Put flowers in tea pots and use them as centrepieces.
- Use all your old lacy tablecloths and overlap them.
- If you are using tea bags, buy them wrapped in individual pouches and display them on trays or in an old cigar or silverware box.
- Use your grandmother's tea cups and decorate your table with old family photographs.
- A suggestion that Sam Twining once told me about — to soften the flavour of Earl Grey, mix it with English Breakfast tea.

- To create a two-tiered tea plate, place a pedestal plate on top of a plain plate. Fill with a selection of cookies, fruits, chocolate-dipped strawberries and mint leaves. This also makes a great, easy dessert.
- Try to find the sugar cubes with little flowers painted on them.
- Strew long-stemmed fresh or dried roses over the table.

MATCHING FOOD WITH WINE*

This menu does not really require wine, but if you would like to serve wine, the salad will go well with a sunny dry rosé. The bright fruit and crisp acidity of the rosé will complement the tuna and dressing.

* See Alcohol (page 274).

POTATO CURRANT SCONES

SERVING SUGGESTIONS

- Sprinkle the scones with coarse sugar just before baking.
- Make individual scones and bake for 12 to 15 minutes.
- Bake the dough in an 8-inch/20 cm round baking pan.

MAKE AHEAD
- These taste best made just before serving.

The mashed potatoes make these scones very tender. Serve them for tea or breakfast. If the currants are hard, soak them in boiling water for 5 minutes before using.

Makes 8 scones

1 cup	all-purpose flour	250 mL
½ cup	whole wheat flour	125 mL
¼ cup	granulated sugar	50 mL
1 tbsp	baking powder	15 mL
¼ cup	soft non-hydrogenated margarine, cold	50 mL
½ cup	mashed potatoes	125 mL
⅓ cup	currants	75 mL
1	egg, beaten	1
½ cup	milk	125 mL

1. In a large bowl, combine flours, sugar and baking powder.

2. Cut in margarine until it is in tiny bits. Rub mashed potatoes into flour mixture with your fingers. Mix in currants.

3. In a small bowl, combine egg with milk. Reserve 2 tbsp/25 mL for topping. Drizzle flour with remaining egg mixture and gather dough together into a rough ball.

4. Shape dough into a 7-inch/18 cm disc and place on a baking sheet lined with parchment paper. Score top into 8 wedges. Brush with reserved egg mixture.

5. Bake in a preheated 400°F/200°C oven for 25 to 30 minutes, or until golden brown and cooked through in the middle.

Savoury Scones

Reduce the sugar to 2 tbsp/25 mL and omit the currants. Serve the scones with smoked trout topping (page 184).

PER SCONE

Calories	202
Protein	4.4 g
Fat	6.8 g
Saturates	1.1 g
Cholesterol	27 mg
Carbohydrate	31.9 g
Fibre	2 g
Sodium	190 mg
Potassium	179 mg

Chopped Salad Niçoise

Salad Niçoise is usually arranged on a large platter with all the ingredients separated. In this version I chop everything into small pieces so that every bite bursts with the flavours of Provence. This is best made when local tomatoes are in season, but if not, use plum or cherry tomatoes. You can also use smoked chicken instead of tuna.

Makes 8 servings

4	ripe tomatoes, diced (about 1 lb/500 g)	4
½ lb	green beans, cooked and diced	250 g
2 cups	diced cooked potatoes (about 1 lb/500 g)	500 mL
1	hard-cooked egg, diced	1
2 tbsp	black olives, pitted and halved, optional	25 mL
2	7-oz/198 g cans white flaked water-packed tuna, well-drained	2
2 tbsp	capers	25 mL
3 tbsp	red wine vinegar or sherry vinegar	45 mL
½ tsp	salt	2 mL
¼ tsp	pepper	1 mL
1 tsp	Dijon mustard	5 mL
1 tbsp	chopped fresh tarragon, or 1 tsp/5 mL dried	15 mL
3 tbsp	olive oil	45 mL
3 tbsp	chopped fresh chives	45 mL
3 tbsp	chopped fresh basil	45 mL
3 tbsp	chopped fresh parsley	45 mL
4 cups	chopped Romaine lettuce	1 L

1. In a large bowl, place tomatoes, beans, potatoes, egg, olives (if using), tuna and capers.

2. In a small bowl, whisk vinegar with salt, pepper, mustard and tarragon. Whisk in oil. Stir in chives, basil and parsley. Taste and adjust seasonings if necessary.

3. Combine salad ingredients with dressing and allow to marinate for about 30 minutes. Just before serving, toss in lettuce. Serve immediately.

Serving Suggestions
- Serve on large leaves of Romaine lettuce.
- Serve in large hollowed-out tomato halves.
- Serve on glass salad plates mounded like a pyramid.
- Make savoury version of scones and fill with salad to make little sandwiches.

Make Ahead
- This can be made ahead, but add the lettuce just before serving.

Per Serving

Calories	167
Protein	12.4 g
Fat	7.3 g
Saturates	1.3 g
Cholesterol	43 mg
Carbohydrate	14.1 g
Fibre	2.6 g
Sodium	354 mg
Potassium	566 mg

Excellent: Niacin; Folacin; Vitamin B_{12}
Good: Vitamin A; Vitamin C; Vitamin B_6

LIME CHIFFON MOUSSE WITH CARAMEL AND FRESH FRUIT

SERVING SUGGESTIONS
- Make the mousse in an 8 x 4-inch/1.5 L loaf pan. Unmould and cut into slices to serve.
- Make the mousse in twelve 4-oz/125 g ramekins. Unmould onto individual plates.
- Sprinkle servings with edible flowers (page 22).
- You can also make this in a trifle bowl and serve in scoops.
- Serve a scoop of mousse in a phyllo cup (page 272).

MAKE AHEAD
- The mousse, sauce and compote can be made a day ahead. The mousse can also be made up to a month ahead and frozen. Defrost for 5 to 6 hours or overnight in the refrigerator.

PER SERVING

Calories	280
Protein	5.2 g
Fat	2 g
Saturates	0.7 g
Cholesterol	56 mg
Carbohydrate	63.5 g
Fibre	1.3 g
Sodium	59 mg
Potassium	228 mg

Excellent: Vitamin C
Good: Vitamin B$_{12}$

This lovely dessert is wonderful for tea but also makes a refreshing and light dessert after a heavy meal. Adding chunks of no-fat angel cake (use storebought or see page 294; you can also use ladyfingers) makes it less rich than a cream-filled version (sometimes I use half yogurt cheese and half whipped cream). You can also use lemon juice and peel instead of the lime.

Leftovers will keep for about three days.

Makes 12 servings

1½	envelopes unflavoured gelatin	1½
⅓ cup	cold water	75 mL
1½ cups	fresh lime juice	375 mL
1 tbsp	grated lime peel	15 mL
1¾ cups	granulated sugar	425 mL
3	eggs	3
2¼ cups	yogurt cheese (page 303) or thick yogurt	550 mL
3 cups	cubed angel cake (about ½-inch/1 cm cubes)	750 mL

Fresh Fruit Compote

2	kiwis, peeled and finely diced	2
1	mango, peeled and finely diced	1
8	strawberries, hulled and finely diced	8
1 cup	finely diced fresh pineapple	250 mL
2 tbsp	dark rum, optional	25 mL

Caramel Sauce

1 cup	granulated sugar	250 mL
3 tbsp	cold water	45 mL
½ cup	apple juice	125 mL
2 tbsp	dark rum, optional	25 mL

1. In a small saucepan, sprinkle gelatin over cold water and allow to rest for 5 minutes. Heat gently over low heat, stirring just until dissolved. Remove from heat.

2. Combine lime juice, peel and sugar in a medium saucepan. Bring to a boil.

3. Beat eggs in a medium bowl. Whisk in hot lime juice mixture. Return to saucepan and cook, stirring constantly, over medium-high heat until mixture just comes to a boil. Whisk in gelatin mixture. Pour mixture into a large bowl and set over a larger bowl of ice and water to cool.

4. When mixture is cool, fold in yogurt cheese and then fold in cake cubes. Spoon into an 8-inch/20 cm springform pan or soufflé dish lined with plastic wrap. Cover and refrigerate for 3 hours or overnight.

5. For fruit compote, in a large bowl, combine kiwis, mango, strawberries and pineapple with rum (if using).

6. To make sauce, combine sugar with water in a medium saucepan and cook just until sugar has dissolved. Brush sugar down from sides of pot with a pastry brush dipped in water. Cook over high heat, without stirring, until mixture turns a deep caramel colour. Watch closely to make sure it does not burn. Carefully, standing back, add apple juice. Cook gently until smooth — about 1 minute. Stir in rum (if using). Cool.

7. To serve, uncover cake and turn upside down to unmould. Remove plastic wrap. Serve in wedges on plates drizzled with caramel, with some fruit compote on the side.

Orange Chiffon Mousse

Use half orange juice and half orange juice concentrate instead of lime juice. Use orange peel instead of lime peel.

Yogurt Cheese
Line a large strainer with cheesecloth, paper towel or a coffee filter and set over a bowl. Place 3 cups/750 mL unflavoured low-fat natural yogurt in strainer and allow to rest for 3 hours or up to overnight in the refrigerator. About half the volume of yogurt will strain out as liquid (the longer the yogurt sits, the thicker it becomes). Spoon thickened yogurt cheese into a container, cover and refrigerate. Use as required. Makes 1½ cups/375 mL.

STRAWBERRIES WITH SPICED SUGAR AND YOGURT CREAM

SERVING SUGGESTIONS
• Serve berries in a silver or crystal bowl or, for a casual look, a wicker basket.
• Serve dips in small sea shells or little bowls beside the berries.

MAKE AHEAD
• This can all be assembled a few hours in advance.

On their own fresh strawberries are perfectly delicious, but this is a fun way to serve them. This is very pretty to serve at a tea or wedding shower. You could also serve melted chocolate, applesauce, honey or maple syrup as dipping sauces, and Graham cracker crumbs in place of or in addition to the brown sugar mix.

Use leftover sugar in tea or coffee. Leftover yogurt dip can be used to top other desserts. Or simply slice leftover strawberries and combine with the sugar and yogurt.

Makes about 36

4 cups	whole strawberries (about 36)	1 L
½ cup	brown sugar	125 mL
1 tsp	cinnamon	5 mL
pinch	grated nutmeg	pinch
pinch	allspice	pinch
pinch	cardamom	pinch
¾ cup	yogurt cheese (page 303) or thick yogurt	175 mL
1 tsp	grated orange peel	5 mL
1 tsp	vanilla	5 mL
1 tbsp	orange liqueur or orange juice concentrate	15 mL

1. Wash and dry strawberries well, leaving hulls on.

2. In a small bowl, combine sugar, cinnamon, nutmeg, allspice and cardamom.

3. In another small bowl, stir yogurt cheese with orange peel, vanilla and liqueur. Guests can dip berries into either mixture or into yogurt and then sugar.

PER STRAWBERRY

Calories	24
Protein	0.6 g
Fat	0.2 g
Saturates	0.1 g
Cholesterol	1 mg
Carbohydrate	4.9 g
Fibre	0.4 g
Sodium	5 g
Potassium	54 g

CANADIAN DIABETES ASSOCIATION FOOD CHOICE SYSTEM

The following Canadian Diabetes Association Food Choice Values have been assigned to the recipes in this book in accordance with the Good Health Eating Guide (1994) which is used for meal planning by people with diabetes. The Food Choice Value for a certain serving size has been calculated for each recipe to make it easy to fit into a personalized meal plan. Servings must be measured carefully, since changing the serving size will increase or decrease the Food Choice Value assigned. Some recipes may include an inappropriate portion of a certain food group for a person with diabetes. For these recipes, it is recommended that the portions in excess be reduced to help include the recipe in a meal plan. Food Choice Value calculations following do not include optional ingredients listed in recipes.

The Good Health Eating Guide (1994) reflects the Canadian Diabetes Association's position on the intake of sugar by people with diabetes. Added sugars can be incorporated into a meal plan according to the Good Health Eating Guide (1994) and with the help of a dietitian-nutritionist.

The Food Choice System used in the Good Health Eating Guide (1994) is based on Canada's Food Guide To Healthy Eating. For more information on diabetes and the complete Good Health Eating Guide (1994), contact the Canadian Diabetes Association National Office:

15 Toronto Street, Suite 800, Toronto, Ontario, M5C 2E3

E-mail: info@cda-nat.org   *Internet:* http://www.diabetes.ca

FOOD CHOICE VALUE PER SERVING

PG RECIPE (PORTION SIZE)	STARCH	FRUITS & VEGETABLES	MILK	SUGARS	PROTEIN	FATS & OILS	EXTRA
APPETIZERS							
34 Hummos with Roasted Squash (¹⁄₄₈ of recipe)		½					
35 Caramelized Onion Dip with Roasted Potatoes (⅛ of recipe)	1	½	½ 2%			1	
36 Shrimp and Asparagus Sushi Rolls (¹⁄₂₄ of recipe)	½	½					
38 Shrimp Mousse on Sugar Cane Sticks (¹⁄₂₄ of recipe)					½		
39 Quesadillas with Caramelized Onions and Grilled Peppers (¹⁄₂₄ of recipe)	½	½			½		
40 Roasted Tomato and Garlic Bruschetta (¹⁄₂₀ of recipe)	½	½				½	
42 Sushi Pizza (1 piece: ¹⁄₁₆ of recipe)	1½						
44 Chickpea Bruschetta (¹⁄₂₆ of recipe)	½					½	1
45 Baked Chèvre on Black Bean Salsa (1 tbsp: ¹⁄₈₀ of recipe)							1
46 Spiced Lamb Cigars (¹⁄₃₆ of recipe)	½				½	1	
48 Corn Pancakes with Salsa (1 pancake: ¹⁄₂₄ of recipe)	½					½	
50 Curried Chicken Pot Stickers (2 dumplings: ¹⁄₁₇.₅)	½				1		
52 Grilled Shrimp with Charmoula (⅙ of recipe)		½			2	½	
53 Southwest Chopped Shrimp Cocktail (⅛ of recipe)	1½	½			1½		

PG	RECIPE (PORTION SIZE)	STARCH ▯	FRUITS & VEGETABLES ◪	MILK ◈	SUGARS ✳	PROTEIN ⊘	FATS & OILS ▲	EXTRA ⋯
HOLIDAY OPEN HOUSE MENU								
56	Sparkling Passionfruit Berry Punch (¹⁄₁₂ without fruit)		1		1			
57	Asian Eggplant Dip (1 tbsp: ¹⁄₂₄ of recipe)		½					
58	Roasted Garlic and Potato Crostini (¹⁄₃₂ of recipe)	½						
59	Teriyaki-glazed Chicken Meatballs (1 meatball: ¹⁄₄₀ of recipe)					½		
60	Baked Spring Rolls (¹⁄₃₂ of recipe)	½					½	
62	Chicken Satays with Peanut Marinade (¹⁄₁₆ of recipe)					1		
63	Chewy Spice Cookies (1 cookie: ¹⁄₆₄ of recipe)				1		½	
SOUPS								
66	Carrot and Ginger Soup (⅛ of recipe)		1½			½	½	
67	Barbecued Tomato and Corn Soup (⅛ of recipe)	½	1			½	½	
68	Roasted Tomato Soup (⅙ of recipe)		2			½	½	
70	Split Pea Soup with Cilantro Salsa (⅙ of recipe)	1½	1			1		
71	Celeriac and Potato Soup (⅙ of recipe)	1				½	½	
72	Caramelized Onion and Parsnip Soup (⅛ of recipe)	½	1			½	½	
73	Sweet Potato Chowder with Red Chile Paint (⅛ of recipe)	2	½				½	1
74	Pasta e Fagioli (⅛ of recipe)	1½				1		
76	Mexican Lentil Soup (⅛ of recipe)	2½	½			2		
77	Wheat Berry Minestrone (⅛ of recipe)	1	1			½	½	
78	Chicken Soup with Matzo Balls (⅛ of recipe)	½				1		
80	Ruby Red Beet Borscht (⅙ of recipe)	½	1½			½		1
81	Japanese-style Chicken Noodle Soup (⅙ of recipe)	2½	1			2½		
COSY WINTER DINNER MENU								
84	Hot Apple Cranberry Drink (⅛ of recipe)		1½		1½			
85	French Onion Soup (⅛ of recipe)	½	1½			1	½	
86	Pot Roast of Beef with Root Vegetables (¹⁄₁₀ of recipe)	1	1			4½		
87	Succotash (⅛ of recipe)	1				½		1
88	Apple Crisp Strudel (⅛ of recipe)	1	1½		2		1	
SALADS								
90	Roasted Potato, Chickpea and Arugula Salad (⅛ of recipe)	2½	½				1	1
91	Antipasto Pasta Salad (⅛ of recipe)	1½				1½	½	
92	Serious Syrian Salad (⅛ of recipe)	3½	1			1	1½	
93	Russian Beet and Potato Salad (⅛ of recipe)	½	½	½ 2%		½		

PG RECIPE (PORTION SIZE)	STARCH	FRUITS & VEGETABLES	MILK	SUGARS	PROTEIN	FATS & OILS	EXTRA
94 Green Mango Salad (⅙ of recipe)		1½		½		½	
95 Marinated Vegetable Salad (1/12 of recipe)		1			½	½	
96 Roasted Vegetable Pasta Salad (⅙ of recipe)	3½	2			½	1½	
98 Warm Breaded Chicken Salad (⅛ of recipe)	½	½			4½		
99 Salsa Spaghetti Salad (⅛ of recipe)	2½	1				1½	
100 Asian Chopped Salad (⅙ of recipe)	½	1½		1	1½	½	
102 Noodle Salad with Barbecued Chicken and Peanut Sauce (⅙ of recipe)	2	1½			3		
104 Rice Noodle Salad with Lemongrass Chicken (⅛ of recipe)	1½	½		1½	3		
FLAVOURS OF ASIA BUFFET MENU							
108 Smoked Salmon Sushi Balls (1 ball: 1/32 of recipe)	½	½					
110 Samosas with Cilantro Chile Dip (1 samosa: 1/36 of recipe)	½					½	
112 Lamb Biryani (⅛ of recipe)	2½	1			4		
114 Ginger Curry Grilled Chicken (1/12 of recipe)	4	2			5		
116 Grilled Vegetable Salad with Tomato Soy Dressing (⅛ of recipe)		2				½	
117 Raita with Tomatoes and Cucumber (⅛ of recipe)		½			½		
118 Caramelized Pears with Tiramisu Cream (⅛ of recipe)		1		2½		½	
MEATLESS MAIN COURSES							
120 Vegetarian Pad Thai Noodles (⅙ of recipe)	2	½		1	½	1	
121 Portobello Egg Cups with Salsa (⅙ of recipe)	1				1	1½	1
122 Pasta with Caramelized Onion Sauce (¼ of recipe)	4	2			1½	1½	
123 Bucatini with Fennel and Chickpeas (⅙ of recipe)	3½	1			1	½	
124 Crazy Lasagna (⅛ of recipe)	2	2			2	1	
126 Frittata Burgers (⅙ of recipe)	2	1			1	1½	
127 Scrambled Tofu with Onions and Mushrooms (½ of recipe)	1				4		
128 Nasi Goreng with Tofu (¼ of recipe)	3½	½	1 2%	½	1½	1	
130 Stir-fried Tofu and Broccoli with Sweet and Sour Sauce (¼ of recipe)		1½		1½	2	1	1
132 Sushi Salad with Grilled Tofu (⅛ of recipe)	2	½		½	½	½	
134 Pineapple Upside-down French Toast (⅛ of recipe)	1	½		2½	1	½	
135 Broccoli and Gorgonzola Quiche (⅙ of recipe)	1				1	1	
136 Vegetarian Burgers with Tomato Salsa (⅙ of recipe)	9½	½				2	
138 Roesti Potato Pizza (⅛ of recipe)	1				½	1	
139 Leftover Fried Rice (¼ of recipe)	5½	1			½	1	1
140 Beet Risotto (¼ of recipe)	5	1½			1	1½	

PG	RECIPE (PORTION SIZE)	STARCH	FRUITS & VEGETABLES	MILK	SUGARS	PROTEIN	FATS & OILS	EXTRA
141	Wild Mushroom Risotto (⅙ of recipe)	3½	½			½	1	
	VEGETARIAN FEAST MENU							
144	Sesame-seared Tofu Salad Rolls (1 piece: ¹⁄₂₄ of recipe)		½			½		
146	Black Bean and Corn Hummos (1 tbsp & chips: ¹⁄₃₂ of recipe)	½	½				½	
147	Roasted Squash and Garlic Soup with Beet Splash (¹⁄₁₀ of recipe)	½	2			½		
148	Mediterranean Vegetable Strudel (⅛ of recipe)	2	1			½	2	
150	Carrot Cake with Marshmallow Frosting (¹⁄₁₂ of recipe)	1	2		4½		2	
	SEAFOOD AND POULTRY							
154	Roasted Halibut with Fennel and Artichokes (¼ of recipe)	2½	½			3½		
156	Cilantro-roasted Sea Bass (⅙ of recipe)		½			4		
157	Roasted Sea Bass with Balsamic Vinegar (⅙ of recipe)				½	4		
158	Tandoori Salmon (⅙ of recipe)					3	½	1
159	Sweet and Sour Pickled Salmon Appetizer (¹⁄₁₂ of recipe)		½		½	2	½	
160	Smoked Salmon Soufflé Roll (¹⁄₁₀ of recipe)	½		½ 1%		1½		
162	Swordfish Sicilian (⅙ of recipe)		1			3½		
163	Roasted Red Snapper with Tomato and Herb Salsa (⅛ of recipe)		½			4		
164	Gefilte Fish Loaf (¹⁄₁₂ of recipe)				½	3½		
165	Mussels Provençale (⅛ of recipe)	3				1½		
166	Thai Shrimp Wrap (⅛ of recipe)	4	½			2½	½	
168	Cilantro-grilled Chicken Breasts (⅛ of recipe)		½			4½		
169	Spaghetti with Chicken Meatballs (⅙ of recipe)	3½	1			3		
170	Chicken Tagine with Honeyed Tomatoes and Couscous (⅛ of recipe)	3½	½		½	4½		
171	Hoisin-glazed Chicken Satays (¹⁄₂₀ of recipe)				½	½		
172	Coq au Vin (⅛ of recipe)		1			6½		1
174	Thai Mango Chicken Stir-fry (¼ of recipe)	6	2½		½	3		
176	Red Curry Chicken (⅙ of recipe)	4½	1			4		
178	Old-fashioned Roast Turkey (¹⁄₁₆ of recipe)				½	5		
180	Turkey Pastrami-style (¹⁄₁₂ of recipe)				½	2½		
181	Italian Turkey Meatloaf (⅙ of recipe)	1				2½		1
	CELEBRATION DINNER MENU							
184	Buckwheat Blini with Smoked Trout (1 pancake: ¹⁄₂₄ of recipe)	½				½		
186	Smoked Salmon Napoleons (⅛ of recipe)	1		1 2%		2	½	1
187	Roast Cornish Hens with Herbs (⅛ of recipe)		½			6		

PG	RECIPE (PORTION SIZE)	STARCH ▯	FRUITS & VEGETABLES ▱	MILK ◈	SUGARS ✳	PROTEIN ⊘	FATS & OILS ▲	EXTRA ✚✚
188	Polenta with Wild Mushrooms (⅛ of recipe)	2		2 1%			1	
189	Fennel, Endive and Red Pepper Salad (⅛ of recipe)		½				½	1
190	Frozen Lemon Meringue Cake (¹⁄₁₀ of recipe)	½	½		5½	1		
MEAT								
194	Teriyaki Noodles with Beef (⅙ of recipe)	3	½		½	3	½	
196	Grilled Flank Steak and Vegetable Salad (⅙ of recipe)		2			3	1½	
198	Striploin Roast with Wild Mushrooms (¹⁄₁₀ of recipe)		1			5½		
200	Southwestern Barbecued Brisket (¹⁄₁₆ of recipe)		½		1	2½		
202	Grilled Steak Sandwiches with Melted Onions (⅛ of recipe)	3½	½		½	3½		
204	Pot Roast of Lamb with Tomatoes and Orzo (¹⁄₁₀ of recipe)	2	1			5½		
206	Moroccan-spiced Lamb Shanks (⅛ of recipe)	4½	1			5		
208	Miso-glazed Lamb Chops with Caramelized Soy Drizzle (⅙ of recipe)				1	2½		
209	Rack of Lamb with Honey Crust (⅙ of recipe)				1	2		
210	Crown Roast of Pork (¹⁄₁₀ of recipe)	2	2½			4	1	
212	Boneless "Sparerib" Roast with Polenta (¹⁄₁₀ of recipe)	1½			½	5		
BACKYARD BARBECUE MENU								
216	Cranberry Orange "Sangria" (⅛ of recipe)		½		2½			
217	Spicy Thai Shrimp (¹⁄₃₂ of recipe)				½	½		
218	Balsamic Maple-glazed Lamb Chops with Sweet Potatoes (⅛ of recipe)	2				1½	½	
219	Wheat Berry and Grilled Corn Salad (⅛ of recipe)	3					1½	
220	Grilled Tomato Salad (⅛ of recipe)		1				1	
221	Raspberry Upside-down Cake (⅛ of recipe)	1½			3½	½	2½	
VEGETABLES AND SIDE DISHES								
224	Glazed Fennel with Balsamic Vinegar (¼ of recipe)		1½		1		½	
225	Tian of Eggplant and Zucchini (⅛ of recipe)	½	1			½	½	
226	Stir-fried Eggplant with Miso (⅙ of recipe)		1				½	
227	Dal with Spiced Yogurt (⅛ of recipe)	1½				1½		
228	Pureed Carrots and Ginger (⅛ of recipe)		1½		½		½	
229	Grated Squash with Pears and Cranberries (⅛ of recipe)		2		½		½	
230	Double Roasted Smashed Potatoes (¼ of recipe)	2½					1	
231	Stuffed Baked Potatoes (⅙ of recipe)	1½				½	½	
232	Lynn's Lemon Potatoes (⅛ of recipe)	1½						1
233	Celeriac and Potato Mash (⅛ of recipe)	2					½	

PG	RECIPE (PORTION SIZE)	STARCH	FRUITS & VEGETABLES	MILK	SUGARS	PROTEIN	FATS & OILS	EXTRA
234	Caramelized Roasted Root Vegetables (⅛ of recipe)		2				½	
235	Sauteed Peppers with Garlic and Balsamic Vinegar (⅛ of recipe)		1					
236	Vegetable Stir-fry (⅙ of recipe)		1½			½		
237	Sauteed Brussels Sprout Leaves (⅛ of recipe)		½				½	
238	Sauteed Green Beans with Bean Sprouts and Green Onions (⅙ of recipe)		½				½	
239	Braised Red Cabbage and Apples (⅛ of recipe)		1		½		½	
240	Bread Stuffing with Herbs (1/12 of recipe)	1½	½			½		
242	Sliced Wild Mushrooms and Shallots (⅙ of recipe)						½	1
243	Couscous with Vegetables (⅛ of recipe)	3½	½				½	
244	Fragrant Rice with Aromatic Spices (⅛ of recipe)	2	1				½	
245	Sushi Rice "Pilaf" (⅙ of recipe)	3½	½				½	
TASTE OF SUMMER MENU								
248	Double-wrapped Shrimp Salad Rolls (1 roll: 1/20 of recipe)	½				½		
250	Asparagus Soup with Fresh Tarragon (⅙ of recipe)		1			1	½	
251	Cedar-planked Salmon (⅙ of recipe)				½	4	1	
252	Potato and Arugula Salad with Mustard and Roasted Garlic (⅙ of recipe)	2					1½	
253	Bumbleberry Cobbler (⅛ of recipe)	1	1		2		2	1
BREADS, CONDIMENTS AND BEVERAGES								
256	Asiago Drop Biscuits (1 biscuit: 1/16 of recipe)	1			½	½	1	
257	Five-grain Muffins (1 muffin: 1/12 of recipe)	1	½		1		1	
258	Chunky Banana Muffins (1 muffin: 1/12 of recipe)	1½	½		1½	½	2	1
259	Southwest Cornmeal Scones (1 scone: 1/12 of recipe)	1			½	½	½	
260	Fresh Cilantro and Mint Chutney (1 tbsp: 1/12 of recipe)							1
260	Caramelized Cranberry Sauce (1 tbsp: 1/32 of recipe)							1
261	Spicy Red Pepper "Ketchup" (1 tbsp: 1/64 of recipe)							1
262	Strawberry Lemonade (⅙ of recipe)		½		3½			
262	Hot Spiced Apple Cider (⅙ of recipe)		2½		½			
263	Spiced Chai (⅛ of recipe)			½ 2%	½			
264	Mint Tea (⅛ of recipe)				½			
264	Lemon Rosemary Herbal Remedy (⅓ of recipe)				2½			
265	Ginger and Honey Tea (⅛ of recipe)				½			
SPRING BRUNCH MENU								
268	Sparkling Orange Juice Jelly (⅛ of recipe)		1½		1			1

PG	RECIPE (PORTION SIZE)	STARCH	FRUITS & VEGETABLES	MILK	SUGARS	PROTEIN	FATS & OILS	EXTRA
269	Southwest Frittata (⅙ of recipe)	1				1	1½	
270	Roasted Salmon Salad Niçoise ⅛ of recipe)	2	½			3	2	1
272	Phyllo Baskets with Mango Ice (⅛ of recipe)	1			2½		1	
273	Dried Cherry and Hazelnut Biscotti (1 cookie: 1/50 of recipe)				1		½	

DESSERTS

PG	RECIPE (PORTION SIZE)	STARCH	FRUITS & VEGETABLES	MILK	SUGARS	PROTEIN	FATS & OILS	EXTRA
276	Oatmeal and Ginger Florentines (1 cookie: 1/72 of recipe)				1			
278	Cranberry Oatmeal Cookies (1 cookie: 1/16 of recipe)				1½		½	
279	Nick Malgieri's Fudge Brownies (1 square 1/16 of recipe)	½			2		½	
280	Chewy Chocolate Oatmeal Cookies (1 cookie: 1/34 of recipe)				1½		½	
281	Chocolate-coated Strawberries (1 berry: 1/20 of recipe)		½				½	
282	Caramelized Pineapple and Bananas (⅛ of recipe)		3½		3			
283	Fruit Salad "Margarita" (⅛ of recipe)		2		½			1
284	Crêpes with Orange Marmalade (⅛ of recipe)	½			2	½	½	
285	Amaretti Pear Crisp (1/12 of recipe)	½	1½		1½		1½	
286	Cranapple Crisp (⅛ of recipe)	1	1½		3½		2	
288	Phyllo Nests with Caramelized Winter Fruits (⅛ of recipe)	1	3		3½		1½	
290	Poached Meringues in Rhubarb Strawberry Sauce (⅛ of recipe)		1	½ 1%	3	½		
292	Chai-spiced Rice Pudding Brûlée (⅛ of recipe without topping)	1		1 1%	½			
293	Strawberry Shortcake Napoleons (⅛ of recipe)	1½	½		1½	1	1½	
294	Almond Angel Cake with Cinnamon Apricots (1/12 of recipe without yogurt drizzle)	½	1		4	½		
296	Angel Berry Shortcake with Raspberry Sauce (1/12 of recipe)	½	½		3½	1	½	

TEA IN THE AFTERNOON MENU

PG	RECIPE (PORTION SIZE)	STARCH	FRUITS & VEGETABLES	MILK	SUGARS	PROTEIN	FATS & OILS	EXTRA
300	Potato Currant Scones (1 scone: ⅛ of recipe)	1½			½		1½	1
301	Chopped Salad Niçoise (⅛ of recipe)	½	½			1½	½	
302	Lime Chiffon Mousse with Caramel and Fresh Fruit (1/12 of recipe)		1½		4½	½		
304	Strawberries with Spiced Sugar and Yogurt Cream (1/36 of recipe)				½			

* Alcohol in recipes is counted as ▲

INDEX

Butterflied Leg of Lamb with Wild Mushrooms, 199

C

Cabbage
    Braised Red Cabbage and Apples, 239
    Ruby Red Beet Borscht, 80
Caffeine, 287
Cakes
    Almond Angel Cake with Cinnamon
        Apricots, 294
    Angel Berry Shortcake with Raspberry
        Sauce, 296
    Carrot Cake with Marshmallow Frosting, 150
    Chocolate Angel Cake, 297
    Chocolate Chip Angel Cake, 295
    Frozen Lemon Meringue Cake, 190
    Raspberry Upside-down Cake, 221
Calcium, 125, 129
Cancer, lowering risk of, 101, 129, 133, 152, 175, 230
Caramelized Cranberry Sauce, 260
Caramelized Onion and Parsnip Soup, 72
Caramelized Onion Dip with Roasted Potatoes, 35
Caramelized Pears with Tiramisu Cream, 118
Caramelized Pineapple and Bananas, 282
Caramelized Roasted Root Vegetables, 234
Carrots
    Caramelized Roasted Root Vegetables, 234
    Carrot and Ginger Soup, 66
    Carrot and Orange Salad, 207
    Carrot Cake with Marshmallow Frosting, 150
    Pureed Carrots and Ginger, 228
Carving, 27–29
Casseroles. See also Stews.
    Chicken Biryani, 113
    Crazy Lasagna, 124
    Lamb Biryani, 112
    Shepherd's Pie, 201
    Tian of Eggplant and Zucchini, 225
Cauliflower
    Marinated Vegetable Salad, 95
Cedar-planked Salmon, 251
Celeriac
    Celeriac and Potato Mash, 233
    Celeriac and Potato Soup, 71
Celery and Potato Soup, 71
Centrepieces, 21
Chai
    Chai-spiced Rice Pudding Brûlée, 292
    Spiced Chai, 263
Charmoula, 52
Cheese. See also Yogurt cheese.
    Asiago Drop Biscuits, 256

Baked Chèvre on Black Bean Salsa, 45
Broccoli and Gorgonzola Quiche, 135
Herbed Asiago Biscuits, 256
Roasted Tomato and Garlic Bruschetta with
    Cheese, 41
Cherries
    Dried Cherry and Hazelnut Biscotti, 273
    Fudge Brownies with Dried Cherries, 279
Chèvre on Black Bean Salsa, Baked, 45
Chewy Chocolate Oatmeal Cookies, 280
Chewy Spice Cookies, 63
Chicken. See also 168–176.
    Chicken Biryani, 113
    Chicken Pastrami-style, 180
    Chicken Satays with Peanut Marinade, 62
    Chicken Soup with Matzo Balls, 78
    Curried Chicken Pot Stickers, 50
    Ginger Curry Grilled Chicken, 114
    Homemade Chicken Stock, 79
    Japanese-style Chicken Noodle Soup, 81
    Moroccan-spiced Chicken, 207
    Noodle Salad with Barbecued Chicken and
        Peanut Sauce, 102
    Rice Noodle Salad with Lemongrass
        Chicken, 104
    Teriyaki-glazed Chicken Meatballs, 59
    Warm Breaded Chicken Salad, 98
    Wheat Berry Sushi Salad with Grilled
        Chicken, 133
Chickpeas
    Antipasto Pasta Salad, 91
    Bucatini with Fennel and Chickpeas, 123
    Chickpea Bruschetta, 44
    Devilled Eggs with Hummos, 34
    Hummos with Roasted Squash, 34
    Nutty Chickpea Sauce, 62
    Roasted Potato, Chickpea and Arugula
        Salad, 90
    Serious Syrian Salad, 92
Chiles, 73
    handling hot chiles, 67
    Samosas with Cilantro Chile Dip, 110
    Sweet Potato Chowder with Red Chile Paint,
        73
Chipotles, 73
Chocolate
    Chewy Chocolate Oatmeal Cookies, 280
    Chocolate Angel Cake, 297
    Chocolate Chip Angel Cake, 295
    Chocolate Sauce, 272
    Chocolate-coated Strawberries, 281
    Fudge Brownies with Dried Cherries, 279
    Nick Malgieri's Fudge Brownies, 279
Cholesterol, 101, 133, 205, 222, 241

Chopped Salad Niçoise, 301
Chunky Banana Muffins, 258
Chutney, Fresh Cilantro and Mint, 260
Cilantro
    Cilantro-grilled Chicken Breasts, 168
    Cilantro-grilled Shrimp, 168
    Cilantro-roasted Sea Bass, 156
    Fresh Cilantro and Mint Chutney, 260
    Samosas with Cilantro Chile Dip, 110
    Split Pea Soup with Cilantro Salsa, 70
Classic Rice Pudding, 292
Cobbler, Bumbleberry, 253
Coffee, 287
Cookies
    Chewy Chocolate Oatmeal Cookies, 280
    Chewy Spice Cookies, 63
    Cranberry Oatmeal Cookies, 278
    Dried Cherry and Hazelnut Biscotti, 273
    Oatmeal and Ginger Florentines, 276
Coq au Vin, 172
Corn
    Barbecued Tomato and Corn Soup, 67
    Black Bean and Corn Hummos, 146
    Breakfast Corn Pancakes, 49
    Corn Pancakes with Salsa, 48
    Succotash, 87
    Wheat Berry and Grilled Corn Salad, 219
Cornish Hens with Herbs, Roast, 187
Cornmeal
    Southwest Cornmeal Scones, 259
Couscous
    Chicken Tagine with Honeyed Tomatoes
        and Couscous, 170
    Couscous with Vegetables, 243
    Israeli couscous, 243
Cranapple Crisp, 286
Cranberries
    Caramelized Cranberry Sauce, 260
    Cranapple Crisp, 286
    Cranberry Oatmeal Cookies, 278
    Cranberry Orange "Sangria," 216
    Grated Squash with Pears and Cranberries,
        229
    Hot Apple Cranberry Drink, 84
Crazy Lasagna, 124
Crêpes with Orange Marmalade, 284
Crisps
    Amaretti Pear Crisp, 285
    Amaretti Rhubarb Crisp, 285
    Apple Crisp Strudel, 88
    Cranapple Crisp, 286
Crostini. See also Bruschetta.
    Roasted Garlic and Potato Crostini, 58
Croutons, 77, 85

Grilled Tomato Salad, 220
Grilled Tomato Salad with Fennel, 220
Grilled Tuna Salad Rolls, 145
Grilled Turkey Sandwiches, 203
Grilled Vegetable Salad with Tomato Soy
    Dressing, 116
Quesadillas with Caramelized Onions and
    Grilled Peppers, 39
Sesame-seared Tofu Salad Rolls, 144
Sushi Salad with Grilled Tofu, 132
Wheat Berry and Grilled Corn Salad, 219
Wheat Berry Sushi Salad with Grilled
    Chicken, 133

H

Halibut, 155
    Roasted Halibut with Fennel and Artichokes,
        154
Ham
    Antipasto Pasta Salad, 91
Harissa, 206
Heart disease, lowering risk of, 43, 152, 155, 175,
    222, 230, 241, 274
Herbs. See also individual herbs.
    Bread Stuffing with Herbs, 240
    Herbed Asiago Biscuits, 256
    Lemon Rosemary Herbal Remedy, 264
    Roast Cornish Hens with Herbs, 187
    Roasted Red Snapper with Tomato and
        Herb Salsa, 163
High blood pressure, 64
Hoisin-glazed Chicken Satays, 171
Honey
    Ginger and Honey Tea, 265
    Lemon Rosemary Herbal Remedy, 264
    Rack of Lamb with Honey Crust, 209
    Rack of Lamb with Honey Nut Crust, 209
Horseradish, Homemade, 164
Hot Apple Cranberry Drink, 84
Hot Spiced Apple Cider, 262
Hummos
    Black Bean and Corn Hummos, 146
    Devilled Eggs with Hummos, 34
    Hummos with Roasted Squash, 34

I

Ice cream sandwiches, 278
Iron, 125, 195
Israeli couscous, 243
Italian Turkey Meatloaf, 181

J

Jalapeños, 73
Japanese-style Chicken Noodle Soup, 81

K

Kids, cooking for, 16

L

Lamb. See also 204–209.
    Balsamic Maple-glazed Lamb Chops with
        Sweet Potatoes, 218
    Butterflied Leg of Lamb with Wild
        Mushrooms, 199
    carving, 28–29
    Grilled Lamb Sandwiches, 203
    Lamb Biryani, 112
    Red Curry Lamb, 177
    Spiced Lamb Cigars, 46
Lasagna, Crazy, 124
Leftover Fried Rice, 139
Lemongrass
    Rice Noodle Salad with Lemongrass Chicken,
        104
Lemons
    Frozen Lemon Meringue Cake, 190
    Lemon Rosemary Herbal Remedy, 264
    Lynn's Lemon Potatoes, 232
    Strawberry Lemonade, 262
Lentils, 76
    Dal with Spiced Yogurt, 227
    Mexican Lentil Soup, 76
    Serious Syrian Salad, 92
Lime
    Lime Chiffon Mousse with Caramel and
        Fresh Fruit, 302
    Thai Lime Dressing, 105

M

Mangoes
    Green Mango Salad, 94
    Phyllo Baskets with Mango Ice, 272
    Thai Mango Chicken Stir-fry, 174
Manners, 30–32
Maple syrup
    Balsamic Maple-glazed Lamb Chops with
        Sweet Potatoes, 218
Margarine, 280
Marinated Vegetable Salad, 95
Matzo, 78
    Chicken Soup with Matzo Balls, 78
Mayonnaise
    Charmoula, 52
    Garlic, 202
Meatballs
    Spaghetti with Chicken Meatballs, 169
    Teriyaki-glazed Chicken Meatballs, 59
Meatless main courses. See also 120–141.
    Corn Pancakes with Salsa, 48

Mediterranean Vegetable Strudel, 148
    Southwest Frittata, 269
    Tian of Eggplant and Zucchini, 225
    Vegetable Stir-fry, 236
Meatloaf, Italian Turkey, 181
Mediterranean diet, 241
Mediterranean Vegetable Strudel, 148
Menopause, 133
Menu planning, 16–17
Menus, 16–17
    Backyard Barbecue, 214
    Celebration Dinner, 182
    Cosy Winter Dinner, 82
    Flavours of Asia Buffet, 106
    Holiday Open House, 54
    Spring Brunch, 266
    Taste of Summer, 246
    Tea in the Afternoon, 298
    Vegetarian Feast, 142
Meringues in Rhubarb Strawberry Sauce,
    Poached, 290
Mexican Lentil Soup, 76
Minestrone, Wheat Berry, 77
Mint
    Fresh Cilantro and Mint Chutney, 260
    Mint Tea, 264
Miso, 226
    Miso-glazed Lamb Chops with Caramelized
        Soy Drizzle, 208
    Stir-fried Eggplant with Miso, 226
Mixed Vegetable and Ginger Soup, 66
Moroccan-spiced Chicken, 207
Moroccan-spiced Lamb Shanks, 206
Muffins
    Chunky Banana Muffins, 258
    Five-grain Muffins, 257
Mushrooms
    Butterflied Leg of Lamb with Wild
        Mushrooms, 199
    Polenta with Wild Mushrooms, 188
    Portobello Egg Cups with Salsa, 121
    Sauteed Asparagus with Enoki Mushrooms,
        238
    Scrambled Tofu with Onions and Mushrooms,
        127
    Sliced Wild Mushrooms and Shallots, 242
    Striploin Roast with Wild Mushrooms, 198
    Wild Mushroom Risotto, 141
Music, 19–20
Mussels Provençale, 165
Mustard
    Mustard Horseradish Vinaigrette Dressing, 196
    Potato and Arugula Salad with Mustard and
        Roasted Garlic, 252

N

Napkin folding, 24–26
Nasi Goreng with Tofu, 128
Nasi Goreng with Tofu and Shrimp, 129
Nick Malgieri's Fudge Brownies, 279
Noodles
Japanese-style Chicken Noodle Soup, 81
Noodle Salad with Barbecued Chicken and
Peanut Sauce, 102
Noodle Salad with Barbecued Tofu and Peanut
Sauce, 103
Rice Noodle Salad with Lemongrass Chicken,
104
Teriyaki Noodles with Beef, 194
Vegetarian Pad Thai Noodles, 120
Nori, 43
Nutrient analysis, 11
Nuts. *See also* Peanuts.
Dried Cherry and Hazelnut Biscotti, 273
Rack of Lamb with Honey Nut Crust, 209
toasting nuts, 295
Nutty Chickpea Sauce, 62

O

Oats
Apple Crisp Strudel, 88
Chewy Chocolate Oatmeal Cookies, 280
Cranberry Oatmeal Cookies, 278
Homemade Oatmeal Mix, 287
Oatmeal and Ginger Florentines, 276
Old-fashioned Roast Turkey, 178
Olive oil, 241
Onions
Caramelized Onion and Parsnip Soup, 72
Caramelized Onion Dip with Roasted Potatoes,
35
French Onion Soup, 85
Grilled Steak Sandwiches with Melted Onions,
202
Pasta with Caramelized Onion Sauce,
122
peeling pearl onions, 173
Quesadillas with Caramelized Onions and
Grilled Peppers, 39
Sauteed Green Beans with Bean Sprouts and
Green Onions, 238
Scrambled Tofu with Onions and Mushrooms,
127
Oranges
Carrot and Orange Salad, 207
Cranberry Orange "Sangria," 216
Crêpes with Orange Marmalade, 284
Orange Chiffon Mousse, 303
Sparkling Orange Juice Jelly, 268

Orzo
Pot Roast of Lamb with Tomatoes and Orzo,
204
Osteoporosis, 129, 133

P

Pad Thai Noodles, Vegetarian, 120
Pancakes. *See also* Blini.
Breakfast Corn Pancakes, 49
Corn Pancakes with Salsa, 48
Panko breadcrumbs, 98
Pantry, 15
Papaya
Thai Papaya Chicken Stir-fry, 175
Parsnips
Caramelized Onion and Parsnip Soup, 72
Caramelized Roasted Root Vegetables, 234
Passionfruit
Sparkling Passionfruit Berry Punch, 56
Pastas
Antipasto Pasta Salad, 91
Bucatini with Fennel and Chickpeas, 123
Crazy Lasagna, 120
Japanese-style Chicken Noodle Soup, 81
Noodle Salad with Barbecued Chicken and
Peanut Sauce, 102
Noodle Salad with Barbecued Tofu and Peanut
Sauce, 103
Pasta e Fagioli, 74
pasta tip, 123
Pasta with Caramelized Onion Sauce, 122
Pot Roast of Lamb with Tomatoes and Orzo,
204
Rice Noodle Salad with Lemongrass Chicken,
104
Roasted Vegetable Pasta Salad, 96
Salsa Spaghetti Salad, 99
Spaghetti with Chicken Meatballs, 169
Teriyaki Noodles with Beef, 194
Vegetarian Pad Thai Noodles, 120
Peanuts
Chicken Satays with Peanut Marinade, 62
Noodle Salad with Barbecued Chicken and
Peanut Sauce, 102
Noodle Salad with Barbecued Tofu and Peanut
Sauce, 103
Tofu Satays with Peanut Marinade, 62
Pears
Amaretti Pear Crisp, 285
Caramelized Pears with Tiramisu Cream, 118
Grated Squash with Pears and Cranberries,
229
Peppers, 230
Fennel, Endive and Red Pepper Salad, 189

Hummos with Roasted Red Peppers, 34
Quesadillas with Caramelized Onions and
Grilled Peppers, 39
roasting peppers, 49
Sauteed Peppers with Garlic and Balsamic
Vinegar, 235
Spicy Red Pepper "Ketchup," 261
Pesto
Hummos with Roasted Squash and Pesto, 34
Phyllo pastry
Apple Crisp Strudel, 88
Baked Spring Rolls, 60
Mediterranean Vegetable Strudel, 148
Phyllo Baskets with Mango Ice, 272
Phyllo Nests with Caramelized Winter Fruits,
288
Smoked Salmon Napoleons, 186
Spiced Lamb Cigars, 46
Spiced Vegetarian Cigars, 47
Strawberry Shortcake Napoleons, 293
Pie, Shepherd's, 201
Pineapple
Caramelized Pineapple and Bananas, 282
Pineapple Upside-down French Toast, 134
Pine nuts, 162
Pizza
Roesti Potato Pizza, 138
Sushi Pizza, 42
Placecards and seating arrangements, 20–21
Poached Meringues in Rhubarb Strawberry Sauce,
290
Polenta
Boneless "Sparerib" Roast with Polenta, 212
Polenta with Wild Mushrooms, 188
Pork
Boneless "Sparerib" Roast with Polenta, 212
carving crown roast, 29
Crown Roast of Pork, 210
ordering crown roast, 211
Portobello Egg Cups with Salsa, 121
Potatoes. *See also* Sweet potatoes.
Caramelized Onion Dip with Roasted Potatoes,
35
Celeriac and Potato Mash, 233
Celeriac and Potato Soup, 71
Celery and Potato Soup, 71
Double Roasted Smashed Potatoes, 230
Lynn's Lemon Potatoes, 232
Potato and Arugula Salad with Mustard and
Roasted Garlic, 252
Potato Crostini with Smoked Salmon, 58
Potato Currant Scones, 300
Roasted Garlic and Potato Crostini, 58
Roasted Potato, Chickpea and Arugula Salad, 90

BONNIE STERN

Bonnie Stern is the owner of the Bonnie Stern Cooking School in Toronto.
She is the author of eight cookbooks, including the national bestsellers *Simply HeartSmart Cooking*
and *More HeartSmart Cooking*. She writes a weekly food column for the *Toronto Star*
and contributes regularly to *Canadian Living* magazine.
Bonnie is also the host of "Bonnie Stern Cooks" and "Bonnie Stern Entertains,"
both of which can be seen nationally on the Women's Television Network.

HEART AND STROKE FOUNDATION OF CANADA

Heart and Stroke Foundation of Canada is a voluntary non-profit organization
that provides Canadians with the most current information and skills to help prevent
heart disease and stroke. The Foundation's HeartSmart programs include
helpful information on grocery shopping, cooking and eating out.

*Also available
from Bonnie Stern
and the
Heart and Stroke
Foundation of Canada.*